Daily Cornbread

BROADWAY BOOKS

New York

Daily Cornbread

365 Secrets for
a Healthy Mind, Body, and Spirit

Stephanie Stokes Oliver

BROADWAY

A hardcover edition of this book was originally published in 1999 by Doubleday, a division of Random House, Inc. It is here reprinted by arrangement with Doubleday.

Broadway Books titles may be purchased for business or promotional use or for special sales. For information, please write to: Special Markets Department, Random House, Inc., 1540 Broadway, New York, NY 10036.

PRINTED IN THE UNITED STATES OF AMERICA

BROADWAY BOOKS and its logo, a letter B bisected on the diagonal, are trademarks of Broadway Books, a division of Random House, Inc.

Visit our website at www.broadwaybooks.com

First Broadway Books trade paperback edition published 2002

Book design by Ellen Cipriano

The Library of Congress has cataloged the hardcover edition as follows:

Oliver, Stephanie Stokes.
Daily cornbread: 365 secrets for a healthy mind, body, and spirit / Stephanie Stokes Oliver.—1st ed.
p.   cm.
1. African–American women—Health and hygiene.
2. Mind and body.
I. Title.
RA778.4.A36   043   1999
613'.04244'08996073—dc21   99-24396
CIP

ISBN 0-7679-0553-9

1 3 5 7 9 10 8 6 4 2

This book is dedicated to

THE CREATOR,

*who gave me this day my Daily Cornbread
and from whom all blessings flow, including this one.*

My Parents,
Josephine Stratman Stokes
and the late
Judge Charles Moorehead Stokes,

*for a loving, happy childhood
and a close, supportive adulthood.*

Acknowledgments

I found that it takes a village to write a book! With grateful appreciation and affection, I thank the following folks who have passed through the *Daily Cornbread* tribal community.

My husband,
Reginald Oliver
Thank you for the love and laughter, peace and harmony that support writing and creating

My girls,
Anique (my computer consultant), **Amena, Aleeyah, Ahmondyllah**
My siblings,
Vicki Stokes, André S. Wooten, my cousin, **Gloria Leonard,** and my sister-in-law, **Daphne Barbee-Wooten**
My powerful publishing trio:
Agent **Victoria Sanders,** editor **Janet Hill,** attorney **Gizelle Galang**

The contributors to this book:
Tracy E. Hopkins, Research Associate; Shelia Baynes, Rosemary L. Bray, Ronald B. Brown, Julia Boyd, Leah Chase, Deborah Tutt Chisholm, Sherrill Clarke, Harriette Cole, J. California Cooper, Herbert Daughtry, Leah Daughtry, Gerald W. Deas, Gary C. Dennis, Maria Dowd, Katherine Dunham, Marian Wright Edelman, Debrena Jackson Gandy, Nikki Giovanni, Teresa Lyles Holmes, Victoria Johnson, Julie Kembel, Ann Lemon, Carol Lindner, Bessie Love, Barbara Mitchell, John P. Mitchell, Sharon Morgan, Daniela Morrisey, Katie Garber Penner, Donna Richardson, Teresa Ridley, Maryanne Russell, David Satcher, Tuti Scott, Attallah Shabazz, Maggie Spilner, Roberta Spivak, Vicki Stokes, Jewel Diamond Taylor, Patrick Taylor, Damon Thompson, Marlene F. Watson, Roniece Weaver, Grace Wilson-Woods

The sister-friends who gave support:
Shelia Baynes, Audrey Edwards, Brenda Stone, Susan Long-Walsh, Helena Mitchell, Olivia G. Shaw, Geraldine Smith, Marlene F. Watson, Nina Wells, Erlene B. Wilson, and the sister-mothers of North Jersey Jack & Jill

My circle of sister-writers:
Bertice Berry, Julia Boyd, Rosemary L. Bray, Bebe Moore Campbell, Harriette Cole, Audrey Edwards, Debrena Jackson Gandy, Benilde Little,

Jill Nelson, Susan L. Taylor, Linda Villarosa, Marlene F. Watson, Valerie Wilson Wesley, Erlene B. Wilson

People who said particularly encouraging words (which I remember, even if you don't):
Clarence Brown, Helen Gurley Brown, Marie Brown, Maya Browne, Faith Hampton Childs, Marlene Connor, Susan Crandell, George Curry, Carole Hall, Lisa Hunt, Dallas Jackson, Lonnie Jones III, Marlene Kahan, Vanesse Lloyd-Sgambati, Claire McIntosh, Teresa Ridley, Lena Sherod, Tracy Sherrod, Lorraine West, Fo Wilson

The writers "out there" who inspired me:
Maya Angelou, James Baldwin, Sarah Ban Breathnach, J. California Cooper, Nora Ephron, Nikki Giovanni, Alex Haley, Laurie Beth Jones, Langston Hughes, Zora Neale Hurston, Anne Lamott, Terry McMillan, Toni Morrison, Danielle Steel, Iyanla Vanzant, Alice Walker, Laura Ingalls Wilder

Every reader of this book—you!
Thank you! Enjoy!

Introduction

We all remember our first kiss, but do you recall the first fitness tip anyone ever gave you? I recall some advice my great-aunt Dorothy gave me when I was eight years old. "From a seated position, raise your foot to your mouth and kiss your big toe. If you do it every day, you'll still be able to do it when you're my age." At the time, I thought Aunt Dorothy was a bit nuts, and I had no idea why I would want to kiss my toe at age eight or sixty-eight, but now I realize that she was giving me, my brother, and my cousin a message about exercise, stretching, flexibility, and longevity. I remember the first kiss I got from a boy, but I also recall that first time I kissed my big toe—and I still do it.

It's that kind of down-home wisdom mixed with New Age advice that *Daily Cornbread* endeavors to deliver. Hopefully, a tip a day will keep the doctor away. The information collected here provides steps toward achieving a strong mind, body, and spirit, and a lifestyle of good health for the new millennium. You'll find out how to get more fiber in your diet, how to stay motivated to work out, how to replace stress with joy, ways to stay spiritually grounded, and more.

I call this wisdom "cornbread" because most of the worthwhile lessons we learn in this life are not of the white bread variety. Plus, cornbread, which has more fiber and began with Southern roots, is becoming increasingly mainstream, more all-American. I mean, if most corner delis in New York City serve corn muffins, and most supermarkets across the country sell Jiffy cornbread mix, it must be the common folks' food. Yet it's becoming quite chic, too. A very upscale restaurant I dined in recently served it instead of the usual crusty bread. Cornbread is food for the soul.

I eat cornbread just about every day. Growing up in Seattle, I started out enjoying my mother's good ol' Southern-style cornbread made from scratch. But now that I live across the country from Mom's cornbread, I make it at home (from the box), or order a toasted corn muffin from the deli for breakfast. One wintry morning as I was preparing to get off my commuter bus, after reading the inspirational pamphlet *Our Daily Bread,* I began to anticipate the warm cornbread muffin I would soon order, along with a cup of English breakfast tea, at the deli near my job in New York City. I thought to myself, *I just finished* Our Daily Bread; *now it's time to eat* my *daily cornbread.* The notion of "daily cornbread" struck me as pretty funny. The Lord's Prayer may say "Give us this day our daily bread," but most days for me that bread is cornbread—literally, figuratively, and culturally.

. . .

Since cornbread is comfort food, *Daily Cornbread* was written to provide words of comfort to all. Here you'll find reassurances that you're on the right track, as well as new information about African American health and well-being. It addresses most specifically African American women, much like the magazine of which I was the first editor-in-chief, *Heart & Soul,* because of the higher incidences of diabetes, hypertension, heart disease, and obesity among us and our families. In addition, after centuries of enslavement, segregation, and the struggle for civil rights, black folks have been totally worn out. As the late activist Fannie Lou Hamer would say, we're sick and tired of being sick and tired. But we've kept on pushing, and now, with affluence among African Americans on the rise, we are slowly allowing a healing to begin. So black folks need a targeted message that we are not getting from other books for the "general population." However, everyone is welcome to share and enjoy the secrets of a strong mind, body, and spirit.

Use it as a book of days—366 (an extra day for leap year), to be exact—of inspiration and motivation. Each day is labeled either "Mind," "Body," or "Spirit," with special sections on observances of Valentine's Day, Black History Month, Black Health & Fitness Week, Men's Health Week, Breast Cancer Awareness Month, Kwanzaa, and other special holidays. Read it day by day. Read a week's work of pages in one day, or take it a month at a time. If you prefer, read it all at once and start using the information right away! You can even read it starting from the end of the book (perfect for lefties, like me): Be sure to check out the "Afterword," written by the United States Surgeon General David Satcher, an inspiring message about what you can do to improve our health and keep it strong far into the new millennium.

If *Daily Cornbread* were rated as movies are, I would say it's PG-13, because I wrote it as a guidebook, not only for African American women, but for our children, teenagers going off to college, sister-friends starting a family, and our elders. At every age, we need good health—from the womb to the tomb. Everything we want in life, and every high purpose we pursue, begins with the power of robust well-being. You *can* have a balanced life and maintain a strong and fit mind, body, and spirit. What follows are some secrets for how to do it—because I *know* you can!

—*Stephanie Stokes Oliver*

Daily Cornbread

❋ JANUARY 1 ❋

Put God first.

"Put God first, then you won't be looking for love in all the wrong places," said Salt of the rap group Salt N Pepa on BET's *Teen Summit*. Salt was talking about sex and relationships, but for all the reasons we individually might need to put God first, this first day of the year would be a good time to make this our first resolution of the new year.

Often we take it for granted that we do put God first, but sometimes we need to check ourselves. Recently, I had to stop and reflect. I was packing my suitcase for a much-needed vacation during which I planned to lounge on a beach and read to my heart's content. The hardest part of packing was deciding what book to take. Should I take the hot-off-the-press book by one of my favorite authors or the novel about the life of Christ that I had picked up to help me understand the Bible better?

After entirely too much deliberation, the thought came to me: *Put God first.* That was it. That was the decision, as clear as could be. And that simple phrase made me evaluate a lot of other things in my life, helping me to make decisions about both complex and simple matters.

Choosing between two books to read may seem like a simple matter. Making the more complex decision that Salt referred to of not choosing a compromising relationship may make you feel lonely at first. But when grappling with which way to go, which road to take, which direction to follow, if you go with the one that puts God first, you can't go wrong.

Here are some everyday ways to put God first:
- ❖ Make prayer your first activity of the day.
- ❖ Put the word "God" in your computer code, ATM pin number, or voice mail passcode (on the phone the keypad numbers are 463).
- ❖ Do something God-like today. (Treat someone lovingly.)

Secret Ingredient: Today is the last day of Kwanzaa, traditionally the Day of Meditation. Reflect on the Kwanzaa principle of *imani* (faith) and the highest values, ethics, and ideals of the past and future of yourself and our people. On January 1, 1863, the Emancipation Proclamation took effect, declaring slaves in the South free. So on this first day of the year "put your mind on freedom."

❋ JANUARY 2 ❋

Get happy.

"There's nothing wrong with stopping to ask yourself whether you're happy and trying to change your life if you're not," writes Mark Mathabane, in his memoir *Love in Black and White.* Growing up under apartheid in South Africa, Mark Mathabane had many reasons not to be happy. He took stock of them and tried to change his life by coming to America. Fortunately, he was successful.

I think it's interesting that he says, "There's nothing wrong with stopping to ask yourself . . ." because too often we don't stop to assess our situations, and we feel guilty for pursuing happiness. In other words, we do think there's something wrong with trying to make ourselves happy. Doing so may mean leaving others behind. Doing so may mean taking a risk, or seeming selfish. Sometimes it's important to stop. Stop living your life in fast forward, stop running in circles—just plain stop and ask yourself: "Am I happy?"

When I was at *Heart & Soul,* we had a lot of strategic planning meetings, quarterly business meetings, three-year planning meetings, and other periods of assessment to see how well our magazine was doing. How many of us take that much time to take stock of how well our own personal lives are going?

This year, I resolve to do it at the beginning of the year, and to do it quarterly, to do "Stephanie's Three-Year Plan" (with a yearly revision); to have weekly family business meetings with my husband and daughters; to ask myself often if I'm happy, and to try to change my life if I'm not.

How about you?

- ❖ Plan a day for your own personal "Assessment" retreat.
- ❖ Take a pad and pencil and sit in your favorite spot, or take notes at a computer if printing out a plan will help make it all seem more "official."
- ❖ Jot down what makes you happy and what keeps you unhappy. Then think of strategies to eliminate the items in the "unhappy" column. Vow to yourself to focus on the things that make you happy. Follow your plan!

Secret Ingredient: Have your own Happy Hour every day—and I don't mean get drunk! Do something that makes you happy for an hour each day.

❄ JANUARY 3 ❄

Resolve to tap the power of the positive.

The new year signals new beginnings; a time to assess what worked last year and what didn't; a time to change. As editor-in-chief of *Heart & Soul*, the health and fitness magazine for African American women, I researched and wrote an editorial that was published one January that covered seven principles of developing a strong body, mind, and spirit. Many of these healthy habits that start on this page and are presented over the next six days, may seem like common sense to you—and they are. *But what is common sense is not always common practice.* So let these suggestions serve as friendly reminders of inspiration to say, "I can do it!" You can begin to use these ideas right now to help you remain true to your New Year's resolutions.

Resolution Number One: Pursue the positive. Maintaining an attitude of hopefulness, optimism, and positivity is the primary legacy of our ancestors. If they hadn't believed that things would get better, or that there would be a better day ahead for their children and grandchildren, how could those who were enslaved and those who faced bigotry, oppression, and segregation have gone any further?

With the psychological energy of positive living, even the toughest challenge is easier to meet. Living positively includes having a strong sense of spirituality, of tranquillity, or purpose in life, self-esteem, and most important, love and happiness (Al Green was right! Or as the hip-hop group Lost Boyz named a CD: *Love, Peace & Nappiness*—which I can personally relate to).

Are you the type of person who sees the glass as half empty or half full? Do people consider you a positive person, or a "rough customer"? Maybe things haven't worked out for you—but you didn't think they would anyway. Remember the old adage: You've got to believe to achieve.

Jewel Diamond Taylor is a motivational speaker, author, and mistress of ceremonies for the African American Women on Tour Conference. As she says at the conference, "When people give you a hard time about your optimism and try to bring you down, just tell them, 'Kiss my positive attitude!' "

Secret Ingredient: **Create a personal affirmation that will help you develop a more positive attitude. Upon waking each day, write down your affirmation ten times (or more) and then practice re-**

peating it in front of the mirror. Let your affirmation become your own sacred mantra and a protection against negative thoughts. Use it whenever you need it.

 BODY

❄ JANUARY 4 ❄

Resolution Number Two: *Commit to healthy habits.*

To keep your body strong, resolve this year to abstain from smoking and abusing alcohol or other substances. Commit to safe sex *every* time. Think about the little things that can make a big difference—like, getting up early enough to be on time for work (that's a continuing challenge for me!). Work on those simple health and safety precautions, such as using seat belts, putting Baby in the backseat (never, ever on your lap in the front), and installing and maintaining smoke detectors in your home.

When President Clinton said during his campaign that he had tried marijuana but didn't inhale, I didn't laugh, because I could relate. When I was in college, I thought it would look cool if I smoked cigarettes, especially when I was out at a club or at one of those jumpin' Howard U parties. Since I didn't drink alcohol, I thought I needed *some* kind of prop! But I found inhaling the smoke to be unnatural and actually pretty hard to do. I thought, *Well, if it's this hard, then it must not be for me.* (Plus I figured I could use the money I spent on cigarettes for clothes!)

According to my childhood diary, one day my father announced to my two older siblings and me, "I'll give you twenty-one dollars if you don't start smoking cigarettes before you turn twenty-one." That was big money to a little kid back in those days, and my brother, André, and I took him up on the challenge. Unfortunately, Vicki paid more attention to the prevailing glamorous media images and peer messages of how "Kool" it was, and she started smoking at age fourteen.

Thankfully, for Vicki, getting older made her wiser and she began to realize the dangers of smoking. And when her friend Emily told her she would help her quit, Vicki knew she could do it. "Whenever I would tell Emily I felt like having a cigarette, she would say, 'No you don't, Vicki. You're a nonsmoker.' After you make a decision, someone's help can carry you through." Whatever your unhealthy habit, take the first step: Make the decision to stop.

Secret Ingredient: **For more information on how to stop smoking cigarettes, call the American Lung Association at 1-800-LUNG-USA, or visit their Web site: http://www.lungusa.org. Or, if there's another habit you need to abandon, develop a plan to stop it, and follow it.**

❄ JANUARY 5 ❄

Resolution Number Three:
Nourish your body with good food.

Don't use food as recreation or an antidote for stress. Inspirational speaker and comedian Dr. Bertice Berry says that when she was twenty-six years old the stress of writing her doctoral dissertation made her turn to overeating. "I was eating Haagen Dazs bars," Bertice recalled in 1996 at *Heart & Soul's* African American Women on Tour Conference seminar called "Loving Those Big Brown Thighs and Other Healthy Habits." "When I would write a paragraph that I thought was brilliant, I would reward myself with a Haagen Dazs bar. It got down to sentences. After that I was like, 'the use of the word *the*—that was brilliant.' I gained about fifty pounds during that process. I was sitting there eating and writing and eating and writing, until I realized, 'I can't do this!' And I lost the weight quickly."

Like Bertice, we all can create a healthier lifestyle: Eat only when you are hungry. Nourish your body with foods low in fat, and include more vegetables, beans, fruits, and whole grains. Make these, not meat, the centerpiece of your plate. Try new ways to healthy-up old favorites: Next time you decide to make candied yams, hold the sugar and try a baked sweet potato instead. Because I rarely experimented with food, I had been cooking for my family for years before I realized that a yam can be baked just like a "regular" potato. My husband likes to experiment with seasoning greens, so when he makes a pot of greens no one misses the fattening hamhock. Sometimes he uses herbs, sometimes he cooks with smoked turkey. Men who cook just seem to be more adventurous in the kitchen than we sisters (like me) who just want to get the meal done after a long day at work. Take a cue from the brothers and enjoy the adventure of good nutrition.

Secret Ingredient: **And this time I really mean it, as in recipes. Take a dish that you prepare that you know is high in fat, sugar, or salt, and give it a makeover.**

❋ BODY

❄ JANUARY 6 ❄

Resolution Number Four: *Commit to get fit.*

I know it's hard—mainly because getting regular exercise can be such a chore! But I also know (and probably you do, too) that all the evidence suggests that keeping fit is not just a health bonus, but a vital necessity. The good news is that there are so many ways to get in that thirty minutes of exercise at least three times a week. You can jog, cycle, dance, play tennis, work out at home or at the gym, take an aerobics class. Or, get to steppin' like my friend Erlene Wilson, who got a step platform, a video, a cute black unitard, and now feels so good after her basement workout at home in Maryland, that she just hates to go a day without it.

Another great way to get steppin' is to go walking. In a survey of black women, walking for fitness was the number-one activity. It's also the most popular exercise among all women.

Of course, it's hard to stay motivated to walk around your neighborhood, local track, or in the park if you live in parts of the country that have frequent rain, snow, or cold weather at this time of year. And it's easy to indulge the excuse that it's too dark to exercise by the time you get home from work. Well, do as my friend Marlene Watson does: Get a treadmill or use one at your local gym. Marlene, who lives in Pennsylvania, says she has gotten hooked on hittin' the rubber every morning. Here are a couple of treadmill workout tips to get you up and running:

❖ **Start slowly and gradually.** Begin by using a very slow speed to become accustomed to the machine. Work out for only the amount of time that you feel comfortable doing so. Increase the speed and time of your workout as comfort level increases. Try for at least forty minutes at a moderate pace, three times a week.

❖ **Get a grip.** The first time I tried a treadmill, girl, I thought I was going to fall off! Don't worry about looking like a novice—

hold on to the rails until you feel ready to let go and swing your arms naturally. (You'll look cuter holding on than tumbling to the ground!)

Secret Ingredient: Fitness experts say that the best way to commit to exercising is to choose an activity *you* enjoy doing—not what your friends like to do, or what's popular on TV infomercials, but what you enjoy returning to time after time.

 BODY

❄ JANUARY 7 ❄

Resolution Number Five: *Watch your weight.*

Couple good nutrition with regular exercise to achieve a normal, healthy weight. This may be a benefit for vanity, but more important, it can prevent heart disease, hypertension, and diabetes—all life-threatening illnesses that we are more prone to.

The first step? Steer away from "going on a diet." Instead, *change your diet* by eating foods low in fat, and by stressing conscious control over eating habits.

I got a lesson in the relationship between weight and diet when I went off to college. So merry to be "free" of my mother's nutritious meals, I began a dubious, but delicious habit of having a nuked "honey bun" (imagine a huge cinnamon pastry with sugary icing slathered all over) for breakfast, lunch from the local greasy-spoon or hamburger joint (always including fries and a chocolate malt), and an all-you-can eat soul food dinner from the med-school cafeteria across the street from my dorm. This became my daily diet! Needless to say, the phrase "freshman fifteen" became a reality—and then some. I have no idea how much weight I put on because I refused to get on a scale, but when I had gained enough dress sizes that none of the clothes I had brought three thousand miles to college fit me, and I had no money for a new wardrobe, I knew I had a weight problem. Not having had that kind of problem before, I wasn't sure what to do about it, except to tell my schoolmates that I was "on a diet." But I was clueless as to how to diet healthfully and effectively. So I lost no weight.

Then, I started dating a brother who was a vegetarian. If I wanted to go out to dinner with him, that meant dining in places with names like The Golden Temple. We started talking about our bodies as "temples."

When he cooked for me, I never missed the meat. And we began to study up on how to get all the vitamins and minerals our bodies needed. You can probably guess the end of my story: I lost the weight and kept it off. I haven't had a hamburger since 1972, and I don't miss it. Now, I'm not saying that everyone ought to be a vegetarian, but I will say this: I changed my diet, my way of eating, my relationship to food, my dining lifestyle—and if you are determined, so can you.

Secret Ingredient: **Maintain a healthy eating plan of low-fat, high-fiber foods, including "5 a Day"—that's five servings of fruits and vegetables, which is as easy as fruit on your cereal, a salad for lunch (counts for at least two servings), and two veggies at dinner. (Serving = ¹/₂ cup.)**

❋ BODY

❋ JANUARY 8 ❋

Resolution Number Six: *Be proactive in preventive care.*

Health care is not just about shots and checkups. It also means actively participating in a relationship with your doctor, dentist, and other health practitioners—and being an advocate for high-quality health care for everyone.

Byllye Avery, founder of the National Black Women's Health Project, is one of my health heroes. In a black history feature in *Heart & Soul,* writer Kirk Johnson reported on how she turned personal tragedy into a health mission. In 1970, Avery was a special-education teacher with two young children when her husband, Wesley, died suddenly at age thirty-three of massive heart failure. Her grief turned into serious contemplation about health and prevention of such loss—and then she took action. Over the next ten years, in Gainesville, Florida, she became a co-founder of a women's health center, an alternative birthing center, and eventually, the National Black Women's Health Project. The now-national organization based in Washington, D.C., began as a support group, Avery says, "so black women could come together and be validated." That validation comes through conferences, the Walking for Wellness program, films made about black women's reproductive rights, sexuality, and prenatal care, and more. She has been honored with an *Essence* Award and a MacArthur Foundation genius award.

Avery practices what she preaches by eating mainly "fish and fruit," she says, and by walking and getting annual checkups. We each can follow her good example by doing these three things:

- ❖ looking after our own health care by eating right and living healthfully;
- ❖ being proactive in the prevention of diseases and seeing a doctor at the first signs of symptoms;
- ❖ caring about the well-being of our community, by advocating for quality health care for everyone. It's a healthy thing to do.

Secret Ingredient: **Call your doctor to make an appointment for a physical today.**

 MIND

❄ JANUARY 9 ❄

Resolution Number Seven: *Relish your relationships.*

Make the people you love a priority. Good love is what we all need and deserve—as a matter of fact, is there any other real love?

Creating a cocoon of loving ties around you is often harder than we want it to be—but it's important work. Strong relationships are a vital aspect of emotional and physical health. Also, because of pervasive domestic violence, we must consider our health when we select a partner. As I once heard Oprah Winfrey say on her show, "If love hurts, it's not real love because real love feels good."

I have a close friend, Marlene F. Watson, who is a psychologist in private practice and is director of the Graduate Program in Couple and Family Therapy at MCP Hahnemann in Philadelphia (in other words, she has a Ph.D. in knowing a thing or two about relationships). She also happens to write the "Good Loving" column in *Heart & Soul.* In the relationship forums that the magazine has hosted in cities across the country in conjunction with African American Women on Tour, Marlene has stated that her philosophy is that we should seek three things in relationships. She calls them the Three As.

- ❖ **Affection:** "Show affection to ourselves first—mind, body, and soul," she says. "And then to others."
- ❖ **Affirmation:** "Affirm ourselves, so that we can affirm others."
- ❖ **Appreciation:** "Show appreciation for the love you get by giving love in return." Start today by showing your loved ones (yourself included) your own special brand of the Three As.

Secret Ingredient: Read *The Best Kind of Loving: A Black Woman's Guide to Finding Intimacy,* by Dr. Gwendolyn Goldsby Grant. Or, you can get it, like I did, on audiocassette. It beats listening to songs on the radio about love gone wrong. Pop it in the car cassette player and get empowered!

 MIND

✳ JANUARY 10 ✳

Cultivate wealth.

Now that we have made our New Year's resolutions, I must ask you a serious question: Would you like to hit the lottery? Okay, okay ... maybe you don't like the idea of gambling (and maybe that wasn't so serious). So let me ask another question: Would you like to have wealth? Uh-huh, me too; most of us have that in common. If you think about it, though, you probably already have a certain degree of wealth; one that you may take for granted, that you might have even gambled with from time to time. You guessed it—that wealth is your God-given health.

What's the most common refrain of expectant parents when asked, "Do you want a boy or girl?" Answer: "It doesn't matter as long as it's healthy." What do most people on the planet want more than wealth? Answer: health.

No matter who we are, from womb to tomb we want optimum health. Yet we tend to value it most when we don't have it. And when we do have it, especially when we're young and kickin', we often take it for granted with risky behaviors of smoking, drinking, drugging, overeating, and underexercising. Add racism, stress, and societal pressures to the mix, and it's no wonder our wondrous bodies break down.

But with faith, commitment, dedication, information, and inspiration, we can become stronger than the negative powers. Here are some ways that you can start today:

❖ Go deep within. Weed out the negative and begin to love the unique you that you are.

❖ Read the books, get the videos (often available at your local library) to learn how to be strong and fit.

❖ During your annual checkup, ask your doctor to advise you on a personal "optimum health plan."

❖ Check out magazine beauty pages for ways to glow with good health.

- Be strong, settle for no less than wholesome and caring relationships.
- Gather your "wealth," cultivate it, and share it with those you love.

Secret Ingredient: Today, do something—anything—that you *know* is healthy. Make an effort and it just may become a habit.

 MIND

❄ JANUARY 11 ❄

Increase your self-worth.

"Your self-worth should always be greater than your net worth," says financial planner Suze Orman, on her audiobook *The 9 Steps to Financial Freedom.* Listening to the tapes, I found Orman's financial philosophy pretty interesting. Her cassette jacket explains: "Before we can get control of our finances, we must get control of our attitudes about money; letting go of anxieties and creating new attitudes are the first steps. . . . Financial freedom is about realizing that we are worth far more than our money."

Unfortunately, for too many of us, both our self-worth *and* our net worth are far too low. But when you think about the ways that financial experts advise us to increase net worth, some of those strategies can also work for our self-worth. Like these:

Net worth: *Make automatic deposits into your bank account.* **Self worth:** *Make automatic deposits into your self-esteem bank. Automatically assume you are worthy of the good things in life. Develop the habit of acknowledging the best about yourself.*

Net worth: *Pay yourself first.* **Self worth:** *Pay yourself compliments before you head out the door. Did you look especially good this morning? Are you wearing a shade of nail polish that particularly complements your skin tone? Each time you pay a compliment to someone else, think of one for yourself.*

Net worth: *Learn about investments.* **Self worth:** *Invest in yourself. Buy clothes in lesser quantity, and invest in higher quality. Go back to finish school, or if you've already graduated, take specific classes to make yourself more marketable—or just more knowledgeable.*

Net worth: *Make sure you have a will.* **Self worth:** *Develop strong will and couple it with personal integrity. As the saying goes, "where there's a will, there's a way."*

Secret Ingredient: Make financial decisions that increase your self-worth, rather than your materialism, and your fiscal fitness will stay well balanced.

✳ JANUARY 12 ✳

Count your pennies from heaven.

The show was *Lifestyles of the Rich and Famous.* The guest was Sinbad. "I'm glad you had me on this show," he said to host Robin Leach, "because I did grow up rich—I had a mother and a father and a happy family."

I've heard similar remarks from my mother. Looking back on her early life in segregated Selma, Alabama, she says her family probably was "poor," but she adds, "we didn't know it. My sister and I had the love of our family, our community, our church. And we were well dressed because our aunt sent us the beautiful, hardly worn clothes of the wealthy Hollywood children whose families she worked for."

Nikki Giovanni expressed her thoughts on the subject in this excerpt from her poem "Nikki-Rosa":

> *. . . if you become famous or something*
> *they never talk about how happy you were to have*
> *your mother*
> *all to yourself . . .*
> *And though you're poor it isn't poverty that*
> *concerns you . . .*
> *but only that everybody is together and you*
> *and your sister have happy birthdays and very good*
> *Christmases*
> *and I really hope no white person ever has cause*
> *to write about me*
> *because they never understand*
> *Black love is black wealth . . .*

Secret Ingredient: Read the poem above in its entirety in *The Selected Poems of Nikki Giovanni,* then flip to my other Nikki favorites, "My House" and "A Certain Peace."

❋ JANUARY 13 ❋

Celebrate the day of your birth.

Today is my birthday. I was fortunate to have a mother who celebrated the birthdays of her children with wonderful parties that made each birthday seem very special. Memories of those birthdays, along with my parents' gifts and cards long after I was grown, and my husband's enthusiastic sharing in the day, has always put me in the mood to celebrate my own birth each year. As my friend Kathryn Leary says, "Birthdays signify the new year in our personal lives." Keeping that in mind, I've created some birthday rituals. Feel free to use them for yourself!

Par-tay! Of course, the most obvious way to celebrate is to have a party. When I turned thirty-five, I threw a party for myself. When I turned forty, I threw a party for myself! A friend said to me that she would never think to give herself a party, that that was something she would leave to her husband. I asked if he had ever given her a birthday party. She said no. "Well, then don't wait on a man or anyone else. Create your own fun!" I told her. My husband threw me a great thirty-ninth birthday, but I didn't want him to feel anxious about planning the kind of party *I* wanted to have for my fortieth, and I also didn't want to wonder if I would get a repeat surprise, so I planned the party at a restaurant myself and he volunteered to help. We've got to get over these notions that it's not okay to do for yourself. Plus, it relieves the pressure on others.

Take the day off. I once had a boyfriend who never worked on his birthday. His rationale was, "If I have the day off for Martin Luther King's birthday, and Lincoln and Washington's birthdays, why shouldn't I take off for my own birthday?" Since I met him around the time that I started my career, I've always taken my birthday off. And when I became a manager, I encouraged the staff to do the same.

Send your parents flowers. At some point, it occurred to me that it really didn't make a lot of sense that we expect the people who brought us into the world to give us gifts and parties, too. After all, I thought, it was my mother who endured labor on that day, and my father had his own waiting-room anxiety. So do as I do; give thanks with a single flower or a bouquet.

Secret Ingredient: If you can't afford to send flowers, there are lots of wonderful, poignant greeting cards these days. Or, better still, make a card or write a letter. Whatever you decide, send your mother, parents, or guardian a note of thanks.

❄ JANUARY 14 ❄

Say thanks; it makes room for more.

James Cleveland sang about it. Your mama told you to do it. Say thanks.
  It may seem like a trivial thing. Of course you say thanks; you say it all the time, you're probably thinking. Well, I'm discovering that it really isn't something that happens naturally. To make the expression of gratitude a part of your natural attitude, consider these examples.

When a stranger gives you a courtesy: What I've observed to the point of pet peeve, is that many folks now substitute "okay" for "thank you." When I'm on line for the commuter bus, someone inevitably comes by and asks anyone, "Is this the line for the number thirty-three bus?" Then someone else will answer "Yes." Then the original person will just walk off muttering, "Okay." Say what?

When you know you need to write a thank-you note: We all get busy after someone has done us a pleasantry, but it's always worth it to express your gratitude, even after the time you think the person may have forgotten about it. When my brother was in college, he brought home a classmate who became a house-guest pest. He was a nice guy, charming, and handsome (fine, actually; I remember him well!). My parents were more than happy to extend their gracious hospitality to anyone that André called a friend. However, it turned out that Mr. Fine stayed longer than originally planned, eating my mother's cooking paid for by the grocery money my father provided, lounging around the house, and generally driving me to distraction. After he (finally) left, my parents began to anticipate a note of thanks for all their trouble. A couple of weeks went by that became months and years, no thank-you note. Then the nonexistent note of thanks became fodder for family stories at the Christmas table. "Hey Jo, remember that boy that came and stayed here all that time and never sent us a thank-you note?" my father would start. Just goes to show that people do remember your inaction.

When you have a blessing to acknowledge: God should get thank-yous, too! For the big things and even for the little things. My cousin Gloria Leonard once told me that she says "Thank you, God," even when she comes up on a hard-to-find parking space.

Secret Ingredient: **Keep a gratitude journal. Commit to writing down three things every day for which you are grateful. You'll quickly see all that you have to be thankful for.**

✳ JANUARY 15 ✳

Rev. Dr. Martin Luther King, Jr.'s Birthday

Strive to be a doer.

It really irks me that each year on the birthday of Martin Luther King, Jr., the television coverage, commercials, and print advertising mainly characterize this great man as a "dreamer." "Celebrating the Dream," "Live the Dream," "Remembering the Dream" become the sound bites, catchphrases, and one-liners of the day. But to me, King was not just a dreamer but a *doer.*

I'm old enough to remember when King was alive. The headlines were much different then, more along the lines of "King Leads Bus Boycott," "King Gets Jailed," "King Leads Peaceful March from Selma to Montgomery," "King Wins Nobel Peace Prize." He definitely wasn't sitting around dreaming.

And neither should we. Now that King has been saluted with a national holiday, use the day off to make a difference. Here are some options:

❖ **Agitate.** Go to a conference on activism. As an example, for the King holiday in 1999, Rev. Al Sharpton's National Action Network took the opportunity to schedule a conference at the Waldorf-Astoria Hotel in New York City to bring attention to disparities in the advertising community.

❖ **Fund-raise.** An organization in my town gives a $20 breakfast each year to raise money for scholarships in King's name.

❖ **Serve others.** In his radio address to the nation in 1999, President Clinton encouraged Americans to take part in community service in observance of the King holiday.

❖ **Make a pilgrimage.** Go to Atlanta and participate in the activities of the Martin Luther King Center for Nonviolent Social Change. In recent years, an animated film on King's life was premiered, and Coretta Scott King bestowed the Martin Luther King Peace Prize to people working toward international unity and peace.

❖ **Read.** Ever think about what else besides "I have a dream," Martin Luther King, Jr., said in his other speeches? It's all in *A Testament of Hope: The Essential Writings and Speeches of Martin Luther King, Jr.,* edited by James M. Washington. Excellent resource!

Secret Ingredient: For updated information on events at the Atlanta King Center visit www.thekingcenter.com.

✳ JANUARY 16 ✳

To find your purpose, follow your passion.

What did Martin Luther King, Jr., and Diana the princess of Wales have in common? A first inclination might be to say "not much." One was born black in the segregated South of the United States and struggled against injustice all his life. The other was born white into British aristocracy, married a prince, and, some might say, lived a fairy tale life.

But think again. Both died tragically during the height of their contributions to society. News reports after Princess Diana's tragic death in a car accident in Paris in 1997 portrayed a young woman passionate about humanitarian issues, about helping the poor, advocating for more AIDS research, influencing decisions to ban landmines. Martin Luther King, Jr., who was assassinated almost thirty years before Diana's death, was also passionate about humanitarian causes, about helping the poor, and stopping war efforts. Although both were just in their thirties when their lives ended, it could be said that both had found their purpose in life by just following their passion.

As *Essence* magazine editor-in-chief Susan L. Taylor says in her speeches, "We were created *on purpose for a purpose.*" Bertice Berry talks about purpose in her speeches, too: "I have a dream," she says, "that everyone will fulfill their purpose. Sometimes we're so busy helping other people get on the right path that we get off our own path."

But many people wonder just what their purpose in life is. Just what are we here on earth for? One thing is sure: Only *you* can determine that for yourself; not your mama, not your daddy, not your man, your sister, or your pastor. It's something you must grapple with within your soul. As a matter of fact, you could call it soul-wrestling. You may decide on a purpose, and then change your mind. That's okay, too.

I always thought my purpose would come to me in some lightning and thunderbolt way. You know, like in that *Ten Commandments* kind of way. But when the thought came to me, it made me laugh. A children's church song that I had thought was pretty corny when I was a kid in the junior church choir came into my head one day when I was feeling love for the sun: "A sunbeam, a sunbeam/Jesus wants me for a sunbeam/A sunbeam, a sunbeam/I'll be a sunbeam for Him." As an adult I began to relate to the lyrics in a way I didn't as a child. I knew I wanted my personal life and my work to exude a certain warmth, to be a light to others, to help folks feel good and happy—like the sun.

What's your purpose? Whatever it is, it can come only from within you.

Secret Ingredient: Today, take time out and allow yourself to let *any* thoughts form that could help you formulate your purpose— silly thoughts, corny ones, outrageous ramblings, *whatever.* Be un- inhibited on purpose.

 BODY

❄ JANUARY 17 ❄

Claim your own beauty.

I don't have to tell anyone who's black that our beauty is rarely recog- nized—much less celebrated. And because of that, we're often struggling to accept our unique beauty, frequently falling into the trap of trying to adapt to the impossible beauty standards of the American dominant cul- ture. How can a brown-eyed, black-haired brickhouse constantly see her beauty when she's bombarded with images of blue-eyed, blond waifs?

In all fairness, women of all races are waging a backlash against the prevailing standards of body image. Many women are tired of seeing stick-thin women in magazines and other media, and are pressuring im- age makers to portray more realistic body types. But you can change your attitude without waiting for the media. Here are ways to take the lead in celebrating your own beauty:

Make "Black Is Beautiful" an affirmation. Keep repeating the phrase, continue to believe that African Americans are, indeed, a beauti- ful people, and that you as one of that tribe are a beautiful person.

See beauty from inside out first. Like your mama said, beauty is as beauty does. Be a warm, loving person, and you'll exude a quality more important than outward superficiality.

Take pride in our unique features. Our full lips should be a source of pride in our African heritage. Many white models and celebrities are getting collagen injections to create the illusion of what we have natu- rally—so why are we still ashamed? The flare of our nostrils may give us some indication of our tribe of origin. Plus, as we know from certain celebrities whose nose jobs have been blatantly botched, there's no reason to think any plastic surgeon can do a better job at shaping noses than God did. Our tightly curled hair is unique, special—and it's all good!

Secret Ingredient: Don't let America's media images be your only images. Every so often, open up a photography book of Africa. Study the beauty of our African sisters and brothers. In the late

1980s after seeing the Broadway musical *Sarafina*, I was so touched by the short naturals the cast wore that I cut my hair to emulate them. We don't have to get our inspiration only from fashion magazines intended for other women. Do the research about your own beauty.

 MIND

❄ JANUARY 18 ❄

Feel good about your achievements, as well as your goals.

Like most folks always striving for toward future goals, I rarely acknowledge current successes. One day over lunch, my book editor, Janet Hill, asked me if I had attained my "dream job" as editor-in-chief of *Heart & Soul*. The question took me aback. I had to put down the fork with which I had been devouring a delicious Caesar salad to think about it. As a budding young journalist I had said in every job interview in response to the question, "What is your ultimate career goal?" that I would like to be "editor-in-chief of a major national women's magazine." I achieved that. Yet, my goals of making the magazine a big success, and writing books that might make a difference had become such obsessions that I hadn't taken time to reflect on my hard-earned achievement. I hadn't realized until Janet brought it up that I rarely sit back, pat myself on the back, and think: *Job well done, Steph; you did what you set out to do!* I think there's a self-perception that to "sit back," even for a second, will result in a "setback."

The reality is that if we don't take at least a moment every once in a while to sit back, reflect, and praise ourselves, who else will? How can we see ourselves as winners if we don't acknowledge what we've already won? In self-help books and tapes, we're often asked to write down our goals for the future. I suggest that each time we do that we also jot down our achievements thus far. It may make you feel good about your personal progress. You may be able to take pride in what that success has contributed to your family, your community, our country, our world, even the universe.

There's a gospel song that says, "We've come a long way. We've still got a long way to go." But the reverse is also true: We've still got a long way to go, but, boy, have we come a long way! And that's an achievement that's just as important to be acknowledged.

Secret Ingredient: Sometime today sit down and list your achievements. (Don't be embarrassed: No one has to see this list but you!) As the old saying goes, you won't know where you're going if you don't know where you've been.

✳ JANUARY 19 ✳

Stay spiritually grounded.

A sister in the audience of the *Ricki Lake Show* asked guest L. L. Cool J, "What do you attribute your longevity in the business to?"

Lazily watching the show on a day off from work, I was surprised by L. L.'s answer. "I just try to stay spiritually grounded, and to treat other people the way I want to be treated," he said earnestly.

I was surprised, because I really didn't expect him to go there—in that spiritual direction. In addition, he said that he follows the Golden Rule of doing "unto others as you would have them do unto you."

It's easier said than done to "stay spiritually grounded." And what does that really mean? To stay grounded in spirituality? To let spirituality keep you grounded? I would say both. But there are many temptations to be grounded in earthly things. You can be grounded in the belief that money will cure all that ails you. You can be grounded in jealousy and envy of others. You can even get "grounded"—for bad behavior, if you're a teenager. No, it's not often that someone says they are grounded on a spiritual path. I commend L. L. Cool J. for that.

Think today of what you can do to stay spiritually grounded in your own life:

- ❖ Is it church attendance that does it for you?
- ❖ Is it reading the Bible or Quran?
- ❖ Maybe it's prayer or meditation.
- ❖ Is it just watching a beloved baby sleep (especially one who is hyperrambunctious when awake!)?

Whatever it is that keeps your faith on solid ground is a beautiful thing.

Secret Ingredient: Remember that spiritual ground is always the high road. When deciding which road to take—the low road or the high road—try to reach for higher ground.

✳ JANUARY 20 ✳

Reach out and touch . . .

I used to think that Diana Ross song about reaching out and touching somebody's hand was pretty corny. That was probably because when the song came out, I was young enough to be more interested in reaching out and touching some *boy's* hand.

But with age comes certain wisdoms—or at least a different take on things. And I reconsidered the power of touch more recently when I heard Henry D'Souza, the archbishop of Calcutta, say on TV in eulogizing Mother Teresa that "the warmth of her hands conveyed the compassion of her heart." Mother Teresa was a small woman with a big heart, and the feelings of caring she had for strangers was often first expressed through a word, a touch, a gesture. A dying baby, a homeless man—both could equally feel compassion through Mother Teresa's gentle stroke of the head, pat on the arm, touch of the cheek.

Touch, though nonverbal, can say so much. It can convey happiness or harassment. Love or abuse. And many things in between these extremes. What does your touch most often say about you? Does it most often convey something compassionate?

I had a loving aunt—you know, the "other mother" kind of aunt, my mother's big sister—whose birthday is today, January 20. In the many years I was blessed to have her in my life before she died in 1996, we shared, among lots of things, the bond of being left-handed. With her left hand, Aunt Katie touched many a person—literally. As one of the first African American nurses in the State of Washington, she soothed thousands of sick people who needed a caring touch. With a specialty in obstetrics, hers were often the first "laying on of hands" a newborn received. You can be sure that with Aunt Katie, those babies were welcomed into the world with the kind of touch any mother would want for her child.

As Gladys Knight said in a televised concert at the White House, "I'm trying to be like the phone company: Reach out and touch somebody."

Secret Ingredient: **Start today to develop your compassion. Using Mother Teresa's example, begin by conveying warmth to someone who least expects it.**

✳ JANUARY 21 ✳

Praise the good.

You know how you can sometimes meet a person, and feel that you've known him all your life? That's how I felt upon meeting Alex Haley, the author of the American epic *Roots,* in Egypt, while on one of the most fortunate business trips I've ever had.

The trip was already magical for me. In 1990, as editor of *Essence* magazine, I went to Egypt to lead a photoshoot of the Dance Theatre of Harlem (DTH) in front of the pyramids. At a reception for DTH at the Cairo Marriott, I met Haley, who was there for the opening of the movie *Roots.* Over dinner with him and his host, an African American consulate officer, I gained many wisdoms about writing and truly felt as though some great ancestral griot had bestowed this precious time of sharing, laughing, and storytelling with me. One of his most memorable adages was, "Find the good, and praise it."

Unfortunately, too soon thereafter, Alex Haley passed away, and actually became an ancestor. I would say that he died before we had a chance to cultivate a friendship, but because meeting him was a sublime pleasure (made all the more special because of the surrounding pyramids, the Nile, the museum treasures of King Tut, and the awesome performance of DTH), I knew that the meeting was as blessed as a friendship.

Alex Haley's life was about finding the good and praising it, and I could tell that he practiced what he preached. Why don't we use his example and look for goodness today?—and when we find it, let's be sure to praise it!

Secret Ingredient: **Catch someone you love doing something right. We're always catching someone doing something we disapprove of. Instead, let your child, your man, your mother, your boss know you noticed their good behavior ("I saw that—you washed the dishes! Thank you!").**

❋ JANUARY 22 ❋

Let Grace help you win the race.

Lately, I've been thinking about the concept of "grace"—a word that is common in religious language, but uncommon in everyday speech. But most of us have heard of the song "Amazing Grace," and many may even know the words well enough to sing along.

My dictionary says that grace is "divine love and protection bestowed freely upon mankind."

Now, black humankind likes to mime and rhyme, whether we're speaking the "King's English," like, say Jesse Jackson, or the language of hip hop, like say, Puffy Combs. Myself included. So, during a sermon at my church that I was just about zoned out of (not because of anything that reflected negatively on the preaching, but because I was holding somebody's cuddly baby and totally distracted), my ears perked up when the guest pastor, Rev. Dr. Calvin G. Sampson, Sr., said, "In the word 'grace' is the word 'race.' In the word 'race' is the word 'ace.' " Then his voice hit a crescendo that only preachers can achieve. "God gives you *grace* to run this *race*—and He is your *ace!*" Make that your thought for the day. And here's an easy assignment:

For most of your life have you been mindlessly repeating the same grace before you eat a meal? Before your next meal, decide not to utter anything you've ever said before. Give some thought to how grace has made a difference in your life, and how it allows you to receive the blessing of food for the nourishment of your body. *Amen.*

Secret Ingredient: **Today, consider how grace has intervened in your life. What were the occasions on which you knew the turnaround was "amazing"? Reflect and give thanks.**

✴ JANUARY 23 ✴

Stop whining and start winning!

Once upon a time, I had a supervisor who totally intimidated me. Physically attractive, yet tough as fake nails, she took great joy in calling me into her office for the most trifling infractions. On one particular occasion, she had me shaking in my platform boots after she couldn't make out something I had written and began screaming, "Use number-two pencils, Stephanie! *Number-two!*"

As fate would have it, this person with the powerful job and stern manner was abruptly fired. She was the first person I ever knew to get fired, so this caused me some anxiety. The next time I had a one-on-one with our top boss, I gathered up enough nerve to ask her if she wouldn't mind sharing with me why my supervisor had been fired. I wanted to know, I said, so that I would avoid her mistakes.

"She was a whiner and complainer," she said matter-of-factly. "She always came in with problems, but never with solutions."

I hadn't witnessed the whining manner, but I didn't doubt that my former supervisor was always complaining. Her interaction with me had been one complaint after another! I vowed then to always think of a solution—even if it seemed like a dumb one—to the problems I took to my boss. As time went by I became known for being a problem solver, for offering solutions. And I started to win! I got promoted and I gained the respect of my team.

What's your *modus operandi?* Whining or winning? Take stock of your M.O. and start winning today. You can do it!

Secret Ingredient: Why be a whiner when you can be a winner? Take note of the winning strategies of people with whom you work and socialize. Then next time you have a complaint, use the strategy to develop an unemotional, constructive solution.

❄ JANUARY 24 ❄

Work that body!

If you've already reneged on your New Year's resolution to work out more often, it may give you consolation to know that according to a federal health study, January could be called the laziest month of the year. That's right. Although more than 25 percent of adults in this country admit to not working out at all—regardless of what month it is—the number of nonexercisers rises to 35.3 percent in January.

My excuse in January is the snow. Where I live, there could be snow on the ground just about every day—and who wants to go for a power-walk in slush? To tell the truth, it's easy to think of excuses for not exercising no matter what the time of year; here are some doozies I've collected in David Letterman's Top Ten Countdown list style:

Top 10 Excuses That Sisters Have for Not Exercising

10. "Been there, done that when I was in school."
9. "I'm afraid of getting funky."
8. "I need to lose twenty pounds before I'm seen in spandex."
7. "I'm allergic to exercise."
6. "Working out is boring."
5. "I'm already slim, so I don't need to exercise."
4. "My new love is taking up all my free time!"
3. "I'm too tired to exercise."
2. "I don't know what to do with the kids while I work out."
1. **And my favorite excuse:** "I'll sweat and my hair will 'go back.'"

If exercise is such a bother, why bother? Well, for good reasons (that most of us already know): Becoming more physically active helps make us more fit. Becoming more fit, helps us to feel more in control of our health. It wards off health problems that can compromise our quality of life, such as heart disease, high blood pressure, diabetes, and obesity. And it's vital to a long, strong life.

Secret Ingredient: **Over the next few days, I'll give you some ways to excuse-proof your fitness lifestyle. Start your warm-up now: Put your arms up above your head; now *stretch* and try to touch the sky!**

❄ JANUARY 25 ❄

Exercise excuse proof tip: Don't think of it as a **workout.**

If you consider your workout just more work after your workday, you'll be less likely to get motivated and to stick with it.

Here's how to change your mind about it: Think of your workout as playtime. When you were a kid, didn't you love to go outside and play after school? Wasn't it fun jumping up and down on your bed until you got busted by your mom?

Just change "going outside to play" to "going outside for a jog around the park." When I was a child, the house I lived in was near a playground called Garfield Park next to the "black" high school, Garfield High (Quincy Jones and Jimi Hendrix went to that school, but that's another subject). Looking back, I think of how much exercise I got hanging out there: First, there was the seven- or eight-block run to get there (I was always so excited, I ran the whole way). Then I had to hit every piece of equipment there—the swings (pumping your legs to go high took energy!), the merry-go-round (getting it started with one leg pushing off the ground was hard!), the tetherball (all that jumping up and hitting the ball was strenuous!), and the monkey bars (climbing to the top took leg and arm strength!). Now that I'm grown, I live 3,000 miles from that park, but thank goodness for the one near me. In Brookdale Park, I may pass up the playground, but the track and the walking trail are my haunts; for some of my neighbors, the tennis courts are their playground.

Now I wouldn't advise jumping up and down on the bed . . . But, hey, an exercise trampoline is reasonably small and can fit just about anywhere in the house, and slide under the bed when you're not using it.

Secret Ingredient: **Exercise trampolines are inexpensive. Look for them wherever sporting goods and exercise equipment are sold and start your playtime soon.**

❋ JANUARY 26 ❋

Excuse-proof exercise tip: Do it in spurts.

Perhaps you're not inclined to run an exercise marathon, but may I interest you in a few hundred-yard dashes? Research indicates that three ten-minute periods of activity may add up to nearly the same fitness payoffs as a solid half hour spent sweating it out at the gym.

Nix a routine that you do only a few days a week, and make fitness a part of your life every day. Here are several activities that are breakable into ten-minute spurts:

* **Walking.** Walk to your bus or train stop. Better yet, walk to work! Walk in the morning, and again on the return trip. A quick lunchtime stroll makes three spurts, and it will also give you a slight energy boost for the rest of the afternoon.
* **Housecleaning.** Vacuum one part of the house in the morning, another in the afternoon, the rest that night.
* **Dancing.** Come on baby, let's do the twist for ten minutes in the morning, pony with your partner for ten more, and get your hip-hop groove on for the last ten.
* **Running.** Run to the bank. Run around the mall. Run around the block (or after the baby).
* **Stretching.** Do ten minutes before you get dressed. Stretch for ten more at work. Do the last ten before you call it a day.
* **Weight lifting.** Ditto the stretching times. I have been known to keep a mini-weight on my desk at work. It comes in handy during long phone calls.

Of course, as Chaka Khan would say, "once you get started . . ." it may be hard to stop, but that's all good!

Secret Ingredient: To keep up with your workout sessions, you may find it helpful to keep a fitness logbook. Look for them in sporting-good stores, or in bookstores (January is a good time to find a yearly log). You can also use a spiral-bound weekly calendar, found in stationery or office-supply stores. Jot down the exercise and the amount of time you spent doing it. At the end of a month, look back at how consistent you were, and which exercises you stick with most.

❄ JANUARY 27 ❄

Excuse-proof exercise tip:
Put on your "play" clothes as soon as you get home.

Now that is probably the easiest tip I'll ever give you. You gotta change clothes anyway, so instead of putting on your same ol' couch-potato uniform, slip into something that will make you feel like working that body! Even if you end up just puttering around the house, at least you'll be more physically active than usual. It's as simple as throwing on a sweatshirt and some leggings. As soon as you tie the sneaks, you'll start to feel like bouncing around instead of lying around.

My colleague Teresa said this tip worked for her. I had written it in one of my editorials and the next thing I knew, I heard her say, "I just read somewhere that if you go home after work and put on your workout clothes, it will help you to get in the mood to work out. I tried it and it worked!"

"That's great! It really works!" I said, immodestly reminding her I was the source of that information.

She added, "Yeah, I put on my jogging suit, and the next thing I knew, I was outside raking leaves, when ordinarily I would have been stretched out on the couch!"

But don't take our word for it. Try it yourself. Today.

Secret Ingredient: **When you lay out your work clothes for the day, also put out your workout clothes. Then, when you get home from work, you won't have to look for them (and have an excuse to throw on something else). Your "play" clothes will be ready for you to jump into.**

❄ JANUARY 28 ❄

Excuse-proof exercise tip: *Work out with your honey.*

Okay, you've done the candlelight dinners, the sensual baths together, the scrumptious homecooked meal. But have you ever said to a brother,

"I'll race you around the track"? Or, "I bet I can do more push-ups than you!" Believe me sisters, it really doesn't matter at all whether you can deliver. It's just the spirit of competition that will turn him on!

I would say that the couple that exercises together, stays together, but I have no proof of that. However, the couple that exercises together does work out more often, according to an Indiana University study.

But with so many women having participated in sports at some time in their life, surely you can challenge him at something. Maybe you're a good swimmer—do some laps that end up in his lap. Maybe you can stage a dance contest for two—and make him forget he ever *heard* of Janet Jackson.

Other ways to work out together:

❖ In-line skating.
❖ Tennis.
❖ Side-by-side at the gym in the weight room or on treadmills.
❖ Riding bikes (try a tandem to really test your teamwork!).
❖ Hiking.
❖ Volleyball.
❖ Skiing.
❖ Sharing a personal trainer.
❖ Spot checking each other's at-home fitness routine.
❖ Shooting hoops.

Secret Ingredient: **If your man's the kind of jock who likes to dominate the game, set up ground rules in the beginning that you'll alternate between his favorite sports and your choice of activities.**

 BODY

❄ JANUARY 29 ❄

Excuse-proof exercise tip: *Get active with your kids.*

Just about all of the sports activities listed on the previous day could also be shared with your children; hitting tennis balls with them, going swimming, riding bikes together. A full day at the amusement park is a workout in itself—even if you don't get on a ride, the walk around the park is great exercise.

I still have fond memories of going roller-skating with my mother. Each year for several years straight, my mother hosted my Jack & Jill children's group at the local roller rink. My mother loves to dance, so roller-skating, which is like dancing on skates, seemed to come easily to her. In fact, her stories of growing up in Selma, Alabama, often include tales of using her skates as her own form of "public transportation" to get from one end of town to the other.

Using her example, even though I was always a fraidy-cat about falling, I am proud to say that I taught my youngest two stepdaughters to roller-skate. On their weekend visits with their dad, the girls loved being active—and Reggie and I enjoyed coming up with fun activities to keep them from bouncing off the walls of our tiny, New York City apartment. There was a roller rink in our Upper West Side neighborhood, and our family spent many Sunday afternoons there.

It's good for our children to see us as physical beings. As vibrant and active. Many mothers complain that they can't work out because they don't know what to do with the kids, but there are many ways to get your exercise that can include the children. If you jog around a track, sit your little one down on the grassy center to play as you make your rounds; you'll be able to see him from every point. At *Heart & Soul*, we once photographed the late Olympic champion Florence Griffith Joyner working out on a stationary bike. And right next to her was her young daughter, Mary, who was pedaling her own pint-sized replica of Mom's bike. Look for children's exercise equipment at sporting-goods stores and major retailers, such as Toys R Us.

Secret Ingredient: **Inquire about "Mommy and Me" workouts during which the mom uses the infant as a weight. Or if Baby's too big for that workout, check out the programs at the YWCA and at health clubs for women; many provide child-care services for your convenience.**

 BODY

❄ JANUARY 30 ❄

Excuse-proof exercise tip: *Don't wear spandex . . .*

. . . that is, if your excuse is that you need to lose twenty pounds before you're seen in spandex. If that rings a bell for you, you can do one of three things: don't wear spandex, exercise at home, or lose twenty pounds. Seriously, though, if you do one of those things, at least you will be doing *something*.

Don't wear spandex. Wear cut-off jeans, wear cotton gym shorts, play a sport that calls for other types of clothing. Actually, though, whether at the gym or in the park, the exercise "uniform" I see most often is spandex bike shorts under an oversized T-shirt that just about covers everything!

Exercise at home. If you feel self-conscious at a gym or health club, create your own workout routine in the privacy of your own home. Or take daily health walks in your 'hood—and wear whatever feels comfortable. There's a video called "Women at Large: Breakout." The description says: "Designed for large women by large women, here's a low-impact, high-result way to begin shaping up."

Lose twenty pounds. I know, I know, this is easier said than done. But it can be done! Exercise! Most folks think the best way to lose weight is to "go on a diet." One thing I've learned is that the word "diet" should not be used to mean something temporary, but rather, something that is permanent—a way of eating, a lifestyle. As in, pursue a healthy diet with fruits and vegetables as the cornerstone, not meat. Couple that with exercise, say walking at a brisk pace, five times a week for forty-five to sixty minutes, and you'll be on the way to achieving your weight-loss goal.

My sister Vicki changed her diet, and saw a TV news story on a black male trainer named Zarif, of Zarif Fitness Center in Inglewood, California near her home, that inspired her to want to join his class. Next thing I knew, she said she had gotten her two grown daughters to join her. And in no time, they had all lost weight and were having fun, too! Hard to believe that these were three folks who wouldn't have been caught dead in spandex just a year ago. Go, Vicki! Go, Tina! Go, Lisa! And *you* go, Girl!

Secret Ingredient: **The main way to excuse-proof your workout is to make sure you are comfortable in your clothes, are doing an exercise you enjoy, and working out in a supportive environment.**

🌸 BODY

❄ JANUARY 31 ❄

Excuse-proof exercise tip: *Use mind over body.*

When it comes to exercise, for most of us the mind is willing, but the body just ain't.

You know the scenario: You worked hard all day, or you studied hard at school, or you did both in one day with children to feed, a man (or woman) to love, bills to pay, chores to do. You're *tired*. Just where is fitness supposed to fit in that scenario?

The answer: You've got to change the picture. Here are some new scenes to visualize:

Work out as soon as you wake up—before you shower, or wake the kids.

Do it simultaneously with something you're in a habit of doing. Say you always look at the evening news. Put your exercise bike in front of the TV and watch the news sitting on the bike working out, instead of sitting on the couch nodding out.

Take lessons. When I was about twenty-three and had a tennis-playing boyfriend, I was inspired to take up tennis and found that I really enjoyed it. Soon, I let coworkers know about my new passion (both the boyfriend and the sport, of course), and in turn, someone told me that there was an indoor tennis club that offered lessons at lunchtime just a block from our office. Twice a week at noon, I was hitting balls and having fun.

Take Geritol. I know it sounds funny, but I'm just sharing what works for me. I don't know how I got into taking Geritol. . . . Oh, wait, yes, I do: As a child, I had a problem swallowing pills, so I took liquid vitamins. The habit followed me to adulthood, but I didn't want to continue taking children's vitamins, and the only other liquid supplement I could find was Geritol, the old folks' tonic; except I didn't know it was regarded as that, so I bought it and acquired a taste for it. Anyway, it really does make me feel more peppy. If you think about it, you probably have your own secret energy booster. So just put it to use, and stop your tired excuses.

Secret Ingredient: **Start your day by getting a move on. After you turn off your alarm clock, turn on your TV to ESPN2 for the station's morning exercise shows. Look for Kendell Hogan's program (if I can do this brother's workout, so can you).**

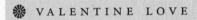 VALENTINE LOVE

❄ FEBRUARY 1 ❄

Believe in love.

If you don't believe in love, you may as well not believe in *anything*.
That's a line from August Wilson's Broadway play *Seven Guitars*. I

had the pleasure of hearing Wilson read some of his favorite parts of the script, and then I heard the line again when I went to see the play on Broadway. I've often wondered why, of all the many lines in the story, it struck me so. But maybe one reason is that it was written by a man and that a male character said it onstage. It seemed so refreshing to hear a brother speak so passionately about love.

Don't you think that's a pretty good philosophy? I do. Romantic at heart that I am, I truly believe in love. To have a strong, loving, supportive, healthy relationship in your life is a wonderful blessing. Of course, we all know that—that's why we seek such good loving, and why we work hard to keep it once we have it.

Remember that song from the soundtrack of *The Preacher's Wife* called "I Believe in You and Me"? Well, that song is evidently the one that Pauletta and Denzel Washington call "our song." I was watching the NAACP Image Awards on television the year that Denzel won an award and his wife presented it to him. In so doing, she chose that song to be played in dedication to him and their relationship. She was saying to him, in front of millions of people, I believe in our love.

If you are looking for love, believe that it can happen. If you have love, believe that it can grow strong. If you have lost love, believe that you can find healing.

I put love in the blessings category because if "God is love," it must be sacred. So let's believe in it, as we believe in God, as we believe in ourselves.

Secret Ingredient: **Do you have a favorite love song that expresses your belief in love? Picking favorite songs affirms our beliefs and philosophies. Choose one, like the Washingtons, that expresses your own feelings.**

❋ VALENTINE LOVE

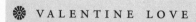

❋ FEBRUARY 2 ❋

Take your time entering a relationship.

When you meet that special person and just know he's got it going on, the adrenalin rush is enough to make you feel it must be love. And if you are in love, and the other person feels the same way, then you must be in a relationship. Right?

Well, maybe. But it's helpful to study the anatomy of relationships.

Like anything else you want to succeed in, relationships are enhanced when you have examined some research, some wisdom on what makes them successful—just like anything else you want to succeed in. In my car recently, I listened to the audiobook of Deepak Chopra's *The Path to Love*. When I heard the following gem of wisdom, I pulled over to the highway shoulder to write it down: "There are four distinct phases of romance: attraction, infatuation, courtship, intimacy . . . the next stage is relationship."

Years ago, like anyone else, I dove into love blindly. When I met my husband, I felt like *Okay, I'm getting this yearning pain in my gut every time I'm with you. When people mention your name, a smile spreads across my face and I get light-headed. It must be love, so let's get married.*

Fortunately, Reggie was a bit older and wiser than I when it came to marriage. One reason was because he had been married before and had learned some things about himself and relationships. Each time I would whine and pine to get married, he would say, "I wouldn't marry anyone without knowing her at least three years."

Three years! When you're twenty-four, three years is an eternity. I smiled sweetly to him, but I thought to myself, *I'll get you faster than any three long years!* So when did we get married? You guessed it—three years later. And I'm so glad. It took us that long to get to know each other through all seasons, through difficult and fun situations, through family get-togethers and company parties.

Take time to get to know a person. If you're going to be together "forever" anyway, what's a year or two of mutual exploration and discovery? It's all time that you'll both recall lovingly.

Secret Ingredient: **After you've moved through each joyous stage of attraction, infatuation, courtship, and intimacy, *then* you can claim relationship. Pay attention to your feelings as you experience each stage.**

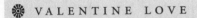 VALENTINE LOVE

❄ FEBRUARY 3 ❄

Give a care.

"Sex is when you don't give a damn; making love is when you care." Guess who said that? Barry White. Well, sho' you right, Barry.

On a New York television show called *Like It Is,* I once heard a scholarly brother say he thought it was sad that love had been replaced by sex. Well, if sex is when you don't give a damn, and love is no longer important, we are lost!

As a parent of a teenager, I get pretty frustrated with all the media studies and experts who say that parents don't talk to their children about sex. My question is: What are we supposed to say? What would be considered an age-appropriate conversation? What kind of talking should we be doing to effectively prevent teen pregnancy, STDs, HIV/AIDS? Aside from the simplistic "just say no" conversation about abstinence, what should we say to our kids so they'll listen without sucking their teeth and rolling their eyes? Maybe a lot of us don't know because we haven't figured it out for ourselves. Some adults are still searching for love and settling for sex (and some are just settling without searching), or using sex as recreation. So how can we guide our children on the right path?

One day, I took my daughter and her friend to the mall and as we were eating in the food court, the friend started cooing over a baby passing by with its young mother. Seizing the opportunity to advocate against premature sex, I said, "Yeah, the baby's cute, but don't think it's so cute that you start to feel you need to have one." My daughter's friend's answer was calm and confident. "Oh, I'm not going there, Mrs. Oliver. I haven't yet met anyone that I've had strong enough feelings about to take that risk, and I really think I'm too young for that kind of relationship anyway." Even at fifteen, one can know that love and caring come first.

Secret Ingredient: **If you feel you may need help talking with your adolescent about sex, call your local Planned Parenthood. Many chapters offer free counseling, seminars, videos, and brochures.**

❋ VALENTINE LOVE

❋ FEBRUARY 4 ❋

Love your neighbor.

In these days leading up to Valentine's Day, I've been talking, primarily, about love relationships. But today, there's another kind of love I want to discuss. In honor of Rosa Parks's birthday, I'd like to talk about loving your neighbor. Having neighbors of varying ethnicities, I feel indebted to Mrs. Parks for refusing to give in to segregation. Integration has benefited our country. I feel touched when white people in my town of Montclair,

New Jersey, are quoted in articles about how great our community is, saying that they chose to live in Montclair because of the ethnic diversity. On my street there are black, white, and Asian families, and all are cordial and friendly with each other. When my daughter was a latchkey kid, forever losing her housekeys, she knew she could knock on the door of either the Pulitzer Prize–winning African American composer next door, or the white sculptor married to an Asian businessman, on the other side. Anique was welcome in either home, and we were grateful for such kind neighbors.

Other examples of neighborliness:

❖ Maybe the elderly lady down the hall could use some help with heavy lifting or other chores her deceased husband used to do.

❖ The pregnant teen at church might need some motherly advice over a carefree lunch, like the kind my friend Kim, who had just had a baby at forty, shared with a young lady about to have her first baby at eighteen.

Speaking of babies, I'll never forget one particular act of kindness bestowed on me and my husband by a neighbor of ours when we lived in an apartment building in New York City. I was about to go into labor; Reg was desperately trying to hail a taxi to take us to the hospital. Our downstairs neighbor, Arnie, came out to move his car (as New Yorkers habitually have to do to avoid tickets). Seeing our distress, Arnie passed up a very desirable parking spot to offer us a ride to the hospital. Now that was a random act of love that allowed our little Baby Love to come into the world inside Lenox Hill Hospital—rather than on Amsterdam Avenue!

Secret Ingredient: Today, commit a premeditated or random act of love. And remember "neighbors" aren't only people who live near you, but they are also people you encounter on your life's journey: folks on buses, in the ATM line, driving next to you on the freeway.

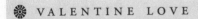 FEBRUARY 5

No one can make your life complete but you.

One thing I love about women's friendships is the deep understanding between us. I remember hearing about a study that said that when women tell their problems to other women, the response is sympathy and agreement: as in "Uh-huh," "Yeah, girl," "You got that right!" When we share with men, the response from the guys is more often advice: "You should go in there tomorrow and tell her what you think!" Sometimes, I think, men should be more like us, but there was one time in particular when I wished I had responded more like them.

At a Christmas party at a swanky hotel many years ago, my husband and I double-dated with some newlywed friends of ours. In the lobby taking a breather, I listened as my sister-friend went on and on about how her husband hadn't changed his ways since they got married, and how he still hung out with the guys. I nodded, letting her vent. Then she said she had assumed marriage would have made her happy; that in becoming a husband, he would have automatically changed his ways and made her happy. I stopped nodding, but kept silent. But when she said, "I can't even smile anymore!" I was dumbfounded.

To be truthful, I don't remember what I said in response, but I know it wasn't adequate. In the years since, I have thought about what I wish I had said: "My sister, don't ever give a man—or anyone else—that much control over you. Who made smiles? Is the Creator still on the throne? Did you smile before you met that Negro? Isn't he smiling right now, as we speak, upstairs dancing with somebody else? Love you first, love what you bring to the marriage, love your own smile, and then you'll get the love you want.

Being in a habit of listening with sympathy, I probably didn't think fast enough to switch to the masculine role of advice giver, but I did learn that it's necessary to do that sometimes, and that no one can make you feel complete but you. Marriage won't make you happy if you're not happy single. No man—or woman—can be the source of your smile. It has to come from within.

My mother always says, "No one can take care of you better than you can take care of yourself." And to that I add: No one can love you better than you can love yourself. Remember: No one can make your life complete but you.

Secret Ingredient: "Expand your definition of love. Allow your conception [concept of love] to go beyond your emotional needs, and your whole perspective will change." —Deepak Chopra, *The Path to Love.*

❄ FEBRUARY 6 ❄

Look for a heart of gold.

There's nothing wrong with being attracted to someone progressive, ambitious, and hardworking. Folks like that usually "get paid." And there's a reason for the popularity of the song that went: "You've got to have a J-O-B if you want to be with me."

But, let's not define a person by his paycheck. Or to be more specific, let's not define the depths of our love by the depths of his pocket. A "fiancé" is not to be confused with a "financier."

When my eldest stepdaughter, Amena, was president of her college's Black Student Union, she invited me to visit her West Virginia school to moderate a panel of students on the topic of interracial relationships. It seems that many of the brothers at her school preferred dating white girls over going out with sisters. This made the sisters pretty peeved, so they wanted to put the issue out in the open.

I started the session by asking the black female students in the theater-style auditorium, "How many of you would date white men?" No hands went up. Then I asked, "How many of you would date Donald Trump?" Just about every hand shot up. I was surprised; I had only thought of Trump because he had been in the news that week.

"Why would you date Donald Trump?" I asked one of the students who had just high-fived her girlfriends excitedly but had looked totally bored two seconds ago. "Isn't he white?"

"Yeah, but he could get me straight!" she answered, explaining that Trump could pay off her bills and get her a house, a car, and all the trappings of her imagination. In other words, dating him would be like winning the lottery.

"Why would you think that someone who took you on a date would get you straight?" I asked. "I just wanted to know who would *date* Trump."

She looked at me like I was the crazy one. I guess gold-digging dies hard. But I still believe that if you want real love, lasting love, look for a *heart* of gold.

Secret Ingredient: **Find love on the Internet (but use caution). Rather than initial physical attraction, online chats allow you to ask probing questions that get to the heart of the man. I know of a couple of successes!**

❋ FEBRUARY 7 ❋

Accept the ups and downs of love.

"There will be valleys and there will be mountains," said the Rev. Dr. Samuel B. McKinney, pastor emiritus of Mount Zion Baptist Church in Seattle, in advising Reggie and me when we got married. I have found this simple statement to be a good way to describe the ups and downs that are bound to happen in any long-term intimate relationship.

The ups are what we all live for; the way we form opinions about our relationship. The good times define what we want our marriage to be about. They are the face we put on our relationship for others to see. The mountains are the good times together: the lustful can't-get-enough-of-each-other early days, the virtual honeymoon period, the joy of babies born, the pride of another milestone anniversary. You're on the mountain top each time you dance together, share a private joke, brag about each other's accomplishments, catch a wink across a crowded room.

The valleys are the down days. The times when you wonder what in the world you are doing with this person, when you're arguing too much and laughing too little, when you've lost that loving feeling. Often the valleys are caused by things over which we have little or no control: the loss of a loved one, the stress of a layoff, bills not paid, the sting of racism. Most of us have known valleys all too well.

But often, we can climb back up those mountains. We can put on our hiking shoes and get to stepping. A harsh word can be followed by a sweeter one. A sweet word can become a loving sentence. A loving sentence can become a healing dialogue.

When you're in a valley, just think about the tops of those mountains you've reached together, and make your way, step by step, to the next one.

Secret Ingredient: **For more ways to make the best of your valleys, read** *The Value in the Valley: A Woman's Guide Through Life's Dilemmas,* **by Iyanla Vanzant.**

❄ FEBRUARY 8 ❄

Agree to disagree.

During a sermon a few years ago, Rev. McKinney said another thing I remember: "The key to good relationships is not agreement but rather acceptance." It's so true—no two people will ever agree on everything, but we can live together peacefully with mutual acceptance.

My mother once told me that. "As long as two people are two different people, they will never be the same," she said. "There will always be things they disagree about, ways in which they are different."

They may be little things: One likes to get up early, the other likes to sleep late; one likes the window open even in cool weather, the other prefers to snuggle under the covers—the proverbial "one likes it hot, one likes it cold."

And of course, things can get more complicated: One person's a spender, the other is a saver. One likes to hang out, the other likes to hang at home—and wants the hang-out partner to stay put, too. Ah, that's when the trouble starts; when one partner demands total agreement. But often, the resolution to the disagreement is acceptance of the differences.

When touchy situations like that occur, it's helpful to think to yourself, *Is this really hurting me, or just hurting my feelings? Am I being reasonable or do I just want my way?* Consider all the things you can do if you accept the other person's behavior. For example, if he goes out on Friday nights, that can be the night that the new reading club you start can meet, or the night that you can call your best friend and talk in privacy for hours, or the time when you can write in your journal or take a soothing bath. When you accept benign things that you cannot change, you open the door for self-discovery.

Secret Ingredient: For pillow talk sometime, discuss the things you accept about each other that you're not in agreement about. It's helpful to know not only what things about your mate are difficult for you to accept, but what things he uneasily accepts about you. Then agree to disagree with a kiss.

❋ FEBRUARY 9 ❋

Give each other space.

"Let there be spaces in your togetherness," advises *The Prophet*. No one can be together *all* the time. We all know that. I mean, hey, we've got to go to work *sometime*—and most folks don't work with the ones they love. But everything after that seems up for consideration and negotiation. How many business trips are too many? Should you live together or keep separate apartments? Does a separate vacation have to signal something awful?

We've all heard of relationships that have broken up because one mate said, "I need space." When you love being with someone, it's natural to want that good feeling all the time. But we must remember another old adage: "Absence makes the heart grow fonder."

I know one marriage that endured a three-year separation while the wife pursued her dreams of living in New York and Paris. The husband continued to run their business in Jamaica. What was the glue? He wanted his wife to be happy, and he went to visit her on many occasions, staying as long as he could. And, of course, their phone bills were astronomical!

Another couple I know had twin boys. They decided that the husband should follow his goal to become a lawyer and get his law degree at Howard University in Washington, D.C., while the family stayed in their home in New Jersey. The secret? Belief that what he was doing would benefit the family in the future. Instead of dwelling on their temporary feelings of missing each other, they stayed focused on their long-term goals. He came home on weekends whenever he could, too.

Of course, strong relationships have always endured military separations, long-distance commuting, and even prison terms! But the best of them also allow for each partner to grow—and sometimes that means spending time apart. But it doesn't have to mean that the relationship falls apart.

Secret Ingredient: **Assess your relationship: Is there space in your togetherness? If not, decide today to do something about it—give yourself and your mate room to grow. If you aren't in a relationship right now, assess your relationship with yourself. Are you allowing yourself the freedom to do what you want, or are you hemmed in by others' expectations of you?**

❋ FEBRUARY 10 ❋

Love and learn.

Having loved a few brothers myself, and having been married to the most special one for almost twenty years, I've discovered that whether a relationship ends in marriage or just ends, you come out wiser for having tested the waters, from having followed your heart. When we love, we learn.

For example, from my high school sweetheart, I learned that even young guys can have the wisdom to treat you with respect and care. The five years we went together taught me about monogamy and relationship longevity. And I also learned that you don't have to hate the person, or even get mad at him for it to be time to end a relationship. Sometimes, you just grow apart.

From my college heartthrob, I learned things both positive and negative. On the downside, I learned how it felt to be hurt, to feel betrayed, to love more than I was loved in return. Because I've "been there, done that," I can empathize with women who are going through it. On the up tip, I was given the gift of vegetarianism—something that has lasted much longer than the relationship that has been of value to my way of life (and to my weight!).

From my first fiancé, I learned a love of travel. He had an adventurous spirit that took us from Washington, D.C., to backpacking through Central America. That same spirit made it almost impossible for him to settle down to marriage though, which is why our engagement never made it to a wedding, but I have no regrets over the beautiful three years we spent together.

From my husband, I have learned so much—and I'm still learning: compassion, patience, to be a more nurturing person. I have learned to say "I'm sorry," a phrase that was not in my pre-Reggie vocabulary. And together we have made the love of each other grow into the love of our family.

Secret Ingredient: **Think about the loves you've thought of as "lost." It's easy to dwell on how much the relationship may have hurt you, but try focusing on the ways in which you gained from it. Consider the lasting, positive effects of the good times you had together—and what a lesson loving is.**

✼ FEBRUARY 11 ✼

Consider your personal safety when you choose a mate.

I was watching Oprah one day when I heard her say this: "If someone hits you, he doesn't love you—because love feels good."

Because of pervasive domestic violence, we must consider our personal well-being when we consider establishing an intimate relationship. Of course, it's not always easy to tell. A light in a partnership can last for years before the fuse gets blown.

My mother always taught me the One-Hit Rule. "If someone ever hit me one time, that would be the last time," she would say. It was passed down through generations that if a man hit you, you would have to leave. My great-aunt Dorothy, a tall, dark, statuesque beauty, became the heroine of family legend by doing just that. It seems that she married quite young, and her older husband decided to try to control her strong will by abusing her. Aunt Dorothy fought back and knocked his teeth out. Fortunately, she escaped. Growing up, I only knew her as an independent, elegant woman who was ahead of her time; she lived alone in beautiful homes and catered parties for Hollywood stars such as Spencer Tracy. But she had made it clear that she'd rather live alone in peace than live in marriage with a man who would hit her.

Hopefully, fewer and fewer of us will have to "go there." Surely, the message that domestic violence "ain't cool" will make more men think twice before they strike. And although many couples make up by making love, a relationship is really stronger when love and respect are shown during anger, as well as after things have cooled down. Although I once had a boyfriend who had the nerve to slap me (and that was the end of that relationship!), I am fortunate to be married to someone who has taught me about showing love even when you're burning mad. One reason our relationship has endured for twenty years is because during some of our most heated arguments, Reg has completely disarmed me by saying, "I love you—and that's why I'm telling you this!" I'm still trying to learn to do the same.

Love should make you feel safe, respected, and cared for. Just ask Oprah.

Secret Ingredient: **If you've never had a discussion with your mate about domestic violence, do it right away! It's an essential conversation. If you or someone you know is at risk, please call the National Domestic Violence Hotline, 1-800-799-SAFE. For the hearing impaired: 1-800-787-3224.**

❋ FEBRUARY 12 ❋

Answer the call of love's duty.

"It's not the booty call—it's the duty call!"

After conducting a pretty sedate health-and-fitness workshop at Washington State University one wintry Saturday in the month of March, I sat in the student center listening to the keynote speaker of the school's annual African American student conference, P. Eric Abercrumbie, Ph.D., very boldly make that exclamation. The timing was perfect. The movie *Booty Call* had just been released and this was the University of Cincinnati's Director of the African-American Culture and Research Center's way of getting the restless high school and college students' attention. He got it. The kids in the room went wild.

The theme of his speech was "doing the right thing." In relationships, duty often calls us to do the right thing. The American Social Health Association (ASHA) has a campaign that emphasizes the upcoming Valentine's Day as the perfect time to do the right thing in loving someone by protecting his or her sexual health—and your own. February 14 is National Condom Day. "Because STDs are so often symptomless, sex partners must talk to one another about any risk for STDs, even if neither person has symptoms," says Linda Alexander, ASHA president. "We know it's a sensitive subject, but this is the only way to make sure that you both stay healthy."

If either partner has had unprotected sex at any time, ASHA recommends that both be tested for STDs in a physician's office or clinic. The partners should also use condoms correctly, every time they have sex, to help prevent against transmitting an infection.

Alexander emphasizes that abstaining from sex is the only completely safe choice. "For those who are having sex, unless both partners are one hundred percent certain that they are free of infection, condoms are essential," she says.

Secret Ingredient: Free, confidential information about STDs and condom use is available through two hotlines operated by ASHA under contract with the Centers for Disease Control. They are: the National AIDS Hotline, 1-800-342-2437; and the National STD Hotline, 1-800-227-8922.

❋ FEBRUARY 13 ❋

Show your love.

On Valentine's Eve, thoughts often turn to presents. *I wonder what my baby's going to buy me,* may be the most common reflection of the day.

I was never one to think that Valentine's Day was "Christmas for Lovers." That's because my earliest Valentine's remembrances are of my mother buying everyone in the family—not just my dad—something red to wear. One Valentine's I got red pedal pushers that I vividly recall because I just knew that I was on the cutting edge of fashion—at least as edgy as a second-grader could be.

My mother's gift giving was later to seem like such a womanist act. I mean, most women I came across seemed adamant about only being on the receiving end of the presents. Rarely giving. I am sure that I surprised (and hopefully delighted) more than a few boyfriends as I was growing up, when they got Valentine's gifts from me—whether or not they had given me one. (However, I'm not above saying that if that was the case, it was probably the last gift they got from me!)

The lovers have got the day covered. It's romantic, beautiful, and sentimental. But if we agree with both the cliché that "love is a two-way street" and the biblical phrase that "it is more blessed to give than receive," then let's experience real love by giving it away this Valentine's. Make an effort to "show your love" as Steve Harvey, the host of *Showtime at the Apollo* would say:

Send Valentine's cards to all your friends—just as you did in grade school! If you have children and have to buy the obligatory packages of Valentines for the party at school, pick up an extra box for you. (Even better: Send them to old classmates with whom you may have exchanged them back in the day.)

Give a gift of love to someone who least expects it. The folks at work, the babysitter, a sister-friend.

Show your love to someone less fortunate. If it's time to clean out the closet, do it in time to give the clothes to someone who could use them on Valentine's Day.

Secret Ingredient: **If you'd really like to have an extraordinary Valentine's Day, volunteer at a nursing home or AIDS hospice. That's expressing love for humankind.**

❋ FEBRUARY 14 ❋

See God's face in the one you love.

"When you are in love with someone, you can see God. God is love; real love is perfect."

Who do you think made that beautiful statement? Here are three guesses for your very own Valentine's Day quiz. Was it:

1. Iyanla Vanzant
2. Deepak Chopra
3. Your mama
4. The Artist (formerly known as Prince)

Maybe Mama said there'd be love like this, but according to *Jet* magazine, it was The Artist (formerly known as Prince). He was talking about his own feelings for his wife, Mayte Garcia-Nelson, whom he married on Valentine's Day 1996, in Minneapolis.

That's the voice of a newlywed talking. But as time goes by, and most folks get into the daily routine of just trying to make it, it can get harder and harder to see God in the face of the person who shares the bills, the heartaches, the problems, and the day-to-day drudgery. Sometimes when you look in that person's face, you don't know who you see— much less God.

But if that person is truly your soul mate, then he or she is the divine right person for you. And if that is so, then he or she is God-sent. And if you can look in your honey's face and remember how you felt when love was new, then maybe, just maybe, you can see God.

Secret Ingredient: On this day of romance, write a poem for the one you love, or exchange poems to read aloud from *Love Poems,* by Nikki Giovanni, or *Full Woman, Fleshly Apple, Hot Moon: Selected Poems of Pablo Neruda,* by the Pulitzer Prize–winning Chilean poet, or his *One Hundred Love Sonnets.*

✳ FEBRUARY 15 ✳

Love your black history; love your black self.

You've heard the Sankofa saying: If you don't know where you came from, you don't know where you're going.

What better time to investigate where you came from than during Black History Month? First, let's talk about where this time of commemoration came from. It was started in February 1926 by the founder of the Association for the Study of Negro Life and History, Dr. Carter G. Woodson, as Negro History Week. According to the book *African American Holidays,* by James C. Anyike, Dr. Woodson "communicated with other influential African Americans, all of which supported the idea. They agreed on the second week of February for the observance of the achievements of the 'Negro' . . . because it is the week of the birthdays of Frederick Douglass and Abraham Lincoln, both highly respected at that time." In 1972, the name was changed to Black History Week, and in 1976 the week was expanded to a month as part of the country's yearlong bicentennial celebration, and the month stuck.

The study of history should not be just a school-required task. Its lesson of triumph can boost our collective self-esteem, and lay out the map as to where we should be headed. Not only do you not know where you are going if you don't know from where you came, you also can't imagine how far you've come.

Secret Ingredient: **Share your knowledge today! Tell four or five coworkers about Carter G. Woodson and the history behind Black History Month.**

✳ FEBRUARY 16 ✳

Remember that our history didn't start in slavery.

Alex Haley once told me, "Our history didn't begin in a cotton field." And we all know now that it didn't even start on this continent, right? Even a major newsweekly magazine acknowledged that archaeologists agree that the earliest known ancestor was a black woman they call "Lucy," whose roots can be traced to Ethiopia. Many black scholars have found a treasury of history in studying Nubian culture and the building of the pyramids in Egypt. The great East and West African cultures of Kemet, Dahomey, Benin, and others have shown African Americans that we are descended from great people.

Some of those great people were the queens of Ethiopia and Egypt described in the wonderfully informative book *Black Women in Antiquity* edited by Ivan Van Sertima. The stories of these ancient warrior women in Ethiopia and Egypt smash the myth of female inferiority. There's Andromeda, daughter of the Ethiopian king, Cepheus. Makeda, the queen of Sheba, is known in the Bible as the great black beauty who melted King Solomon's heart into a song. There's Tiye, who was born in Nubia, but reigned in Egypt for half a century, and set the style for female beauty in the royal court. Her daughter-in-law was Nefertiti, who poet-writer Sonia Sanchez describes in the book this way: "Nefertiti was not some harem girl randomly selected for wedlock. No. She was perhaps the most admired woman of her day. . . . She could not relegate herself to the traditional role of subservient-queen. She envisioned an active role for herself in reshaping civilization." Hatshepsut, the queen who ruled like a king, donning male attire, sporting the beardlike accessory of the day, was a born leader. She's my personal favorite, because of her philosophy of nonaggression against other nations (although she had to fight the enemies of her own camp and country—doesn't that sound familiar?). One of the most exciting parts of my trip to Egypt in 1990 was visiting her fabulous palace (the White House should look so palatial!) that has withstood the ages. Now *that's* an enduring legacy.

Secret Ingredient: **Make a vow to learn more about ancient African culture—you may be enlightened by what you find!**

❄ FEBRUARY 17 ❄

Honor your history heroes.

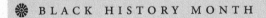

Harriet Tubman is, without question, my favorite hero of the oppressive period of African American enslavement. I just think it's amazing that in 1849 at about twenty-nine years old, she escaped slavery in Maryland and made her way all by herself amid enormous dangers to freedom in the North. And on top of that, she risked her life nineteen more times to miraculously lead her parents and many others to freedom. It wasn't enough that she was free. She wanted everyone to be free, and she wouldn't settle for anything less than she thought she could do toward that end. In the face of unimaginable life-threatening risk, the obsession with freedom made Harriet Tubman a woman of enormous courage and unshakable faith.

Because of her struggle and those that came after her, we no longer have to run from bounty hunters and yapping dogs. But there are still major obstacles that call for us to tap into our own courage and faith. In 1970 human rights activist Angela Davis fled into hiding when charges were made against her—trumped-up charges of which she was eventually acquitted. Revolutionary Assata Shakur risked her life by breaking out of a New Jersey prison and fleeing to political asylum in Cuba in 1979. These are African American women in our own era—who live today—who found the courage to flee to freedom. Like Harriet Tubman, they won over their enemies.

For most of us day-to-day, the flight to freedom may mean something less nationally high-profile, yet still harrowing or frightening, like planning that escape route from an oppressive job or crime-torn neighborhood. Maybe it's domestic violence or sexual harassment. It may be something more personal, like finding the courage to step out on faith that the predominantly white college you chose so far from home will be the right one for you. Or that the new job you've been offered will be more rewarding than the one that you've held for so many years, but without advancement. Often it's hard to trade in the known evil for the unknown future. Just remember that the brightest stars shine in the darkest night.

Secret Ingredient: **Freedom for our ancestors didn't mean "no work," but the liberty and independence to make a difference on one's own terms. What is your idea of freedom?**

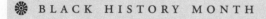 BLACK HISTORY MONTH

❄ FEBRUARY 18 ❄

Reflect on our health heritage.

What does history have to do with health? Plenty! Black History Month is a perfect time to reflect on our health heritage. How much do you know about African American health-and-fitness history? Here's a little quiz to tease your brain:

1. Who was Charles Drew?
   A. A brother who was good at drawing
   B. The first black man to become a medical doctor
   C. The physician who discovered blood plasma could be preserved and stored for later use

2. Who was Mary Eliza Mahoney?
   A. The author of *Uncle Tom's Cabin*
   B. The first African American to become a nurse
   C. The woman who did all those experiments with peanuts

3. Who was the first African American to hold the position of United States Surgeon General?
   A. M. Joycelyn Elders
   B. David Satcher
   C. Henry Foster

4. In what year was the National Medical Association (the organization of black physicians) founded?
   A. 1968
   B. 1903
   C. 1895

This quiz featured major accomplishments of African Americans to the health and well-being of our country. However, our health heritage isn't just about the big splashes made by folks in history books. It's also the little ripples, the well-intentioned attempts of everyday people who are advocates for good health and wholesome living. People like you and me.

Secret Ingredient: **The answers: 1. C.; 2. B.; 3. A.; 4. C. During this month of emphasis on black history, do your part in seeing that our health history does not go overlooked. Share health tips and knowledge of our health heritage with your children.**

❋ FEBRUARY 19 ❋

Enjoy your plans.

What are your plans for the day? To go to work? Drive to the mall? Attend a church service? Do nothing?

Whatever your plans, reflect on this: You are blessed to be able to have plans. In the novel Family, author J. California Cooper writes that the former slave she calls Always had no reason to think that she would be free one day, but she planned for it anyway:

> Chile, I'm tellin you this FREEDOM was really somethin if you had any sense to work with it! My chile, Always, had planned when she didn't even know what she was plannin!

Always gathered her strength and faith and came up with a winning plan for success in her newfound freedom. We can be inspired by this fictitious character who represents the very real lives of many of our ancestors. We can also be motivated after gaining the dubious freedoms of a job layoff or a divorce to make new plans to move our lives forward. Stepping into the darkness from the known to the unknown can be difficult, but never as hard as it was a hundred years ago, a generation ago, even yesterday. At least we know today that we always have the freedom of choice to make plans for everything from the most mundane chores of the day to plotting a second chance for our futures. As the saying goes: Those who fail to plan, plan to fail.

Freedoms our ancestors prayed for have come to pass for us. The hopes they had for their descendants have been realized. We are a highly literate people because the country that once prohibited us from learning to read and write now requires that we attend school and obtain an education. By law, we are free to live in any neighborhood we please. We can pursue any job we feel qualified for. The freedom is ours to travel the world and see God's creations anyplace on the planet.

As Maya Angelou expresses it best in her poem "Still I Rise": Bringing the gifts that my ancestors gave, "I am the dream and the hope of the slave."

Secret Ingredient: **Plan for your freedom now. Think of what a day totally free would mean for you. No work? Lots of travel? Your own business? Free your mind to dream today.**

✳ FEBRUARY 20 ✳

Teach our children the lessons of black history.

Marian Wright Edelman, the founder and president of the Children's Defense Fund in Washington, D.C., and author of the best selling book *Measure of our Success,* is one of my heroes. She's forthright, clear-thinking, and committed to the well-being of all our country's children. Most important, she's a doer.

Ten years ago as editor of *Essence,* I had the pleasure of editing an article by her that was adapted from a speech she delivered at the Congressional Black Caucus awards dinner the year before. Called "An Agenda for Empowerment," the article started off: "Many of us are moving on up. Some of us are going down and under. But none of us can be empowered until we throw lifelines to our children, our families, our communities."

Today, and especially during Black History Month, her words still ring true: "We must recapture and care about our lost children and help them gain the confidence, self-esteem, values, and real-world opportunities—education and jobs—that they need to be strong future guardians of the black community's heritage. How do we do this? Edelman suggests the following:

> Remember to teach children that black folks have never been able to take anything for granted in America and that we better not start now. . . . Frederick Douglass put it bluntly: "Men may not get all they pay for in this world, but they must certainly pay for all they get."
>
> Tell our children that they're not going to jive their way up the career ladder. They have got to work their way up—hard and continuously. Too many young people want a fast elevator to the top floor and resist walking up the stairs or stopping on the floors of achievement between the bottom and the top. Tell them to do their homework, pay attention to detail and take care and pride in their work. People who are sloppy in little things tend to be sloppy in big things. Tell them to be reliable, to stick with something until they finish and resist jumping from pillar to post. And tell them to take the initiative in creating their own opportunity. They can't wait around for other people to discover them or to do them a favor.

Secret Ingredient: Do you know some young people who could use that advice? Share it with them. Or is there something you can learn from Ms. Edelman's words of wisdom? One thing black history teaches us is that if "getting over" is your goal, "you're history." If honest achievement and honorable accomplishment are your goals, you can make history.

✳ FEBRUARY 21 ✳

Know the difference between substance and style.

Another step to empowerment recommended by children's activist Marian Wright Edelman is to know the difference between substance and style. I truly love the anecdote she tells about one of my favorite heroes of black history, Fannie Lou Hamer, and I often quote Edelman in my keynote speeches. Here's Edelman's advice that's suitable for Black History Month (or any other month for that matter):

> Too many of us think success is a Saks Fifth Avenue charge card or a "bad" set of wheels. Now, these are things to enjoy, but they are *not* life goals.
>
> I was watching former President Johnson's inaugural ball on television with a black college president's wife in Mississippi, when Mrs. Hamer, that great lady of the Mississippi Civil Rights Movement, who lacked a college degree but certainly not intelligence or clear purpose, came onto the screen. The college president's wife moaned, "Oh my, there's Miz Hamer at the President's ball, and she doesn't even have on a long dress." My response was: "That's all right. Mrs. Hamer with no long gown is there, and you and I with our long gowns are not."
>
> So often we miss the real point—we buy BMWs and fur coats before we think about whether where we're going to drive and wear them is worthwhile. Nobody ever asks about what kind of car Ralph Bunche drove or what kind of designer suit Martin Luther King, Jr., bought. Don't confuse style with meaning. Get your insides in order and your direction clear first, and then worry about your clothes and your wheels.

Style has its place, but few people make history—or even pay the rent—based on style alone. What's more important is something more enduring, more meaningful, more deep; what always takes first place is substance.

Secret Ingredient: Spend a few moments in reflection on how style versus substance has affected your life. Maybe there was a job you didn't get because you were more concerned about what to wear to the interview than about what to say during it. Or maybe you judged someone else on her appearance instead of listening to what was in her heart and mind. Forgive yourself, and start anew by making an effort to put substance first.

❋ FEBRUARY 22 ❋

Know when to stand up for what's right
(and know when to keep your seat).

"Stand up and fight!" is how we usually think of taking a stand for what is right. In the case of Rosa Parks, in 1955, she kept her seat on the bus for the cause of justice.

In her book *Rosa Parks: My Story* written with Jim Haskins, Mrs. Parks makes it clear that she was not the first person to keep her seat on a bus and get arrested. She even lets us know that during the incident that made history, there were three other black passengers in her row of seats who refused to get up the first time the bus driver demanded that they give their seats to the white man who was standing. After the second time, she alone was left seated.

"People always say that I didn't give up my seat because I was tired, but that isn't true," she writes. "I was not physically tired, or no more tired than I usually was at the end of a working day. I was not old, although some people have an image of me as being old then. I was forty-two. No, the only tired I was, was tired of giving in."

What happened next is the spark that set off the Montgomery, Alabama, bus boycott: After her arrest, Rosa Parks consented to be the test case that the NAACP president, E. D. Nixon had been looking for. A year later, the boycott ended in victory with a federal injunction against segregation on buses, Dr. Martin Luther King, Jr., became a national figure, and the Civil Rights Movement became a national cause.

But Mrs. Parks should not be defined by her single act of defiance. She had been involved with the Montgomery NAACP long before the boycott, and now she continues to be an outspoken speaker for equality long after the boycott.

Secret Ingredient: Surely, there are ways that each of us can make a difference. Have you ever committed an act of defiance that you are particularly proud of? During this Black History Month, be assured by the spirit of those that have come before us that it's an effective, nonviolent tactic to stand your ground for what is fair and just.

❋ FEBRUARY 23 ❋

Wait on freedom.

One day on television, I heard a black intellectual refer to February as African American Heritage Month. Although I do use the appellation "African American" with pride, I prefer to call the observance Black History Month because it sounds more inclusive of our sisters and brothers throughout the African diaspora.

During a trip to South Africa in 1997, I learned from Blacky Komani, the North America manager of the South African Tourism Board that the country would be sponsoring along with Selma Edwards of E-Z Tours in New York City a music festival in February 1998 in honor of Black History Month. The event, held in Cape Town, was a lovely and touching tribute to African Americans from our South African cousins, and featured both American and African musicians.

If we expand our thinking about black history, it should be noted that there was a major event in 1990 that had a great impact on South Africans, African Americans, and the world: On February 11, Nelson Mandela was released from incarceration after twenty-seven years as a political prisoner. Several years later, in 1994, apartheid was dismantled, the first free elections were held, and Nelson Mandela was named president of South Africa. Amazing!

In 1997, I was able to tour the Robben Island prison in South Africa and see Mandela's jail cell. To think that a man so big in character and integrity could be imprisoned in a cell so small is unfathomable. Yet, it is clear that although the body was imprisoned, the spirit was not. Three decades of incarceration did not stop Nelson Mandela from his destiny to lead his country and be respected and admired throughout the world.

Think of how low Mandela must have felt at times during his incarceration. But look how high he has risen, with the grace of God; from a prison cell to a presidential palace; from an oppressed political prisoner to one of the most admired statesman on the planet. See how high the spirit can fly?

Secret Ingredient: Freedom, however you define it in your life, may not come when you want it; it may take years, as it did for Mandela. But keep the faith, because God can make even clipped wings fly again. Mandela remained physically and emotionally strong by exercising every day while he was in prison. Think about how you can create similar discipline and resolve.

❋ FEBRUARY 24 ❋

Start something.

"Don't you start . . . !" That's an admonition most of us have heard—or said—at some point. It's often said sternly, sometimes humorously. But sometimes we are moved to do just the opposite.

In February 1960, four North Carolina A&T students—Jibreel Khazan, Franklin McCain, Joseph McNeil, and David Richmond—made history by starting something important. These African American young people are credited with starting the first sit-in—meaning they sat down at a luncheonette in a Greensboro, North Carolina, F. W. Woolworth store reserved for "Whites Only" and kept their seats even in the face of violent mobs of whites who tried to intimidate them into ending their protest. On July 25 of that year after repeated sit-ins, Woolworth's began to serve all customers at its lunch counters. The tactic was used to integrate other luncheonettes throughout the South.

Just because it's not the sixties anymore doesn't mean you can't start something positive today. Many people—black, white, Asian, Hispanic, Native American—started positive programs and dialogues in Los Angeles after the 1992 riots. In the early days of *Heart & Soul*, we reported on lots of folks across the country that we called "Champions": unsung community activists starting all kinds of good stuff, like James ("Rocky") Robinson and Joe Perez. After watching the quality of emergency medical care in their proud yet crime-plagued Brooklyn community go from bad to worse, they founded the Bedford-Stuyvesant Volunteer Ambulance Corps (BSVAC), the nation's first volunteer corps run by people of color.

Get inspired by these folks who are making history; go ahead and start something!

Secret Ingredient: As the saying goes, there is strength in numbers. To work most effectively toward change, identify a need, then gather together like-minded people to strategize and work together: E-mail is changing the traditional "meeting place," and "letter writing" campaigns can now be waged online.

❋ FEBRUARY 25 ❋

Remember the names of the "four little girls."

I've always enjoyed the movies of Spike Lee, but when he released the film "4 Little Girls" in 1997, I had to give him all his "props," as they say in the 'hood; and "respect," as they say in Jamaica. Thank you, Spike, for bringing that piece of history to international attention. And congrats on the Academy Award nomination—it was a winner in our hearts.

Props and respect to Angela Davis, too. What is little known is that Angela Davis, who is originally from Birmingham, Alabama, knew the families of two of the four young girls who were killed during the height of the Civil Rights Movement in the racist bombing by the Ku Klux Klan of the Seventeenth Street Baptist Church in Birmingham on September 15, 1963. On the occasion of the thirtieth anniversary of the bombing, I had the privilege of asking Davis if she would write an article about that horrible day and the children who died. What sticks in my mind most about working with her on the story that ran in *Essence* in the September 1993 issue, is that Davis was very adamant that we remember the *names* of the girls who died: Addie Mae Collins, Carole Robertson, and Cynthia Wesley, all fourteen years old; and Denise McNair, just eleven.

Even though they were young, they died for our freedom and their lives had meaning. Angela Davis wrote that she would like us to know not only the terror of their deaths but the positive lives they lead as teenage girls. Carole Robertson, for example, the younger sister of a friend of Davis's, was excited about joining a newly formed organization of blacks and whites called Friendship and Action, which would challenge racism in the recently desegregated schools.

On that horrific day, I was exactly the same age—eleven—as Denise McNair. Many years later I discovered that I also had something in common with Carole Robertson: membership in Jack and Jill. In memory of her, the Jack and Jill of America Foundation instituted in 1966 the Carole Robertson Memorial Award. Each year at their teen conferences nationwide, members of Jack and Jill who are high school graduating seniors are chosen by their chapters to receive recognition for outstanding community service.

Secret Ingredient: Spend a few minutes remembering the spirits of the four little girls. Call a friend or family member and start a dialogue: "Do you know the names of the four little girls?" If the answer is "No," share what you know. Talk about the Civil Rights Movement. What can you do today in the name of peace (and/or tolerance)?

To support young achievers like Carole, you can make donations to: Jack and Jill of America Foundation, 346 Commerce Street, Alexandria, VA 22314. To honor Carole, Addie Mae, Denise, and Cynthia, start by knowing their names.

❋ FEBRUARY 26 ❋

Wear your crown.

I first heard *Essence* editor-in-chief Susan L. Taylor say it, quoting the illustrious author James Baldwin in the mid-eighties after she had had lunch with him. Then more recently, I heard TV mogul Oprah Winfrey say it in an interview with journalist Bryant Gumbel and attribute it to *Beloved* author Toni Morrison. Here it is: *Your crown has already been bought and paid for, so put it on and wear it!*

Toni Morrison and the late James Baldwin were friends who shared a knowledge and appreciation for the history and the struggles of our ancestors. It doesn't matter who originated that inspirational adage, what matters is that you believe it. Dues have been paid with the sweat and toil of our enslaved ancestors who built this country. Our "crowns" have been purchased with the money that was exchanged at slave auctions, the fortunes that were made in cotton and tobacco and rice. They were bought with lives that were lost to lynchings, to securing the right to vote, to police brutality. The price was greater than money.

In that TV interview, Bryant asked Oprah, "What scares you?" She answered that her experience filming *Beloved* and visiting Ile de Goree, the slavery historical site in Senegal, led her to believe that "there's no reason to be afraid of anything, because there's *nothing* worse than where we came from."

It may be a crown that no one sees you wear but you. It may be one that others may try to knock off its rightful perch. But just keep your head held high, walk like the queen or king you were born to be, and wear it with pride.

Secret Ingredient: If imagining your crown is not sufficient to give your spirit a boost, get yourself a more tangible one. Make one with African fabric ala Queen Latifah, or buy a tiara. Put it on and look in the mirror and see who you really are.

✳ FEBRUARY 27 ✳

Never give up.

Congressman John Lewis of Georgia visited my area recently and spoke about his journey from his childhood on a cotton farm in segregated Alabama to his rise as the highest ranking African American in the United States House of Representatives. "If someone had told me fifty years ago when I was preaching to the chickens on our farm that one day I would be speaking from the floor of Congress," he told the group, "I would have said, 'You're crazy.' "

In the ensuing years, John Lewis developed an unwavering commitment to the Civil Rights Movement. As a student at Fisk University, he organized sit-in demonstrations at segregated lunch counters in Nashville, Tennessee. In 1961, Lewis volunteered to participate in the Freedom Rides, which were organized to challenge segregation at interstate bus terminals across the South. As a freedom Rider, Lewis risked his life and was beaten severely by mobs as a result of his activism. As a founder of the Student Nonviolent Coordinating Committee (SNCC), at the age of twenty-three, Lewis was one of the planners and a keynote speaker at the historic March on Washington in August 1963. On March 7, 1965, Lewis and activist Hosea Williams led 525 marchers advocating for voter registration across the Edmund Pettus Bridge in Selma, Alabama. The march ended in a confrontation with state troopers that left Lewis with a fractured skull and became known as Bloody Sunday. A subsequent march two weeks later, one of the most dramatic nonviolent protests our country has ever seen, between Selma and Montgomery, led to the Voting Rights Act of 1965. John Lewis is surely a hero.

I heard him talk about his life and his autobiography *Walking with the Wind* to a group of teenagers in an intimate home gathering where he kneeled on the floor and spoke with the ease of a Southern storyteller. A few days later I saw him share his triumphant story at an elegant corporate luncheon hosted by Sony Music Entertainment's, LaBaron Taylor, and attended by attorney Johnnie Cochran, and actors Ossie Davis and Ruby Dee, among others. To both groups, his earnest message was the same: "Never give up. Never give in. And never give out."

Secret Ingredient: **I'll bet there was a time when your perseverance paid off that you can remember with pride. Recall it today to be your own example and inspiration. And when adversity appears, call on your inner strength—and never give up.**

❋ FEBRUARY 28 ❋

Keep your eyes on the prize.

Did you see the documentary series *Eyes on the Prize?* I thought it was an excellent documentation of African American history, and that it particularly captured the spirit of the Civil Rights Movement even in its title, taken from a song used to motivate protest marchers.

Each of us can learn to keep our eyes on the prize in our own lives:

Follow the goal in your soul. Not everyone has vision. Even if others can't comprehend your passion for what you know you can achieve, persevere anyway.

Keep focused. In sports, they call it "keeping your eye on the ball." Don't get distracted. Maintain your focus. Concentrate.

If you get off course, make your way back to the path. The narrator of *Eyes on the Prize* was a black history hero for me—Julian Bond. As a founding member of the Student Nonviolent Coordinating Committee (SNCC), Bond helped organize protests, sit-ins, and Freedom Rides. During the tumultuous 1963 Democratic National Convention, held several months following the assassination of Martin Luther King, Bond was nominated as a protest candidate for Vice President of the United States. Just twenty-eight, he was too young to actually receive the nomination, but he made history anyway, and continued to show his commitment to human rights through his work as a Georgia legislator and a national public speaker.

Like you and me, even revolutionaries have setbacks and troubling periods in their lives. Bond, a father of five, experienced a difficult divorce, and was rumored to have used drugs. Having given up his Georgia state senate seat to focus on an unsuccessful 1986 congressional race against John Lewis (see previous page), he moved to the Washington, D.C., area. There, out of the spotlight, he began to repair his life. In February (Black History Month!) 1998, Julian Bond was back on top—elected chairman of the board of the National Association for the Advancement of Colored People (NAACP). Through his time of hardship, Bond kept his "eyes on the prize." Although most of us don't go through our "trials and tribs" publicly, we can still use his example and get our lives in order.

Secret Ingredient: Have you had trouble briefly sticking to your plans or long-term goals? Whether your goal involves a weighty social issue or even personal weight loss, spend a half hour to an hour today thinking about how you can get back on track. Recommit to keeping "your eyes on the prize."

�֍ BLACK HISTORY MONTH

✲ FEBRUARY 29 ✲

Take a leap. Make history.

Today is Leap Day! You don't have to be a John Lewis or Harriet Tubman to make history. You don't even have to be on Oprah or The Tom Joyner Show. You just have to be yourself.

Your name may never make the history books, but you can still make history by being "a drum major for justice" as Martin Luther King, Jr., said. Here are some ways to make the leap into history:

- ❖ **Vote during every election.** Honor our ancestors who died for the right to vote. Make sure our elected officials are held accountable for their actions. Remember: Your vote *can* make a difference.
- ❖ **Serve on a jury.** Don't try to get off every time you're called and you will ensure that the disproportionate numbers of blacks accused of crimes get a fair trial. (My former brother-in-law, Lionel "Lon" Cryer, was called and served on the jury of the O. J. Simpson trial; for performing his civic duty, he'll go down in history as Juror Number Six.)

- **Be a good parent, grandparent, or friend.** Be a hero to that little person in your life who watches every move you make more intently than any TV camera—and who records it in his memory longer. My grandmother, Flossie Levingston, did many good works as a "club woman," active in black women's organizations and in our church, but to me she will always be my hero for the love, attention, and sweetness she gave *me*.
- **Make a difference in your community.** Touch lives while making the world a better place. There are many unsung heroes in this world. I'll bet you know a few (you may even be a local hero yourself). Pay homage to the heroes in your life by "writing them down in history"; list their names here: _____

_____

Whether you call it history, her-story, or *your*-story, just do what you know is right, make a contribution to society, and the reward will be great. Get ready for it. Write your name here: _____

_____

Secret Ingredient: If you are not currently registered to vote, call your local League of Women Voters, NAACP, or Urban League for information on how to register in your area. If you are already registered to vote, and know of people in your family or neighborhood who aren't, call them up and encourage them to get registered.

❋ WOMEN'S HISTORY MONTH

❧ MARCH 1 ❧

Be proud to be a strong woman.

She just couldn't take it anymore. Sitting there on the steps of the pulpit, she hadn't been invited but because she wanted to sell copies of her self-published book, she was there anyway. Listening to the dialogue about how women should be denied equality because they couldn't even get into a carriage or jump over a puddle without being helped, she hadn't been asked to make a speech, but she decided to speak up anyway.

Dat man over dar say dat womin needs to be helped into carriages, and lifted over ditches, and to hab de best place everywhar. Nobody eber helps me into carriages, or ober mud-puddles, or gibs me any best place! And a'n't I a woman? Look at me! Look at my arm! [and she bared her right arm to the shoulder showing her tremendous muscular power]. I have ploughed, and planted, and gathered into barns, and no man could head me! And a'n't I a woman?

Sojourner Truth's words of 1851 still ring true over a hundred years later. Asserting herself as a strong black woman, Sojourner Truth made others take notice. On this first day of Women's History Month, let us remember that early feminist.

Be inspired by her strength. Sojourner Truth was proud to show that she had a strong, healthy body, and it was obvious that she had a strong, healthy mind.

Think of her courage. How brave it was of her to stand up when she hadn't been invited, much less asked to be one of the dignitaries on the dais! She had something to say—and she said it eloquently!

Be self-defining like Sojourner. Even her name was from her own mind. Born Isabella to James and Elizabeth Baumfree around 1777, at the age of forty-six she said she obeyed the voices in her head by taking the name Sojourner, then she added Truth. When her first, much older, husband died, she married a younger man. Even though she never learned to read or write, she published a book, spoke out against slavery, and was received in the White House by President Abraham Lincoln.

Listen to God. Like most of our foremothers, Sojourner Truth let God lead her. She said God told her to travel and tell her truth. And all she did was obey.

On March 1, 1982, I gave birth to a beautiful girl. May Anique, and all our daughters, be inspired by Sojourner Truth and embrace the proud strength of our foremothers.

Secret Ingredient: Read up on black women in history in *Epic Lives: One Hundred Black Women Who Made a Difference,* by Jessie Carney Smith.

Honor yourself for being a strong capable woman by taking a long, relaxing candlelit bath. Light a candle in homage to Sojourner Truth, and vow to keep her spirit and message alive.

❀ MARCH 2 ❀

Identify sheroes outside your race.

Just as Sojourner Truth demanded to be acknowledged at a conference on the status of white women, we all need to acknowledge women of achievement of different races. Why? Because if we want to be respected, we've got to respect others. That's what "mutual respect" means. If we want to be admired, we need to show genuine admiration. Unity, equality, and common goals can bring women together for greater good.

That's exactly what happened as a result of the friendship between Marcia Ann Gillespie, the African American editor-in-chief of *Ms.* magazine, who was formerly the editor of *Essence,* and Gloria Steinem, the well-known feminist activist and author, who is Jewish. In a move that proved their common belief in equality among women of varied races, Steinem, Gillespie, and several other women investors forged a partnership that raised over $3 million to buy *Ms.* A foundation of mutual respect turned into a history-making women-owned business triumph.

Besides Gloria Steinem, Native American tribal chief Wilma Mankiller, former Philippines president Corazon Aquino, the late president of India, Indira Gandhi, and the late First Lady Eleanor Roosevelt are other non-black women I admire. In studying the stories of great women, I learned that black folks aren't the only ones who can boast of being "the first" when it comes to their achievements. For example, in the sixties Bella Abzug was the first Jewish woman elected to Congress. When she died in 1998, a newscaster said she was born in 1920, the year women got the vote, and died on March 31, the last day of National Women's History Month. It was just like her to be part of history coming and going. As an attorney, she once defended a black man accused of raping a white woman in Mississippi. And she was known for her love of wearing wide-brimmed hats. Now many a sister can relate to that!

Secret Ingredient: In observance of Women's History Month, write down the names of women of other races you admire below, and then share the stories of their greatness with someone today.

1. _____

2. _____

3. _____

❀ MARCH 3 ❀

Be an activist about your health.

As I mentioned before (see February 21), Fannie Lou Hamer is one of the women in history I most admire. Born in poverty in Mississippi, Mrs. Hamer rose to challenge the Democratic Party at the 1968 Presidential Convention. As an advocate of civil rights through voter rights, she endured humiliation, imprisonment, and was beaten by her white jailers. Yet her spirit prevailed as she led freedom marchers to victory singing "This little light of mine/I'm going to let it shine."

Eventually, Stress and Duress took its toll on Fannie Lou Hamer. As she weakened and took to her bed, visitors would come to her home to pay their respects. When they would ask her how she was feeling, she would reply with a now-familiar phrase: "I'm sick and tired of being sick and tired."

We now know that her feelings of being "sick and tired" translated to the medical conditions of breast cancer, heart disease, hypertension, and diabetes. In 1979 at the age of just fifty-nine, Fannie Lou Hamer died.

It's my opinion that anyone whose death comes before they get to be a senior citizen has died prematurely. I said this at a speech I gave recently, and a woman told me afterward that she thought that Mrs. Hamer had run a hard race and went home to Heaven to get her reward. This lady and I proceeded to have a gentile debate. Like Rev. Dr. Martin Luther King, Jr., said in his last speech, I feel that "Longevity has its place." Maybe if Mrs. Hamer and the people in her community had had access to the best possible health care, she would have been able to enjoy her family longer. If she had been told that taking a thirty-minute walk three times a week around her beloved Delta (waving to her neighbors on the way), would be good for her heart, we may have been able to honor her in person today. If she used the low-fat soul food recipes popularized in *Heart & Soul* magazine and *Essence* food editor Jonell Nash's cookbook *Lowfat Soul*, perhaps she may have controlled or even prevented her diabetes. If someone had given her permission to take time for herself and slipped her a copy of *Sacred Pampering Principles*, by Debrena Jackson Gandy, it may have kept her blood pressure down. But all of us still have a chance to live a long, vibrant life. Strive toward the longevity that Lena Horne and Rosa Parks have achieved. We need you.

Secret Ingredient: **Take control of your health now, so in your golden years you can reap your earthly rewards before going on to your heavenly one.**

❀ MARCH 4 ❀

Drink water.

Not only is it Women's History Month, it's National Kidney Month. To observe it, here are some simple bits of advice: Drink two quarts of water a day.

Yep, that's eight eight-ounce glasses daily. It's the same advice your mother gave you. Drinking that much water in one day sounds easy, but for me it has always been a problem. I'm just not that thirsty. I'm too busy to be bothered. And I hate drinking water—it tastes so blah.

Several years ago I experienced a painful kidney ailment, and now I'm a believer! Yes, my sisters, I can testify that bread is not the only staff of life.

Do you know how much this liquid investment can pay off? Let me count the ways (and remind myself to boot):

Payoff #1: It'll roll the stones away. Experts say that drinking eight to ten glasses of fluid a day significantly reduces your chances of developing kidney stones—and their attendant agony. By increasing your water intake, you dilute your urine and help prevent the formation of salt crystals that can lead to kidney stones.

Payoff #2: It'll calm your cough. The next time you have a wet cough, rather than grabbing the cough syrup, chug a glass of water instead. It's the best expectorant you can take.

Payoff #3: Water can zap your headache without the bellyache. The more water you drink to dilute medicines that can cause stomach distress—aspirin, ibuprofen, and antibiotics—the less chance of stomach upset.

Payoff #4: You'll spend less time on the throne, my queens. Constipation is often the result of not drinking enough water.

Secret Ingredient: Examine your attitude toward drinking water. Are you a relentless guzzler, a reluctant sipper, or something in between? Track your water intake this week to see how close you come to two quarts a day. If you're one of those lucky sisters for whom the minimum intake is no problem—good for you!

❧ MARCH 5 ❧

Get close to your new friend.

Make water a friend, not a foe. Here are a bunch of ways to change a dehydrated lifestyle and guzzle down sixty-four ounces of water a day. Before you read this, go get yourself a tall glass of water!

❖ "Start the day with two glasses of water upon rising," suggested Dr. Barbara Justice Muhammed, M.D., when both of us were guests on Imhotep Gary Byrd's WLIB radio show in New York City.

❖ Keep water on your desk at work. If you don't have a "desk job," think of someplace comparable.

❖ Take a water bottle with you to meetings, to the movies, to the mall!

❖ Each day, put a fresh bottle in your car's cup holder instead of a coffee mug.

❖ Sip during your commute—even if it's on the bus or train.

❖ Always have a water bottle in your purse, totebag, backpack, or briefcase.

❖ Put an eleven-ounce bottle in your pocket when you go to the movies. (Hey, if we feed a baby with a bottle in these places, why not discreetly quench our own thirst?) A two-hour sit is a good time to get hydrated.

❖ Stop and sip: Make it a habit to drink from every water fountain you pass.

❖ Buy a special, unique, or beautiful glass that you'll find pleasure drinking from. That's what I did. I found a bright-red, plastic stemmed glass that sits on my desk at work, and that I take to meetings with me.

❖ Order water with a twist of lime or lemon when you're out partying.

❖ Buy six-packs of water along with the other beverages when you're throwing a party. My daughter's friend Dayna's mom, Carolyn, did this for their eighth-grade graduation party and after a few minutes of serious dancing, the first thing all the kids grabbed was the water—not the sodas. Teach your children good habits early and they won't have to try to change later when it's harder.

Secret Ingredient: **A friend asked me after I wrote about water in my *Heart & Soul* editorial, "If I hate water, won't other liquids do** the job?" Well, the experts say that juices, soups, milk, and herbal tea count toward daily totals, but it's best to make water at least half your daily liquid intake because other beverages may contain more sugar, caffeine, or calories than you want.

🌻 MARCH 6 🌻

Make "diet" what you eat, not what you don't eat.

I went on a diet once. What a disaster! After gaining the proverbial "freshman fifteen" when I was in college, I decided to lose the weight. What did I know about dieting (except that it meant not eating a bunch of stuff that I was eating—and enjoying)? I went home for Christmas, and told my mother I couldn't eat this, and I wouldn't eat that. Amused, she announced to her friends that I was "reducing," but I didn't lose a pound.

When I got back to school, I started dating a brother who was a vegetarian. As I mentioned before, dining with him meant going to restaurants with names quite different from the grills and fast-food joints I had been frequenting. I traded in Wings and Things for the Yes! Health-Food Restaurant. Like going on a new and exciting journey, my honey and I explored the delights of our new cuisine. On lazy Sunday mornings, he prepared banana pancakes and served them to me in bed. Who wouldn't be seduced into going vegetarian? And when I noticed that I had lost all the weight without "dieting," I was hooked.

In addition, I found that being a vegetarian, I could eat all I wanted and never have that overstuffed feeling. While I was gaining the weight, my roommates and I would eat soul food dinners night after night. Our ritual was to go to the all-you-can-eat cafeteria, chow down, then go back to the dorm and complain about how much we had pigged out! After I stopped eating red meat and began to enjoy new foods like tofu and eggplant, I never had that pigged out feeling again. I just felt like I could run around the block after dinner! And best of all the weight stayed off—to this day.

If you'd like to try lightening up your diet, don't think about what you can't eat or what you'd be depriving yourself of. Look forward to eating new, more healthful foods.

Secret Ingredient: If you've been considering becoming a vegetarian, but are reluctant, here's the secret: Start gradually. Begin by eating a meatless dinner, say, spaghetti loaded with your favorite vegetables in the sauce, instead of meatballs. Or just prepare the foods you love in a new way that lowers the sugar and fat content. Do it once a week, then twice a week. Buy cookbooks that you can use to experiment with. Find the nearest health-food restaurant and check it out. Eating healthfully could become a habit! *Vegetarian Times* magazine can give you some pointers.

✱ SPIRIT

✿ MARCH 7 ✿

Try the balm.

Growing up attending Mount Zion Baptist Church in Seattle, I used to love to hear a song the choir sang called "There is a Balm in Gilead." I had absolutely no idea what in the world they were singing about, but I enjoyed the harmony and the feeling of the song. Just going with how something feels is what happens when you're in touch with your soul. I think children trust the soul more than adults do.

Recently, I heard about the good works of an organization called Balm in Gilead. A resource center based in New York City, Balm in Gilead helps black churches nationwide establish AIDS ministries through training, workshops, seminars, displays, and distribution of materials to congregations. According to Rev. Meriann Taylor, the National Black Church Week of Prayer, the first week of March each year, was created to "help those infected and affected by HIV/AIDS."

Explaining the biblical connection with the name of the organization, Rev. Taylor says that "balm is what they used to call ointment. The Balm in Gilead is taken from a story in the Book of Jeremiah in the Bible." That passage, Jeremiah 8:22, is the inspiration and the healing spirit of her organization.

What can we do?

❖ Help someone with HIV/AIDS get treatment, find support, and obtain the care he or she needs.

❖ Volunteer at an AIDS hospice organization.

❖ Organize AIDS awareness programs in your community.

❖ Acquaint yourself and your loved ones (this includes elderly people, who are single, a growing HIV/AIDS population) with the requirements of safer sex.

❖ Pray for people who are affected by HIV/AIDS and their families. Pray also for an end to this devastating virus.

Secret Ingredient: **If you would like to establish an AIDS ministry in your church or community, contact Balm in Gilead in New York City. Take time today for several minutes of silence in honor of those who have passed away from AIDS as well as the people who are living with HIV.**

 BODY

❀ MARCH 8 ❀

Create your own health-and-fitness path.

Today is my husband's birthday, and I must say that he is far more diligent than I am in following a lifestyle of good health. When we met, I was impressed that as a Muslim he didn't eat pork and had already made the pilgrimage to Mecca before he was even thirty years old. Here's Reginald Oliver's recipe for strong mind, body, and spirit:

Eat low-cal foods for high energy. His is "a basically vegetarian diet" with occasional fish. Reg recommends a "low-cal diet with salads and fresh fruits and vegetables to keep your weight down and your system clear." The benefit: "It keeps my energy up."

Cleanse your colon with herbs at least twice a year. "It strengthens the central nervous system," Reggie says. "To live in this life, you need to be as strong and as vital as possible."

Exercise. Reg practices what he preaches by doing yoga daily, and by jogging or swimming at least three times a week. Why? "To maintain a toned body and to keep my weight down."

Practice deep breathing daily. His reason: "To send oxygen throughout my body and mind. Your body needs oxygen, just like it needs water."

Meditate. Always on the path to self-enlightenment, Reg recently took a course in Transcendental Meditation, and now he practices it twice a day. The course, he says, taught him that "meditating keeps your blood pressure low, it relaxes you from tension and stress, and allows you to come in contact with the deeper parts of your spirit."

How can each of us come in contact with the deeper parts of our body, mind, and spirit? Be open to learning new things: Study, take courses, read books, check out Web sites, consult with your doctor—then pursue your new endeavor as easily as you try on a new pair of shoes.

Secret Ingredient: **Are you on a path to optimum well-being? Have you ever laid out the points of your plan? Today, think of what you are doing for the betterment and maintenance of your body, your mental health, and your spirituality.**

For information about free Transcendental Meditation Program lectures in your area, call toll-free 1-888-LEARN TM or visit www.tm.org.

 BODY

 MARCH 9

Pursue your own "independent study."

In high school, I thought about becoming a fashion illustrator. As a result, my art teacher allowed me to take a course of independent study, learning about fashion illustration while everyone else in class followed the usual general art curriculum. In college, when I considered majoring in African American Studies, I was privileged to have distinguished professor Stephen Henderson guide me through independent research in African American literature. When I was a young career girl, I took an after-work, adult learning course in calligraphy. That one class has given me much joy—and an extra income—for years ever since. These courses that I took independently taught me the benefit of following my own agenda, and that the wisdom you gain becomes your companion. Not everyone is on the same schedule. You may be interested and open to a new experience that your friends or family members may not be ready for yet. But don't let that hold *you* back!

As I mentioned yesterday, my husband, Reggie, recently took a class in transcendental meditation—even though I was not ready to do the same. Reg went to the classes in the evenings after work alone and made new friends. One weekend, he even drove several hours from our house to a weekend transcendental meditation retreat. It was a journey he delighted in taking on his own.

If you have any interests that might move your life forward, or help you understand something better, or help you learn a new skill, don't wait for other folks to validate you by showing their interest, too. It's pleasant if other people want to share in your interests, but if you can't convince others to care about a pursuit as much as you do, follow your inner voice. It shows strength of character and pushes your self-confidence for you to do what you *know* you need to do. If you follow your own paths, you'll strengthen your character and increase your self-confidence.

Secret Ingredient: Decide on a subject you'd like to learn more about. Then be open and alert to receiving the information to further you along that path. That happened to me; I decided to learn more about Ayurveda, and as fate would have it, the next week someone put an Ayurvedic book on my desk at work! Knowledge works in mysterious, amazing ways.

 BODY

❧ MARCH 10 ❧

Pick parts of your own body to rave about.

Are you in a habit of comparing your body to those of other women? If so, it's a habit you really need to break in order to appreciate your own body fully. If you keep wishing you had Tyra Banks's breasts and Tina Turner's legs, that's counterproductive thinking that detracts from your own unique features. Complimenting other women is healthy; obsessing about what you perceive you lack is not healthy.

I have made peace with my flat chest (see how tomorrow). But more important, I have decided that there are parts of my body I feel as proud of as Tyra and Tina must feel about their breasts and legs. I also think I have pretty nice hands, too—inherited from my mother.

Think about it. I bet you've got some family assets you feel proud of. Is it full, fabulous, healthy hair? Luscious lips? Curvaceous hips? Perfect feet? Loving little parts of yourself can add up to loving all of you.

Secret Ingredient: Take inventory today: Totally nude, look at yourself at all angles in a full-length mirror. Find at least five things that please you about yourself. Appreciate them often.

❀ MARCH 11 ❀

Turn your flaws into flowers.

When I was six years old, I went to the Orpheum Theater in Seattle with my older girlfriend Olivia (who was all of nine) and stepped up to the window to pay for my movie ticket. "Before you go in," the woman who took my money whispered, "you might want to know that one of your boobs is falling down!"

Humiliated and astonished that my "falsies" had collapsed into my undershirt, I put my arms across my chest, threw the ticket at the male ticket-taker, and ran into the ladies' room to fix my bust line. Of course, Olivia was in hysterics by this time, and we laughed so hard I doubt that we paid much attention to the show we went to see.

Unfortunately, years later it seemed that my real breasts *still* hadn't grown in. Even by the time I was a teenager, the cups of my bra seemed to stay half-collapsed. In college, I remember one particular night of dormitory "dissing" when a "big girl" on my floor called me no-chested. "Well, all it takes is a handful!" was my well-rehearsed comeback (actually a whimper).

About ten years later, I got married, and two years after that, pregnant. As my stomach grew to accommodate the creation inside, my breasts blossomed to accommodate feeding my baby. When she was born, my lactating breasts were plenty big enough to feed little Anique. I remember that Olivia, whom I had followed to New York City by then, remarked that I must feel sexy at last with those enormous breasts. I recall trying to explain that it wasn't "sexy" that I felt; it was something greater—maternal.

A few years later, I went to Africa for the first time. There, in the Ivory Coast, I saw women walking around bare-chested, with absolutely no concept of breasts as sexual objects. Breasts were for feeding babies. Many of the women had sagging breasts, and it didn't seem to bother them in the least. They still strutted around with the pride and beauty of Nzinga, the eighteenth-century Angolan warrior queen. Like any good mother, the Motherland had taught me a lesson; the obsession with breast size is a Western concept. Now my whole outlook on my breasts has changed, and I appreciate the "little things" (pun intended!) in life.

Secret Ingredient: Like yesterday's exercise, check out your nude body. This time, choose one feature you're not totally happy with. Now think of reasons to love it anyway; appreciate yourself just the way you are.

❀ MARCH 12 ❀

Interview yourself.

If a hot new magazine was publishing a special issue for National Women's History Month and asked you to share the secret of your greatness, what would you say?

In the thirtieth-anniversary issue of *Rolling Stone,* Diana Ross is quoted as saying: "I'm pretty satisfied with who I am, and I think that shows."

It's likely that Queen Latifah's secret stems from the best advice she said she had ever received (revealed in the same *Rolling Stone* issue). "To believe in myself," was her reply. "My mother always said you can accomplish anything you want if you put your mind to it. That was real important because it gives you confidence and it doesn't make you afraid if you open your mouth and speak."

The secrets of greatness from these two super achievers of the music world are to believe in yourself and be satisfied with who you are. What's the secret of your success? What would you say if a reporter were jotting down your every word? Whatever that "sound bite" or great quote of advice would be, give it to yourself right now. Famous folks aren't the only ones with motivation to share. You have some, too, I'm sure, even if neither *USA Today,* Barbara Walters, nor Tom Joyner has called you to share it with the world just yet. Was it something your mama told you? Something a friend shared? A tip from a magazine, or a directive from a sermon? Remind yourself and share it with your loved ones, your children, your friends, and your colleagues.

Secret Ingredient: Interview yourself. Then put it "in print," below.

The Secret of My Greatness Is:

_____

_____

_____

❧ MARCH 13 ❧

Take your own advice.

Good advice doesn't always have to come from someone else—most of the time, you've got to admit, you know what's best for you. But sometimes taking your own advice is difficult to do.

I'm not sure that it was the best advice I ever gave myself, but I definitely remember the euphoria I felt when I followed my own counsel. When I was about twenty-three, I was crazy about a guy who wasn't so nuts about me. He invited me to spend the weekend with him, but when I got there, he told me he had a conference to go to. The next night he had a dinner to attend. The "business dinner" was followed by a "breakfast meeting" (on a Sunday, no less). As I sat there waiting and waiting, eventually, I got the message that there was someone else he was, in fact, spending the weekend with! Trying to act "like a lady" always kept me from dramatic outbursts, but while I was miserably waiting for him to return hours after the time he had promised to, it occurred to me that I didn't have to wait any longer—I could just leave! My inner voice said, *Get outta here—right now!* I had the power to turn the tables of confusion on him and have *him* wondering what happened to *me*. When I realized I didn't have to take his rudeness and disrespect for me, my adrenalin began to flow. I grabbed my stuff and ran out of there, caught a train back from Washington, D.C., to New York City, and didn't speak to him again until he called to apologize. That was the last time he ever treated me like that.

Can you think of a liberating act you performed after following your own good advice? Actually, we all do it all the time. We wonder what is the best thing or the right thing to do, and we end up following our best judgment. We don't always have the on-the-spot opinions of our mother, father, mentor, or therapist. You gotta give yourself credit for following the advice of the person who knows you best—you.

Secret Ingredient: **Think of the best advice you ever gave yourself. Exchange "best judgment" recollections with a friend. Discuss if you're both still following your advice. If not, why not?**

❧ MARCH 14 ❧

Maintain your integrity.

Do you know how something can be sitting right under your nose, then one day you look at it and see something you never noticed before? Well that just happened to me. On my desk was a church program that had been tucked in the corner of my desk blotter for months. But since I'd just had a very stressful experience with someone with whom I felt lacked integrity, all of a sudden the following sentence caught my eye: "Integrity is Christlike character in work clothes." I felt like I was looking at the church program for the first time.

What is integrity? It's firm adherence to a set of moral and ethical values. I know it's important to me. It's a character trait that I feel is necessary to my own self-image and reputation. When I was going through my "terrific teens" and would leave the house saying I was headed for a basketball game, or Baptist Youth Fellowship (BYF), or some other wholesome-sounding activity that really meant ending up driving around with my girlfriends looking for our boyfriends, my father would simply say, "Remember, you're a Stokes." And I would think, *Yeah, whatever that means!* But not everything that is told to you is made clear at the time. Some things take time to become incorporated into the wisdom of your inner voice. Over the years, I would come to know that Daddy was trying to instill a sense of integrity in me. It was his way of saying that I had a good name—so don't go out and bring dishonor to it. Be a person of integrity and high character. Remember who you are. His message seeped through: Since I couldn't forget that I was a Stokes, I couldn't give up the name even when I got married.

Too often, over my years of being a manager, I've seen young people risking their integrity: lying on their resumes, taking advantage of perks they would like to have that aren't theirs to enjoy, doing just enough work to "get over," never taking initiative or making an extra effort. Sometimes I wonder what has happened to integrity. So I was pleasantly surprised when I noticed the church program.

We all must remember to wear our integrity as obviously as we wear our work clothes. Keep it clean, neat, and pressed. Be proud to show that you're a person of good character.

Secret Ingredient: What is integrity to you? Think of the most important moral and ethical values you were raised to adhere to. What did you do when they were challenged? For inspiring stories of women and men of exemplary character, read *The African American Book of Values,* edited by Steven Barboza.

❧ MARCH 15 ❧

Get fiscally fit.

Ann J. Lemon is a very high-powered sister. A vice president at an investment firm in midtown Manhattan, she has her share of clients whose portfolios are worth millions of dollars. Yet, her overriding message to everyday people like you and me is pretty down to earth: Save your money.

"I was talking with a man today who told me he didn't have any money," she says. "I said, 'Well, you have enough to call me, don't you?'" Meaning if one has money to pay the phone and utility bills, they have enough money to start saving. "He said he was a teacher, and I told him he didn't need to make lots of money to start saving. All he needed was a plan." Lemon helped this man get a plan, so I asked her to formulate one for you. Here are her top tips to start saving now:

Have gratitude for the resources: Write down five things about your financial life that you're grateful for. Glad to get paid weekly? Grateful to be able to pay for child care? Happy you bought a house?

Gather the evidence: Collect your pay stubs to see how much income you have. Go through all your bills to compute your monthly expenses. How much money do you spend each month?

Make a plan: Using the above information, make a monthly budget. Be sure it includes savings, even if it's only 5 percent of your monthly income.

Enlist buddy support: Get your spouse or best friend to agree to help you stick to your plan.

Conduct plastic surgery: To avoid credit card usage, determine which bills you will pay by check. Pay all other expenses with cash.

Divvy it up: Divide cash expenses into four envelopes, one for each week of the month. When the envelope is empty, you're finished spending for that week.

Write it down: Get a small notebook. Each day, write down your purchases, even if it costs less than a dollar, to see where your money is going. Don't procrastinate.

Secret Ingredient: **Ann Lemon suggests you educate yourself, attend financial seminars, and read books and magazines.** *Money* **magazine is a good start. Then find an advisor to help you prepare an investment plan that fits your goals. Contact the National Association of Personal Financial Advisors at 1-888-333-6659; Web site: www.napf.org.**

 MIND

🌺 MARCH 16 🌺

Dig yourself out of debt.

It's hard to feel strong, healthy, and happy—and sometimes to even sleep at night—when you're buried under a mountain of debt. I know; been there, done that. But I also know that you can become debt-free; I'm a living, breathing testament.

Once I decided I hated bills and never wanted to feel bad about not being able to pay them again, I focused on my goal of being debt-free with the same fervor I used for everything else I had been successful at: total determination. I got fierce! First I had to stop buying so much stuff. But so that I wouldn't feel totally deprived, I never denied myself certain things like books and magazines. To consolidate my monthly payments, I destroyed all my credit cards except one and another one for backup (in case an establishment didn't do business with my primary card company). Then I targeted bills to pay off one by one, starting with the lowest balances. I would earmark paychecks, bonuses, and monetary gifts for certain bills. When I would pay off the balances, I would feel like screaming, "Yes!" I became as addicted to paying off the bills as I had been to shopping and spending money.

If you're under a mountain of debt and feel you need professional help, here are the names of some sisters in finance who may be able to help you out, and I've added some other resources too.

- ❖ **Cheryl D. Broussard,** financial advisor and author of *The Black Woman's Guide to Financial Independence,* Palo Alto, California; 1-415-688-1188.
- ❖ **Glinda F. Bridgforth,** financial advisor, and author of *The Basic Money Management Workbook,* Oakland, California;

1-888-430-1820; e-mail: glindab@aol.com. www.electra.com
(AOL Keyword: Electra); www.bridgforthfmg.com.
❖ **Debt Counselors of America,** 1-800-680-3328; Web site:
www.getoutofdebt.org.
❖ **Consumer Credit Counseling Service,** 1-888-462-2227; Web
site: www.credit.org.

Secret Ingredient: Dig yourself out of debt with the three Ds: Desire, Determination, Discipline. For a free booklet called "Managing
Your Debts," write the Consumer Information Center, Pueblo, CO
81009 or call 1-888-8-PUEBLO. Visit their Web site at
www.pueblo.gsa.gov.

❀ SPIRIT

❀ MARCH 17 ❀

Celebrate our differences.

Do you wear green on St. Patrick's Day even though you're not Irish? If
you do, I wish you the luck of the Irish!

You may think, *That's not my holiday.* But is Martin Luther King, Jr.,
Day ours alone? No, it belongs to everyone. As folks say in New York
City on St. Pat's Day at the Fifth Avenue parade, "Everyone is Irish to-
day!"

Born on St. Patrick's Day, Karen Callaway Williams is a sister who
always wanted to visit Ireland. In 1998, she became the first woman tap
dancer to join the Irish dance performance "Riverdance" at Radio City
Music Hall in New York City. "When I arrived," Williams is quoted as
saying in the *Newark Star-Ledger* newspaper, "the Irish girls were very excited to see me."

As with Williams's experience, expanding your vision and embracing other cultures can make a difference for the people of another culture
as well. When I was seventeen, my high school choir toured Ireland. We
stayed in the homes of Irish families and performed in concerts all
around the country, and then in Britain, Scotland, and Wales. The
twenty or so African American kids in the choir of one hundred were the
first black people many of these Irish folks and their neighbors had ever
seen. The community actually came outside their homes to watch us ar-
rive! Their warm hospitality is something I will carry with me forever.

In 1998, after President Clinton visited Africa, he and the First Lady were pictured on the cover of *Jet* wearing kente cloth with their arms up in triumph. African Americans could feel proud that the President chose to honor our heritage by donning kente, the exquisite West African fabric that's a symbol of our pride in our Motherland. We can return the favor to other Americans who are just as proud of their heritage. Small gestures go a long way.

Secret Ingredient: **Wear green today as a sign of respect for our Celtic brothers and sisters.**

 BODY

 MARCH 18

Strut your stuff (and get in shape).

If you've ever had the pleasure of being asked to participate in a St. Patrick's Day Parade or African American Heritage Parade or Chinese New Year Parade or any other parade, there's one thing they all have in common—walking. And even if you never plan to do anything beyond rain on someone's parade, you can strut your stuff to fitness.

That's right. Fitness walking can take off fat and reduce stress, and may prevent heart disease and a whole lot of other ills. By doing what comes naturally—walking that walk—all of us can reap a multitude of health benefits. Did you know that . . .

* A brisk walk for as little as half an hour a day may keep a heart attack away?
* Walking regularly keeps you "regular"?
* Brisk walking, or other exercise, done three times a week for at least twenty minutes each time may reduce the pressure within the eye that leads to glaucoma?
* Walking not only tones your legs but can take off fat anywhere—from arms to thighs?
* A study of mostly black women in Florida with stressful jobs showed they had a 30 percent reduction in work stress after eight weeks of fitness walking?

Maybe you do know what walking can do for you because walking is the most popular form of exercise for American women of all backgrounds. Remember walking to school when you were a kid? Well, if you haven't taken a stroll since then, get up and go! Walking is an exercise that can last a lifetime. Free your legs, and your mind will follow!

Secret Ingredient: Before the day is over, walk for ten minutes, either outside or inside. (If you're inside, turn on your favorite music and march in place.) Tomorrow, walk for five additional minutes. To help you make walking a part of your fit lifestyle, pick up a copy of *Walking* magazine.

❋ BODY

MARCH 19

Walk this way!

Run-DMC and Aerosmith said to do it. And though I'm still not sure they were talking about what I'm talking about, I do know that if you were to get the CD and listen to that early rap jam on a Walkman and head to a track or park, you couldn't help but be motivated to move it!

I don't know what motivated me to finally get with it. I didn't learn to walk until I was twenty-two months old. For years my father would joke that I had been thinking, *Why should I walk when these fools will carry me?* But once I got started, there was no stopping me. And by high school graduation, I was voted "Most Soulful Strut." A dubious distinction, but nevertheless, I do love to walk, and now that I know that walking not only gets one from point A to point B but also is great exercise, I'm down with it.

Here are some basics for doing the stroll:

Start out slowly. For the beginner, the word is take it slow. If you've never exercised regularly, try just five minutes at first (pay no attention to all those jocks racing around you on the track). Work up to a half hour three times a week—slowly.

Choose a comfortable pace. You should never feel tired or sore after your walk—nor should you be gasping for breath.

Don't go too far. Don't get so carried away that you're too tired to walk back. Gradually you will get to know your limits.

Keep your body aligned. Think about the racewalkers you've seen who walk fast but don't lean forward. Leaning will create a strain on your back. Walk tall!

Secret Ingredient: Set a goal, and stick to it. Three times a week for thirty to forty-five minutes at a time should be the minimum. To lose weight, especially if it's only ten pounds, you'll want to walk at least five days a week, the longer the better. A lot depends on your needs and lifestyle. If you walk at a fifteen- to twenty-minute-mile pace, you can probably walk an hour every day without harm. If you love speedwalking, then you may need to take days off. You can walk fast one day, rest or stroll the next.

 BODY

❧ MARCH 20 ❧

Plan a walkathon.

A healthy trend I've observed among African American women's organizations is increasing sponsorship of walkathons. What a wonderful thing! It's a great way to welcome spring (or summer or fall), exercise for a good cause, and raise money for charity. Walking for health is something young and old can do together.

In the November 1996 issue of *Heart & Soul,* we ran a small item about a walkathon sponsored by The Links, a prestigious national-service organization for African American women. The story informed readers about the annual Project Walking Fete: Making Health a Habit, which is hosted by Links chapters across the country and in Germany and the Bahamas. With the item, we ran a small photo of about a dozen people with their jogging outfits and visors on, ready for the event. At the time the magazine was published, I recognized a couple of people in the picture, such as the former Links president, Patricia Russell McCloud, and TV weatherman Spencer Christian. But it wasn't until months and months later, when going through back issues of the magazine, that I looked at that same page again and noticed that Dr. Betty Shabazz, who had recently passed, was also in the picture. In the photo, she's looking healthy and energetic, with a visor and jogging suit on, ready for the walk. What a wonderful, vibrant image of her! I was so excited that I called one of her daughters, my friend Attallah, and told her about it, then sent her a copy of the magazine. "Yes," she told me, when I asked if Dr. Betty had been in the habit of exercising, "originally a nurse and nutritionist, Mommy was very health conscious." Well, my sisters, that's a powerful, spiritual message from a woman who holds an esteemed place in our history, who will always be a role model. If she was committed to fitness, so should we be.

Another great organization that sponsors a walking program is the National Black Women's Health Project in Washington, D.C. Their Walking for Wellness program has spread to several cities.

Strut your stuff in support of a good cause; it's definitely a step in the right direction.

Secret Ingredient: **Consider starting a walking group with friends, family, or a community organization. If you'd like to be a part of the Walking for Wellness program, contact the National Black Women's Health Project in Washington, D.C.**

❀ MARCH 21 ❀

Bless your house.

If our bodies are our temples, what are the houses we live in? Holy cities, maybe?

There's no question that our homes need to be sanctuaries of peacefulness and tranquility in order for us to have a reliable refuge from the unpredictable outside world. As in the gospel tune "Bless This House," which Mahalia Jackson sang, we can evoke the connection between how we feel about our homes and how we revere God's house, the church. Here are some ways to think of our homes as our temples:

Surround yourself with people you love. Only allow in your home people whom you know to have good vibes. So often we invite people— or let them invite themselves—into our homes out of habit. I found this out the hard way. Several years ago, someone whom my intuition told me was not "on the up-and-up" made several unannounced visits to our home. But because he had never done anything to us that we could point to, we kept letting him in. Soon after, our house was robbed—and we had reason to believe that this man may have been involved in some way. To prevent something like this happening to you—honor your instincts and invite into your home only those people you know well and whose energy is positive and uplifting.

Bring goodness into the house. It's an old tradition that when a couple marries, the groom carries the bride across the threshold. Imagine that picture (if you had the experience, remember it)—a happy scene with the hope that good luck will follow. Make an effort to have good things cross your threshold, such as happy babies, spiritual vibes, groceries that will provide good health, furniture on which you can relax and de-stress, and most of all positive people. Avoid bringing in the negativity that comes with drugs, cigarettes, excessive alcohol, or violent behaviors.

Keep the cleanliness in, the chaos out. If cleanliness is next to godliness, then a clean house is a godly house. It's hard to keep a dorm room, apartment, or house spotless when you're a busy woman, but cleaning or tidying up at least one area in your home each day is a step toward keeping the clutter out.

Stay safe and secure. Have you checked the locks lately? Does your neighborhood crime rate call for an alarm system? Do what you can to make your home a haven from the mean streets of life.

Secret Ingredient: **Repeat the prayer you probably know from childhood:** *Bless this house, O Lord I pray. Make it safe by night and day.*

❀ MARCH 22 ❀

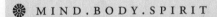

Spring clean.

It's spring cleaning time! If you are truly diligent—and who of us really is?—you might consider cleaning out your closet, washing windows, clearing out the refrigerator, maybe rearranging furniture.

Have you ever considered that in the same way you clean your home in the spring, you can clean your self? Here's how:

Body: Organize your fitness routine. If your treadmill has been serving as a valet instead of an exercise device, donate it to your local YWCA or senior citizen home. Don't beat yourself up for not exercising—just regroup. Try something new. A trampoline, maybe? A line-dance class? Swim lessons? Golf is all the rage—find a city course and take a lesson.

Mind: Clean out the clutter. Take a day to clear your mind of stress, of negative feelings, of worries you can't do anything about. Are you holding on to a dream, idea, relationship, or emotion that is no longer seeing you? If so commit to releasing it and freeing yourself of negative feelings. I love the Angela Bofill song, "This Time I'll be Sweeter." Forgive yourself of past mistakes and vow that next time you'll do it differently . . . and better.

Spirit: File it under "Faith." In that classic Bofill song, the last lines are "Have faith in me." Develop fresh faith in yourself. Spring is a good time to get out to visit a new church, take that meditation class you've been thinking about, or visit the ashram you heard about. Springtime is a good time to be born again!

Secret Ingredient: After you've given yourself a good spring cleaning of body, mind, and spirit, don't forget to clean the house! Commit to clearing out clutter and to cleaning one room a week for the next several weeks. If you haven't worn a garment or used an item in over two years, either give it to a friend or family member, donate it to a worthy cause, or simply throw it away.

✺ MIND

❧ MARCH 23 ❧

Make peace with your hair.

"When black women make peace with their hair, they'll lead the world," my husband, Reggie, said to me one day several years ago when I was flip-flopping over whether to straighten my hair or stop straightening it. I like to think that we'll prove him right one day.

But right now a lot of us are still grappling with how to wear our African textured hair and feel accepted in America—especially in the workplace, where our natural styles may not be as well regarded, or even tolerated, as we would like. And for too many of us, memories of "bad hair," "nappy edges," and "kinky kitchens" have eroded our self-image and left emotional scars that are slow to heal.

And no wonder. Such negative attitudes have been ingrained in us for centuries. Hair historian Willie L. Morrow writes in his self-published book *400 Years Without a Comb* that when our ancestors were snatched from their homeland, they were forced to leave behind their elaborately decorated combs—symbols of their culture, and part of their concept of beauty. "Having no comb and no time in which to groom or fashion the thick growth into a stylish hairdo the slave began to resent his hair even more."

As time went by, our collective assimilation of white beauty standards negated our hair's strong, tight-curl pattern and made us see its natural texture as something to be ashamed of. Even now, too many of us remember when nothing less than hair that was "bone straight" would do.

Fortunately, the "Black Is Beautiful" movement of the 1960s helped to turn that shame inside out. We proudly sported our "bushes," and photographic images of that pride are still part of popular culture today. As the political winds of change blew toward the right, though, many of us returned to what we knew to be safe in this society in which ours is not the dominant culture. Now that the Reagan-Bush years are over and more blacks are in government and generally gaining power, I'm seeing more choices—locks, natural styles that a friend of mine calls "freedom hair," as well as chemically relaxed bobs. But we should never relax our effort to instill in ourselves and our children positive feelings about our unique textured hair. Remember, what's important is that our hair is healthy.

Secret Ingredient: **The children's book *Nappy Hair,* by Carolivia Herron, affirms the beauty and pride in the natural texture of black hair.**

 MIND

❀ MARCH 24 ❀

Have a good hair day for the rest of your life.

I know everything I said yesterday about "good hair" and "bad hair" are habits that are hard to break. Even the general population has adopted the phrase "bad hair day"—though of course, that means something entirely different for black folks. If you're black and think you've got "bad hair," it's something you live with every single day of your entire life—not just days when you need a haircut or didn't have time to wash it. It's emotionally damaging and it's downright sad.

I certainly haven't been immune to the hair thang. My hair has a very African, very tight curl. Like many of you, over the years I've had my hair fried, lyed, and laid to the side. I've been through perms, braids, twists, hot-combing, warm-combing, and blow-drying. A few years ago my reliance on perms began to feel more and more like a "chemical dependence." I grew tired of spending hours in the beauty shop, but didn't have the patience to do my hair myself. I also wanted low-maintenance hair that would allow me to get over my swimming phobia, let me get caught in the rain, and to wash it whenever I wanted to. Finally, I just cut it all off. Now, as the saying goes, "I'm happy I'm nappy."

Several years ago, after having a good laugh over a photo in *Jet* of a brother whose 'fro was cut into the shape of a bowler hat, Patricia Copeland, my late aunt-in-law, remarked: "Since we black folks are the only ones who have this unique texture of hair, it must be divine and special." Who else has hair that can stand straight up, be cut in the shape of a garden bush, or hang like the strongest ropes? Our natural hair has inspired people of other ethnicities to make peace with their own non-straight hair. We're not the only ones using "picks" or growing dreads.

I've even taken to considering the spiritual aspect of it: If God gave me this hair, who am I to mess with it and alter it and deny His creation? Everyone isn't at the same place, and I accept that. But whether your hair is natural or processed, commit to loving it, keeping it healthy, and giving thanks for its unique versatility, resilience, and wondrous texture.

Secret Ingredient: **If you're not happy with your hair, resolve to do something about it! After you do, you'll probably wonder what took you so long.**

SPIRIT

MARCH 25

Go for the goal!

It's not the gold—it's the goal. This sentence came to me in a dream. Sorry, I don't remember the dream, only the message.

It's not the money—it's the mission. This sentence came to me just now—as I was typing, wide awake, but hey, I accept that message, too.

I have noticed that people who are super-successful are always quoted in interviews as saying that they love what they do. If we make the love of a task or job our goal (in other words, if we choose goals that we feel in our heart) we'll reap the financial rewards. For example, if you love to paint, don't be discouraged by folks who may tell you that you'll never "make any money" painting. If it is your goal to be a great painter, and you follow your heart, you will succeed because that was the plan for you. Ask Betye Saar, whose artwork graces the cover of this book.

I think of the great artist Elizabeth Catlett, whom I was honored to interview for *Essence* in 1985. I would say that her goal was to paint scenes that would educate others about the greatness of African American history and the beauty of contemporary life. In so doing, her goal has given her the "gold" of a beautiful home in Mexico with a pool, double artist studios for her and her husband, and a rewarding family life. The black-and-white woodcut of poet Phillis Wheatley that I bought from her and that she inscribed so graciously to me, hangs in my writing room. So the money I gave Catlett for her mission now inspires me toward my own mission—writing—an endeavor I hope will bring *me* money!

Here are ways to put mind over money:

❖ Concentrate on your ultimate goal: What makes you happiest?

❖ Be willing to politely ignore people who try to stifle your dreams.

❖ Read up on your area of interest. Whether it's becoming a hip-hop star, an investor, or a human rights activist, there are manuals, classes, Web sites, and other resources available. All you have to do is diligently search them out.

Secret Ingredient: **Keep a notebook devoted solely to your goal. Write in it dreams, notes, ideas, any information that furthers your belief in yourself. Believe in your goal. Your mission is as worthwhile as anybody's.**

❋ SPIRIT

 MARCH 26

Think "blessed," not "stressed."

For about the last dozen years now, I have recognized that March is the month in which I get totally freaked out. To be specific, in March 1988, when my daughter turned six, I orchestrated a birthday party for her at school, another one for her at home, a third party for my husband's birthday a week later, a business trip I had invited the whole family on—and while I was planning all this, I was in my usual fast-forward mode at work.

By the Saturday my daughter's house party rolled around, I had lost it: Every time the doorbell rang announcing the arrival of another cute, little guest, I would break down and cry. I was acting worse than the kids! Fortunately, my husband and a friend who arrived early with her child took over. Later, as I pondered my situation, I came to realize that everything I had been so anxious about was a blessing. My daughter was healthy, and happy to be celebrating her birthday. My husband deserved a celebration, too. I was blessed to have a great job—one that had the benefit of business trips that I could occasionally share with my family. In just a week, we'd be on our way to Barbados!

Research has shown that there is indeed "good stress" and "bad stress" and that just identifying the difference can help you cope with it more easily. Some "good stressors" include applying to college, a promotion or raise at work, an upcoming marriage, a new baby, a new house.

At the African American Women on Tour conference several years ago, I heard mistress of ceremonies Jewel Diamond Taylor say to the crowd, "You are too blessed to be stressed!" That catchy phrase struck a chord with me. In her self-published booklet called *You Are Too Blessed to Be Stressed,* she writes, "You can continue to be reactive and always in a state of crisis . . . or you can choose to be proactive and live in a state of grace."

Secret Ingredient: **Recognize that good stressors precipitate positive change in our lives. The goal is not to eliminate them, but to manage them better. To order Taylor's booklet, e-mail her at jeweldiam@aol.com. Today take time out to think about your life. Are you stressed or blessed? Is something in your life causing you anxiety? How can you view the situation in a more positive light? Remember, as Jewel Diamond Taylor says: You are too blessed to be stressed!**

 MIND

❀ MARCH 27 ❀

Arm yourself with stress busters.

We all know what the bad stressors are. For African Americans, racism is at the top of the list. Barbara Dixon, R.D., L.D.N., and author of *Good Health for African Americans,* has even labeled it "Black Stress." That is, stress caused by such things as racial jokes in the workplace, job and housing discrimination, being victims of bias attacks. A study of African American women conducted by Duke University identified their most common stressors as loss of a loved one; strained love relationships; concern for children's well-being; caretaking responsibilities; and, one I found startling, *intraracial* segregation—meaning economic, education, and skin-color issues.

This is tough stuff. What to do? Stress by definition is a situation in which we feel we have little or no control. So it's a reality that we can't always prevent. However, we *can* control the following: how we react to it, how we manage it, how we de-stress.

React by maintaining your calm, dignity, and integrity. Don't stoop to the level of the individual who is trying to set you off. It could just further exacerbate the situation.

Manage stress by scheduling times to deal with it. Don't let stress consume all your waking hours. Take charge of the situation by taking constructive action, such as filing a complaint, or confronting the perpetrator—even days later once you've cooled down ("I heard you tell that racial joke the other day, and I want you to know that I thought it was inappropriate and not even funny. I think you should apologize").

De-stress with prayer and music, two of the top ways *Essence* readers once responded to a poll on coping methods. More recently, *Heart & Soul* readers' most common strategies were "take a bubble bath, light some candles, put on some jazz."

Exercise is a proven stress reliever.

Secret Ingredient: When stress hits, evaluate the situation and think of the four methods to help you cope with it.

MIND

MARCH 28

Plan an adventure in bed.

I admit unabashedly that I have had some of my most exhilarating moments in bed. Sometimes with company, but mostly alone. My children have witnessed my adventures, and they've even had a few of their own!

What I'm talking about is my way of heading off stress at the pass: hibernating in bed. It's the closest thing I have to returning to the womb. It's prevention.

On the weekends, my friends know not to call me before 11 A.M. (after I've awakened and watched *Style* on CNN at 10:30). When folks do call and I say I'm in bed, they say, "Oh that's right, it's Saturday." My family knows I ain't going nowhere before at least 4 P.M., if then. I read, I write, I eat, I nap, I administer parental discipline, I talk to my brother six thousand miles away—all without moving from my king-size bed.

Some people think lying around all day is just lazy. But author J. California Cooper isn't one of them. "I live in my bed," she proclaimed when I told her I had heard we had "bed time" in common. "My wardrobe is nightgowns. I don't see any sense in getting dressed if you're at home. I write all my books in bed. That's because in bed is where I'm most relaxed. When you relax, your brain is the only thing you have to work. It doesn't mean you're lazy."

Maybe more people would be understanding (and would even try it) if they knew that staying in bed can make you rich. One day when I was lying in bed, I picked up a book my husband had left around called *Money Is Your Friend,* by Phil Laut. The book explained how self-esteem leads to riches: "Money will not add to your self-esteem, it works the other way around." The author provided some exercises to increase self-esteem, including taking a bath daily, getting a massage weekly, always speaking the best of yourself and others. And the one that hit home: Staying in bed all day once a week. According to Laut, if you schedule time alone to think, this will make it easy to become your own best friend.

Secret Ingredient: **Tonight, get in bed a half hour earlier than usual. Read a book, listen to music, or just sit in silence and think and dream. The next time you feel like spreading out your blanket on the sand, but can't get to the beach, spread it out on your bed. Take the chill-out time to do whatever you want—or do nothing. I assure you, it will be a worthwhile adventure.**

 SPIRIT

❧ MARCH 29 ❧

Sing and rejoice!

What does that old biblical word "rejoice" mean, anyway? It means "feel joy."

That's what I'm talking about. Sing and feel the joy of letting your spirit soar. It really doesn't matter if you can carry a tune or not. It's about expressing yourself through music, rhythm, movement, and inspiration.

I grew up in a household where everyone sang aloud. If you asked my father a question, he might answer you with a lyrical phrase. My mother sang solos at church, then later directed the children's choir, and now sings in three choirs! I once had a boyfriend who couldn't understand why I was always singing. "Do you think you can sing or something?" he would ask, trying to embarrass me into silence. As I explained, it wasn't about ego, it was about self-expression, and experiencing even momentary joy. I could think of a song in my head and didn't have to wait for it to come on the radio—I could sing it myself!

I don't have to tell you that our ancestors sang all the time. In the fields, in the churches, at happy occasions and sad ones. African Americans created "work songs," spirituals, the blues, jazz, R&B, and rap. We are a singing people!

Singing is healthy because:

❖ It makes you happy and doesn't hurt anyone else.
❖ It clears your lungs and keeps your voice strong.
❖ Singing gives you self-expression.
❖ It comes from the soul (as in the lyrics ". . . then sings my soul").

Secret Ingredient: Let your spirit soar with some wacky fun! Grab some friends and go to a club that offers karaoke, and sing along to your favorite songs. This form of entertainment was imported from Japan, where singing to Motown sounds and other popular American music is all the rage!

❋ SPIRIT

 MARCH 30 ❋

Join the choir.

I've got to say something else about singing: To anyone who is moved by beautiful gospel music, especially those sisters who sing in church choirs, how great thou art! You are doing something wonderfully uplifting for your mind and spirit.

Every Sunday, at microphones in black churches across the country, women prove that they are "somebody." In our churches, the high notes of the domestic worker may move to tears the attorney who can't sing a lick. At church, you can be known for decades as the woman who can *sang* (as Aretha Franklin's father, the Reverend C. L. Franklin, said of his daughter on her *Amazing Grace* album)! We all know women who will never get recording contracts, women who will never be seen on BET or MTV, but, these same sisters have reputations for making people "get happy" every time they open their mouths. Their joyful noise is beautiful. And here are some other beautiful things about choir-singing sisters:

❖ No one has to be super-skinny or reflect any of society's warped standards of "mediagenic" beauty standards. Heavy sisters, little ladies, poor women, affluent sisters, those with health challenges, those with spunk, young women, silver seniors—all stand side by side, sing praise, and release their burdens in the church choir.

❖ According to a Duke University study, people who attend religious services on a regular basis have better mental health than those who don't.

Secret Ingredient: **Even if you can't carry a tune, it's never too late to learn! Join a choir, or practice singing in the privacy of your own home. If you'd rather *listen* to music than sing it, here are some suggestions:**

❖ **Throw a gospel brunch at home.**
❖ **Go to a soul food restaurant that features a Sunday gospel brunch.**
❖ **Enjoy a gospel concert.**
❖ **Listen to a gospel radio station.**
❖ **Lift your spirit by playing gospel music in the morning while you get ready for the day.**

❀ MARCH 31 ❀

Learn to pray—then go out to play!

I'm an ol' church-choir girl myself! My mother had me in the junior choir she directed as soon as I was old enough to carry a tune. I still sing alto at church (although I must admit that I'm not in the choir) and love to harmonize to "We've Come This Far by Faith," "How I Got Over," "Sweet Spirit"—don't get me started!

In my house, Mahalia Jackson lives! On one of my old albums, she exclaims, "I found the answer/I learned to pray." Well, I've been singing that song around the house since my father bought the album when I was a little girl. I took it to college with me, and then to my first apartment; I've still got it downstairs with the other LPs (yes, I still have albums—and play them!). When my daughter was little, she once heard me singing the song (at the top of my lungs, of course) and came in the room. After my "performance" was over, she looked thoughtful. "I like that song," she said and started singing. "I found the answer—I learned to play!"

I cracked up. Her young mind thought I was saying "play" instead of "pray." That's what she related to!

We could all use more prayerful and playful spirits. Many of us know how to pray, but rarely take the necessary time out to play. Others play too much, and rarely say a prayer. Prayer can heal, and so can play! Playfulness, humor, and laughter can be "the best medicine," but we could all benefit from the balance of time to pray and time to play.

Secret Ingredient: Reverend Dr. Barbara King's book *Transform Your Life* can tell you how to use prayer for better health. *Go, Girl! The Black Woman's Book of Travel and Adventure,* edited by Elaine Lee, can show you where in the world to have a funky good time!

When we were children, we took time out every day to play and also say our prayers. The Bible says, "Lest ye be as little children, ye shall not enter the kingdom of heaven" (Matthew 19:14). Get back in touch with your child-spirit and reincorporate prayer and play time into your daily routine.

APRIL 1

Don't fool with a fool.

It's April Fool's Day (no fooling!) and I can't think of one joke or prank to write. All I can think of is some advice my husband's eccentric and much-loved (now deceased) Aunt Pat once disseminated in her own colorful style of talking: "Don't f——with a fool!"

Now, who knows what the circumstances were that prompted her never-censored directness, but we got the message. Maybe it was prompted by the story I told her of someone I knew who had recently become pregnant. When I asked the person if she was going to marry the baby's father, she had replied, "Him? He's a jerk!" I remember being amazed that she had sex, much less had not used contraception, thus allowing herself to get pregnant by someone she didn't even *like*, much less love. Since she opted to keep the baby, this meant that she would be a single mother without the support of or parental sharing with this man. Why would she fool around with a fool?

Some attitudes and mores have really changed from generation to generation. For example, my mother says that back in her day, she wouldn't have considered even *dating* someone that she wouldn't have wanted to marry. Most of my girlfriends say when they were in their twenties they wouldn't have had *sex* with anyone they wouldn't have a lasting relationship with. Recently, I heard a twenty-seven-year-old say she'd never have sex with anyone she wasn't at least *attracted* to. (In reaction to that, someone else said that there are men who couldn't care less about being attracted to someone—all they need is a partner with a pulse!)

Things have changed over the years, but what does seem to stay the same is that if you fool with a fool (my variation on Aunt Pat's theme), you could regret it. The consequences could be as irritating as spending an otherwise lovely dinner with an egomaniac who won't stop talking about himself, or as daunting as spending your life with someone who doesn't respect you.

Secret Ingredient: Be careful when choosing a mate—always hold out for the best. Pick a person who is kind, loving, mature, responsible, and most of all, respects you. In your heart of hearts, *you* know what is best for you. Follow your instincts, and don't forget Aunt Pat's advice: Don't fool with a fool—and don't be one!

 SPIRIT

 APRIL 2

Find (and be) someone easy to love.

Just before South African President Nelson Mandela and the former First Lady of Mozambique, Grace Machel, married in July 1998, the bride-to-be was widely quoted as saying that their relationship had "all the elements of mutual respect for each other. There are no destructive elements. He's so easy to love."

What a powerful thing to say! What a blessing that we all should be so fortunate to experience in our lifetime:

❖ Love that is built on mutual respect.
❖ Love without the intrusion of negative vibes or destructive habits.
❖ A lover deserving, open, and receptive to love.

And not only should we seek such a lover, but we should seek to be someone who respects and trusts the one we love, someone who does not bring destruction into the relationship, someone "easy."

Someone close to me was once married to a man who was charming and easy. If you asked him "What do you want for dinner?" or "What movie would you like to see?" he was apt to reply, "Oh, it doesn't matter, I'm easy." He was the first person I ever heard describe himself in such a way, and it endeared him to me. It didn't mean that he was a wimp. It didn't mean that you could run over him. It meant that he was confident enough in himself and in your desire to do right by him to trust you to do so.

President and Mrs. Nelson Mandela are role models in the revolution for freedom and in international statesmanship. They could let that be enough, but fortunately, they have chosen to show us the power of a serious, constructive relationship, and have allowed the world to see the dignity of black love.

Secret Ingredient: **The absence of destruction, added to an abundance of mutual respect, equals an easy kind of love.**

 BODY

❧ APRIL 3 ❧

Learn to love your body.

A few years back there was a study out from the University of Arizona that revealed that 70 percent of black teenage girls were happy with their size, while 90 percent of white teens weren't. More recently, another study reported that Americans are living heavier and happier as they age.

Accepting yourself is important. But according to the National Center for Health Statistics, about 33 percent of people in this country weigh more than 20 percent over standard weight guidelines for good health. In other words, they are obese. Among black women, over 50 percent are above a healthy weight range. Is self-acceptance being confused with complacency?

While it's positive that African Americans seem to appreciate a voluptuous, "brickhouse" body over stick-thin supermodel images, black women have among the lowest levels of fitness activity. And as we know, obesity can lead to health problems, such as hypertension, diabetes, and heart disease.

So what to do? First, learn what loving your body really means. It not only means acceptance, but several things that are more proactive, such as:

Knowing how healthy you really are. If you are getting regular checkups, your doctor should be informing you about your best weight and how to achieve it.

Moving your body. If you feel too stressed to exercise, consider that physical activity is a better stress buster than eating. Get your heart rate going with any physical-fitness activity, sport, or dance that you will enjoy enough to stay with it.

Eating healthfully. Too often we use food for recreation ("Since I'm at the mall, I might as well stop by the food court") or as an antidote for stress ("I know I already had a piece of cake, but after that bad news I just got I deserve another"). Or we go on crash diets only to regain the weight after returning to our previous eating habits. Educate yourself about healthful foods. Make vegetables, not meat, the main attraction of your plate. Make gradual changes from high-fat foods to low-fat foods you love.

Secret Ingredient: **Keep that positive body image while keeping tabs on healthy habits.**

 MIND

🌼 APRIL 4 🌼

Don't rely on the Wall Street Journal.
Keep your own journal.

As I write this, today marks the thirtieth anniversary of the assassination of Rev. Dr. Martin Luther King, Jr. I know that I was sixteen on that sad day in 1968. But now in my mid-forties, my own personal recollection of that day has faded. I remember where I was when President Kennedy was shot and killed—that was the first scary event of national proportion of my life—but for some unknown reason I have no memory at all of the days surrounding King's assassination that occurred almost five years later.

Fortunately, though, I do have a record of my thoughts and what I did in the days following this major world event because I kept a diary. I may not have kept a copy of that day's *Wall Street Journal,* but I still have my own journal, a very serious-looking, brown leather diary with a lock. Here's what it says (don't laugh now, remember I was a kid!):

April 4, 1968: Today the second assassination in my lifetime was committed. REV. MARTIN LUTHER KING, JR., WAS KILLED.

He was a Negro leader for civil rights & a Nobel Peace Prize Winner . . . Survivors include: his wife, his 4 children, & a nation!

April 5, 1968: School let out at 11:00 in honor of Rev. King . . .

April 7, 1968: Dear Diary, After church there was a march downtown to the stadium for a memorial service for the Rev. Martin Luther King, Jr. We marched about four miles or so from Mt. Zion [my church]. 15,000 people participated in the memorial. After that, I went on my first date at night to the show . . .

Because I kept a diary, I know that during the sixties we mourned, we marched, and we went to the movies. Terrible things happened, but we tried to let life move on.

Keeping a journal let me learn a history lesson from my self, not just from other people's records, other people's accounts, or the media's interpretation. If you keep a diary, or would like to, know that what you are doing is not selfish or self-indulgent. It's your personal history. It's documentation that you were here, on the planet, participating in life.

Secret Ingredient: **Did you know that journal writing is a great form of self-therapy? (More on that tomorrow.) Before you go to sleep tonight, take time to write about your day and how you felt. Most often, expressing ourselves on paper helps to ease our burdens.**

 MIND

 APRIL 5

Keep a journal, keep your sanity.

I've kept a journal almost as long as I've known how to write. The first entry I found (written at age eight) reads: "Dear Diary, Kandace [a Japanese-American girl in my class] came over and we had fun." More recent entries, in the silver blank book I bought when I came to New York over twenty years ago, document first dates, my marriage, my pregnancy and my daughter's birth, jobs changed. Over the years, I've gotten too busy to keep it up-to-date, but the last entry, like the first, was also about fun: my fortieth birthday party.

My friend, author Benilde Little, keeps a journal. So, at *Heart & Soul*, we asked her to share her experience with our readers. She wrote, in 1996, that she was introduced to journal writing when she interviewed playwright and author Ntozake Shange. In answer to Benilde's question on how to have a successful and happy life, Ntozake replied, "The most important thing you can do to help you find your way through life is to keep a journal."

Journalist and author Jill Nelson put it even more bluntly: "When you write stuff down, you own yourself—which is especially important in a culture where so often we, as African American women, are not affirmed."

Here are some ways I think journal writing affirms you:

- ❖ It documents that you *are*, that you exist and that you matter.
- ❖ Journal writing relieves stress by helping you to sort out things you are dealing with.
- ❖ It allows you to vent your feelings, to scream on paper, or shout for joy.
- ❖ It gives you a safe place to share your goals, plot your course, chart your progress.

Don't know what to write, or feel reluctant because you don't think you write well? Not to worry. Your journal is for your eyes only, so don't be concerned about grammar or spelling. What's important is that you state the facts and your feelings at the time.

Secret Ingredient: **Be honest with yourself, and your journal will reward you by providing a record of your heartfelt emotions for years to come.**

 SPIRIT

🌻 APRIL 6 🌻

Eat the Fish of Life.

At my church one Palm Sunday, the Scripture was from Luke, so I decided that on Good Friday, when I had off from work, I would read that Book of the Bible. I enjoyed the stories of healing and resurrection, and wondered why I had never before realized that the town of Emmaus in Pennsylvania, where Rodale Press (the company that owned *Heart & Soul* at the time) was based, had been named after a biblical village near Jerusalem (maybe because I didn't read the Bible enough, huh?).

But there was one story in particular that struck my fascination: After Jesus's death, when he appeared to his disciples, they were startled and frightened, thinking they had seen a ghost. Then Jesus invited them to touch him, saying that a ghost doesn't have flesh and bones. And he showed them his pierced hands and feet. "And while they still did not believe it because of joy and amazement, he asked them, 'Do you have anything here to eat?' They gave him a piece of broiled fish, and he took it and ate it in their presence." (Luke 24:41–43)

I know I have a warped sense of humor, and I'm probably the only person who ever read this passage and had these thoughts, but it amused me that while everyone around Him was trippin', Jesus defused the situation by asking the most mundane and humane of questions: "Hey, what y'all got to eat around here?" And what does one feed the Son of God after He has performed the miracle of all miracles, arising from the dead? Ham, which is a traditional Easter food? Pig feet? Hog maws? Barbecued ribs? Chitlins? I don't think so. Broiled fish was what He was served, and what He accepted and ate.

Broiled fish—maybe some blackened salmon or broiled flounder; a nice piece of mahi mahi well done. Let your imagination take you to the best piece of broiled fish you've ever had. Then think about miraculous times of reentry that you've experienced or that anyone could possibly go through: your first full meal after reaching a weight-loss goal, a welcome-home dinner after a hospital stay, a long-awaited home-cooked meal after a long journey or stint in the military. I wonder what Nelson Mandela had to eat for his premiere meal upon release from incarceration? Broiled fish wouldn't be too far-fetched.

Secret Ingredient: **Cook up some broiled fish. It's a good, healthy choice—that comes with a Most High recommendation.**

 MIND

 APRIL 7

Write a poem today.

Like journal writing, self-expression through poetry can be cathartic and fun. It's a creative endeavor that can make you feel you accomplished something enduring in just a few minutes or hours.

When I was in college during the seventies, much of the sentiments of the Civil Rights struggle was articulated through poetry. Poetry readings were "in." Many of us took to collecting books by favorite poets, such as Don L. Lee (now known as Haki Madhubuti) and Sonia Sanchez. I wrote a few verses myself that got published in Howard University's *Hilltop* student newspaper. Work, marriage, children, and the eighties put an end to that reflectiveness, but lately, I've been writing a poem or two to include in my public speaking. Here's one I shared with the women physicians of the National Medical Association recently:

Good Health

People play the lottery
Saying they want wealth,
But you know, there's something greater than money
It's called "good health."

Even before we're born
While we're forming in the womb,
It's something our mothers pray for
A blessing from cradle 'til tomb.

Mind, Body, Spirit
We need to keep them strong,
Or we won't enjoy good health
For very long.

So eat right, exercise
Keep God in your sight,
See your doctor regularly
Then you'll sleep well every night.

Poet Amiri Baraka says, "Poetry, to me, is not a hobby. It's what I want to say about the world." So go ahead/Have your say/Try your hand at a poem today.

Secret Ingredient: In many cities, there's a resurgence of poetry readings. For some inexpensive evening entertainment, check out the literary cafes and bookstore events in your area. Then step up to the mike!

❀ APRIL 8 ❀

Conceive. Believe. Achieve. Receive.

"If you believe, you will receive," I heard a minister say. Are there obstacles that you feel keep you from believing good things can happen to you? Is there something you aspire to but you feel held back by other people's skepticism or criticism? Remember that what *you* believe will result in what *you* receive—you won't receive because *others* believe. What's coming to you has to originate uniquely in you. Others may not understand it, and that's okay. Belief isn't always a group activity.

As the old saying goes, "Whatever you conceive, you can achieve if you only believe." It's more than a memorable ditty or a cutesy rhyme. It's the truth.

Secret Ingredient: **Believe in yourself and the good that you have coming to you. Believe and you will receive . . .**

❀ APRIL 9 ❀

Call on faith.

"Who do you turn to for inspiration when things get difficult?" MSNBC journalist Ed Gordon asked poet, author, and great lady Maya Angelou, at the end of an interview in which she had shared an abundance of inspiration with viewers. Her answer: "I call on my faith, my religion. I try to remember that I am a child of God."

Many of us call on people, or call up people, when we need inspiration. But people don't always do the trick. Faith, however, can work the magic. Religious faith can move—yes—mountains of problems.

What does it mean to be "a child of God?" It means:

❖ If your mama is no longer with you to call on, you may feel like a "motherless child," but you're still somebody's child—you're a child of God.

❖ If you've never known your biological father, you can still get to know your Heavenly Father.

❖ If someone treats you as though you are less than human ("three fifths of a man"), remember that you are a divine creation.

Maya Angelou, like Whitney Houston, goes to the Rock.

I love the soundtrack to *The Preacher's Wife*. As Whitney Houston sings so beautifully and convincingly, "When I need a shelter, when I need a friend, I go to the rock." Amen.

Secret Ingredient: **What He's done for others, He'll do for you!**

 BODY

 APRIL 10

Do some sole searching.

Back in the day, it would've been an insult if someone said, "Your mama wears combat boots!" Now, things haven't changed entirely, but it may not be the biggest compliment for someone to say, "Your mama wears high heels!" Most of us know by now that wearing stilettos or spike heels habitually can lead to aching feet, bad backs, and just plain walking funny. Okay, so neither you or your mama wears high heels *all* the time—who does? Maybe no one, but even though it seems everyone wears sneakers, how many women take the time to pick the best shoe for fit and comfort, as opposed to style? Do you know the difference between a cross-trainer, a runner, a walker, and an aerobic shoe?

I admit that just a few years ago, I just thought "sneaker"—period. But now that I know the difference between them, it makes me feel like a more knowledgeable consumer when I buy athletic shoes. Here's how to find a good sole mate:

Aerobic shoes have extra support in the ankles to take all that side-to-side movement. The soles are specially made so you don't slip around on hardwood floors.

Walking shoes fit snugly and bend easily from toe to heel. Get these for everyday use as well as fitness walking.

Running shoes have serious cushioning for ankle support and knobby soles for bounce.

Cross-trainers are the shoes for just about any fitness activity. If you like to walk a mile, then run around the track; or if you jog to your aerobics class; then your sole-searching may be over.

Pick the right shoes and you'll be spared "the agony of de feet!"

Secret Ingredient: Don't wear the same shoes you use for fitness activities for hanging out. Keep your fitness shoes in tip-top shape by wearing another pair when you want to just look sporty.

 MIND

 APRIL 11

Break type.

There's a theatrical term that I always thought was interesting: typecasting. I first heard it in college when my roommate, who was a drama major, complained that she kept getting "typecast." Meaning that she was cast repeatedly in the same type of role. Of course, we loved her roles, but she wanted her parts to grow and evolve.

In real life, we often get typecast. By teachers who don't see our potential. By bosses who only consider us capable of doing the same type of work year in and year out. By well-meaning friends who think they "know" us. By a society that can't imagine black folks enjoying adventure travel or the opera.

My brother (whose birthday is today) breaks all type, bless his heart. He's an African American attorney who lives in Hawaii (unusual enough), where he goes *surfing* after work (totally rare bird). André recently sent me a picture of himself on the beach, surfboard under arm, dreads blowing in the breeze, body in great shape, with this caption: "The kid at 50." You *go,* boy!

My type, as you might imagine, is a bit more sedate. I can't even swim, much less get up on a surfboard. However, I love shocking people with my passion for parasailing! It's big fun being up there in the sky.

Do you ever "break type"? Here are some ways to stretch yourself a bit, without breaking your neck:

Let your inner "alter ego" out every once in a while. There was a very shy and quiet kid in my high school who rarely said "Boo!" to anyone, but on Halloween every year he would let it all hang loose when he put on a mask. He eventually got a job at an amusement park haunted house.

Minimize the risk by taking a class in your area of interest. Sherrill Clarke, a copy editor at *Essence,* says, "I'd always wanted to learn to fly, so I took lessons after starting out on a self-exploration path. Soaring above the clouds and controlling an airplane unleashed my adventurous spirit and released the exciting, outgoing person inside."

Make a list of things you always wanted to push yourself toward, like being more physically active or being comfortable eating in restaurants alone. Then pick one to try—just once—to see how you like it. Try it, you might keep doing it!

Secret Ingredient: Today, try one thing you've never done before. Or, if it's a big thing that takes planning, start the research today and set your date of execution.

 BODY

 APRIL 12

Cook with love.

Leah and Dooky Chase have been married for over fifty years. I'm sure that they have a recipe for longevity in love just like the Mandelas do. But in New Orleans, they are celebrated for their recipes of another kind. The Creole cooking kind. If you are ever in New Orleans, you *must* dine at Dooky Chase Restaurant. And if you live in "The Big Easy"—boy, are you lucky!

I was lucky enough to meet the Chases many years ago when I wrote a story about them for *Essence.* Just recently, when I was in town I had the pleasure of dining there and seeing Mrs. Chase again. She said she had learned many things since that article that gave her her first taste of national publicity was published almost twenty years ago. One thing she had learned was the value of cooking that is not only tasty, but healthful.

"Chicken," she says, "is served all over the world. In Africa, they make chicken. In America, we cook chicken." Here's the recipe she recommends for a quick and healthy African American chicken dish.

Low-Sodium Creole Oven-Fried Chicken

$^{1}/_{2}$ frying chicken
White pepper
1 cup flour
$^{1}/_{4}$ tsp. ground thyme
$^{1}/_{2}$ tsp. paprika
$^{1}/_{4}$ tsp. granulated garlic

Preheat oven to 375 degrees. Remove skin from chicken, cut chicken in pieces, and season with white pepper. Place flour in bag or bowl. Mix in last three ingredients. Shake chicken in bag in flour mixture. Remove chicken and shake off excess flour. Spray pan with nonstick cooking spray. Place chicken on pan. Bake for 45 minutes.

SERVES TWO.

That's so easy, even I can fix it! New Orleans has had its share of negative press lately for being dubbed "the fattest city in America" by the Coalition for Excess Weight Risk Education. But leave it to Leah to come up with a dish low in fat and sodium—and still be able to call it Creole.

Secret Ingredient: "Cooking is from the heart," Mrs. Chase wrote in our copy of her wonderful cookbook. "Put a little love in the pot."

❀ BODY

❀ APRIL 13 ❀

Be seen cooking red beans.

I'm definitely no Leah Chase. For people that knew me when I was Contemporary Living Editor for *Essence* magazine, it was pretty funny that I would be in charge of the food pages, considering that I hated to cook! If a person who has no luck with plants has a brown thumb, then I had a burnt finger when it came to cooking. Yet, I am proud to say that I could *edit* a recipe with the best of food editors!

Fortunately, I only had to edit the recipes, not create them *(Essence* had wonderful food editors, Venezuela Newborn and now Jonell Nash, to do that). And luckily for me, my husband does most of the cooking (poor man wanted to eat!)—and he does it very well (he's got a rep for a mean blackened salmon)! But there are times when I have a taste for my own meager cooking (and hey, I'm a mom, so I have to cook *sometime),* so I bang a few pots together and come up with one of the easiest, low-fat, high-protein, quasi–soul food meals anyone can make:

Stephanie's Seattle Soul Beans and Rice

Instant brown rice
Canola or olive oil or soy margarine
1 onion
1 clove garlic
2 15.5-oz. cans red kidney beans
Season to taste

1. Prepare rice according to package directions.

2. While the rice is cooking, pour just enough oil or margarine in a skillet for sautéing the onion and garlic.

3. Peel and chop the onion and garlic and add them to the hot skillet. Sauté until transparent.

4. Open the cans and add the beans to the skillet; let heat thoroughly, stirring whenever you feel like it (say, if someone walks into the kitchen and you feel the need to profile).

5. Season to taste—but don't pour a bunch of salt in there and raise the sodium content, please!

6. When you think it looks more like "dinner" than "ingredients," and the rice is all fluffy like in the TV commercials, serve the beans over the rice.

SERVES FOUR PEOPLE, MORE OR LESS,
DEPENDING ON WHETHER THEY HAVE SECONDS
OR NOT.

Secret Ingredient: **This dish will look more like a meal if you serve it with some vegetables, like a big green salad, and some—take a guess—cornbread. Think about how you can make your favorite dishes healthier. Consider enhancing a dish with vegetables or whole-grain bread, and reducing salt and sugar.**

 BODY

 APRIL 14

Be a man (or just cook like one).

One of the stories I used to enjoy writing at *Essence* was called "Men Who Cook." It was fun to find these liberated fellas who could throw down in the kitchen. Fortunately, I'm married to that kind of guy. He started out making dinner because his hunger couldn't always wait for me to get home from work. And on weekends, when his three daughters were with us, he enjoyed delighting them with their favorite Daddy concoction, "Spaghetti Casserole." Over the years, his cuisine and skill have blossomed and now he loves to entertain and feed folks. His signature dish is "Blackened Salmon."

"I like 'Blackened Salmon' because it tastes good, it's quick and easy to make," he says, then adds with pleasure, "and everybody likes it!

"It's a romantic dish," he continues (and I can vouch for that!). "It looks pretty on the plate and is healthier than serving fried chicken!"

It's so quick and easy that it only has three ingredients and takes just ten minutes to prepare. Here's his recipe; try it tonight:

Reg's Blackened Salmon

Salmon filets or steaks (enough for the number of people you are serving)
Blackened fish seasoning
Canola, safflower, or vegetable oil

Wash filets or steaks. While fish is still wet, shake on seasoning. If you like spicy food, pour it on generously; if you prefer it mild, sprinkle it more sparingly.

In a cast-iron skillet or frying pan, pour just enough oil to coat bottom of pan ("Not enough to fry, but just so the fish won't stick to the pan," says chef Reg). Let the oil get hot, but not on the highest temperature; medium-high is best (cooking it on the highest heat can produce a lot of smoke; be prepared to open windows or doors).

Put the fish in the pan. Let it get done on one side, then "flip that bad boy over" and let the spices get nice and black and crusty. This should take about 8 minutes; 10 minutes or more if you like your fish well done.

Remove from the pan and place on a paper towel-covered plate. "Serve with your favorite love potion." (I ask what his is, but he won't divulge it.)

Secret Ingredient: **Reg uses Chef Paul Prudhomme's Magic Seasoning Blends' Blackened Redfish Magic. If you are ever in New Orleans, however, you can get blackened fish seasoning just about everywhere—even where souvenirs are found.**

❀ APRIL 15 ❀

Fire up the passion you need to succeed.

Since we have to pay taxes, we might as well give it up from a job we enjoy. My college classmate Amy Hilliard, of Chicago, not only enjoys her work as president of her own niche marketing and motivational consulting firm, The Hilliard Group, Inc., she has a passion for it.

"Once you find your passion—the success that's in your soul—you'll begin to soar!" Amy says. "But how do you find your passion? By digging deep to discover what really matters to you, and seeking the steps to achieve it in your life. Then, take this knowledge and do something about it. Turn your passion into action."

In the motivational seminars Amy delivers to major companies, she shares these 10 "Passion Principles":

- ❖ Find your **Purpose**
- ❖ Believe in **Possibilities**
- ❖ Identify your **Priorities**
- ❖ Get **Prepared**
- ❖ Have **Patience**
- ❖ Seek **Positivity**
- ❖ Manage **Perceptions**
- ❖ Assume **Prosperity**
- ❖ Stay **Persistent**
- ❖ Develop **Power**

Amy advises that you use these ten principles to make the power of passion work for you in the key areas of your life—your career, relationships, spirituality, and finances. "If you do," she says, "prosperity will follow."

Secret Ingredient: **Faith.** "These principles are supported by a spiritual foundation," Amy explains. "Have Faith. Use Faith. By using Faith as an action word, you can:

Focus on what you want.

Accept your greatness, assume success, and get into alignment.

Intuitively use your imagination and insight with integrity.

Trust in the process of finding your truth.

Heed your heart.

For more information on Amy Hilliard's "The Power of Passion" concept, contact her at: The Hilliard Group, Inc., 4823 South Kimbark Avenue, Chicago, IL 60615; 1-773-924-9997; or e-mail her at HGIMM @aol.com.

 SPIRIT

 APRIL 16

Worship your body, your temple.

How many times have you heard someone say, "your body is your temple"? How many times have you nodded in agreement, then gone off to "desecrate the temple"? It's good to have a positive body image, but if we don't really take care of our beautiful, God-given bodies, then we're just talking trash. Think about it: In your temple, church, or mosque, would you light up a cigarette? In your temple, would you drink liquor? Would you use drugs at church?

Those may seem like extreme examples, but the point is that most of us have considerably more reverence for our place of spirituality than we have for the place in which our own spirit dwells. When we desecrate something, we treat a sacred thing with disrespect. That's what we do when we abuse our bodies, when we don't get enough sleep, when we eat until we're "stuffed like a pig," when we devour a bag of potato chips and rationalize that at least we had a vegetable today. Desecration is what we do when we have unprotected sex, when we don't seek prenatal care, when we're over fifty but have never had a mammogram.

When we worship, we express reverence, respect, and devotion toward a divine being. We show a deep attachment or love. We honor, cherish, and admire. These are all things we can do to worship our bodies.

Our bodies are "divine beings." We express reverence when we avoid habits that we know are destructive. We give our bodies respect when we don't allow others to negatively influence our healthy habits. We prove we're devoted to our well-being when we don't do things we wouldn't want the children to whom we're so devoted to do. Do you honor, cherish, and admire your body, or do you admonish yourself with comments about how fat, unloveable, pitiful—fill in the blank—you are? This day, start anew to establish a deep attachment to yourself, expressed through loving thoughts about who you are, and by considering your body a divine place, worthy of your highest praises.

Secret Ingredient: Make a pact to honor yourself by treating your body as your temple. Create a daily "worship yourself" ritual. Start off simply—adopt three self-care habits (go to bed one hour earlier, eat more fruits and vegetables, meditate/pray at midday) and expand from there.

 MIND

 APRIL 17

Pick your ten best healthy-living books.

In 1998, there was a lot of hoopla over a list of "one hundred best English-language [to distinguish from Zulu-language maybe?] novels" published this century, as chosen by the editorial board of a major book publishing company. Out of one hundred, there were only three books by black authors: James Baldwin, Ralph Ellison, and Richard Wright. All worthy, all men. There were no books at all by African American female authors. Where were books by Toni Morrison, the Nobel Prize winner? Books by Alice Walker, the Pulitzer Prize winner? Just goes to show that it's important for us to know our own personal "bests," even if they're not acknowledged by big shots who get national publicity. Here's *my* list of ten best English-language books for body, mind, and spirit that may never see the light of day in the *New York Times, USA Today,* or *Time:*

For the Body:
- *Body & Soul: The Black Women's Guide to Physical Health and Emotional Well-Being,* edited by Linda Villarosa
- *Health & Healing for African-Americans: Straight Talk and Tips from More Than 150 Black Doctors on Our Top Health Concerns,* edited by Sheree Crute, Foreword by Joycelyn Elders, M.D.
- *A Path to Healing: A Guide to Wellness for Body, Mind and Soul,* by Dr. Andrea D. Sullivan
- *Make the Connection: Ten Steps to a Better Body—And a Better Life,* by Bob Greene and Oprah Winfrey

For the Mind:
- *In the Company of My Sisters: Black Women and Self-Esteem,* by Julia A. Boyd
- *What the Blues Is All About,* by Angela Mitchell with Kennise Herring, Ph.D.

❖ *Sacred Pampering Principles: An African-American Woman's Guide to Self-Care and Inner Renewal,* by Debrena Jackson Gandy

For the Spirit:
   ❖ *Acts of Faith: Daily Meditations for People of Color,* by Iyanla Vanzant
   ❖ *Lessons in Living,* by Susan L. Taylor
   ❖ *Jesus CEO,* by Laurie Beth Jones

Secret Ingredient: My hands-down favorite for the best book ever written for body, mind, *and* spirit is the Bible. On a list all its own is *The African-American Devotional Bible: New International Version,* which features 312 daily devotions from prominent African American Christians. What's on your list?

 MIND

❀ APRIL 18 ❀

Start or join a book club.

One fun way to compile a list of good books is with a group of like-minded friends. From Oprah's Book Club to kitchen table clubs, folks are gathering together to talk about books they love, and the lessons they can draw from them.

My friend Shelia and ten girlfriends started a reading group called the Bibliophiles in northern New Jersey in 1988 that now numbers twenty-five. Why? "The answer is simple and clear," Shelia says, "because I love to read!" She adds that it also helps her "gain the full depth and appreciation for what the author is trying to communicate, and what other readers (and in turn, I) think the message is. I can think of few things better than a rousing discussion with a group of women (and sometimes men) about what Toni Morrison was revealing to us in her Pulitzer Prize–winning novel *Beloved*—the book around which the Bibliophiles was formed!"

Here are Shelia's tips for organizing the first meeting:
   ❖ Call at least three other women you know who love to read— this is the primary criterion!
   ❖ Suggest and agree on a date, time, and meeting place (preferably, where food is available). The Bibliophiles meet bimonthly in the home of a member.

- Agree on a book you would like to discuss; something that generates a lot of excitement!
- At the meeting, after a few minutes of warm-up greetings, introduce the book and offer a statement or question to get the discussion going. Maintain order, but make sure you have fun.
- Decide if this is something you'd like to do regularly. If the answer is "Yes!" set aside time to create a reading list and then decide when and where to gather, and you're on your way!

Secret Ingredient: **The Bibliophiles are willing to help others start their reading groups; just fax (908) 464-3479. Another organization of sister-readers, the Go On Girl! Book Club has over twenty chapters nationally, holds annual conferences, and the founders have recently published** *The Go On Girl! Guide for Book Clubs,* **which includes how-tos on starting a club. Write them at P.O. Box 3368, New York, NY 10185, or visit their Web site: www.goongirl.org. You can also become a member of Oprah's Book Club: on AOL Keyword: Oprah, or www.oprah.com.**

 BODY

 APRIL 19

Healthy-up yourself.

Do you know that Bob Marley song "Lively Up Yourself"? Well, it occurred to me that we all need to "healthy-up" ourselves. To prevent the diseases that African American women are more prone to, we must be on the case! Determine which of the healthy habits that follow you can begin today—and if you're already doing them all, celebrate with some reggae aerobics!

Prevent heart disease. "If you were to ask, 'What is the major health threat to black women?' most black women would say, 'Breast cancer,' " says Anne L. Taylor, M.D., associate professor of medicine at Case Western Reserve University in Cleveland. "But [actually] cardiovascular heart disease has higher mortality and prevalence rates." Keep your weight down below obese levels, abstain from smoking, exercise regularly, and maintain a low-fat diet.

Cancer prevention and detection. Breast, cervical, and lung cancers are the three most fatal kinds of cancer black women face. *Breast cancer:* Regular breast self-exams, yearly doctor's exams, and mammograms upon your doctor's recommendation. The National Medical Association recommends a baseline mammogram for black women age thirty-five and up. *Cervical cancer:* Early detection can make this disease almost 100 percent curable. An annual Pap smear is a must, along with condom use to prevent STDs. *Lung cancer:* Just one cigarette a day can increase your risk. Don't start, do stop, and try to avoid second-hand smoke.

Make the pressure drop. Obesity and high cholesterol levels contribute to high blood pressure, which is a major cause of stroke. Keep weight and cholesterol levels down. Talk with your doctor about the risk of taking birth control pills while smoking.

Dodge diabetes. Postmenopausal hormonal changes and increased weight after age forty-five can cause increased insulin resistance and bring on diabetes. Again, to prevent it or control it, exercise and diet are key.

Secret Ingredient: **Did you know that nausea and vomiting are common symptoms of a heart attack that are often dismissed as indigestion? Other symptoms include crushing, squeezing, or heaviness in the chest that can spread to the jaw, neck, or arms. Know the symptoms and pay attention to your body.**

❋ BODY

🌻 APRIL 20 🌻

Trace your health roots.

Family lore said that my maternal great-grandmother Mary had died young and suddenly "after picking a corn on her little toe." This story made three subsequent generations quite wary of fooling around with their feet. As I grew older and more health-conscious, I began to wonder what the *real* medical story was. My Aunt Katie, an obstetrical nurse, finally cleared up the corn story for me: Most likely, the foot became gangrenous because our foremother, Mary, had diabetes. That made sense of the story, at last.

Diabetes, kidney disease, sickle cell anemia, and certain types of cancers can run in families for generations. Knowing the medical history of your family members can help you and your doctor ward off conditions that you may have a propensity toward by making diet and lifestyle changes or with medical intervention. So do a little sleuthing and find out some lifesaving facts. Here's how to get started:

Document your own history first. Do you know if and when you had chicken pox, measles, mumps, or other conditions? Keep records of shots, medical treatments, illnesses, surgeries, ages at which they occurred, and former doctors' contact information for yourself and your immediate family in one place. I keep mine in an accordion file under "M" for medical records. Computerization can make medical-history organization even easier.

Next, find out your parents' history. Just about anytime you fill out a medical form, you will be asked about your parents' health history. If they are deceased, note the date and cause of death.

Make a family health tree. Consider tracing your roots in this very meaningful way that you can share at family reunions or give as gifts. Inquire about not only your parents, siblings, and grandparents on both sides of the family, but their siblings as well. For each person include name, birth date, illness and age of onset, other illnesses, date of death, and cause of death. If you know each person's place of birth and death, you've got as complete a genealogical record as any.

Secret Ingredient: **Send relatives a health-history questionnaire. The March of Dimes Birth Defects Foundation has such a form that's available for a $1 check or money order from: March of Dimes, Genetic Counseling/Family Tree, P.O. Box 1657, Wilkes-Barre, PA 18773-1657. 1-888-MODIMES, or try www.mod.net. The new iMac computer has a medical history template built in.**

❋ MIND

🌻 APRIL 21 🌻

Find some peace and quiet.

I was already at Canyon Ranch Health Resort in Tucson, a place where one would expect to find peace and quiet. And I was there with my mother for a restful, relaxing Mother's Day weekend. But I had chilled out too quickly, because going by my biological clock of C. P. Time made me miss the afternoon group walk. Deciding to go it alone, I started hiking down a dirt road adjacent to the ranch. After about a mile, at the spot where the road was about to take a sharp turn, I heard the sounds of rushing water. Then looking to my left, I saw the river down the embankment. My mind became instantly peaceful and joyous with this thought: *He leadeth me beside the still waters. He restoreth my soul.* All the blessed stress, responsibility, and busy-ness of my life were laid down by that riverside.

It's not always easy to find peace and quiet. So when you do find it, remember to make a mental (or written!) note of where you found it, how you found it, and how to find it again. Here are some of my favorite places:

- ❖ My bedroom
- ❖ A tub filled with my favorite bath bubbles
- ❖ A beautiful park
- ❖ The beach
- ❖ A bicycle trail

And of course, we have to have fantasy places, like romantic weekends with our honey in a country bed-and-breakfast, or taking an Alaskan cruise! If you can't afford to go away, create a sacred retreat in your own home: Unplug the phone, light candles, turn on your favorite music and enjoy. Dreaming gives you peace and quiet, too! And you just might get there.

Secret Ingredient: **It's best to jot down your list of favorite places to find peace and quiet, so that when you're frazzled and out-of-touch with yourself, you can remind yourself that relief is closer than you think. Write down your five favorite places**

_____

_____

_____

 MIND

 APRIL 22 ❀

Be a sister-friend if you want to have a sister-friend.

Sister-friend—it's a phrase as common among black women today as girlfriend or boyfriend. But I remember when it got its roots. I swear that author-poet Maya Angelou started it all. I don't know how these things get documented, but in the griot tradition, I proclaim that Maya was the first high-profile person to coin the phrase and popularize it. Around that time, in 1983, I was fortunate enough to visit her at her home in Winston-Salem, North Carolina, and talk with her about sisterhood. Here's some of the wisdom she shared with the readers of *Essence* that day that still holds true today:

Me: You call your friends sister-friends. What does sisterhood mean to you?

Maya: Well, I don't believe that the accident of birth makes people sisters or brothers. It makes them siblings. Gives them mutuality of parentage. Sisterhood and brotherhood is a condition people have to work at. You compromise, you give, you take, you stand firm, and you're relentless. The only thing is you don't have sex to further complicate it. But all the responsibility, all the courtesy, all the soft and sweet words, all the teaching words, are called for in those relationships as much as in a love affair.

Sisterhood means that if you happen to be in Burma and I happen to be in San Diego, and I'm married to someone who is very jealous and you're married to somebody who is very possessive, if you call me in the night, I have to come. Whatever I have to pay, I have to be there. So really, it's no small matter.

Me: You have white women friends. Can they be our sisters?

Maya: With those I know to be sisters, we have all paid dues for our sisterhood. Only equals make friends. Otherwise the relationship is out of balance, out of kilter. Without the parity of investment, loss, triumph, bravery, cowardice, fear, the relationship is essentially paternalistic, maternalistic, condescending.

I have many sisters, black and white. But then I've lived a long time. My mother told me early on: If you want to have a friend, you have to be a friend—and I make a good friend.

Secret Ingredient: **Take time today to reevaluate your relationships to the women in your life. Are you being a good sister-friend? Are your sister-friends being good to you? As Maya Angelou says, are your relationships in balance or "out of kilter"? If your sister-friendships are out of balance, make a plan and do something about it.**

✿ APRIL 23 ✿

Know when to say "later" to a friend.

I hate to say it, but sometimes it's best to distance ourselves from certain people who are close to us. I remember when I first realized this. Many years ago, when I was visiting my hometown, an old friend called to update me on all the "happnin's" since the last time I was home. I didn't know what I was in for! She told me more "dirt" than I wanted to hear. In particular, this friend (I'll call her Yvette; not her real name, of course) bad-mouthed the husband of another friend of ours (I'll call her Suzette) in a way that made me very uncomfortable. I had just talked with Suzette, who hadn't given any inkling anything was wrong between her and her husband. After I hung up, I thought about the petty, envious comments Yvette had made and I realized that *I* had changed. In my new life back East, I had begun to surround myself with positive people. We were too busy trying to support each other in our quest for success and happiness to talk negatively about people. Even though we had been friends since childhood, I decided that Yvette could no longer have what *Essence* editor-in-chief Susan L. Taylor calls "a front-row seat" in my life.

One front-row friend of mine, Marlene Watson, Ph.D., has explored women's friendships in her work as a marriage and family therapist. Here is some advice from her on handling sticky relationships: "Like a love relationship that starts out wonderful, but ends in a breakup, a once-solid friendship may dissolve because of betrayal, jealousy, overdependency, lack of common interests, or changing needs. Friendships are like contracts that need to be renegotiated when they're no longer working. But a troubled friendship doesn't always mean that you and your sister-friend should part company. Discuss the situation with your friend, and affirm her as a good person despite your differences."

Secret Ingredient: **Talk honestly with your friends about your feelings. Keep the door of forgiveness open. Saying "later for her!" just may mean you'll make up with her later.**

✿ APRIL 24 ✿

Keep the light on.

Something told me to get up and go to the 8 A.M. church service. Motivational speaker Jewel Diamond Taylor says, " 'Something told me' is just another name for God." When something remarkable happens that makes you look back in wonder, it's divine intervention. That's the way I felt when I got to church for the earlier service than I usually attend and was rewarded by a sermon delivered by a local woman minister I enjoy, Rev. Deborah L. Spivey.

In her sermon she explained that just like our belief that in a dark room a switch turned to "on" will indeed make the room fill with light, faith can turn on the switch of spiritual light. Know that faith can work wonders, just as sure as you know a light will make a room brighter.

Sometimes it's hard to turn on that spiritual light, isn't it? Disappointments can have you groping in the dark for the switch. And horrendous events can make you feel there is no light.

On my way home from church, I picked up a newspaper and read a terribly sad story of a double funeral for teenage sisters who died in the August 1998 American Embassy bombing in Nairobi. As the mother of Gloria and Caroline Mutuiri, age sixteen and seventeen, stood near the twin coffins draped in lace, she said, "I have lost my light."

What can one say to someone who has lost a child? In this Kenyan mother's case, two children? And we all lost out because Gloria and Caroline were in the embassy trying to get visas to allow them to study and work in the United States. Who knows which of us might have met them, and had our lives enriched as a result? Or what contribution longer lives may have allowed them to make to our country and the world, as Kofi Annan has made as head of the United Nations, as South Africans Miriam Makeba and Nelson Mandela made just by touching our shores.

There will be days when the light dims, and others when we can feel blessed to have it shine brightly. Our faith tells us to keep turning on the light of faith—even in a blackout.

Secret Ingredient: **When "something tells us" it's time to try the light switch again—or at least light a candle—heed God's call.**

❦ APRIL 25 ❦

Eat your way to good health.

Collard greens, candied yams, macaroni and cheese, potato salad, fried chicken, barbecued ribs, peach cobbler—is your mouth watering yet? If these are foods you eat on occasion, good for you. If these foods are the mainstay of your homecooking and dining out, watch out.

Most of us love soul food, and with good reason. It tastes so good! Mama made it for us, and served it with love. *Her* mama cooked it and served it lovingly too. And they had the right idea. Many of our traditionally African American favorites are good for us, and the National Cancer Institute states that they may protect us against some cancers. Leafy greens and yams are among the foods recommended for a healthy diet. But it's often the way we prepare them—with too much fat, sugar, and salt—that make them detrimental to our health.

I loved the movie *Soul Food,* but I would have liked to have seen at least one of the sisters (or their husbands) encourage the family to bring healthy soul food dishes to dinner on Sunday. Maybe "Mama" wouldn't have gotten sick and died if the family had come together to serve baked yams instead of sugar-laden candied sweets. I wish there had been a line in the movie about the Vanessa Williams character's greens cooked with low-fat turkey parts instead of fatback. Maybe Vivica Fox's character could have delighted the family with a new recipe for delicious skinless baked or broiled chicken.

Too much fatty food may increase the risk for several cancers and other diseases. Simple changes, such as preparing fish with lemon and other seasonings, then broiling or baking instead of frying, is a tasty and healthy way to greatly reduce the amount of fat in your diet. And you'll be here a lot longer time to eat a lot more delicious food.

Secret Ingredient: **Learn about nutrition, and eat for health as well as good taste. Eating healthy doesn't have to mean giving up the foods you enjoy. It just means eating like the smart, intelligent, food-savvy person you are.**

✿ APRIL 26 ✿

Age graciously and blossom.

On a trip to South Africa, I traveled with a group that included a Nigerian who is living in Los Angeles, Chinyere Charles Anyiam, founder and editor-in-chief of *The African Times*. When I asked Charles if he would ever return to live in Africa, he responded, "Yes, when I retire. I don't want to grow old and die in America."

"Why not?" I asked him.

"Because America doesn't cherish its elders. In Africa, we revere and respect old people. We look to them for wisdom, and we take care of them, and try to make their last days their best days."

It's true that American culture worships youth. There are books on antiaging, cosmetics to stop wrinkles, and plastic surgeons to help wives who want to keep husbands from taking on younger mistresses. There are hair dyes for women and hair clubs for men.

But we shouldn't always follow popular culture. I think it's more honorable to honor age. Seeing Lena Horne turn eighty-one, release a new album, and still be considered one of the most beautiful women in the world is phenomenal. In *People* magazine, she shared the kind of wisdom that only age brings: "Growing older seemed to make me blossom. . . . I'm glad I never hid my age. I can say, 'Yes, I *did* all those things, I *knew* all those people.' . . . Oh, I've had it all. A great life!"

Entertainer Eartha Kitt shares the same philosophy. In 1997 at age sixty-nine, she was quoted in the *New York Times Magazine* as saying, "My voice has become richer as I've gotten older. . . . The older I get, the better I get."

And Tina Turner feels that age is part of her allure. "People like me because I'm unusual," she said on *60 Minutes* when she was fifty-six. "I'm showing sexuality at an old age—and that's unusual."

Maya Angelou sums it up exuberantly: "You should relish getting older—it's a wonderful happening!"

Secret Ingredient: **Appreciate yourself and savor life, regardless of how old you are. Call or write an elder and let them know you appreciate them and are grateful for their wisdom.**

❀ APRIL 27 ❀

Trust God—like the little girl said!

Chiaroscurist. That was the word Jody-Anne Maxwell spelled correctly and won the National Spelling Bee in Washington, D.C., in April 1998. The victory meant a lot to blacks in the Caribbean and United States. The twelve-year-old Jamaican, who says she wants to be a lawyer, was the first black person and the first youngster from outside the United States to win the National Spelling Bee. Prevailing over 248 contestants, Jody-Anne won the grand prize of $10,000. And she did it with charisma and charm.

My daughter and I watched all the media coverage we could find. We saw her on CNN, on the local news, and later in *Jet* and *Ebony.* "When I look back I can say that it was only God," Jody-Anne says in the October 1998 issue of *Ebony.* "I went there with most of the odds against me, struggling with the pronunciations, standing under the hot lights in front of all those people . . . it's only God."

Her strong faith in the power of God, and the courage to articulate it, at such a young age astounded me. Then, I was reminded of another youthful show of faith—this one ancient and biblical. Wasn't Jesus just twelve years old when he first publicly asserted his faith, to the amazement of the temple's teachers, learned people, his parents, and the world?

On CNN, Jody-Anne was asked if she had any advice for other spelling bee hopefuls. Her deliberate and confident answer: "Trust God. Work hard. Never lose sight of your goal."

Secret Ingredient: **Whether you're a chiaroscurist (an artist who works in depth representation using light and shade) or a manicurist (someone who also paints, just on a smaller canvas!), you (and all of us) can use Jody-Anne Maxwell's advice.**

❀ APRIL 28 ❀

Don't be a mouse potato.

Okay, so you're not a *couch* potato. You're too smart to just lie around on your sofa for hours, pointing the clicker at the boob tube. You're one smart lady, surfing the Net, clicking on to the latest Web sites. In fact, a recent Nielson/AOL study found that people with Internet access at home watch 8 percent less TV than those in households with no Web access.

Well, whether you're clicking the mouse or the remote, if you're sitting for hours on end, you're in danger of developing a sedentary lifestyle. And that, my sisters, can lead to excess weight, which can lead to obesity, which can lead to a bunch of health problems, as you know. In addition, sitting at a computer for long hours can cause aches and pains of its own, including carpal tunnel syndrome, back pain, and eye strain.

So what to do? You don't want to be left behind in the race to cyberspace! Here are some strategies to get in the habit of, starting today:

❖ Get up from the computer to walk around at least every half hour.

❖ Do exercises at your desk: Stretch, rotate the head, shake out ankles and wrists, point and flex toes.

❖ Try to schedule exercises after long periods spent in front of the computer. A good jog or swim after sitting for a long time can make you feel refreshed.

❖ If you repeatedly feel pains that don't go away once you're away from your computer station, or if you have abnormal aches that seem to occur only when you're sitting at your PC or laptop, see your doctor right away. The call to her office won't take much longer than the time you spend waiting for that hourglass icon to disappear.

Secret Ingredient: While you're on the Internet, check out the health and fitness Web sites. AOL has a site, most health magazines have their own, and *USA Today* and many major newspapers have links.

✿ APRIL 29 ✿

Say the (other) N-word.

In the 1980s, former first lady Nancy Reagan popularized the slogan "Just Say No" to drug use. I've read lots of articles and heard many speeches about how women should say "no" to all those things on our plate that make us stressed out and harried.

But what I've observed lately is that the reason it's hard to say "no" is because so many of those things on your plate are so appealing! When you have plans to work over the weekend and a long-lost girlfriend calls on Saturday to say she's in town, what are you going to do—not see her? When you know you need to save money, but "everybody" is going to the jazz festival in the Caribbean and your favorite singer is the headliner, what are you going to do—stay home and knit? These are often the kinds of choices we have to make, deciding to refuse to do something fun and pleasurable for the greater good.

I had always wanted to see classical pianist André Watts in concert. Having studied classical piano myself for twelve years, I had promised myself that the next time he came to the New York area, I would get tickets. Well, he came on a Sunday when I was already obligated to host a radio show, so I didn't buy tickets. I said no—points for me. But then, on that Sunday morning, a friend called with two free tickets! How could I resist? I thought about it, and it was a difficult choice, but if I went to the concert I might be late and unprepared for the radio show. I decided to accept the tickets, so my husband could go—without me. As it turned out, he took our teenage daughter, and the fact that she got to experience this culturally enriching afternoon made me feel even better than if I had gone.

When we "just say no," we're not always refusing something terrible—like drugs. Sometimes even too many wonderful experiences, we may receive them in abundance. But can be overwhelming. You can be having a good time and not even know why you keep feeling stressed and stretched. Spread out the fun, pass on your bounty and plenitude to others, and in so doing, you'll gain the fulfilling feeling of balance in your life.

Secret Ingredient: **When your cup runneth over, say no to more, and yes to exchanging "piece of mine" for peace of mind.**

❀ APRIL 30 ❀

Win the fight with faith.

On November 9, 1996, underdog Evander Holyfield defeated Mike Tyson for the Heavyweight Championship of the World. But it wasn't just his jabs that won the fight. Evander's robe was embroidered with this Scripture, Philippians 4:13: "I can do everything through God who gives me strength." After the match, Holyfield said it was faith in God and in himself that made the difference.

"I'm a praying person," he explained on ESPN. "I prayed before the fight. I prayed during the fight. When I get in the ring, I bring everything with me to help me win. It didn't make a difference what everyone said I would do. I believe in Jesus, and nothing [can] stop me when I believe in myself. You have to face a challenge and give it your all.

"I thank Mike Tyson for the opportunity. I'm not here by myself.

"I couldn't quit when people doubted me," he continued. "It gave me a chance to let God use me and put me out ahead.

"My son cried when I lost to Riddick Bowe, but I told him, 'I gave my all. Whether you win or lose, when you give your all you can hold your head up high.' "

Check out the many messages in Evander's quick TV sound bite:
- ❖ Believe in God.
- ❖ Believe in yourself.
- ❖ Graciously acknowledge your opponent.
- ❖ Don't let the opinions of naysayers make you quit. They could all be wrong!
- ❖ Give your all.
- ❖ Whether you win or lose, hold your head high.

Secret Ingredient: **Adopt Evander's winning attitude. Boxing is such a brutal sport that one doesn't expect spiritual words of wisdom to come from a pugilist. But I think that Muhammad Ali and Evander Holyfield have shown that everyone can face formidable challenges and, armed with faith, win!**

✿ MAY 1 ✿

Go ride a bike.

Or fly a kite! It's May Day, and a time to revel in carefree, outdoor activities.

As you know, riding a bicycle is great exercise. But who has time to do what you did *all the time* as a kid? Well, take it from Teresa Lyles Holmes of White Plains, New York. Teresa is married, a mother of three, and a busy public-relations executive. How in the world can she find time for bike riding? She does it with her family. It's part of the family's weekend fun time together. "It's a solo sport that you can also do with the kids," she says. "You can work out, meditate, think—and also bond with your family. And it's free!"

Here are more benefits Teresa—and you!—can get from cycling:

- ❖ It's a great stress buster, because it makes you feel refreshed.
- ❖ Unlike aerobics or jogging, bicycling is low impact, so it won't pound on your system.
- ❖ If you are interested in weight loss, it can burn 450 to 800 calories an hour.
- ❖ Riding a bike is great for shaping up your legs.
- ❖ And while we're talking vanity, just think of how good you'll look in your riding gear (starting with bike shorts).

Some things may have changed since you rode your bike to grandma's house as a kid, though. Now, for example, you would want to wear a **helmet.** It's probably the law where you live, and even if it isn't, you need to be protected from falling off your bike and onto your head! There are also specially made **cycling shoes** that more evenly distribute the support in the sole as you pedal (no more "tennis shoes" for riding your bike). A **rearview mirror,** a **bike-repair kit,** and a **good lock,** may also be options you didn't have on your original Schwinn. The kind of bike I rode as a teenager (not a 10-speed, y'all) is now called a **touring bike.** More than likely, a **road bike** will do the job for you. But if you really get into riding regularly, off-road and rugged, a **mountain bike** may become your style. Ride on, my sister!

Secret Ingredient: **Confused over whether you should ride with or against traffic? Always ride *with* the traffic, and observe the same road rules as drivers. Your rearview mirror will help you gauge approaching cars.**

✿ MAY 2 ✿

Make your wildest dreams wilder.

I was watching *60 Minutes* when I heard country singer Jimmy Buffett say that his book *A Pirate Looks at Fifty* had sold beyond his wildest dreams. I didn't hear much of the rest of the interview because my mind drifted off into a mental discourse into the concept of our "wildest dreams."

It's usually mentioned as a way of saying, "I didn't really plan for it or think about it," or that something wonderful that had occurred was beyond one's expectations. Well, I thought, we need to have wilder dreams! If things happen beyond our wildest dreams so often that there's an expression of speech for it, then maybe we need to do something about that. Are our expectations too low? When was the last time you planned for something exceptional to happen? When was the last time you even *had* a wild dream?

Tina Turner knows about dreaming big; she had a *Wildest Dreams* CD and concert tour. Have your own wild dream right now. Write down your answers, so you can have proof that even the wildest dreams come true!

When you think of your "wildest dream," what's the first thing that comes to mind? Now, if you could make that desire, that happening even bigger, imagine just how good it could get. Visualize yourself enjoying the success, the dream, the blessing beyond anything you've ever experienced or dreamt.

Secret Ingredient: **Maintain your vision by committing it to paper and referring to it frequently. Experts say it's wise to write down your dreams as soon as you wake up. Well, the difference with "wildest dreams" is that you can have them when you're wide awake!**

❀ MAY 3 ❀

Take your prayers to the next level.

Some people pray five times a day, but in 1988 President Ronald Reagan decreed that Americans should pray at least once a year when he signed an amendment making the first Thursday in May National Day of Prayer.

Events to observe this day are held nationwide, including a gathering in Lafayette Park in Washington, D.C., across the street from the White House. Always the day before National Day of Prayer, this racially diverse crowd prays for the President, the First Family, the government, and the nation.

Have you ever prayed for any of them? I would wager that like me, most people pray for ourselves, our families, our relatives and friends. We pray for things we want ("Please Lord, let me get that house, that car, that man . . .") or things you don't want ("Please Lord, don't let that man be loving that other woman, leaving me here with this house note, this car note . . ."). With good reason, we pray for the things that have urgency in our lives. But there is a higher level.

During the Vietnam War, there was a movement to "Pray for Peace." Now that we have it, we need to pray to keep the peace, so that we don't take it for granted. Who says we're immune to a war on our shores?

Pray for enlightened leaders to guide our nation to total well-being, where everyone has health-care coverage, where our infant mortality rate is zero, where all our citizens get nutritious meals to eat, and no one goes hungry. Pray to be such an enlightened leader.

Pray for nonviolence (remember that?). Pray that not one more of our children will be cut down by another child in this country. Ask God for an end to abuse in any and all forms. Pray for a better nation—and a more prayerful world. Amen.

Secret Ingredient: **Pray that your prayers evolve to a higher level, and when they do, so will your spirit.**

MAY 4

Celebrate a week of wellness!

It started as a corporate mandate. Rodale Press, the company that founded *Heart & Soul,* required that every magazine in its fold have a Leadership Initiative. That meant that the magazine had to do something to give back to the community. Those of us on the executive committee of the magazine took a day to brainstorm and we enthusiastically came up with National Black Health & Fitness Week, which has now been extended to one month. With the mission to encourage and empower African Americans to take control of their health, we kicked it off in May 1997 in the magazine and with special events.

The week leading up to Mother's Day was chosen because we know that mothers are the keepers of the family health. Women are the ones who make the doctors' appointments, stay up with sick children, arrange the family's managed care, and make sure everyone takes their vitamins.

Hoping to help build a healthy, strong community to thrive in the next millennium, we suggested three ways to get women, men, and children across the country involved:

1. **Do one thing a day toward your health and fitness goals.** Each day of the week, act on a health concern, such as taking steps to prevent hypertension, breast cancer, diabetes, HIV/AIDS, prostate cancer, and asthma. End with Mother's Day focused on spirituality.

2. **Use this month as a memory trigger to make appointments for checkups.** If you can never remember when you last had a physical, make it during National Black Health & Fitness Month. Get your mammogram, take your children for eye exams, and make dental appointments this time every year.

3. **Increase awareness of health issues in your community.** If you're a member of an organization that sponsors health fairs, walkathons, or other health-related events, May is a perfect time to do it and tie-in with this national celebration. *Heart & Soul* sponsors special events in health clubs across the country, and many black radio stations have supported the effort on air.

Secret Ingredient: Get involved! For more information, see this month's issue of *Heart & Soul,* or visit the magazine online at www.msbet.com.

❀ MAY 5 ❀

Eat healthy.

The first thing we do each morning is eat. The thing we do most often every day is eat. That gives us lots of opportunities to do it right.

But eating right doesn't have to mean doing without the foods we love. Eat that piece of cake (every once in a while), satisfy that sweet tooth (sometimes), feast on fast food (just don't make a habit of it). Moderation is the key.

In addition, there are lots of easy ways to gradually make your diet more healthful. Such as:

- ❖ Make at least one low-cal, low-fat meal a day.
- ❖ Have a "health food" day each week when you only eat foods you know are good for you.
- ❖ Cook with olive oil instead of butter.
- ❖ Substitute a nonstarch vegetable for your usual rice or potato.
- ❖ Make a list of your favorite meatless meals and prepare one each week, gradually increasing the frequency. Enlist the support of your family by getting their input on personal favorites.
- ❖ Bake a yam, as you would a potato, the next time you think about making candied sweets.
- ❖ Experiment with greens. At *Essence,* we once published a recipe for "Collard Green Quiche." Try sautéing instead of cooking them for hours. Have you taken the hamhock out of your greens yet?
- ❖ Eat at least five servings of fruits and/or vegetables every day. Studies show that few African Americans follow this expert advice. The National Cancer Institute recommends fruit or juice with breakfast, a salad with lunch, a piece of fruit as an afternoon snack, and vegetables with dinner.
- ❖ Make chicken dishes with skinless breast meat.
- ❖ Bake or broil instead of frying. Remember the old TV commercial: "It's not fried. It's Shake N Bake—and I helped!" Fill your own plastic bag of seasonings, shake, and bake.

Secret Ingredient: **Cut the fat, ditch the salt, don't sweat the sweets, and your body will thank you.**

❀ MAY 6 ❀

Shape up.

Too often we think that if we are eating right, we won't need to exercise. People tell me that because I'm slim, I'm lucky because I don't have to work out. Wrong.

Exercise is important for everyone.

❖ It helps cardiovascular endurance.

❖ It keeps our bodies strong.

❖ It helps lower high blood pressure.

❖ It reduces stress.

You can tell the difference between a person who exercises and one who doesn't. Like the scene in the movie *How Stella Got Her Groove Back* when Stella and Delilah were exercising on the beach together—or I should say, Angela Bassett as Stella was exercising, and Whoopi Goldberg as Delilah was waffling. It was a funny scene in the movie as Stella goes off down the beach for a jog, while Delilah goes back to the hotel for a meal. But in real life, Delilah's avoidance of exercise would be cause for pause. Hmmm, and now that I think of it, Delilah never fulfills her dreams. And Stella goes on to enjoy her younger man! Now there's a get-fit message if I ever heard one.

Pick an exercise. The one you'll do most often is the one you enjoy doing. What's your thing: walking, swimming, aerobics, dancing, running, cycling?

Choose your sport. Get active with in-line skating, basketball, tennis, volleyball, skiing, or golf. Anything that gets you moving can help improve your fitness level.

Secret Ingredient: Here's my mantra, the key to fitness that you'll hear me say over and over again: Get moving with at least thirty minutes of aerobic exercise at least three times a week. If you're trying to lose a few pounds, work out longer four or more days a week. It will make a difference. Try it.

❀ MAY 7 ❀

Keep the pressure low.

I have a friend who has a healthy outlook on life, who seems to cope well with stress, is always in good humor, and whom I've never known to be sick a day in her life. Yet, she tells me, she has high blood pressure.

Known as the "silent killer," hypertension sneaks up on its victims, often with no symptoms. You can feel perfectly fine and still have dangerously high blood pressure—high enough to bring on a stroke or heart attack. One out of four African Americans has hypertension, and it can run in families. It occurs earlier in life among black folks, is more severe, and is less likely to be treated adequately or early enough to prevent fatal health disorders. The only way to know if you're at risk is to check your blood pressure regularly.

The cause of high blood pressure is still unknown, but common lifestyle behaviors include too much salt in the diet, too much stress, too much weight, and too much alcohol. The good news is that high blood pressure is preventable. And if you have it, with proper medication, and diet and lifestyle changes, you can control it. James Reed, M.D., and Neil Shulman, M.D., leading hypertension experts who spearheaded a national education campaign called "Bring It On Down!" suggest the following:

❖ Add more lean meats, fish, poultry, and nonfat or low-fat products into your diet. Increase potassium intake by eating more bananas, oranges, cantaloupes, leafy vegetable, and dried peas and beans. Reduce cholesterol by broiling, grilling, or steaming food instead of frying.
❖ Exercise and watch your weight.
❖ Reduce your salt intake to less than 6 grams per day.
❖ Drink less alcohol.
❖ Relax. Reduce the stress in your life. Enjoy a new hobby or other personal pursuit.

Secret Ingredient: **Schedule annual doctor visits to monitor your blood pressure. If you are over forty and/or your pressure is higher than 130/85, have it checked twice a year.**

❀ MAY 8 ❀

Help your man stay healthy (let him read this page).

I once took a bunch of brothers out for lunch. On company time, too. I wanted to know what fellas want women to know about men's health. They told me to approach the special men's health section that *Heart & Soul* was preparing by getting this message across: "Brothers, we women love you, we want you, we need you, we got to have you *healthy.*"

And that's just what I said in my editorial for the first-ever issue of a magazine devoted to the health of African American men. Unfortunately, there are some stark realities I also felt compelled to share:

- ❖ Black men have the highest rate of prostate cancer (37 percent higher than for white men) in the United States. One in six African American males will be diagnosed with prostate cancer.
- ❖ Seventeen percent of black men age twenty or older have serum cholesterol levels about 200 milligrams per deciliter, the level at which you should make dietary changes to lower it.
- ❖ Nearly one third of black males in the United States are overweight.

Fellas, even though the stats look grim, the future looks bright because so many of the health problems men face are preventable. Keep working out, even after you feel played out. If you get to the point where you feel benched because you can't slam-dunk the way you used to, don't let channel surfing become your most active workout. Keep jogging, weight training, playing ball, cycling, skiing. As you get older, take up tennis, golf, hiking, rowing, or circuit training. Get physical—and get a *physical.*

The hardest thing to do may be to watch what you eat. You may not have to be a vegetarian, but you don't have to be a carnivore, either. In his humorous 1973 book *Dick Gregory's Natural Diet for Folks Who Eat: Cookin' with Mother Nature,* he says, ". . . for most omnivores, everything is fair game for consumption, and they are limited only by personal preference."

Secret Ingredient: "Real men" make healthful foods and healthy habits their preference. Pass this message along to the men in your life.

❀ MAY 9 ❀

Keep kids fit.

Back in the day when I went to school, gym class was mandatory. Alarmingly, as a result of school budget cuts, only 25 percent of school children took physical education classes in 1995. That leaves a big gap, and means that we parents have to get involved to take up the slack. Our children are increasingly becoming overweight and inactive, spending more time watching television and eating while they do, than being a part of structured sports and other physical activities. Not only is it damaging for their self-esteem to be overweight so young, but it sets a bad habit of inactivity too early in life. And those bad habits can lead to bad health.

So what to do?

❖ **Make sure your child has at least thirty to sixty minutes of physical activity a day.** Dance class did the trick for my daughter; she liked it so much she took classes for eight years from Alvin Ailey American Dance Theater. Our family friend Dwight Jackson, Jr., isn't even ten years old yet, but we're all sure he's going to be one of the first black hockey superstars. Expose your youngster to different activities, see which one he or she takes a liking to, and encourage your child's participation after school and on weekends. Check out the YMCA for low-cost classes.

❖ **Make fitness family fun.** Friends of ours in California work out as a family. They have three stationary exercise bikes, one each for Mom and Dad, and a "jr." size bike for their little daughter. Good habits start young and if you make exercise part of your child's life early on they'll continue the habit forever.

❖ **Be an example.** Don't just talk about how you used to run track "when I was your age." Show your children what you can do today. My kids see my husband jogging, swimming, biking, doing something physical every day. (They see me working out less often, but I'm working on it!)

Secret Ingredient: **Exercise coupled with good eating habits is the ticket! Pack healthy lunches and teach your children about nutrition.**

❀ MAY 10 ❀

Tap into the faith of our mothers.

"When you educate a man, you educate an individual. When you educate a woman, you educate a nation."

You may be surprised to hear that Nation of Islam leader Louis Farrakhan made that statement in a speech televised on C-SPAN in 1997. But it's so true. Women are the nation builders. From our bodies come life, from our breasts come the food of life, from our mouths come life's lessons.

This Mother's Day season is a perfect time to acknowledge that women are the keepers of family wellness. Mothers play a huge role in our health development, and mothers are our ultimate role models. It's often a challenge to be a "good mother," but the effort is worth it. Though no one is perfect or deserves to get stressed out trying to be, there are some ways in which we can strive to keep our families strong in mind, body, and spirit.

Mind. Because those little people in your life are constantly watching, be careful how you handle stress—don't take it out on them! My daughter once got a ride home from a schoolmate's mother who had a short fuse. "She's not good at conflict management," Anique observed. We can't expect our children to behave well if we're always behaving badly. Plus, our unnecessary temper tantrums make our kids unnecessarily uncomfortable.

Body. Never stop trying new things to cultivate family fun and wholesomeness. For example, if you've never been camping, why not try it? Take swim lessons *with* your child if you never learned.

Spirit. There's a hymn that praises the "Faith of Our Fathers," but with 70 percent of black church members women, we know that its Mama's faith that provides the bulk of the family strength. Call on the faith of our mothers, and our children will call on ours.

Secret Ingredient: **Give yourself a Mother's Day present: Educate yourself about health and wellness, and you'll give your "tribe" the legacy of your knowledge.**

MAY 11

Eat an apple today.

Unless you've been living in oblivion, you've heard that "an apple a day keeps the doctor away," right? Well, that's right. Eating a variety of fruits—including apples—and vegetables helps provide your body with many good nutrients and fiber (something black folks don't get enough of). Plus, they're an inexpensive, easy-to-carry snack food.

Nutrition experts say that we should eat at least five servings of fruits or vegetables every day. However, according to the National Cancer Institute, a recent study revealed that few African Americans follow this advice. Hey, let's change that statistic! Eat for good health by consuming more servings of your favorite vegetables and adding fruits (like apples) every day. As nutritionist Grace Wilson-Woods says, "It adds crunch to your lunch." It can be as easy as this:

BREAKFAST: Fruit as a major part of the meal, such as a honeydew melon (one of my favorites!) with whole wheat toast. Or raisins or banana on top of cereal. Drink juice for your beverage (I remember reading once that black folks drink more orange juice than other Americans—now *that's* a positive stat!).   **2 Servings**
LUNCH: Fruit salad, anyone? Or green salad or apple   **1 Serving**
Dinner: Collard greens, sliced tomatoes   **2 Servings**

                              Total **5 Servings**

To reward yourself, for DESSERT, load up on all the fruit cups you want! Cut up a big, juicy piece of watermelon to clean the palate. Or take a tip from the French, and prepare a fruit and cheese plate. Merveilleux!

                      Extra credit 1 Serving

The original "fast food," fruits and veggies are ready to go when you are. Carry them in your totebag or backpack, or keep at work some of these snack-attack foods: a box of raisins, a banana, grapes, cherry tomatoes, carrot sticks, dried apples or apricots, snack-size applesauce, peaches, or mixed fruit.

Secret Ingredient: Eat apples to keep the dentures—I mean, dentist away, too. They're great for strengthening and cleaning teeth. For more information about the "5 a Day—For Better Health" program, call the Cancer Information Service at 1-800-4-CANCER.

❋ SPIRIT

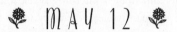

❧ MAY 12 ❧

Make everything a spiritual experience.

Trumpeter Wynton Marsalis was being interviewed by David Frost on a public television show. "Is playing an instrument or composing more spiritual than the other?" Frost asked.

Marsalis had a ready answer. "Everything you do is a spiritual experience." I hear you, Rev. Marsalis.

Here are eleven ways to make the things you do today a spiritual experience:

1. Be prayerful upon rising.
2. Be thankful for being able to see.
3. Be grateful that you can hear.
4. Say grace over that coffee on the run.
5. Give thanks for whatever weather you're having. If it's sunny, be sunny. If it's rainy, be happy to have the water we need for drinking, for keeping our environment green.
6. See the light in the people you encounter—the pleasant police officer, the toll taker that says "thank you," the receptionist that always has a smile.
7. Trade road rage for road respect.
8. Help somebody—a colleague with his computer glitch, a blind person board a bus, an elder cut his meat.
9. Do something creative, such as play an instrument like Wynton (well, no one can play *like* Wynton, but you know what I mean), paint a picture, pick up the needlepoint you put down years ago.
10. Consciously go through the day without saying an evil word to a single person.
11. Forgive somebody today.

Secret Ingredient: Today, get up with a smile and go to bed with one, because God has smiled on you. Read *This Far by Faith: How to Put God First in Everyday Living,* by Linnie Frank and Andria Hall to learn how to incorporate spirituality into your lives twenty-four hours a day.

 MIND

Start something.

Believe it or not, it doesn't take an act of Congress to start a national health week, or any other kind of observance you might consider important. You don't even need a large group of people or a corporation behind you. One person can bring attention to a worthy cause that others endorse and next thing you know, the idea has mushroomed. Think of Carter G. Woodson starting Negro History Week or Stevie Wonder spearheading the drive for a national holiday to honor Martin Luther King, Jr. It just takes initiative and commitment from whatever number of people are involved.

Since today is Stevie's birthday, how about a rousing chorus of "Happy Birthday To Ya!" Stevie Wonder has really shown what a difference one person can make. "We were so proud of him," Berry Gordy said in a TV tribute to his Motown protégé, in reference to Stevie's work to establish the holiday. "What he accomplished was so much more important than a hit record."

National observances are important because they bring attention to significant issues. Increased awareness of a health condition, a person of note, a date in history can only bring about more support and understanding of the cause. Here are five first steps to take:

1. Decide on an observance that arouses passion in you, and that may do the same in others.
2. Start small the first year, such as by just announcing it and getting publicity.
3. Write a press release detailing the observance and its importance to send to media and organizations that might help. Distribute materials in public places in your community.
4. Have a five-year plan that details how you would like the occasion to gradually grow.
5. Solicit the support of influential people that have an interest in your cause. For example, when *Heart & Soul* initiated Black Health and

Fitness Week, we knew that former Rep. Louis Stokes was chair of the Congressional Black Caucus Health Braintrust. County Commissioner Bernard Parker succeeded in convincing the Wayne County Commission to approve a resolution honoring Detroit native Rosa Parks on her birthday.

Secret Ingredient: **Do the doable. An observance can be as local and targeted as starting a Health Day at your church, or a Black History Month program at your child's school. You can do it!**

❀ BODY

🌼 MAY 14 🌼

Pass your Pap test.

Can we talk, my sister, about the importance of a Pap test?

The bad news first: Black American women are far too likely to die from cervical cancer; twice as likely as white women. Because often there's no pain, you can have cervical cancer and not know it.

The good news: Early detection is a way to prevent most cervical cancer deaths. For women eighteen years or older, or those younger who are sexually active, getting a Pap test every year is the best way to find cervical cancer early. The Pap test is inexpensive, quick, and painless.

Still have questions? The National Cancer Institute is happy to provide these answers:

Q. How often should I get a Pap test?

A. Get a Pap test every year.

Q. How is the Pap test done?

A. The nurse or doctor wipes a swab on the cervix in your vagina. This takes only a few seconds.

Q. Who needs one?

A. You do, if you are over eighteen, or under eighteen and having sex. There is no upper age limit for the Pap test. Even women who have gone through menopause need a Pap test every year. It can find cervical cancer early, while it's still curable. And it can save your life!

Secret Ingredient: **Make an appointment for a Pap test today. Write it down.**

✸ MIND

🌻 MAY 15 🌻

Don't be a negaholic.

We were having a ball! Working out, meeting people, funkin' up the place. During National Black Health & Fitness Week several years ago, *Heart & Soul* celebrated with workout events in health clubs in major cities. The team from the magazine wore *Heart & Soul* T-shirts, so the audience would know who to approach if they needed something. Well, at one gym, two sisters let me know that what they needed was a T-shirt.

"Why didn't *we* get T-shirts?" the shorter one asked with an attitude. "You should have had them for everybody."

I was thinking, *Hey, you got goodie bags full of other freebies. You ought to be glad you got that! T-shirts cost a lot of money!* But I swallowed and said, "We're glad you like the T-shirts. Thanks for the suggestion. We'll keep that in mind for next year!"

Then the other one criticized something else, and the first one thought of another thing or two. Finally, I said to them, "You know, it's been so nice meeting you two positive sisters!"

They caught themselves and I saw them grin for the first time. "Oh, we didn't mean anything. It was just that we wanted to know." Then they politely introduced themselves.

I took down their names and addresses, and when I got back to my office in New York, I sent them both *Heart & Soul* backpacks with a note that said "Thanks for coming to our event. Stay positive!"

Sometimes we don't realize when our automatic pilot is set on "negative." It's our *modus operandi* to act evil, to have an attitude, to come on with an edge. As my friend Lynne Scott says, "People who are into 'piss-ativity' love that sparring match." But being evil twenty-four/seven is not good for your health. Being someone who expresses anger constantly shows that one hasn't found a coping method for all the inevitable psychological assaults we all have to deal with on a daily basis. And that can lower your immune system and make you sick.

Don't take pride in being a sister with an attitude. Being strong in the face of adversity doesn't call for being hard in what should be neutral situations. Trade "piss-ativity" for positivity.

Secret Ingredient: **Seek help for "negaholism" that becomes destructive or leads to depression. If however, you or someone you know has become lackluster and lost enthusiasm for regular activities, you may be suffering from depression. Everyday upon waking, affirm to remain positive—no matter what. The Association of Black Psychologists can help you find a caring therapist in your area; call 1-202-722-0808.**

 SPIRIT

 MAY 16

Take a dose of faith.

Did you know that religion and spirituality can help you prevent illness, recover if you do get sick, and live longer?

Faith is good for your health. How? The following are ways in which the spirit affects the body and mind, according to research reported in the *Christian Science Monitor:*

Body
- ❖ Those who attend religious services at least once a week have been shown to have stronger immune system functioning.
- ❖ Greater religious involvement has been associated with lower blood pressure, fewer strokes, lower rates of death from heart disease, lower mortality after heart surgery, and long survival in general.
- ❖ A strong religious faith and active involvement in a religious community appear to be the combination most consistently associated with better health.

Mind

❖ People who are more religious experience greater well-being and life satisfaction, less depression, less anxiety, and are much less likely to commit suicide.

❖ Therapies for depression and anxiety that incorporate religious beliefs in treatment result in faster recovery from illness than do traditional therapies.

It's a whole mind, body, spirit connection that can mean fewer bouts of ill health, shorter hospital stays, and lower medical costs. And that can give you a longer life in which to be a religious, spiritual person.

Secret Ingredient: **Better to "overdose" on prayerful meditation than unnecessary medication. Commit to a daily period of prayer or meditation. Follow this ritual for one week and notice the difference in your life. Read** *The Faith Factor: Proof of the Healing Power of Prayer,* **by Dale A. Matthews, M.D., with Connie Clark.**

 BODY

🌸 MAY 17 🌸

Get pumped!

If your life has you on the go so much that if another person says, "You go, girl!" you'll scream—don't get pooped—get pumped!

Let me spell it out for you:

Get more iron.

Eat healthfully at every meal.

Take vitamins.

Put out the cigarette.

Up the amount of water you drink.

Make time to relax, release, revive.

Pass up the coffee.

Exercise.

Dream more often; get more sleep.

Secret Ingredient: **Don't take drugs, don't drink alcohol, and don't give up. Get pumped the natural way.**

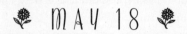

❀ MAY 18 ❀

Laugh to keep from crying.

My father was a funny guy. Sometimes his jokes were morbid, though, like when he got older and took to saying he got most of his exercise by being a pallbearer at his friends' funerals.

When he died, I didn't see much to laugh about. But one day, I was wearing his navy ultrasuede blazer and put my hand in the pocket and found a tiny piece of yellowing newspaper all crumpled up. Unfolding it delicately, I saw that it was a joke cut out from the *Seattle Post-Intelligencer,* the paper he had read every morning. Here it is:

> **Joke of the weak:** They're telling the story about the undertaker who was sliding a coffin into a hearse on a wintry day. The coffin slipped out of his hands, onto the icy pavement, and started skidding down the street.
>
> With the undertaker in pursuit, the coffin gained momentum. It slid through a drug store entrance and past the prescription counter. The breathless undertaker called to the pharmacist, "For heaven's sake, give me something to stop this coffin."

I can't believe you left me a joke about coffins after we just lowered yours! I thought. *And a corny one at that!* I laughed in spite of my grief, and shared the joke with everyone in my family.

Laughter is soul food. Laughing at something funny, remembering a joke, anticipating an amusement can all be good medicine. Humor can defuse difficult situations, ward off stress, take the edge off, and break the ice. If you think you could use a humor fix tonight, here's how to get one:

- ❖ Collect jokes or cartoons from newspapers to make a "joke book" to read when you're blue.
- ❖ Make up your own list of "funniest videos" to pick up at the video store.
- ❖ Go to a comedy club, or turn on BET's *Comicview* or the Comedy Channel.
- ❖ Call up a "crazy" friend or relative.
- ❖ Look in the "humor" section of your bookstore for some real "black" humor.

- Have a party. I went to one once where the host demanded a "one-liner" for admission.
- Hang out with some little kids. You'll be laughing in no time.

Secret Ingredient: **Make at least three people laugh today. It will lift your spirit.**

On Malcolm X's birthday, remember his healthy habits.

Malcolm X was born on this day in 1925 in Omaha, Nebraska. His all-too-brief life was characterized by his dynamic leadership, his revolutionary voice, his commitment to the freedom and self-determination for African Americans, and his love for his people. A family man who left sweet notes for his wife to find when he was away, Malcolm is remembered by his eldest daughter, Attallah Shabazz, as the kind of father "who would get down on the floor with you and play."

I am convinced that much of his strength and personal power came from the healthy lifestyle he pursued that kept him "fit for battle," one might say. Think about it:

He watched what he ate. "He didn't grow up on pork," Attallah tells me. "My grandmother, who was of Egyptian descent, didn't serve it." So when he became a Muslim it wasn't hard to follow the dietary laws, "although he had all kinds of bacon-eatin' friends!"

He didn't drink or smoke. Alex Haley, who assisted Malcolm in the writing of *The Autobiography of Malcolm X,* recalls in the epilogue that Malcolm had a way of discouraging others from smoking, as well: ". . . once when he offered to drive me to a subway, I began to light a cigarette and he drily observed, 'That would make you the first person ever to smoke in this automobile.' "

He married a nurse who was teaching nutrition classes in the Nation of Islam when they met.

He was spiritual. After all, he was a minister and made two pilgrimages, Attallah tells me, to Mecca. He prayed five times a day and led family prayers at the dinner table. He and his wife gave their eldest daughter a name that contains the word "Allah."

He meditated. A little known fact, Attallah says, is that he learned meditation from his parents, practicing it throughout his life, and passed it on to her.

He liked to dance and stayed in good shape (and fine!) all his life. He states in his memoir that when he was a young man and would get out on the dance floor to lindy hop with his partner, the crowd would turn its attention to them and shout, "Go, Red, go!"

Secret Ingredient: If you haven't read *The Autobiography of Malcolm X,* check it out. If you have read it, read it again; this time to study his revolutionary acts of mind, body, and spirit.

✿ BODY

Take a tip from "Skinny City."

You may have heard that New Orleans was dubbed "Fat City" after making the top of a list of metropolitan areas ranked by percentage of adults who are overweight. Conducted by the Centers for Disease Control and Prevention, and the Coalition for Excess Weight Risk Education, the study found 37.55 percent of folks in that city to be overweight.

The *Wall Street Journal Almanac 1998* published the list of thirty cities. Guess which one was at the *bottom* of the list? Washington, D.C. Since both New Orleans and Washington, D.C., are in the top ten list of cities with high black populations, I wondered what made the difference in weight control. Here is my own quirky list of reasons why I think the percentage is lower than the national average in the town where I spent four years getting a college education:

1. Although Washington, D. C. has the unofficial nickname of Chocolate City, the residents never really eat much chocolate. Being the color of chocolate is good enough for them.
2. D.C. does not stand for Dark Continent as rumored, but for District of Collards.
3. Every man, woman, and child in D.C. jogs in Rock Creek Park daily.
4. All that marching from the days of the March on Washington to the Million Man March has done some good, keeping our people in shape.

5. The numerous political scandals in the mayor's office and the White House keep everyone on their toes and running for cover.

Secret Ingredient: If your town can keep up with that, then maybe it can become the next Skinny City. In the meantime, May is a good time to visit Washington, D.C., to appreciate the beauty of the city's cherry blossoms on a walking tour. If you can't get to D.C., take a stroll through your favorite park. If you're from a big city, check out its botanical gardens.

✿ M I N D

✿ MAY 21 ✿

Consider taking a low-stress job.

"If only my job wasn't so stressful!" Have you ever said that? Because we spend so much time at work, it's not hard to assign a major portion of the stress we feel to our jobs. But what if you had a job that was low on the stress scale? Just think of the increased well-being you might experience on a day-to-day basis.

The *Wall Street Journal Almanac 1998* has identified twenty-five "Least Stressful Jobs" by weighing such factors as quotas and deadlines, long hours required, hazards involved, competitiveness, contact with the public, and amount of stamina required. If you are entering the job market, changing careers, or starting a business, these may be some issues to consider (salary, however, is a separate consideration). If you already have one of these jobs, I hope it's living up to its low stress reputation!

Least Stressful Jobs

1. Medical records technician
2. Janitor
3. Forklift operator
4. Musical instrument repairer
5. Florist
6. Actuary
7. Appliance repairer
8. Medical secretary
9. Librarian
10. Bookkeeper

11. File clerk
12. Piano tuner
13. Photographic process worker
14. Dietitian
15. Paralegal assistant
16. Vending machine repairer
17. Bookbinder
18. Barber
19. Medical laboratory technician
20. Electrical technician
21. Typist/Word processor
22. Broadcast technician
23. Mathematician
24. Dental hygienist
25. Jeweler

Secret Ingredient: **Don't run for President—it's Number One on the "Most Stressful Jobs" list (followed by firefighter and senior corporate executive).**

 BODY

 **MAY 22**

Give God a break today.

Even though I've talked a lot about the relationship between faith and health, I want you to know that you can't expect God to bail you out of everything you get yourself into. Let me tell you what I mean.

One day I was riding the Forty-second Street crosstown bus in Manhattan when I overheard an elderly lady talking with the bus driver. Actually, she may not have been as old as she looked, but because she had a cane and appeared to be physically impaired, she looked aged. Evidently, she had never accepted the fact that the foods one eats has a relationship to one's health, because she said to the driver, "Well, my grandson keeps bugging me to change my ways, and stop eating pork and fried foods and things. But I told him, 'God takes care of me! If I get sick, then God will fix it!'"

Poor God. We put so much on him needlessly. Why bother God more than we have to? Plus, as the old adage goes, God helps those who help themselves.

Either we are in denial about the connection between nutrition (or lack thereof) and health, or we think that eating healthfully means denying ourselves of something. The phrase "you are what you eat" is so true, and eating well means *adding* wonderful new tastes, new experiences to your life. You don't have to give up anything, just gradually make it less center stage.

Fortunately, this woman had a caring grandson, who had the right idea. He was just trying to help improve his beloved grandmother's health. But like so many people after a certain age, she's set in her ways. After I helped her off the bus, I hoped that he would continue to lovingly pull her coat. At least she was listening to him. Maybe one day she'll get the message.

Secret Ingredient: Give God a break today—and I don't mean eat a hamburger (if you've never had a veggie burger or a falafel, try one today)! Do your part; take responsibility for your health.

 BODY

Pursue activities with vigor.

Can housework be your workout? Is bowling as helpful to your heart as handball? You hear all this dubious-sounding advice about "taking the stairs" and "parking your car far from the entrance so you can walk," but surely all exercise isn't created equal.

According to the American Heart Association (AHA), the people who should know a thing or two about cardiovascular health, some types of activity will improve the condition of your heart and lungs if they are brisk, sustained, and regular. Low-intensity activities do not condition the heart and lungs much. But they can have other long-term health benefits. And they're fun. This chart, reproduced with permission from the AHA, may help clear things up.

VIGOROUS EXERCISES

Condition heart and lungs when done regularly.

Aerobic dancing, bicycling, cross-country skiing, hiking (uphill), ice hockey, jogging, jumping rope, rowing. Running in place, stair climbing, stationary cycling, swimming, walking briskly.

MODERATELY VIGOROUS

Good choices; can condition heart and lungs if done briskly.

Downhill skiing, basketball, field hockey, calisthenics, handball, racquet-ball, soccer, squash, tennis (singles), volleyball, walking at moderate speed.

LOW INTENSITY ACTIVITIES

Not vigorous or sustained, but they still have benefits of improving coordination and muscle tone, relieving tension, and burning calories.

Badminton, baseball, bowling, croquet, football, gardening, golf (on foot or by cart), housework, Ping-Pong, shuffleboard, social dancing, softball, walking leisurely.

Secret Ingredient: **Mix them up! Do what you enjoy to keep active and help lower your risk of heart disease, *and* do brisk, vigorous exercises for at least thirty minutes, three or four times a week, at more than 50 percent of your exercise capacity for maximum heart and lung conditioning.**

 MIND

 MAY 24

Make reps a way of life.

I read in *Parade* magazine once about a sixty-five-year-old Grand Master in the martial arts who does one thousand push-ups a day. Jhoon Rhee, known as the man who introduced tae kwon do to America, says his goal is to have one hundred years of wisdom in the body of an eighteen-year-old. "I tell people," he is quoted as saying, "you can become whatever you think and do repeatedly."

As they would say in my old neighborhood, "he aint never lied!" If you think about ballet and do ballet repeatedly, you will become a ballerina. If you think about losing weight and eat low-fat foods and exercise repeatedly, you will lose weight. Say you're a smoker, and pass up a cigarette repeatedly, and you will become a nonsmoker.

When you do exercises, you do "reps," or repetitions, meaning you repeat the movement. You might do ten reps or—if you have the uncommon stamina of our martial arts master, Mr. Rhee—you might do one thousand. Regardless, it's the repetition, the repeated action, the habit, the reinforcement, that makes the difference and allows you to master it. It's the discipline to continue the move when you are tired, when you've had enough, but you keep thinking, *Just one more. I can do this. One more time.*

Keep on pushing, and you will be your goal. And your goal will be part of your healthy way of life.

Secret Ingredient: **Think. Do. Be.**

❦ MAY 25 ❦

Take a leap of faith.

It was the conventional type of parental advice we were trying to give out. Our twenty-two-year-old had graduated from college, but continued to work at a well-known fast food chain. Aleeyah had never paid any mind to those flippant remarks people made about not wanting to flip burgers. When asked why she liked working there, she said she enjoyed the camaraderie of the other students in her store, who like her, were working their way through college. The flexible hours allowed her to attend class and study, and she had become a manager before she had even finished college. Her father and I were proud of her, but after she graduated with a B.A. in business, we thought it was time that she look for a job that required her degree.

Eventually, she hooked up with an executive recruiter who lined up several job interviews for her. As she went to the initial and then follow-up interviews, she became more and more confident that she would get another, more lucrative job. So she decided to quit her job at the burger joint. We were stunned; we didn't say to quit one job, even one for which we felt she was overqualified, before getting another one.

"Do you really think it's wise to quit a job before you get another one?" we (okay, so it was me) asked, with a who-in-the-world-do-you-think-is-going-to-support-you? attitude. "What if you don't get one of those jobs?"

After much debate, Aleeyah finally said respectfully but firmly, "I'm taking a leap of faith."

She had faith that she would get the job she wanted! She had faith that things would turn out all right. How could one—even a parent—argue with that? All we could do then was to shut up and give her our blessing. She resigned, giving two weeks' notice. And as fate (another name for God) would have it, on her last day of work, she got the call—the job she wanted most was hers.

I learned some life lessons from my Aleeyah that night. One, that parents can learn something from their children. Though well-intentioned, we're not always right! Second, that faith is a bigger force than traditional wisdom. What we were saying was the "party line" but what she was saying was what she felt in her heart.

Secret Ingredient: **Take a leap of faith and you'll always land on terra firma.**

 BODY

 MAY 26

Be salad-bar savvy.

If you feel like hanging out at a bar, make it a salad bar. Found wherever food is served these days—restaurants, delis, even supermarkets—salad bars are offered as low-cal, healthy additions to the menu. However, loading up on some of the choices that may be displayed to entice diners can make your meal as high in calories, fat, sugar, or sodium as any other.

At the deli on the corner near my job one day, I stood around for a minute deciding what I wanted to eat. As women paid for their salad-bar choices, I noticed that the thinner the woman, the more her salad-bar container looked like, well, salad (i.e., lettuce, tomatoes, cucumbers, beets, sprouts, tofu). The more she weighed, the more her container looked like a barbecue (i.e., fried chicken, macaroni and cheese, yams, potato salad). Yet, I'm sure both of them thought they were having a healthy salad for lunch!

If you want to make sure you're having a low-calorie, tasty salad, follow these doozy do's:

Do start with a lovely layer of leafy lettuce (the greener, the better).

Do pile on lots of raw vegetables, such as tomatoes, cucumber, broccoli, and cauliflower.

Do add beans for protein.

Do have a vegetable salad one day, a fruit salad the next time.

Do walk on by the potato salads and pastas (unless you feel like having a "fat" salad).

Do pass up the fat-laden dressings for those labeled "low calorie."

Do leave alone the hot and fried foods—they don't qualify as "salad."

Do dis' the bacon bits and croutons—they can add unneeded fat and sodium.

Secret Ingredient: **Prepare "salad bars" at home for the family. Try having a salad-bar brunch the next time you entertain. Update the potluck concept by asking guests to bring their own favorite fruit or vegetable, suitable for a yummy, homemade salad.**

 MIND

 MAY 27

Exercise total relaxation.

When I was a teenager, I was very active in a modern dance troupe. Only two students from each high school were chosen to be a part of the all-city dance team in Seattle, and classes were held twice a week. After a jam-packed day at Franklin High School, then the traffic-jam rush to get from the south end of town to the north end where our classes were held at Roosevelt High School, I looked forward to the best part of class—our relaxation technique. Although that was eons ago, I have continued to practice the exercise our teacher taught us. It's a great way to relax after your work day, when you need a time-out from stress, for meditation, or as an anti-insomnia strategy. Here's how it goes:

❖ Dress in completely comfortable clothing (if you can do it, nude and barefoot is even better).

❖ Without music or distractions, lie down flat on your back on a carpeted floor or on a mat or towel.

❖ Put your arms at your sides; feet slightly apart. Close your eyes.

❖ Relax your body, starting with your toes. Mentally check each toe to release any tension.

❖ Do the same with your heels and ankles.

❖ Move up your leg; release all the muscles in your calves; relax your knees and your thighs.

❖ Put your stomach at perfect rest.

❖ Concentrate on your heartbeat.

- Take three deep breaths. Breathe in, breathe out. Suck air in, blow it out. In, out.
- Relax your shoulders. Think about your arms. Release any tension in your elbows, and down through your wrists. Give every single finger a rest.
- Let your neck go limp. Relax your chin and cheeks. Give that stiff upper lip a break.
- Rest your nostrils, your eyelids, your forehead.
- Erase everything from your mind. Listen to your breathing or focus on your heartbeat if you need to concentrate on something. Rest peacefully for at least ten minutes; twenty or thirty, if possible.

Secret Ingredient: **Since you can't read this and relax, too, just remember to mentally move from toe to tip of the head. Or ask someone to slowly and quietly read it aloud for you, then return the favor.**

✸ SPIRIT

 MAY 28 ✿

Keep your head to the sky.

The media says Earth, Wind and Fire is making a comeback. They're touring the country and appearing on *Oprah.* But in my mind, they never left. Their song "Keep Your Head to the Sky" plays in my brain often and it also plays frequently on my stereo (yes, I still play records, folks). The words are so inspirational and the music so beautiful.

I've noticed that many black recording artists include spiritual songs in their repertoire from time to time. To me, that gives the full meaning of the phrase "soul music." M. C. Hammer, for example, said on his VH-1 profile *Behind the Music,* "I always included a spiritual cut on my albums as a way of saying 'Thank you, God.' " His cut "Pray" was spiritual and spirited. Hammer said the song "Keep On" is "the one that is the most emotional for me." It expresses how he felt hurt by "homeys and best friends" but he had to keep on and move on.

Marvin Gaye sang "God Is Love." Sam Cooke knew "A Change is Gonna Come." Patti LaBelle sings "When You're Blessed (Feels Like Heaven)." Aretha Franklin cut two gospels albums (one of which I'm still playing as if it had come out yesterday). Did you know that Nat King Cole and Duke Ellington also created spiritual music?

Nina Simone performed one of her rare American concerts in New Jersey in May 1998, and started the set with "Every Time I Feel the Spirit." But she didn't stop there. She continued the concert with other spirituals and gospel songs (and talked during the breaks about the lack of spirituality in America).

Going back to their gospel roots, these people made spirituality a part of their work. Fortunately for us, all we need to do to "go there"— to keep our heads to the sky, to remember that God is our friend, to keep on—is to play our soul music.

Secret Ingredient: **Go through your own music library and make a list of your favorite spiritual songs, then tape them one by one to create your own "greatest hits album" of music for the soul.**

❋ BODY

Pick your pecs.

If you don't know a deltoid from a hoity-toid, this quick quiz can help you out. If you do know what deltoids, pectorals, biceps, triceps, and quadriceps are, then good for you! You are excused from reading this page (now scoot on off to your personal-training job!).

By the way, the topic of discussion today is muscles. If you can get familiar with the major muscles used in exercising, you can look super-intelligent in workout class, and won't have to be scratching your head instead of lifting a dumbbell when weight-training. And if you never paid attention in anatomy class (or if, like me, you never had it), here's a second chance.

1. Deltoids are:
   A. Pledgees of Delta Sigma Theta sorority
   B. Your shoulder muscles
   C. Alien creatures

2. Pectorals (pecs) are:
   A. Stories told with pretty pictures
   B. What guys in those sexy calendars show off
   C. Your chest muscles

3. Biceps are:
    A. A part of a bicycle
    B. Two muscles in the front of your upper arms (look at your palms, then at the arm underneath)
    C. Ebonics for bisexuals

4. Triceps are:
    A. An important part of a tricycle
    B. The first three sips of a fine wine
    C. The three muscles at the back of your upper arms (look at the back of your hand, then the arm underneath)

5. Quadriceps (quads) are:
    A. Four muscles in your arms somewhere (you're following the pattern here)
    B. What they call it when you have four babies at one birth
    C. The four muscles at the front of your thighs

6. Hamstrings
    A. The muscles in back of your thighs
    B. Rope used to tie your Easter ham
    C. Something like heart strings

7. Abdominals (abs)
    A. The muscles between your chest and pelvis
    B. A beverage that comes in a six-pack
    C. Similar to a washboard

8. Gluteus maximus
    A. The first "big word" you learned in kindergarten
    B. Maximum-strength glue
    C. Da butt

The Answers: 1. B., 2. C., 3. B., 4. C., 5. C., 6. A., 7. A., 8. C. You got them all right, didn't you? Go on with your gorgeous trapezius!

❧ MAY 30 ❧

Be a self-esteem queen.

We admire people for all kinds of reasons. But if you really think about it, those we admire and respect the most usually have high self-esteem. They hold *themselves* in high esteem. And I don't mean in any egotistical way, but in a way that exudes grace and confidence. I call them "self-esteem queens," and I can think of several women who have the varying qualities that fit these descriptions:

Self-confidence. Exudes an "I know who I am" attitude. Doesn't let past adversity keep her from living in the present tall and proud.
- ❖ Maya Angelou
- ❖ Queen Latifah
- ❖ Susan L. Taylor

Intelligence. Maximizes her smarts and creativity to make her contribution to the world.
- ❖ Carol Moseley Braun
- ❖ Oprah Winfrey

Grace in the face of grief. Endures unspeakable loss, but maintains public composure. Instead of withdrawal, she continues her life with a strength that makes a positive example for others.
- ❖ Camille Cosby
- ❖ Coretta Scott King

Grace under pressure. Shows remarkable strength in rebounding from scandal or injustice.
- ❖ Hillary Rodham Clinton
- ❖ Angela Davis
- ❖ Vanessa Williams

Respect. Has self-respect, commands respect, and inspires others to do no less.
- ❖ Aretha Franklin
- ❖ Iyanla Vanzant

Self-deflecting beauty. Realizes that beauty that is only skin deep will get her nowhere. Hones her talent to equal her beauty.
- ❖ Erykah Badu

- ❖ Angela Bassett
- ❖ Lena Horne

Strength in the pursuit of righteousness. Exposes truth and justice even in the face of danger.
- ❖ Rosa Parks
- ❖ Maxine Waters
- ❖ Myrlie Evers-Williams

Secret Ingredient: **Create your own list of self-esteem queens. Consider in which category you would put yourself, and use the women listed in that category as goal models.**

❀ SPIRIT

❀ MAY 31 ❀

Express your sympathy.

I've been buying more sympathy cards lately. Not because more people in my life are dying, but because I now know from personal experience how much such a small gesture can mean. When my father died, there were generous gestures of relatives and friends that meant more than words can say, but there were also simple expressions that touched my heart and helped me heal.

When others face pain, it's easy to brush off what you can do to help by thinking, *Nothing I could do could ease her pain, so why bother?* Or we feel so awkward and concerned that we may say the wrong thing that we say or do nothing. But healing happens, as the song says, with a little help from your friends. The things etched on my heart that I learned we all can do for others include:
- ❖ the quickest hug
- ❖ a supportive nod and wave of long-lost friends in the sea of faces at the funeral
- ❖ a sympathetic e-mail from colleagues
- ❖ cards from friends
- ❖ flowers
- ❖ plants
- ❖ fruit baskets
- ❖ monetary contributions (no amount too small!) to the memorial fund

❖ letters of remembrance from childhood friends

Many of these gestures cost little or nothing. They only take your caring and a few moments of your time. May what we give be what we receive in return.

Secret Ingredient: **Remember that Memorial Day is not just a day off from work, but a commemoration of those who died for our country. Say a prayer, attend a memorial service or parade, or put a flower on the grave of a veteran.**

 MIND

☀ JUNE 1 ☀

Don't give up—stay motivated.

In January, magazines promise to help you "Shrink That Belly Bulge." Weight-loss centers, fitness-equipment stores, and health clubs have their best sales month of the year. All because the health-and-fitness industry knows that people get motivated to get fit as a New Year's resolution. But by June, what happens? Have you fallen off your fitness wagon?

Back in January, I gave you some tips on how to stay motivated, such as taking your gym clothes to work with you, working out with your honey, taking the kids to gyms that have child-care facilities, putting your sweatsuit on when you change from your work clothes. But it may help now, in the middle of the year to remind you of the great benefits of staying motivated.

It's good for your self-esteem. You'll feel better about yourself, and you'll stop feeling guilty if you gradually make time for fitness. Everything you've read so far in this book has recommended that you work out at least three times a week for thirty minutes each day. But if you can fit in only one day this week, that's better than no day. If you can walk briskly for fifteen minutes twice in one day, instead of all at once, that still counts.

You'll look good. When you feel good about yourself, you exude confidence. Plus, in exercising or losing weight, you'll be reshaping your body and getting toned and firm. As the saying goes, "look good, feel good." Who knows, you may meet somebody who thinks you look real good riding that bike.

It will lower your stress level. Exercising has been proven to lower tension, and eating right can lower your blood pressure. A low-sugar diet can prevent that "hyper" feeling. You'll feel calmer and more in control if you get back on that treadmill.

It's good for your family, friends, and coworkers. If exercise is your PMS buster, then the people around you will thank you. If eating right keeps you in good spirits, everyone you encounter will benefit.

Secret Ingredient: **June is a wonderful time of year to recommit yourself to maintaining optimum health. Recharge your fitness batteries. Go play outside, the weather's fine!**

 BODY

 JUNE 2

Create your own medical research file.

One friend of mine recently discovered she has sarcoidosis. Another has an ulcer. A third has a thyroid problem. Everybody, it seems, has fibroids.

If you have a medical condition or have a family history of a particular health risk, then it may do yourself a service to create your own medical research file. In it, you can keep:

- ❖ Records of your family history of that condition (see April 20 for tips on tracing your medical history roots).
- ❖ Magazine and newspaper articles you read on the subject.
- ❖ Copies of book pages that deal with your particular health risk.
- ❖ Health-organization contact information and hotline numbers
- ❖ Brochures from resource organizations
- ❖ Medical journals that publish studies of latest advances, such as the *Journal of the American Medical Association (JAMA)* and the *New England Journal of Medicine.*
- ❖ Support group information

Your local library would be a good place to start your search. The Internet is an excellent at-your-fingertip source. However, be careful about following online advice or that of experts or doctors in health-site chat rooms; always discuss this advice with your own health professional first.

I keep all the info I can get my hands on dealing with kidney disease, a health risk that's a biggie in my family. I also keep the film from my mammograms, and I ask for copies of any records that specialists send my primary-care doctor. Why should the doctors have access to more information about you than you do? To hold the records, I suggest those three-and-a-half-inch-wide pocket folders. They come in a variety of bright colors that look nice on your book shelves—while helping you to lower your health risks.

Secret Ingredient: Acting on media reports, news bulletins, or the grapevine can be more harmful than helpful to your health. The most reliable advice comes from a "primary source," meaning directly from a scientific study or peer-reviewed journal.

✸ JUNE 3 ✸

Find your own church home.

My daughter has discovered that her parents are a case study in "opposites attract." "My mother goes to church every Sunday, my father's church is the woods," she remarked to our family friend Audrey recently.

As I explained to Anique, I feel that everyone has their own path to spirituality. Religion is a matter of family tradition, personal preference, and individual choice. Some people come to faith through a traumatic fall, others just wander into it. Some have to have a cathedral, others find God in the bush.

My husband's cousin Jill had moved from Queens, New York, to seek a better life in Alexandria, Virginia. She called me from her job one day, first cracking that "You know you're 'office ghetto' when you make your long-distance phone calls from work!" Then she proceeded to tell me how she was getting her life together—moving to a new apartment, getting a second job, going back to school, losing weight.

I listened, then asked, "How's your spiritual life? Have you found a church home down there?"

"Oh yeah! Let me tell you!" she exclaimed. "I was driving around looking for a church one Sunday, and saw one with a sign that said Calvary Baptist. So I went in. Then I noticed that there were all white people there, singing from hymnals. I crept out of there." I was in stitches visualizing my down-home cousin wandering into a staid, prim church.

"Then I drove farther down the street and saw another church," she continued. "This time, there was a brother standing outside with white gloves on. I took that as a sign that I was in the right place. I went in—and when I came out I had sweated out my perm!" I knew what that meant, that she had found a church that *rocked.* Tambourines instead of hymnals for the parishioners, dancing in the aisles instead of sitting in the pews, a preacher rather than a minister.

Jill had found her church home, but for someone else, that first church may have been the right place. Only your soul knows when it's home.

Secret Ingredient: **Don't be afraid to wander into the wrong house of worship. It sometimes takes weeks of "house hunting" to find the right church home.**

 MIND

 JUNE 4

Practice self-care.

Debrena Jackson Gandy wrote the book on self-care and inner renewal. It's called Sacred Pampering Principles. Knowing that Debrena is not only an author but a motivational speaker who travels the country, owner of two businesses, a wife, and a mother of three children under the age of five—whew!—I just had to ask, "How do you do it all and stay so up, so positive, so incredibly motivated?" Here's the answer she shared with me exclusively for you:

"I have discovered a powerful, but simple formula that has transformed the way I live. This 'formula for power-full living' is based on two key principles.

"**Principle Number One: Put self-care first.** Tare care of your mental, emotional, and spiritual needs first, before you take care of the world's. Truth be told, many of us are living our lives by a self-last creed. Change this sequence and you can change your life. Instead of kids, boss, girlfriends, husband, relatives, or church first, switch the order of your priorities and tend to your own needs first and foremost. Fortify your self first, before all else. It's not selfish, it's smart.

"**Principle Number Two: Treat your body as a temple.** For a long time I was treating my body like it was a practice model. I was critical of parts of my body that I thought were too wide or too big, and I did a darn good job of hiding and camouflaging them behind oversized shirts or long jackets. I was putting food into my body that I knew didn't serve it, and I was not giving my body enough exercise and movement. A few years ago I really began to take the phrase from the Bible, "treat your body as a temple," very seriously. I started pampering myself more, feeding by body healthier food and drinking more water to keep it well hydrated. I stopped pushing so hard and started building renewal time into my weekly schedule. I began to accept and appreciate all my body parts just as they were. Remember, the body you have is for keeps. No trade-ins or exchanges."

Secret Ingredient: "Be gentle with yourself as you begin to make the shift to living according to this formula," Debrena advises. "I guarantee that you'll begin to experience more joy, peace, pleasure, fulfillment, and aliveness in your life!"

Draw a bubble bath, pull out Debrena's book, and start using the principles for self-pampering today.

❋ BODY

☀ JUNE 5 ☀

Exercise your right to bare arms.

Weight training isn't just for guys who want to look good in videos or for actresses shaping up to play ageless rock stars in movies. It's for everyday people like you and me. That's because of training's many benefits.

❖ It helps develop stronger muscles, which not only look good but give you strength for your physical chores. Your arms will look great in that spaghetti-strap top when you're carrying the groceries!

❖ It raises your body's metabolism, allowing you to eat more without getting "fat."

❖ Weight training builds bone density, which for a woman can give her a reserve of minerals to prevent brittle bones, or osteoporosis.

❖ Lifting weights, like many types of workouts, can give you a feeling of confidence, improved self-esteem and self-image, and inner (as well as outer) strength.

Just three thirty-minute strength-training sessions a week can yield you positive results, particularly in the upper body where there are more small muscle groups than in the lower body. You'll start to see a difference in as soon as three or four weeks. But don't stop there!

The key to a successful training is learning to lift properly. I suggest, from personal experience, you ask a trainer at your health club, gym, or

Y to instruct you. I got a personal training session when I went to the Canyon Ranch Spa in Tucson. Exercise physiologist Mike Siemens, M.S., showed me how to use free weights and gave me printed information with photographs on how to do bench presses, single-arm rows, lateral raises, squats, bicep curls against the wall, triceps dip off the bench, and abdominal crunches. Strength training for the first time at forty-six, I looked in the mirror and thought I was *all that!*

Secret Ingredient: **Commit to working out with light weights for three half-hour sessions a week for at least six weeks straight. And don't worry about starting to look like a man. It would take more of the male hormone testosterone and an extreme weight lifting program to even begin to change your physique drastically. Just think "more toned" and "shapely" like that fabulous actress who played the ageless rock star in that blockbuster movie.**

✺ SPIRIT

✺ JUNE 6 ✺

Shine, even in the dark.

I had a big decision to make. Was I going to leave my comfortable position at nationally known and successful *Essence* to take the top job at a new, fledgling magazine nobody'd heard of named *Heart & Soul?* The prospect was both exciting and scary. I had been offered the new job, but hadn't yet resigned from the old one the Sunday I fell into church and heard Rev. Deborah L. Spivey deliver the message to the congregation's graduates.

"You may not know what's ahead for you," she said in her sermon. "If you're going to college, you may not know what to expect. If you're graduating from college and getting a job, you may not know if it's the right career. But just remember this: Stars shine in the dark."

Rev. Spivey's message may have been intended for the young people, but it struck a chord with me that day. Leaving a job I loved for one I hoped to love was certainly a risk. In my heart, I felt it was time to take what I had learned in my sixteen years at one magazine and apply it to build something else that had the potential to make a difference, too. So why the hesitation? Fear of the dark.

Yet something kept pushing me into the darkness, and it felt like the giddy anticipation I used to have when I was a college student and a bunch of us would drive around in the pitch-black night determined to find "the function at the junction," knowing that once we stopped being lost we'd have a funky good time. Sure enough, once I got to the new job, it was hard to remember why I ever thought twice.

Most of the time when we face these major decisions of job changing, going off to college, moving to another state, getting married, or getting divorced, we are the only ones who can do the decision making. We can talk to friends, family, clergy, and bosses, but the ultimate decision must come from within. Think about it, though; when you walk in the dark, what do you do? You take one step at a time, put one foot in front of the other, do it again, and when you don't fall, you do it again. And soon, you get to a place where you can flip the switch and see the light.

Secret Ingredient: **Always remember: You are a star! Shine on.**

 BODY

JUNE 7

Be cosmetic cautious.

Cleopatra wore eyeliner. Most visual representations of her have that distinctive feature in common.

If women throughout the ages have applied kohl to their eyes, and worn braids in their hair, enhancing one's beauty can be considered an ancient ritual. But conjunctivitis and skin irritation may be just as old.

Cosmetics, which the Federal Food, Drug, and Cosmetic Act defines as "articles other than soap which are applied to the human body for cleansing, beautifying, promoting attractiveness, or altering the appearance," can enhance us, but can also cause problems associated with contamination, product flammability, or allergies. To stay beautiful and safe, follow these tips from *Your Guide to Women's Health, An FDA Consumer Special Report:*

Never share. When using makeup, sharing is definitely taboo, whether you're at home, at work, or out shopping. Shared testers at department store cosmetic counters are even more likely to become contaminated than the same products in your home, according to a Food and Drug Administration report.

"At home, the preservatives have time—usually a whole day—to kill the bacteria that is inevitably introduced after each use," says John E. Bailey, Ph.D., director of the FDA's Office of Cosmetics and Colors. "But in a store, there may be only minutes between each use. The preservatives can't handle it." Sterile, disposable swabs or cotton balls should be available for use when testing at cosmetic counters. If you don't see them, ask.

Keep makeup containers tightly closed when not in use.

Don't use eye cosmetics if you have an eye infection, such as conjunctivitis, and throw away all products you were using when you first discovered the infection.

Don't dye your eyelashes or eyebrows; doing so could cause blindness.

Secret Ingredient: **Throw any makeup away that changes color or if an odor develops. Use caution when opening, storing, and applying cosmetics.**

MIND

JUNE 8

Simplify.

Neat freak. Organizationally gifted. Call it what you like. I just think it's about simplifying your life.

For me, it takes less time to touch something once and put it away, than to use it, put it down, and then have to pick it up to put it away later. Plus, it prevents clutter (which I hate).

Here are some super-easy suggestions for simplification.

1. Wear a low-maintenance hairstyle. My strategy: cutting it as close as I can take it. Dreads or braids also can save time getting out of the house in the morning.
2. Don't wear fingernail polish unless it's a special occasion.
3. Get one handbag that's a neutral color that you can use for casual or dressy wear; you'll save time changing bags. That's getting to be a trend among busy women. Handbag designer Kate Spade says in the *Newark Star-Ledger* newspaper, "For someone who wants the same bag all the time, we have our black nylon bags that go with just about anything and still look smart."
4. Look through mail daily for anything urgent, throw out the junk, open the rest twice a week.
5. Bank online; you'll save time standing on line.

6. Buy a box of special occasion cards to prevent constant trips to the card store.

7. Gang all your medical checkups (physical, eye doctor, dentist) for everyone in your family at the same time every year. Going together saves trips; going during a particular month of the year saves time.

8. Go through your medicine cabinet and throw out expired medicines; it'll be easier to find what you want when you need it.

9. Invest in an electronic organizer. It'll save space as well as time looking between calendars, address books, Rolodexes, appointment books, and notepads.

Secret Ingredient: **Have you heard of KISS? The saying goes, "Keep it simple, stupid." But if you do keep it simple, you'll be smart.**

❋ NATIONAL MEN'S HEALTH WEEK

❋ JUNE 9 ❋

Give a man a hand at good health.

Our fathers, our brothers, our husbands or boyfriends, our sons, and other precious men in our lives—we love them to death, but we want them to live long and not experience premature death. We want to see them excel, achieve, succeed. For them to do that, and live long enough to enjoy it, they need to be at peak performance, at maximum health.

That's the goal of National Men's Health Week, which is held the week leading up to and including Father's Day each year, the period that men receive the greatest attention and focus in our society. If that sounds vaguely familiar to the reason National Black Health & Fitness Week is held the week before Mother's Day, there's a reason for it: National Men's Health Week, originated by the editors of *Men's Health* magazine, was an inspiration for the observance that *Heart & Soul* created when both magazines were owned by Rodale Press.

The purpose of National Men's Health Week is to raise awareness in our country, and especially among men, of the importance of preventive health behavior in the early detection and treatment of health problems affecting men. In other words, if we could just get the guys to think about their health—and better yet, to do something about it—it just may save their lives. It's a fact that women outlive men, on average, by seven years.

So women, who visit doctors 30 percent more than men, must be doing something right. If we could simply encourage our men to take as active a role as women do in regularly visiting their physician for basic examinations, the rate of male mortality could be significantly reduced. Seeking treatment before symptoms reach a critical stage is key. If our men have longer to live, we'll have longer to love them. And together we'll have the good life.

Secret Ingredient: To receive a free booklet on healthy living written just for men, call toll-free 1-800-955-2002 or visit the Web site www.menshealth.com. If you order far enough in advance, you can put the guide in a large-size greeting card and give it to your honey as a Father's Day gift.

❀ NATIONAL MEN'S HEALTH WEEK

❀ JUNE 10 ❀

Be an advocate for men's health.

They're our warriors, our heroes, our helpmates. And though a visible percentage who are super-athletes represent to the world an image of strength and virility, African American men in general face some grim statistics when it comes to their health. The first step to eradicating a problem is to face it. Let's face the following facts from the National Men's Health Foundation and work together to change them:

❖ One third of African American males in the United States are overweight.

❖ Almost half of black males age twenty years and older have serum cholesterol levels over 200 mg/dl, the level above which indicates an increased potential for developing heart disease.

❖ The death rate from cardiovascular disease is 33 percent higher for African American males than the rate for white males.

❖ African American men have the highest prostate cancer incidence rate of any racial or ethnic group in the United States (double that of white men).

❖ The five-year survival rate for African American males with prostate cancer is 75 percent; it's 90 percent for white males.

❖ HIV infection is the leading cause of death for black men ages twenty-five to forty-four, according to the Centers for Disease Control and Prevention.

❖ The death rates for black men ages thirty-five to forty-nine are about 175 percent higher than the death rates for white males in the same age group.

We've got to do something to improve the quality of life for *all* our men! See the next page for steps men can take for maximum health, fitness, and well-being. In the meantime, if you can just get a brother to go get a physical you can feel that "ya done good."

Secret Ingredient: **Read up on ways to keep our men healthy in** ***Brothers on the Mend,*** **by Ernest H. Johnson, and** ***The Black Man's Guide to Good Health,*** **by James W. Reed, M.D., Neil Shulman, M.D., and Charlene Shucker.**

❀ NATIONAL MEN'S HEALTH WEEK

❀ JUNE 11 ❀

Use your charms to stay in his arms.

You talk with your man about *everything*—your dreams, your job, your mom; his hopes, his goals, his mom. But does that everything include how to stay together? There are ways men can beat the odds of disease and decline—by pursuing a healthy lifestyle and taking control *now.* Feel free to use these tips for pillow talk! Just start the conversation using any of the following come-ons—oops, I mean, lead-ins:

When am I going to get to see you bust a move?
What you really mean: "It would be good if you would get some exercise." If you haven't seen him dunk lately, or race his bike, or lift a weight, or show how great he used to be on the track team, let him know you think it would be a sexy date to see him active in his gym clothes.

You have such a brilliant mind! What's your food philosophy?
What you really mean: "Are you health conscious when it comes to food and nutrition?" Encourage him to eat at least five servings of fruits and vegetables a day, to fill up on fiber, to pass up the salt, and lay off the sugar. Discuss the foods you both love that are low in fat—and eat them most often.

You are one cool brother, you know that?
What you really mean: "I want to know how you handle stress." Swap stories of how you successfully overcame a racist situation. Ask if he knows if he has high blood pressure. Discourage the use of drugs, alco-

hol, or marijuana as his "chill pill" of choice. Talk about your ideal scenarios for R&R.

Baby, let's schedule a big night out after your next doctor's appointment.

What you really mean: "If you won't go to the doctor, I'm willing to bribe you." If you go to the same family physician, schedule your annual appointments together. Or, make the appointment for him, if he'll go on the day you say. Let him know it means so much to you to know he's "healthy, wealthy, and wise."

Secret Ingredient: **One of the most sexy things you can do for your man's health (and your own HIV/AIDS protection) is to ask him to show you where he keeps his condoms—and how he puts them on. Take it from there, girl!**

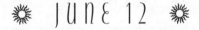

☀ JUNE 12 ☀

Test your health knowledge.

If you've got a guy who never shirks from a challenge, sic him on this quiz, courtesy of the National Men's Health Foundation. And if he insists on competition, take it yourself and see who wins!

1. As a man, what nutrient should make up the bulk of your diet?
   A. Fat
   B. Protein
   C. Carbohydrate

2. As a general rule, at what age should you have your first PSA test for prostate cancer?
   A. 30
   B. 40
   C. 50

3. The doctor takes your blood pressure and tells you it's 170 over 90. This is considered:
   A. Low
   B. Normal
   C. High

4. You've taken a cholesterol test. The results indicate your LDL reading is low, but your HDL is very high. You should be:
    A. Placed on cholesterol-lowering drugs
    B. Slightly concerned
    C. Very pleased

5. Of all AIDS cases in the United States, approximately what percentage is male?
    A. 50 percent
    B. 79 percent
    C. 84 percent

6. As a man, which disease don't you have to worry about?
    A. Breast cancer
    B. Osteoporosis
    C. Cystitis

The Answers:
    1C. The average man should get a minimum of 60 percent of his daily calories from carbohydrate, no fewer than 10 percent from protein, and no more than 30 percent from fat.
    2B. African Americans and any man with a family history of prostate cancer should begin testing before the general recommendation of age fifty.
    3C. Blood pressure is expressed as two numbers: systolic pressure (during a heartbeat) over diastolic pressure (between heartbeats). Repeated readings of 140/90 or greater denote high blood pressure.
    4C. HDL cholesterol is the "good" kind; it helps clear your arteries of the fatty deposits, or plaque, that can cause heart attacks and strokes. LDL is the "bad" fraction—high blood levels tend to stimulate plaque buildup.
    5C. The Centers for Disease Control and Prevention reports that through June 1997, 516,003 men in the United States have been diagnosed with AIDS.
    6. Caught ya! It's a trick question. Though not as common among men as women, all of these conditions can threaten a man's health.

✸ JUNE 13 ✸

Hey man, take care of that prostate gland.

Bill Cosby has a hilarious stand-up routine about it. Many strong, masculine men act like big ol' babies when it comes to doing it. "It" is the rectal examination performed with a gloved-finger probe to detect the presence of prostate cancer. What's not even funny is the fact that black men have the highest prostate cancer incidence rate of any racial or ethnic group in the United States. Ask Harry Belafonte, Sidney Poitier, or Marion Barry. Prostate cancer is no joke.

The prostate is a walnut-size gland located at the base of the bladder that produces the seminal fluid that transports sperm (so it's a major contributor to ejaculation). The cause of cancer of the prostate is still unknown, but according to Barbara M. Dixon's book *Good Health for African-Americans,* a man is at risk of developing it if he is African American and over forty years old, has a family history of it, had sex at an early age, has a history of multiple sex partners, eats a high-fat diet, has toxic job hazards, or has had a vasectomy.

A man may not have any symptoms at all of prostate cancer until it's too late to do anything about it. If one does have symptoms, they may include pain or a burning sensation during urination, frequent urination, an inability to urinate, a decrease in the amount of force of urine flow, blood in the urine, and lower back or pelvic pain. The only sure way to know is to start at age forty having annual checkups that may include a prostate-specific antigen blood test (known as a PSA), an ultrasound probe, and the rectal exam.

Men can cut their risk by decreasing their consumption of red meat and fat. Asian-American men have the lowest incidence of prostate cancer, so follow their example of a diet more typically high in soy, fiber, and vitamins A and C. Exercise has also been shown to lower the risk. And that's no joke.

Secret Ingredient: **Brothers, get your prostate exam. Don't let a minor discomfort hold you back from the major importance of saving your life. For more information, read Prostate Disease, by W. Scott McDougal with P. J. Skerrett.**

❋ JUNE 14 ❋

Don't let the R-word get the best of you.

The R-word I'm talking about is a four-letter word, "rage." That emotional excitement set off by intense anger—such as perceived racism in the form of police harassment, workplace discrimination, and everyday slights. Although African American women are affected by what was coined in the sixties as "black rage," arguably, African American men get hit hardest with it.

The effective management of rage can influence the ability to do your work, get promotions, raises, and ultimate success. Its ineffective management can have an adverse effect on your relationships, health, impacting on high blood pressure, headaches, stomach problems, feelings of distress, even mental illness.

Ronald B. Brown, Ph.D., is president of Banks Brown, a San Francisco company specializing in workplace diversity, self-development, power, leadership, and rage management. You could call him a "rage doctor." I asked Dr. Brown what his prescription would be for the following typical scenario:

Your manager treats you well in front of his boss, knowing his boss hired you. But you suspect he sees you as a threat to his job security, that he's thinking, "If I slip on a banana peel, this person might get my job." That same manager criticizes your work constantly, rewrites all your reports, gives you no respect. What do you do?

"There are two types of responses," says Dr. Brown, "the rage response, which is where we blow it; and the healthy response."

The rage response: You go in his office and curse him out. Or, you let him know where you're coming from (i.e., "Don't you know who I am? Mr. X hired me. I graduated from Harvard, and ran three departments in my last job!") Or, you do nothing and go on and on in the same situation, internalizing your anger.

The healthy response: "The first thing to do is to acknowledge when you're having a rage response," explains Dr. Brown. "Then evaluate the situation by finding out if this is how he treats everyone, or just you. Try not to take it personally, and try not to sink into self-doubt." Dr. Brown also advises talking with the manager about his work style and standards. And as far as the boss's insecurities, "Tell him, 'I'm here to help you.' Praise the positive things he does."

Secret Ingredient: "Rage is good," says our rage doctor. "It fuels your drive. There's no one more motivated than a black person dissed. But how you harness it is what matters, so it doesn't take you down."

❋ JUNE 15 ❋

Keep faith in fatherhood.

A father's love is so precious, so special. I know. As I told my father many times during our life together, I had "the best Daddy ever done it; the best ever was one." And it is my prayer that every child born in the world could experience the unconditional, blessed love of a father who pursues a healthy mind, body, and spirit. These are some ways in which a father can have a positive, everlasting effect on his children:

Mind

- ❖ He works on his own self-esteem, problem solving, and conflict resolution in constructive ways, never taking stress out on his family, always serving as an example of how to deal with life's challenges.
- ❖ He affirms his children's worth, courage, and beauty every chance he gets. And of course, he is never mentally or physically abusive.
- ❖ Whether he lives with his children or not, he puts their welfare first. He spends quality time with them. He keeps his promises, showing integrity. He is participatory and involved in their lives.

Body

- ❖ He sets an example for good health by exercising and keeping himself robust and fit.
- ❖ A concerned father is knowledgeable about nutrition, not just taste, and makes sure his family eats well, not just abundantly. He doesn't just "leave that up to your mama."
- ❖ He gets regular checkups and makes sure his children do, too.
- ❖ He avoids addictive the behaviors of smoking, drinking, and drugging.

Spirit

- ❖ In partnership with his children's mother, he articulates moral and ethical family values.
- ❖ A good father stays on a spiritual path, and raises his children to tap into the Greater Power. My own father made his family-faith message clear: "As for me and my house, we will serve the Lord."

Secret Ingredient: **"Be there" for your children. That's the most important thing a father can do.**

☀ JUNE 16 ☀

Pick up pointers from America's papa.

Bill Cosby wrote the book *Fatherhood*. But although he has been known as "America's Favorite Father" for his award-winning television sitcom, *The Cosby Show,* his most important job has been his starring role as father of his five children. Some years ago (when break dancing was big!), I interviewed him for *Essence* on parenting. His wisdom stands today.

Me: What makes a good father?

Cosby: A person who gives love and wisdom and who has a bottomless well of perseverance directed toward guiding the child to a better physical, mental, and intellectual life than he had.

Me: How can we tell if our children are heading in the right direction?

Cosby: After you listen to the words in some of the songs that are popular and watch your daughters and sons singing along with these words, that's where they'll be going.

Me: How can single mothers raise children effectively without a father present?

Cosby: In many of the lower economic areas, people constantly say that the children have no positive images. So they ask entertainers to come out and give speeches. Sidney Poitier and I have gone to different neighborhoods and visited the schools and found that these kids were not interested in hearing us telling them to study and stay in school as much as they were interested in how many cars we had and how big our house was.

But I tell kids, don't tell me that you don't have a positive image in your house. Look at your mother, if she is a single parent, and see how she has to get up and do your clothing, do your food, give you money so that you can have lunch. Then she goes out and works and comes home to fix your dinner. What kind of image is that? This is something we have to teach our children: to look around and see what their parents are doing—for them. To take this and understand it is to have a positive image. There are very few parents who would not hold down two or three jobs if the children showed some sign of talent in any particular area—other than break dancing.

Secret Ingredient: "Whenever you decide to punish them, you must follow through on that punishment," Cosby said. "Once your anger subsides, there's a tendency for you to say, 'Okay, go ahead.' But I'm a firm believer in adhering to whatever punishment you said you were going to give out."

❋ **BODY**

☀ JUNE 17 ☀

Fill up on fiber.

We just don't get enough fiber. Experts recommend at least 25 to 30 grams per day, but most folks get 10 to 15 grams. I think one reason is because we don't realize which foods can do the trick. Check out this list and load up on your favorites (have at least one at every meal today):

- ❖ Apples
- ❖ Apricots
- ❖ Baked potato with skin
- ❖ Barley
- ❖ Brown rice
- ❖ Figs
- ❖ Kidney beans
- ❖ Lentils
- ❖ Oat bran
- ❖ Oranges
- ❖ Peaches
- ❖ Pears
- ❖ Pinto beans
- ❖ Raisins
- ❖ Wheat bran
- ❖ Wheat germ

Secret Ingredient: **Eat a variety of fiber-packed foods. Doing so can stave off constipation, lower cholesterol and your risk of cancer. Get it going through your body by drinking lots of water.**

✳ JUNE 18 ✳

Love you.

In any self-help book, on all the talk shows, at any gathering of women, sooner or later someone will say, "Love yourself." If you're a natural-born skeptic like me, you say, "Yeah, yeah. I love me already. Okay?"

But then the journalist in me comes out to explore just what that concept means. I've been intrigued by how self-love is defined, what it can do for you, and what happens if you don't really love you. So I started writing down what I heard some very important people say on the subject:

> "To love yourself, you have to love all of who you are, not just your clothes, or where you're from . . . but everything about you . . . the truth of all that has happened to you, and what you have experienced and have to offer. You have to set boundaries of what you want from life and expect from people—and boundaries for yourself. You have to be at peace with where you are. Be happy with yourself."
>
> —Iyanla Vanzant

> "If you don't love yourself, then you go into relationships looking for the love."
>
> —Susan L. Taylor

> "Learn to love yourself. Because if you can't love yourself, how the hell are you going to learn to love anybody else?"
>
> —RuPaul

Secret Ingredient: "Love yourself" sounds like a simple phrase, but it's really complex work that gets to the root of our self-esteem.

☀ JUNE 19 ☀

Celebrate Juneteenth!

A terrible thing turned into a wonderful thing. In January 1863, the Emancipation Proclamation declared America's slaves in the eleven rebel states of the Union "forever free." But as enforcement of the law came only after defeat of local Confederate forces during the Civil War, freedom spread slowly from the White House in Washington, D.C., across the South. The war ended on April 9, 1865, but slaves were not informed in Texas until June 19, 1865, that they had been set free by law two and a half years before! Even if you consider the end of the war, they had remained slaves months longer than they should have (never mind they shouldn't have been slaves in the first place!)—but once they didn't have to "study war no more" or enslavement either, they began to celebrate and their descendants haven't stopped yet! And that's how June 19 became the date of the annual celebration known as the Juneteenth National Freedom Day.

Celebration is a healthy thing to do. In the midst of our daily routine and travails, it helps our well-being because:

❖ It gives us something positive to focus on and anticipate.

❖ The planning of local parades, cookouts, community festivals, and public readings of proclamations let us come together with others around a common cause.

❖ The actual events themselves provide us with a party for a purpose.

❖ Acknowledging our past is a way of honoring our history and our ancestors.

Ethnic holidays such as the Chinese New Year, the Mexican Cinco de Mayo, or Juneteenth allow us to express our commonality, our kinship, and our history with those of our extended human family. And as the Jewish saying goes, "We must never forget."

Secret Ingredient: **Participate in a Juneteenth commemoration. The biggest events are held in Texas, but wherever you live you can celebrate our freedom from oppression and honor the spirit of our ancestors. For more information, read** *African-American Holidays,* **by James C. Anyike.**

❋ JUNE 20 ❋

Vibe with some vitamins.

Sure, you read *Vibe*, you took your SATs, maybe your GREs, and you don't play when it comes to STDs, but do you know your ABCs? I'm talking vitamins, y'all. And I don't mean popping pills.

Just think of how those print ads featuring Spike Lee, Tyra Banks, and Vanessa Williams would look if they had a vitamin D pill instead of a milk mustache on their upper lips. The message would lose its impact. Well, that's comparable to what happens when you rely on vitamin pills for your nutrition. What's better is building your nutritional needs around "whole foods." That is, dairy products, fruits, vegetables, grains, and lean meats. Most of these foods have a combination of vitamins, minerals, and other healthy substances rather than just one thing. So, for example, if you ate an orange you would get calcium and carotene, in addition to vitamin C. Hard to get all that in a pill. Even if you take a multivitamin, it's still best to eat balanced meals. That said, here are some ABCs and the whole foods that provide them:

Vitamin A: Like your mother said, "Eat your carrots; they're good for your eyes." Vitamin A also gives you good skin, strong teeth, and healthy hair. Whole food sources include greens and other dark green veggies, eggs and other dairy products, apricots, cantaloupes, corn, liver, peaches, squash, sweet potatoes—oh yes, and carrots. *A word of caution:* Recent findings suggest high levels of vitamin A can cause birth defects. If you are pregnant now or plan to be soon, consult a midwife or obstetrician.

Vitamin B$_1$, or thiamin: Helps burn carbohydrates for fuel (you know, like a car burns oil). Whole food sources include asparagus, avocados, grains, lean meats, legumes, oranges, and peas.

Vitamin C, or ascorbic acid: Helps increase immune system functions that resist infections. Commonly linked with easing symptoms associated with the common cold, although it hasn't been proven to be a "cure." Whole food sources include asparagus, broccoli, Brussels sprouts, citrus fruits, cauliflower, cabbage, tomatoes, strawberries, and good ol' greens.

Just as A, B, and C are only the beginning of the alphabet, these vitamins are three of many. For more information, check out health books and nutrition Web sites, or ask your doctor or a dietitian for a more personal assessment of your nutritional needs.

Secret Ingredient: Read *Good Health for African-Americans,* by Barbara M. Dixon, L.P.N., R.D., for the vitamins of particular importance to black folks.

 MIND

Take a news break.

I wish I could put my hands on the study, but I distinctly remember reading that when African Americans look at television news, our blood pressure rises higher than that of white Americans. Is that any wonder? Often, the news shows more "bad" news than "good" news, and negative media images of African Americans are internalized. It's a "sad-news" day today as I write this, because of the sense of foreboding around the release of the videotapes of President Clinton's August 1998 deposition ("African Americans are uniquely qualified to recognize unfairness," remarked Rep. Maxine Waters), and particularly because four-time Olympian Florence Griffith Joyner died this morning of a heart seizure at age thirty-eight. Having met Flo Jo, and having been inspired by her, my heart has been heavy and I'm thinking of the loss experienced by her husband, Al Joyner, daughter, Mary, sister-in-law Jackie Joyner-Kersee, and our country. The news of the world can touch us emotionally, even when what happens doesn't affect us directly.

Every once in a while, we all just need to take a news break. Turn off the television, wake up naturally instead of to the radio blasting the on-the-hour news, and keep the newspaper rolled up on the porch. Even toning it down a bit each day can help. My husband, Reggie, used to keep some news on most of the day—from morning TV news programs, to radio talk shows, to the 6 o'clock, then 11 o'clock news—and read the local newspapers, too. He'd often be outraged at the injustices he read about or disturbed by the heated discussions on the radio. Then one day a couple of years ago during a time of introspection, he announced, "I've decided to stop looking at TV, to stop watching even the news. I've decided to listen to silence, to listen to my own self."

Secret Ingredient: Meditate on your own internal "videotape" sometime. Although we all want to be informed, it's healthy to occasionally turn off the noise of the news and listen to the sounds of silence. Read a book, pursue a hobby, talk with a child, play a game, walk your dog, take a hike, get your house in order. Give solitude a chance to have a calming effect on your mind and well-being.

 SPIRIT

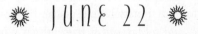 JUNE 22

Cherish the ancient.

Love is as old as creation. It's enduring and everlasting. As my minister, Rev. V. DuWayne Battle of St. Paul Baptist Church in Montclair, New Jersey, says, "Just think: When we love someone, the love doesn't stop when the person dies." Like God, love is Alpha and Omega. God *is* love.

Considering the ancient can give us a firm hold on what's really important in this all-too-fleeting life, our technological age and fast-paced lives have us focused on the temporary, the deleted, the expired, the quickie, the instant. All those things give us high anxiety and keep our attention span timed about as long as a music video. But when we "look what man has done," as the song says, and compare it to what God has done, God wins hands down every time. Here are some things that have endured the test of time:

❖ Faith
❖ Earth's beauty
❖ Rainbows
❖ Smiles and laughter
❖ Night and day
❖ Moonlight
❖ Sunshine
❖ Family
❖ Lovemaking
❖ Breathing

Because these things are ancient and God-given, they are sacred. Pay homage to these and other cherished gifts in our lives.

Secret Ingredient: Make your own list of ancient influences in your life. Also consider those that have "brought you through," such as unconditional parental love, or sibling support. And bless any other spiritual gifts you will cherish "forever."

✺ JUNE 23 ✺

Jump, jump, jump to it.

It may not be what Aretha Franklin had in mind in her song, but jumping rope can be good for your heart.

I bought a jump rope the other day in the supermarket. I saw the ropes on display for only ninety-nine cents, and I thought, *I can afford this, and I know jumping rope is good exercise.* I threw it in the grocery cart. An impulse buy for sure, but all for a purpose: Anything to get me motivated. The ropes had looked enticing, all high-tech with their plastic coating—much more chic than the frazzled ropes of my childhood. And looking at them, I was mentally transported back to my young years of double Dutch, and jumping to my favorite chant of "High ho, Texico/Over the hill to Mexico."

That didn't last long, however. As soon as my daughter saw that I had bought a jump rope, she brought me back to middle-age reality by becoming instantly hysterical.

But if I ever get to jumping, here are the benefits I'll have (and so will you if you do it, too):

- ❖ **Aerobic exercise.** Jumping gets that heart rate pumping!
- ❖ **Calf workout.** Look at any boxer's legs for proof of how jumping rope works all the major leg muscles (didn't Muhammad Ali have pretty legs?).

Try it for just two minutes continuously, then work up to five minutes, and more if you can stand it. Jump feet together, then skipping, then jumping jacks. Turn the rope with your hands at your sides, then criss-cross, get fancy, go on! Now you're jumping!

Secret Ingredient: **If you really get into jumping rope, then take it to the next level—use your rope work for warm-ups for aerobic boxing or kickboxing. There's a class at the gym waiting just for you.**

❋ JUNE 24 ❋

Go for the goal.

I think one of the greatest legacies of the late Olympian Florence Griffith Joyner will be that she showed what can happen when you go for your goal—in her case, the gold. She wanted to win right down to her very fingernails. At one race, she had one long nail painted red, another white, a third blue, and another gold—for her goal. And win, she did.

We can be winners, too, in whatever race we're competing in. Like Flo Jo, we can use our creativity and humor to come up with ingenious schemes to psyche ourselves up.

A great thing about sports is that the goal is so clear: beat the highest record, surpass your own best time, win over the opposing team, make the championship, be an all-star. We can all use those goals as metaphors for our own, and work toward our success with training, preparation, practice. Warm up. Stretch. Have a game plan.

And get yourself a coach. Even Michael Jordan says he couldn't do it without his coach. Whether your goal is giving birth by Lamaze, making it to the top of your job ladder, or singing on key, a good coach is worth her weight in, well, gold. Everyone needs one to push you harder toward your goal, to keep you motivated, to tell you, "You can do it!"

As fate would have it, the day *after* Flo Jo's death, she appeared on a pre-taped show of the Whoopi Goldberg–produced *Hollywood Squares*. The host asked her, "How did you get to be the world's fastest woman?" After explaining that she saw the Olympics when she was seven years old and decided to be a runner, she credited her "great family," and added that she had had, "Belief in myself, faith in God, and the world's greatest coach—my husband, Al Joyner!"

Whatever your goal is, get ready, set, go!

Secret Ingredient: **If you've ever played sports, use the training techniques and the discipline required as examples to help you plot out your game plan for success.**

❋ JUNE 25 ❋

Observe religious dietary laws.

For some people, the dietary laws of various religions can seem rigid, but the bottom line is that most of the commonly held guidelines are pretty beneficial for good health. Consider the following:

Catholics: Abstain from meat on Fridays, especially during Lent.

Jews: Keep Kosher; refrain from pork.

Orthodox Muslims: Refrain from "dead meat, and blood, and the flesh of swine," according to the Quran.

Nation of Islam: Refrain from pork; popularized a delicious alternative to the sweet potato pie—the bean pie!

Seventh-Day Adventists: Mainstay diet: Fruits, vegetables, nuts, and grains prepared free of spice and grease; no meat. Refrain from "pastries, cakes, desserts, and other dishes prepared to tempt the appetite," according to Counsels on Diet and Foods, by Ellen G. White.

Secret Ingredient: **Conduct your own research of religious dietary laws, and analyze how they affect health and fit in with your specific spiritual beliefs. Then "eat to live."**

BODY

❋ JUNE 26 ❋

Be well at work.

Summer's here and the time is right for . . . pursuing good health when you're at work. Here are thirteen things you can do to pursue a healthy workstyle:

1. Take a walk-around-the block break instead of a coffee or smoking break.
2. Go to the gym or take a jog at lunchtime three times a week; take a nap other days.
3. Make it a habit to have a nutritious lunch. Summer salads are a best bet.

4. Keep healthy snacks in your desk, such as rice cakes, granola bars, nuts, dried fruit, microwave no-salt popcorn.

5. Get up and walk around your work area at least once an hour to avoid computer eyestrain, carpal tunnel syndrome, and becoming sedentary.

6. Do neck rolls, stretches, and point and flex your toes.

7. Drink herbal tea instead of coffee.

8. If you have a radio at work, keep it on a jazz, easy-listening, or classical station to keep yourself calm.

9. Try to resolve problems quickly so that they don't fester. Bringing closure to difficult situations is better for your mental health than procrastinating.

10. At work celebrations, bring sparkling cider instead of alcohol. Have bottled water, juices, fruit punch, or lemonade instead of soda.

11. Control your anger. Talking with people respectfully and maintaining dignity is a strategy for getting the same in return.

12. If you have an opportunity to suggest company activities, give ideas that promote wellness, such as blood pressure screenings, CPR classes, blood donation, community service, free mammograms.

13. Give gifts of health for coworkers' special occasions, such as sports or fitness accessories, aromatherapy products, and gift certificates for beauty treatments.

Secret Ingredient: **Take your healthy workstyle habits home with you. For example, if you don't eat ribs or chitlins at work, why eat them at home?**

 MIND

 JUNE 27

Exercise your memory.

Is it as hard for you to remember names as it is for me? For the life of me, I can't remember a person's name two seconds after we've been introduced. I rarely forget a face, but often forget a name. I'm trying to do better, though, by using these strategies:

❖ Repeat the name as soon as you hear it. "Hi, Alexis, nice to meet you."

- Use name association. Think: *Alexis. I have a niece named Alexis.*
- Write it down immediately. If you're making a call to a customer service hotline, for example, be prepared to write down the name as soon as the person answers the phone and identifies himself. "Hello. Thank you for calling Continental Airlines. This is Marlon. How may I help you?" Write down "Marlon" right away.
- Ask, if you forget. Say, "I'm sorry, I know you just told me your name, but would you repeat it, please?" Chances are the person you've been introduced to may have forgotten yours, too! So say your name again as well, as a courtesy.
- Exchange business cards. It seems that everybody has a business card these days. The other day someone on the street handed me a card—and it was for a warehouse sample sale! Even if you don't need business cards for your job, you can make up calling cards. I've created calling cards for my husband and me and as a gift for my sister. I've found the vending machines in a Paris, France, mall and a New York City greeting card store. Insert a five-dollar bill, type in your info, and out come fifty cards.
- Eat humble pie. If someone always remembers your name, but you just can't keep up with theirs, just 'fess up and say, "I'm so sorry, I keep forgetting your name. Please tell me one last time."
- Ask somebody else. "Who was that masked man, anyway?"

Secret Ingredient: **In addition to business card vending machines, you can now get software to make cards on your computer. Look for these inexpensive packages at computer stores, office-supply stores, or wherever software is sold.**

❀ SPIRIT

 JUNE 28 ❀

Let us pray.

Did you know that spirituality has positive health effects on your body? According to Dale A. Matthews, M.D., in his book *The Faith Factor,* a study of 451 African American men and women evaluated the impact of church attendance and other measures of religiosity on depression and found that people with higher levels of religious involvement reported significantly less depression.

In addition, Matthews reports, prayer specifically has *temporary* measurable, definable physiologic effects on the body, including:

- ❖ a decreased heart rate
- ❖ a lower metabolic rate (the rate at which the body burns oxygen)
- ❖ a lower rate of breathing
- ❖ slowing of brain waves

The effects of prayer on healing are unproven, but don't you feel better after you've asked for direction, guidance, healing, renewal, or forgiveness? And just hearing your mother say, "I'll be praying for you!" can give you relief. You know that's going to be a powerful weapon in your defense!

In 1979 when I was a young editor at *Essence,* there was a period when I would hear the editor-in-chief at the time, Marcia Ann Gillespie, singing softly to herself, "I'll be prayin' for ya." After I heard her do this several times, I got nosy enough to ask her what song that was. "It's Andrae Crouch," she said. Not one to badger my boss for more information, but wanting to understand what made her tick, I just went out, and without ever hearing of Andrae Crouch or his music, bought the album on which the cut "I'll Be Thinking of You" appeared. It's a beautiful song that's been one of my favorites ever since. This upbeat yet mellow song about prayer has a soothing effect—like prayer. Just goes to show that prayer can be sung as well as spoken or thought, and the healing effect is just as strong. So next time you want to "feel better fast," don't reach for the aspirin. As they say in church, take it to the Lord in prayer.

Secret Ingredient: **If you'd like to hear Andrae Crouch's "I'll Be Thinking of You," it's on his compilation CD** *The Light Years.*

❋ BODY

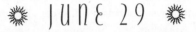

Clean your teeth with a chew stick.

Hedging a question from my dentist, Dr. Neville Thame, on whether I flossed regularly, I told him that I used toothpicks. "Toothpicks can harm your teeth at the roots," he advised. "Try a chew stick instead."

That answer delighted me. When I met my husband, he never once had a cigarette or cigar to his lips, but he was known to have a twig hanging out of his sumptuous mouth. He explained that this was the "African" way to clean your teeth. I thought he looked very hip, sexy, and cool. And I wasn't the only one—people would stop him on the street and ask, "What *is* that?" and "Where'd you get that?"

Since I equated it with my man, though, it was a "man's thang" to me. It didn't occur to me to use one myself until many years later when I became editor of a health magazine, and was thinking of stories that would put "Afrocentric" and "dental" together. Sally Jones, who researched the story, got lots of sticks from sources that market them and shared them with the staff. The photograph of a cute sister-model with a stick in her mouth is still one of my faves.

Dr. Thame tells me that the wood is softer than that used in toothpicks. Also, because the stick is wider, it can massage your gums, remove plaque, as well as clean particles from your teeth. To use it, rinse it off well, just as you would a toothbrush, then using a rotating motion, clean each tooth. The aftertaste of the chew stick is minty and fresh, which encourages the user to just let it hang out the mouth for that cool look.

So don't let your teeth get sick, pick up a chew stick.

Secret Ingredient: **Chew sticks can be found in health-food stores, or from street vendors who sell incense and other Afrocentric products.**

 MIND

☀ JUNE 30 ☀

Give your baby the best milk, breast milk.

My sisters, we just *must* make an effort to breastfeed our babies. With the high infant mortality rate we have in the black community, there's no excuse for not giving our babies the best shot at life by providing them their God-given nutrients. I breastfed my daughter for seven months, and the bonding experience was precious and irreplaceable. When she cried in the middle of the night, there was no stumbling to the kitchen to heat a bottle with one eye open. Nope, just cuddle her up and go back to sleep.

Most important, breast milk is made solely for your baby. It will help to protect your infant from disease, infections, allergies, and tooth decay. I can testify to the fact that when my daughter was exposed to chicken pox when she was two years old, she didn't even get them! I knew it had to be because of the immune system boosters I passed on to her through my breasts.

The first sign of pregnancy a woman gets is often breast tenderness, which indicates preparation for lactation (milk production). For many women, this carries a sense of shame that must be changed; breastfeeding is the *function* of the breast. Our ancient African wisdom tells us this is right! The "modern" bottle-fed way works, but it's not the best way.

Breastfeeding saves money. You won't have to buy expensive prepared formulas or a sterilizer.

Breastfeeding doesn't have to tie you down. You can express your milk and leave a bottle of breast milk for your baby if you have to be away or if you are working.

You can feed your baby without being noticed by lifting your blouse or sweater from the waist. I had a favorite kente shawl I threw over my shoulder and the baby's head that gave us complete privacy, even in public. No one had any idea what was going on under there! Many organizations that encourage breastfeeding also sell shirts and blouses that make discreet breastfeeding easy for all women.

Breastfeeding helps you regain your figure sooner because it causes your uterus to shrink back faster to its normal size, and your body fat is needed for milk production.

Secret Ingredient: Remember, *some* breastfeeding is better for baby than none. If you have difficulty getting started, hospitals offer classes, or you can call the LaLeche League at 1-800-LA-LECHE or visit www.lalecheleague.org. Supportive, been-there-done-that mothers are on the line to help.

 MIND

 JULY 1

Take time out.

Time out! It's not just for toddlers and basketball players. It's something that's good for you and me.

I believe in taking time out. As a matter of fact, I may be the queen of time out. My personal philosophy is: If you work hard, you've got to take time to chill. Of course, it's not easy to get away from the daily grind and your many responsibilities, so taking time out takes some planning.

During the month of July, vacation time is what we're most likely to plan as time out. But just in case you can't get away until next month, or you've already taken all the vacation days you're allotted at work, here are some other ways you can get some R&R, from as quickly as one second to as long as one week:

One second: Take a second out of a hectic day to think of an affirmation. If you're at a loss for one, try "God Is." My colleague writer Michelle Lodge says she writes the affirmation she thinks of each day in her journal.

One minute: Take one minute to sing one of your favorite songs. When things get overwhelming or you find yourself in a tense situation, pause, get quiet, and count to ten.

One hour: Take yourself out for a serene lunch break at a health food café. A solid hour at the gym can make you feel refreshed. Go surfing on the World Wide Web.

One day: Spend several restful hours in your favorite park, where you can munch a packed lunch, then inline-skate the day away. Take a day trip to a nearby town. For example, from my hometown in Seattle, there are so many day trips to take, such as a boat trip to Victoria, Canada, or up to the mountains of Snoqualmie Pass, or down to Portland, Oregon, for tax-free shopping!

One weekend: Escape into a good book. Go away with your honey or to a personal enrichment retreat like African American Women on Tour (call 1-800-560-AAWT).

One week: Take a course to learn a new skill. In just a few consecutive days I learned the art of calligraphy, which has given me joy and stress release for years.

Secret Ingredient: **The power of "one" is great—and so is the power of taking one time-out!**

 BODY

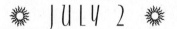 JULY 2

Give your doctor a check-up.

If you don't have a family doctor or pediatrician whom you trust and are fond of, now's a good time to look for one before the holidays and summer vacations. Kids often need back-to-school medical checkups, and establishing a strong relationship with a helpful and concerned doctor for any reason doesn't hurt.

When considering a new doctor: Before the usual questions to the prospective doctor about medical insurance acceptance and payment fees, there's an important question to ask yourself: *Do you feel comfortable with this person?*

- ❖ Is the tone of her or his voice and the demeanor comforting, concerned, and caring?
- ❖ Does the doctor talk straight with you—not down at you?
- ❖ Is the waiting time to get an appointment a few days, or more like weeks and weeks?
- ❖ In the waiting room, is the wait time for your appointment reasonable (assuming *you* were on time, of course)?

When to call on her: Besides the usual annual checkups, there are urgent times to call your doctor and be advised on whether you need to make an appointment. They include:

- ❖ Fever over 102 degrees F, especially if it lasts more than eight hours
- ❖ Accidents such as falls, burns, cuts, or head injuries
- ❖ Bleeding, pain, vomiting, rashes, or infections
- ❖ Prolonged diarrhea or constipation
- ❖ Flu, cold, chicken pox, measles, strep throat, or allergy symptoms
- ❖ Any flare-up of something unusual.

Secret Ingredient: **Too many African Americans use emergency room care as their primary health care. Don't be one of them. Save the ER for life-threatening emergencies or urgent conditions that require quick attention, and see your doctor for medical visits to help prevent them.**

 JULY 3

Have gratitude, not an attitude.

I have these pet peeves about human public interaction. Maybe it's because I grew up in friendly, polite Seattle, Washington, and now live in the snooty, often rude New York City area. But I get all bent out of shape when I hold a door open for someone and the person doesn't even nod my way, much less say "thank you," especially if it's a man! Or if someone asks for directions, and after you give them to the person, he or she *might* say "Oh, okay" before walking or driving off. But in my book, "okay" is not a synonym for "thanks," or " 'preciate it!" These types of people leave you with attitude instead of gratitude.

Acknowledging when someone does you a courtesy is a boost not only to the other person's spirit, but to your own. It makes you feel positive and lets the recipient know you've recognized the positive in him. It shows you have "home training." It's something that would make your mama proud.

We're doing a good job of teaching our children courtesy. I've started frequenting a corner store that has very narrow aisles. Every single time a child passes in front of me while I am gazing at the magazines, he says "excuse me" first. The adults, who are bigger and taller and therefore more of an obstruction, generally just walk in front of me saying nothing—as though I weren't even there, invisible. Makes you want to put your hands on your hips and say, "You're *excused!*" It's as if the adults are tired being polite. We're teaching our children what we're too lax to do ourselves. We can't be bothered.

I'm trying to restrain myself from copping an attitude over these trivial absences of respect. But I'm also checking myself, and making an effort not to "dis" anyone either. The Golden Rule is still in effect as far as I know.

Secret Ingredient: **Be a person who expresses more gratitude than attitude, and that's the karma you'll get in return.**

 BODY

Get out the grill!

It's the Fourth of July, the day that could be renamed National Barbecue Day. There will be cookouts here, picnics there, good food everywhere. It's a great time to try preparing at least *one* dish more healthfully.

Traditionally, when folks cook out, that means grilling the meat. But have you ever considered grilling the *vegetables?* I hadn't—that is, until Reggie and I were dinner guests of Barbara Smith and her husband, Dan Gasby. As owners of three B. Smith restaurants, they know a little about innovation on the grill. On the waterfront deck of their summer house in Sag Harbor, New York, Barbara grilled a meatless meal of fresh foods from her own garden: eggplant, zucchini, and bell peppers served over couscous. It was a chic treat!

Since then, I've done a little research on grilling vegetables. This method of food preparation has its advantages. For example, it's a low-fat way to cook them. The preparation is quick and easy. It's inexpensive and doesn't require a laundry list of ingredients. It's an alternative to making meat the centerpiece of the meal. And, hey, it tastes good!

Whether you cook the vegetables *with* meat (or fish), or *instead* of meat, the results are sure to make you the talk of the cookout! Here are some vegetables to throw on the grill—then sit back and chill:

- ❖ Fresh corn on the cob (cook in the husks)
- ❖ Eggplant (cut in strips or rounds)
- ❖ Red, green, or yellow peppers (cut in half, remove seeds, grill on both sides)
- ❖ Zucchini (cut lengthwise in strips)
- ❖ Squash (ditto)
- ❖ Asparagus spears (the heartier, the better)
- ❖ Portobello mushrooms (make great, low-fat veggie burgers)

Secret Ingredient: **For Barbara's special herb marinade recipe for the vegetables, see her book** *B. Smith's Entertaining and Cooking for Friends.*

 MIND

 JULY 5

Revisit your roots at a family reunion.

Too often funerals become the family reunion. That's where I was, at the funeral of my father's brother in West Virginia, when I learned that the Stokes family had biannual family reunions in Georgia. I asked to be put on the mailing list but never could make the dates, so I guess that's why they stopped sending me the notices. But I've kept every correspondence and plan to attend one of these days. I want to meet my cousins!

Travel-industry studies show that Black folks are primarily the ones doing just that. As if to say "Amen," the National Council of Negro Women even published *The Black Family Reunion Cookbook* in 1991, and the O'Jays recorded a song about it. Typically, reunions are planned for the summer months, scheduled over a weekend, and sometimes have as many as five hundred people in attendance. Some meet occasionally, some every year.

The most elaborate reunions require planning committees to organize as much as they would for a national conference. Some of the events at a reunion could include:

❖ Getting-to-know-you kick-off receptions
❖ Genealogy sessions
❖ Field trips to African American history sites, family heritage locations, or the family cemetery
❖ Talent and fashion shows
❖ Group church attendance
❖ T-shirt and other family memorabilia giveaways
❖ And, of course, food, food, and more good food!

After the reunions, some highly organized (and enviable) families produce newsletters that keep the family up-to-date on promotions, marriages, births, illnesses, and deaths. Even hardship and scholarship funds have been set up. Family reunions are enjoyable ways to bless the ties that bind.

Secret Ingredient: **Compile your own reunion cookbook of your family's most healthy original dishes. Have the recipes copied at the local copy center. Use a three-hole punch and tie with a colorful ribbon.**

 BODY

 JULY 6

Everybody into the pool!

Swimming is hard to beat as an aerobic exercise. Unlike other fitness activities such as cycling, running, and rowing, swimming uses nearly all the major muscle groups. It places an effective demand on the heart and lungs and also improves posture and flexibility. A refreshing change of pace from other fitness regimens, putting in a half hour of laps three times a week is a good outlet for tension and stress.

Even if you don't know how to swim, you can benefit from the new trend in water fitness classes, dubbed "aquarobics," "aquacise," "aqua tone," and "aqua step," to name a few. These are just about my speed, because I 'fess up: I can't swim worth beans! As a kid, I flunked the "guppy" classes at the Y. If I hadn't had to pass Swimming 101 to graduate from Howard University, I wouldn't even be able to tread water. Still don't do it well. But I first tried a water aerobics class at a wonderful beach resort and spa in Grenada called La Source, and I've been hooked ever since.

I can't use the hair excuse anymore, but if that's yours, get it braided for the summer and you'll be ready to jump in anytime you want. Ask your braider for a style that would be particularly easy for swimming, such as one with all cornrows, or rows in front with loose braids in back. If you want to keep your permed 'do, when you get ready to swim, brush it back into a French style, a French braid or French roll. Cover it up with a swim cap. It's best to wash the chlorine out after every swim, and to let it air-dry if possible, especially if you plan to swim three or more times a week.

Some sisters say their inhibitions about swimming come from "race memory" of the Middle Passage, real memory of segregated pools, or shame remembered when their hair "went back" unexpectedly in a public pool. If these psychological scars strike a chord with you, start the healing process by thinking of how our African ancestors must have loved bathing on the shores of the Niger and Nile rivers, and the coasts of the Atlantic and Indian oceans. Work on overcoming your fears for the millennium. Do it for the ancestors—and your health.

Secret Ingredient: **If you're already a swimmer, stroke on, sister! If not, try a special swim class for nonswimmers, hire a personal swim trainer, or do water aerobics. Just get wet.**

❋ SPIRIT

❋ ❋

Ask the questions of the spirit; find the answers of the soul.

Do you know the difference between spirituality and religion? I've been trying to figure it out myself. Having made a mental note to search for clues, I got a lesson in it one night while watching public television. On *Bill Moyers with Sister Wendy,* the nun being interviewed by the journalist said, "Spirituality deepens our awareness of things that matter . . . of things greater than ourselves. . . . When that meets faith, it becomes religious."

For many of us, religion comes first. As I told my pastor when he ministered to my bereavement when my father died, I realized that I had always been a religious person, having grown up in the church and having been baptized at age eight. But it wasn't until my father died, when I was forty-four, that I became spiritual. That's because I began to feel that my father, who was no longer in a physical place, was in a spiritual place, and so I began the spiritual journey in order to connect with him.

Generally, religion is defined as organized systems of beliefs and rituals in worship of God. Spirituality is the quest for answers to life's (and death's) meaning, purpose, and God's plan for us. Religion holds answers. Spirituality asks questions. There are some close similarities, however.

- ❖ Both acknowledge the existence of a Higher Power.
- ❖ Both seek closeness to God.
- ❖ Both overlap in joy and gratitude for blessings, mercy, and grace.
- ❖ Both have what I call "quiet consciousness" with religion's prayers and spirituality's meditations.

And, of course, there are some differences:

Religion: Usually involves formal, organized worship
Spirituality: Informal and more often individual

Religion: Dictates structured behaviors and ancient traditions
Spirituality: More free-thinking and changing with the times

Religion: Focused on divinity in heaven; peace in the afterlife
Spirituality: Focused on finding the power within and inner peace.

Secret Ingredient: There is no right or wrong or "better than thou" in the pursuit of religion versus spirituality. Some people are religious, some are spiritual, some are both. What about you?

❋ MIND

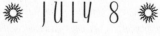 JULY 8

Be cool.

My favorite part of the *Eyes on the Prize* documentary about the civil rights movement is when the mother of a young activist relates her feelings of fear for her son. "He came home from jail and said, 'Be cool, Mother,'" she says with a laugh that holds back tears. "And I tried to be cool."

It's July, the weather is hot. It's the time of year when race riots broke out during the 1960s. When tempers can flare like the heat. The aftermath in Los Angeles of the first Rodney King verdict proves that unrest is always a possibility, not something just for history books. Day by day we encounter situations in which we make split-second decisions about whether to jump violent or to be cool.

During one of our weekly Sunday phone-therapy sessions, my sister, Vicki, told me about a horrible day at work she had had that week in which she was informed that a coworker had referred to her as the B word. Now, let me set this up: My sister does not play. This was not a thing to say about her if that person wanted to live in peace and harmony. I thought to myself, *The woman who said that will definitely regret it.* Thoughts of vicious childhood fights my sister had won flashed in my head.

So you can imagine my surprise when Vicki started talking about how she had *not* confronted the woman. Instead, she took her grievance to her supervisor and filed a complaint. She had handled it the corporate way, and luckily for the employee, the cool way. "It's not the heat of the moment that's important," Vicki said, explaining the wisdom that had come with maturity. "It's the victory, and sometimes you have to wait for that."

Vicki got her victory. So did my *Eyes on the Prize* mother and her heroic son—along with the rest of us because of the struggles won in the civil rights movement. And when we decide to "be cool" and to face our problems constructively, we win every time.

Secret Ingredient: **Martin Luther King, Jr., may have called it nonviolence, but it's just another way of saying "be cool."**

❈ BODY

❈ JULY 9 ❈

Release your inner watermelon woman!

I love watermelon! I don't care what anybody says. Later for the stereotypes, for the bigoted caricatures. I'm going to eat my watermelon. I collect watermelon art (my kitchen is full of it), and I serve watermelon to anyone who stops by on a hot summer day.

Why? Because it tastes good. But also because it's healthful. Did you know that watermelon:

- is high in vitamins A and C?
- provides iron and potassium?
- is low in calories?
- has "Black" history? Watermelons originated over 4,000 years ago near the Kalahari Desert of Africa. It comes from the Motherland, y'all!
- seeds were brought to the United States, the Caribbean, and to Brazil by slaves (and enslavers)

So slice it, dice it, make a smoothie out of it, make melon balls, freeze pieces on sticks, serve a colorful fruit salad, cut out a creative centerpiece from the rind. Cool off with a refreshing, cold, juicy watermelon.

Secret Ingredient: **Watermelon is really a vegetable—not a fruit! It's in the cucumber family. If you don't believe me, contact the National Watermelon Promotion Board, P.O. Box 140065, Orlando, FL 32814-0065; Web site: www.watermelon.org. Or call Susan O'Reilly, Director of Communications, at 1-407-895-5100.**

❋ SPIRIT

❋ JULY 10 ❋

Be a baby in the spirit.

"Babies are the most spiritual of us all, because they just got here," quips comedian and activist Dick Gregory. When I went to see Gregory perform a few years ago, I jotted down that he said this. And although he didn't expound on it, and I can't recall the context, it still provokes thought. But Dick Gregory should know—he's fathered lots of babies!

When my daughter was a newborn, I used to tease her, asking, "Where were you a year ago? What was it like in the spirit world?"

For some, it may be hard to imagine the spiritual life of babies, because they can't talk. But think of how infants live their little lives:

- **With faith.** Babies believe that if you say you're their mommy or daddy, you are! They have faith in your ability to be responsible for them. *Isn't the first step in spirituality to really believe there is a God? Have faith that you are, indeed, a child of God.*
- **With trust.** Newborns totally trust us to love and care for them. They place their lives in our hands. They trust that we'll hold

them without letting them fall. *Wouldn't it be a spiritual thing for us to trust in God that way? For us to trust that we are divinely loved and cared for? To trust that He'll keep us from falling?*

❖ **With obeyance.** Babies pretty much do as you say. They're too young to talk back (they can't talk!), suck their teeth (they don't have any!), or walk away (they can't walk!). They may cry in protest, but the adult caretaker really is in control. *Trust and obey, the church song says. Obey the will of God. Obey the laws of morality and goodwill. And remember, when things get tough, God is still in control.*

Secret Ingredient: Read about the inner world of our little ones in *The Spiritual Life of Children,* by Robert Coles. To explore "pre-birth existence," check out *Coming from the Light: Spiritual Accounts of Life Before Life,* by Sarah Hinze. Deep, right?

 MIND

 JULY 11

Go spa trippin'.

This is the season of the year I like to take some time to ease my mind. Several years ago, armed with ammunition in the form of a great spa guidebook called *Fodor's Healthy Escapes,* I convinced my husband Reggie that going to a spa was not just a "woman thing." *Healthy Escapes* lets you choose your spa based on your interests. Reg wanted a sports and fitness destination; I wanted pampering. We both wanted a Caribbean beach resort. In all three categories we found La Source in Grenada. Sounded good, so we went.

As it turned out, Reg got hooked on the pampering and I got into the fitness. The staff at La Source is almost totally black, and by the time Reg finished getting a facial at the hands of one of those gorgeous sisters, he was walking around telling me and other guests that he had enjoyed the experience so much, he had seen God! My water aerobics wasn't quite that heavenly, but it was big fun.

So now I have a list of favorite places to vacation and get spa treatments. They are pricey, but I plan and save all year for my week of renewal. (Of course, some cost less than others; call for prices.)

Jackie's on the Reef, Negril, Jamaica: This American-sister–owned spa is intimate and *Irie!* (think massage to a gentle reggae beat); one of the most affordable too. Contact Jackie Lewis (and tell her I said hi!) in New York at 1-718-469-2785.

New Age Health Spa, Neversink, New York: Had my virgin spa experience here, so it has a special place in my heart. Popular among black women because of the budget-conscious price. Accommodations a lot like summer camp. Call 1-800-682-4348.

Rancho La Puerta, Tecate, Mexico: Just over the border from San Diego, "the ranch" has a week-long program of swimming, tennis, hiking, spa treatments, exercise—anything you want. For reservations and availability, call 1-800-443-7565; Web site: www.rancholapuerta.com.

Canyon Ranch, Tucson, Arizona: Took my mother here for Mother's Day weekend. Much pampering and features "life enhancement" programs. Upscale, with price to match. Call 1-800-742-9000.

Secret Ingredient: Can't get away? Try a day spa near you. For **personal help in choosing the destination or day spa for you, call Spa Finders 1-800-255-7727; in New York City, 1-212-924-6800.**

 BODY

 JULY 12

Wash your hands.

Admit it: We pick our noses. We scratch our eardrums. We get gunk out of our eyes. We hold on to subway straps and escalator rails. We open doors. We change diapers. We eat fries with our fingers. We pick up germs, germs, and more germs.

Fortunately, our bodies build up antibodies so that these common germs don't kill us. But eighty percent of the illnesses we do get, such as colds and flu, can be traced to germs we picked up by touching, stroking, scratching—you get the picture. I know someone who carries Lysol everywhere she goes, spraying her computer workstation (that others use on different shifts) before she starts work each day, and she hates to travel because of "those nasty sheets! Other people slept on them!"

You don't have to be *that* obsessive. Experts say, just wash your hands often. Using soap and comfortably hot, running water, rub hands together for at least ten to fifteen seconds. Don't forget to wash the back of your hands, the crevices in between your fingers, and under your nails. To dry, use a clean or disposable towel.

Wash before you:

- ❖ Prepare or eat food
- ❖ Handle contact lenses

Wash after you:

- ❖ Go to the bathroom
- ❖ Change a diaper
- ❖ Blow your nose, cough, or sneeze
- ❖ Handle raw meats
- ❖ Touch a pet
- ❖ Handle garbage

Wash before and after:

- ❖ Nursing someone who is ill

Secret Ingredient: **You needn't restrict yourself to antibacterial soaps (the jury's still out on their effectiveness). Experts say plain old soap (or a moist towelette) will do.**

 SPIRIT

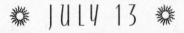 JULY 13

Let God use you.

On the *Motown 40* television tribute, Smokey Robinson tells an anecdote about visiting Marvin Gaye, who lived around the corner from him. Marvin was working on the *What's Going On* album about the Vietnam War and social unrest. When Smokey walked in, he says, Marvin told him, "Smoke, God is writing this album. I'm only being used here."

That album did go on to become one of Marvin Gaye's masterpieces. And it's highly possible that it's because he submitted to the Master. He was humbled in the act of creation.

Have you ever felt like that? I can testify that it's a divine feeling. When you are doing your best, yet you know that your hand is being guided by something greater than your earthly talents, or your feet are being moved toward destiny, it makes you just stop and wonder. And you know how you got over.

It's that profound sentence you wrote on your college essay. It's the conversation you had with your child that you *know* got through. It's that project at work that no one thought you could pull off.

You can't always orchestrate when *the feeling* is going to come. It's often when you don't expect it. But when it does happen, acknowledge the awesome, and recognize that the miraculous has come not *from* you but *through* you. Then give God the glory.

Secret Ingredient: **Know that divine intervention isn't anything you can *make* happen, but expect that it *will* happen.**

 BODY

 **JULY 14**

Eat like The Artist.

In *Interview* magazine a couple of years ago, Spike Lee and The Artist had a conversation that I thought was very entertaining and informative. Who would know just by listening to "1999" or seeing him perform that The Artist is a vegetarian? Or that he has a spiritual side? (Or that black folks keep calling him Prince?)

When Spike (who was a very good interviewer, I must say) asked how he picked his band members, The Artist said, "I have been blessed with having these people come to me. . . . I was looking for a group of four vegetarians. . . . Our people have the worst diet of anybody. I'm ready to put a farmer on my payroll. We've got to get back to growing our own food. You are what you eat!"

I wondered if he had ever read Nation of Islam founder Elijah Muhammad's book by that name, but regardless, it was interesting to know that The Artist was so passionate about vegetarianism and natural foods. Maybe that's the secret to his high energy on stage and his ageless, ever-slim body!

Don't say I never told you that health tips come from unexpected sources.

Secret Ingredient: **If you are interested in becoming a vegetarian, start gradually by eating one meatless meal a week, move to one a day, then to more meals a day. There are tons of books on the subject to help you become an educated vegetarian, loads of cookbooks to make those meals scrumptious, and Web sites that can provide both. *Vegetarian Times* magazine is also a good resource, along with their *Vegetarian Times Complete Cookbook.***

✵ JULY 15 ✵

Know your personality type.

Julie Kembel, the education director at Canyon Ranch health and fitness resort in Tucson, Arizona, conducts a fascinating seminar at the ranch that I had the pleasure of attending. Called Personalities and Stress, it helps you determine your personality profile and stress reactors, based on four dominant temperaments. Symbolized by the words **R**ational, **O**rganized, **L**oving, and **E**nergized, they are called **ROLE** Play. Think about how you see yourself most of the time, and see which personality style is most like you:

Rationals are the intellectuals. Naturally bright and conceptual, they excel at problem solving and coping with complex issues. Often remote and content to be alone, R's are self-critical and impatient with their own and other people's faults. Least likely to show physical or verbal affection, and are uncomfortable with outward displays of emotion.

Organized personalities are hardworking, orderly, and decisive people that most of us rely on. O's are detailed and knowledgeable, steady and dependable. They view life as serious business. Exceptionally neat and tidy, they have a procedure for everything from making breakfast to making love. They are warm and sincere people, but they don't make jokes or act silly unless that is the business at hand.

Loving folks are kind and patient and see the best in others. Compassionate and sensitive, L's are caring and care-giving. Spiritual, they like to explore the deeper meaning of life. They focus on the broad picture and less on practical details.

Energized types are optimistic and good-natured with a natural energy and zest for life. They are free-spirited and resist being constrained by rules or obligations. E's prize freedom, and excel in careers that require daring and innovation. They are typically tolerant and unprejudiced in their approach to people.

Did you find your type? Can you identify other people you know? Kembel says we each have specific reactions to stress and ways of coping with it. When severely stressed:

R's are reclusive reproving, rigid, rude. *Need to restore balance:* time to think, to conceptualize. *You can best deal with them by:* not hovering, using reason rather than emotion.

O's are officious, obstinate, obsessive, opinionated. *Need:* time to organize, to plan specifically. *Deal with them by:* being tolerant, avoiding arguments, offering to help.

L's are listless, leaden, lonely, lost. *Need:* time to talk, to receive support from others. *Deal with them best by:* listening and being patient, supportive, and caring.

E's are evasive, erratic, excessive, egotistical. *Need:* time to get grounded, to do something concrete. *Deal with them by:* being flexible, fun, and not too demanding.

Secret Ingredient: **For more on personality types, read Julie Kembel's book *ROLE Play*. Call her publisher, Northwest Learning Associates, in Tucson, at 1-520-881-0877 for ordering information.**

 SPIRIT

 JULY 16

Follow "The Rules."

The Ten Commandments may seem outdated and antiquated, but they are still "The Rules." Think of them as "oldies but goodies." As a reminder:

1. **Thou shalt have no other gods before me.** Meaning: bow down to none other. Don't put money, men, or material things before your love of God. Love the Lord with all your heart and soul.
2. **Thou shalt not make unto thee any graven image.** Don't pray to any statues or artwork. God can't be represented.
3. **Thou shalt not take the name of the Lord in vain.** Do you say things like "for Christ sakes, what is the problem?" Or curse using God's name? Rename your frustration, starting now.
4. **Remember the Sabbath Day to keep it holy.** Probably not the best day to go to a Las Vegas casino or volunteer for overtime. Use it to worship, and to rest as God did. He's your God model.

5. **Honor thy father and mother.** As a society, we do a bang-up job of honoring our mothers, but our fathers . . . Many people have been blessed with two loving parents. But if either of yours did not give you the love you think you deserve, at least try to give them respect.

6. **Thou shalt not kill.** I still kill spiders and feel guilty; some people kill other people and don't. Considering the debate over the death penalty, this continues to be a complex subject.

7. **Thou shalt not commit adultery.** If I hear another song or see another talk show about someone sleeping with someone else's wife/husband/girlfriend/boyfriend, I'm going to scream. Adultery is out of control. Continue to seek trust and restrain from hurting the ones you love.

8. **Thou shalt not steal.** . . . . Not a dime from your child's piggy bank, not something you didn't pay for at the drugstore, not office supplies for your home, not embezzlement from the company. Don't "borrow" and "forget" to return either.

9. **Thou shalt not bear false witness against thy neighbor.** Susan Smith bore false witness when she said a black man carjacked her van with her children in it. Your lies on others may never be that big, but they are still destructive and out of order.

10. **Thou shalt not covet they neighbor's goods.** On *The New Newlywed Game,* the host asked, "What does your wife envy that someone else has?" as though that was a given! And the husbands did come up with the answers easily. But remember, every house isn't a happy home. Fabulous luxury cars are putting some people in big debt. As the R&B song says, be thankful for what you've got.

Secret Ingredient: **Review the Ten Commandments and discuss with loved ones what they mean to you.**

 BODY

 JULY 17

Drink up.

It's summer, it's hot, you're constantly thirsty. What should you drink for health (regardless of the time of year)?

Water, water, and more water. Can't say it enough. Drink at least eight eight-ounce glasses a day, and more during periods of physical activity. Drink all day long to prevent dehydration. By the time you feel thirsty, you're probably already dehydrated. Bottled spring water is a good choice.

Juices. Drinking fruit or vegetable juice is an excellent way to quench your thirst and get nutrients too. They're also less high in sugar than soda pops, and lower in caffeine than colas. Remember the commercial "I coulda had a V-8"? Well, you still shoulda.

At an organization's family-picnic day recently, there were coolers full of sodas and coolers full of juices. The adults drank all the sodas and gave the juices to the children. When one man was asked, "Is there anything left to drink?" he replied, "No, just juices." What's wrong with this picture? As you become an adult, it doesn't mean that you can't benefit from the healthful benefits of juice. It's not a childish thing to do. It's smart.

Iced tea, lemonade. Make them heavy on the water, low on the sugar. Try honey.

Secret Ingredient: **Now that the weather is hot, if you have a caffeine addiction, it's a perfect time to ease back on your coffee, tea, or soda intake, and drink water instead.**

 M I N D

✺ JULY 18 ✺

Protect yourself.

Howard University, in Washington, D.C., is in the middle of what one could call an inner-city neighborhood. As a freshman, I went with my dorm mates to a takeout on Georgia Avenue one evening in search of something to call dinner. Although it was after dark, there were several little boys, all under twelve, hanging out, unsupervised. As we interacted with the kids ("What are you doing out so late?" "Where's your mama?"), one adorable Denzel-to-be with a serious expression pointed to my long fingernails.

"Look, man!" he called out wide-eyed to another *enfant.* "Look how long her fingernails are." Then he turned to me. "How do you fight?"

My girls busted up laughing. But it was also sad. I could tell that fighting was a routine, an expected part of this child's life.

No one should have to feel the anxiety of constant assaults on your safety. Living or working in urban communities where crime is a frequent occurrence can have you watching your back. And living in the 'burbs doesn't always make you feel any safer. Arm yourself against the bullies with:

- ❖ **Street smarts.** When you're new to a town, ask other sisters for the rules. When men make comments on the street, for example, should you speak to them and keep walking, or ignore them altogether? In some places, the latter encourages even more confrontation.
- ❖ **A self-defense class.** Find one in the Yellow Pages, your neighborhood YM/YWCA, or ask your local police department for a referral. Ask your child's karate teacher if he instructs adults.
- ❖ **A whistle, Mace, a pocket-size flashlight, even a stern expression** can help you feel more secure when alone.

Secret Ingredient: **Take time to think about how you might react if attacked or assaulted. Contrary to what the little boy thought, my long nails could be an effective weapon—right in the eyes. Fortunately, I've never had to use them.**

 SPIRIT

☀ JULY 19 ☀

Create a sacred space.

Jennifer J. Harrison has one in her Baltimore home. As soon as you peek in, you instantly know this is a special spot. Unlike the common areas where guests are entertained, or the room full of toys her twin boys share, this is a personal, intimate space. It's spare, yet full—of candles, crystals, pictures of ancestors, "personal belongings." A woman's room. The focal point of the space is an altar Jennifer created.

"It all started about twelve years ago when I was praying one day, and I felt I needed a place to put my candle," she says. "I got a table, then I added things to it until, before I knew it, I had created an environment." Jennifer says she began in a closet, then she got a room, and now it's a space that people can see upon entering. "It doesn't have to be elaborate."

Her morning starts there. "It's part of my morning ritual—like brushing my teeth," she says. "Whenever I feel stressed, I go into this sanctuary. It's like therapy for me. Forcing me to commune with myself, it's elevated my level of consciousness and my level of spirituality."

If you would like to create a sacred space of your own, start by collecting whatever accoutrements you feel you need to help make life calmer, gentler. Some suggestions, depending on the size of your space:

❖ Candles, crystals
❖ Photos of loved ones, ancestors, saints
❖ Music
❖ Spiritual books
❖ Incense, potpourri
❖ Treasured gifts
❖ Floor pillows, throws
❖ Ethnic cloth, antique lace
❖ Massage products, oils
❖ Decorative jewelry, cowrie shells
❖ Artwork
❖ A chaise longue

Use the room as you like. It can be place in which to pray, meditate, read, write, nap, keep a journal, compose poetry, play an instrument, de-stress, think—or do nothing.

"It's not just important, it's imperative," said Maya Angelou on HGTV about having a room of your own. "In quietude one might hear the voice of God—and we are all healed in that moment."

Secret Ingredient: **Search within and create a sacred space for yourself.**

 BODY

❋ JULY 20 ❋

Take an active-adventure vacation.

Going to a spa isn't the only way you can travel and get fit. There's a whole industry dubbed "active travel" that specializes in outdoor vacations that feature fitness activities. "Adventure travel" takes it to the next level, challenging mind and body limits. Now, if visions of climbing Mount Kilimanjaro are enough to keep you home watching the Discovery Channel, consider these other options:

Active Travel:

❖ **Walking tours.** For starters, you can find sightseeing tours conducted on foot in just about any major city in the world. There are walking tours of lovely countrysides. And if you really get into it, you can join a walking club that plans vacation trips. *Prevention* magazine has such as club. Look for information in

each issue of the magazine, or check online at
www.prevention.com.

- ❖ **Bike tours.** Sisters *are* doing this kind of stuff. My friend
  Deborah J. Mitchell called one day to tell me all about her bike
  trip in Italy. She even had the courage to go alone, knowing that
  when she got there, she'd be part of a group. She booked her
  tour through Cielismo Classico (which also sponsors walking
  tours) at 1-800-866-7314. Want to stay closer to home? VBT is
  a tour operator that can hook you up for bicycling vacations in
  the States, Canada, and Europe. Call 1-800-BIKE TOUR.
- ❖ Backroads [1-800-GO-ACTIVE], the largest bike tour operator,
  offers a five-day sampler of mountain biking, inline skating,
  sailboarding, and rock climbing. The trip, which takes place in
  Northern California, welcomes first-timers.

Adventure travel:

- ❖ For the experienced and adventurous, this kind of trip takes you
  parasailing, backpacking, canoeing, kayaking, white-water
  rafting, mountain climbing, or wherever you dare. Outward
  Bound exhibitions promote wilderness skills and teamwork. Call
  them at 1-888-88 BOUND.

Secret Ingredient: **Make sure you ask the sponsors how to get
physically fit for the journey. You'll have to be in top shape for this
kind of travel.**

 MIND

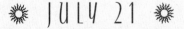

Make the mind-body connection.

It's pretty common knowledge that many experts now espouse a mind-
body connection. That is, that there is a relationship between mental and
physical health. The immune system of our bodies responds to our
thoughts and emotions. You can try to make that connection with these
mental exercises:

- ❖ **Optimism.** Are you a person who sees the glass half empty or
  half full? If you insist the glass is half empty, that will affect your
  reality. On the other hand, if you are optimistic instead of
  pessimistic, you can at least expect a positive outcome.

- ❖ **Creative visualization.** Susan Anderson, my former sister-in-law, gave me a book by this name many years ago, which I still have. The premise is to mentally see yourself healthy, happy, and experiencing wellness. The author, Shakti Gawain, provides meditations and affirmations to help you discover your conscious connection with your higher self in order to fulfill your desires and make dynamic changes in your life.
- ❖ **Stress strategies.** When you develop fatigue, a headache, a cold, PMS, or other common ailment, do you have a set plan of attack? You've experienced these conditions periodically throughout your life, so you may have effective ways of dealing with them—from Mama's chicken gumbo to bedrest. Let your mind control the illness before it controls you.
- ❖ **Positive outlook.** A New York high school grad, Clemente Robles, who received a college scholarship, was interviewed during WNBC-TV's coverage of the National Puerto Rican Day parade in 1998. Advising young people to stay on the positive path, he said, "Positive things happen to positive people!"

Secret Ingredient: **Follow these principles, create a mind/body connection, and watch the transformation in your life.**

❀ SPIRIT

☀ JULY 22 ☀

All hail the power of church worship.

*W*hy bother to go to church? I posed the question to Reverend Daniela Morrisey, minister of Christian Education and Special Projects at St. Paul Baptist Church in Montclair, New Jersey, and offered to let her be a "guest preacher" for this page. Here's the lovely story she shared.

I remember as a child trying to get out of going to Sunday school and church. I would tell my mother that I didn't feel well. My mother would reply, "Okay, then you can't go out and play this afternoon if you feel sick." I tried to convince my mother that I would feel better in the afternoon (after church was over), but she wasn't going for it.

I came to realize that going to church wasn't so bad. I made friends, all of whose parents had the same idea about church attendance as mine did. We went on trips and did all kinds of fun activities, all while learning about God. I think the most valuable lesson I learned was to give God priority in our lives.

Adults with similar rearing to mine say that God is important to them, but they don't put God first. We let our children decide whether or not they want to go to church. We set the example that church is not important when we are more interested in watching the game, or catching up on work or sleep. We complain that two hours in church is just too long, while many of us spend well over ten hours a day at work. We think if we listen to gospel music at home, or watch preachers on television and do good things, that this is good enough.

God calls us to be in relationship—in relationship with God and with each other. When we go to church and worship and study together, we are in relationship. Going to church creates a space for you to fellowship and be in a community. Sometimes, in the midst of community, God will use someone to touch you in a special way. Our ancestors understood the power of worshipping in a community.

In this individualistic society we have been duped into believing that on our own we can please God, that by ourselves we can honor God. But God created us to interact with other people. To make the ultimate connection with God, we need to make the connection with other believers in study, worship, and fellowship.

Secret Ingredient: **Read Acts 2:44–47, in the Bible.**

 BODY

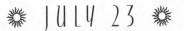 JULY 23

Love yourself clean.

Here's one of the easiest tips I may ever give you: Wash yourself lovingly. It's something you can do starting today.

When you wash your face, massage it gently—don't attack. A dermatologist told me this when I was fourteen years old and had a face full of acne; I've never forgotten it. Your face is not the enemy. Why do we think we need to rub it vigorously in order to clean it? Most of us are not working in coal mines every day. Put a dollop of liquid cleanser in your hand or use a moisturizing facial soap. Gently massage your skin; touch every nook and cranny. Love every wrinkle and feature. Bless your eyes. Caress your cheeks. Using your washcloth, feel the curvature of your ears as you clean them. Rinse off your face as though you were using holy water.

Do the same for your teeth. Brushing your teeth and gums too hard can cause eroding of the enamel and the gumline. Taking at least two full minutes, brush slowly (using a soft-bristled brush), but thoroughly, the surface of the teeth where you chew, uppers and lowers; then with teeth together, brush horizontally the outside from one side of your smile to the other. Finally, place your brush at a forty-five-degree angle against your gums and brush where the teeth meet the gums, and brush horizontally inside and outside.

Floss your teeth afterward to remove any remaining food or plaque between the teeth. Again, take your time and don't snap the floss. You could damage your teeth with harsh action. Heed your dentist's advice: brush and floss after every meal.

Secret Ingredient: **Does your toothbrush look like a Mack truck ran over it? Replace your toothbrush regularly (dentists suggest every three months). To get in the habit, buy one every other time you purchase toothpaste. Look for *soft* bristle brushes. To make flossing more fun, buy the mint-flavored kind. If you haven't had your teeth cleaned in the past six months, make an appointment today.**

 MIND

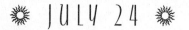 J U L Y 24

Keep on pushin'.

Few, if any, great things are accomplished with ease. It's almost inherent in the definition of greatness to push the boundaries of being just plain good or adequate. You've got to push and push, sometimes against a wall of resistance. When you're trying to raise children, go to work, *and* go to school, you've got to push yourself. You've got to cook dinner, do your homework, and check your *children's* homework even when you don't feel like it. You've got to keep on pushin'.

People thought that winning was easy for Chicago Bulls basketball player Michael Jordan, that he was a natural. After winning the National Basketball Association championship following his father's death, and his return to the game after playing baseball, Jordan showed that success is a challenge—even for a superstar. On MSNBC's *Time & Again*, in an interview with Jane Pauley, Jordan explains earnestly: "You can't do it unless you push yourself."

Another great person agrees. Author Toni Morrison was asked in *Essence* magazine by writer A. J. Verdelle how she managed in the early days of her writing career to work full-time, raise two young sons, and write great books. "All the women I knew did nine or ten things at one time," Morrison replied. "All important things are hard."

As Susan L. Taylor, the editor in chief of *Essence,* says: "Life is work."

Secret Ingredient: **Keep pushing toward your goal. If the work gets hard, that's a sign that you're doing the right thing and that the reward will be all the greater.**

 SPIRIT

☀ JULY 25 ☀

Follow the spirit of life.

Hurdles. That's what I call them. Those invisible blockades that you get to when your spirit is running free. And when you encounter them, you have to decide whether to stop running, to walk around them—or to jump over.

In accepting the 1997 NAACP Image Award for Best Actor in *Amistad,* actor Djimon Hounsou said, "Steven Spielberg is in devotion with the spirit of life. When you have that, it doesn't matter whether you're black or white." That made me ponder my admiration for filmmaker Steven Spielberg, first for daring to direct *The Color Purple.* I'm sure Spielberg, the director of the blockbuster mainstream flicks *Close Encounters* and *Jurassic Park,* took much heat from whites for bothering to make a black movie. I remember all the controversy that surrounded the movie about the portrayal of black men. And when he was snubbed for the Oscars for his work on *The Color Purple,* I figured that Spielberg would give up on making movies with an African American theme. But then along came Debbie Allen's project, *Amistad.* It would have been easy for Spielberg not to listen to Allen's reasons about its importance and let his past experience jade him. Fortunately, he listened to his inner voice and took on another extraordinary black movie. I also found out that Spielberg was inspired to make *Amistad* for his adopted African American son.

In devotion with the spirit of life. That's deep. So many of us find the spirit of *American* life too restrictive, literally too black and white, with lines we dare not cross. Making friendships across racial lines—why bother? Embracing knowledge of some other culture? Too much trouble. Traveling to countries that don't speak your language—out of our feeling of control. We don't make these small steps, much less any of the hard or major hurdles of the racial divide, such as hiring people of various colors to achieve diversity in the workplace, or live a life that can be characterized as inclusive. For many of us, our acceptance of another race is limited to our consumption of foreign cuisine.

As an African living in America, Djimon Hounsou knows what he's talking about. His own incredible journey from homelessness to achievement is a testament to the magnificent spirit of life.

Secret Ingredient: **Take time today to think about what's necessary for the enrichment and empowerment of your spiritual life.**

❋ BODY

❋ JULY 26 ❋

Know what we're doing right.

There are so many studies that point to disheartening statistics about the state of black health. We all know by now that African Americans are more prone to obesity, hypertension, heart disease, diabetes, HIV-AIDS, and sickle cell anemia. But did you know that there were some diseases we are *less* likely to get? Here are a few, first reported in *Heart & Soul:*

Alcoholism: Black women are less likely than white women to drink alcohol, and we report fewer personal and social problems related to alcohol consumption.

Certain cancers: *Skin cancer:* Our melanin-rich skin protects us and serves as a barrier to sunlight. Most commonly, when we do contract skin cancer, it is usually on the bottoms of our feet or the palms of our hands, the parts of our bodies with the fairest skin. *Ovarian cancer:* We have lower rates than white women. *Breast cancer:* We also have lower rates of contracting breast cancer, but because we don't seek treatment as early as white women, we have lower survival rates.

Multiple sclerosis: Nine out of ten people who get this disease of the central nervous system are of white ancestry; for example, the Bantus in Africa never get it.

Suicide: One of the reasons deaths such as that of singer Phyllis Hyman affect us so deeply is that very few African American celebrities have committed suicide.

Secret Ingredient: By knowing the areas in which we are succeeding in taking control of our health, we can contemplate what we are doing right and apply the tactics to areas of our wellness that need our attention. The first step toward turning around negative statistics: early detection.

 MIND

Instigate!

You're determined to lose weight. You've decided to get fit. You've made a pact to cut fat from your diet. No matter what your wellness goal is, you can plan a strategy for accomplishing it with the following guidelines.

- ❖ **Educate:** Learn all you can about the basics of your goal. Read books on the subject. Go online and read more. Cut out magazine and newspaper articles. Ask experts how to achieve your goal. Keep notes.
- ❖ **Investigate:** Find out how much the cost will be. Comparison-shop. Get second opinions. Make sure you understand the pros and cons, the benefits and side effects.
- ❖ **Facilitate:** Decide where the best place would be to carry out your goal—at home? at a gym? If you are going to start a new fitness class, for example, make sure you check out the facilities on a day before the class starts. Know what to expect in terms of the dressing room, shower, even parking availability.
- ❖ **Dedicate:** Once you've decided to commit yourself to the goal, commit yourself to a trial period that will let you see if you feel it's a "can do" task. Once you know how long it will take before you see results, stick with it.
- ❖ **Celebrate:** When you have achieved your goal, give yourself praise by doing something that affirms the goal. For example, if you had treatment for a dental problem, buy yourself a snazzy new toothbrush or a luscious new lipstick. If you completed your first fitness class, pick out an affordable outfit for your next class!

Secret Ingredient: **Enlist your mate.** Having a buddy to help you reach your goal is always helpful. If you have the same goals, doing it together can double the fun.

☀ JULY 28 ☀

Ask God what's up.

When we pray, I truly believe we don't have to be concerned with using biblical language. It's okay to use "thou" and "thine" and "shalt" if that makes you feel the connection to the ancient. But don't let anxiety over the right way to talk to God stop you from having the conversation.

What is important is worship, respect, glorification, submission, and humility. In talking with Spirit, bring who you are to the prayer.

After a lifetime of starting prayers with a parental greeting of "Our Father" or "Father in Heaven/Mother Earth" or something on that order, one evening in exhaustion I let out a huge sigh and heard myself say in prayer, "What's up, God?" Then I got a feeling of amusement and rejuvenation. "What's up" could have myriad meanings, such as:

❖ What's going on in heaven?
❖ What is important and on the up-and-up?
❖ What is positive?
❖ What is uplifting?

At that moment of fatigue I wanted to know how to get up! I needed to get back up to my usual peppy self. I needed some information on getting on up, and not being down and depressed. I actually needed God to tell me what was up. No disrespect intended.

Marvin Gaye sang a song called "God Is My Friend." Most Christian churches sing "What a Friend We Have in Jesus." If God is your friend, feel free to confide in Him in a way that is intimate for you. Ask what's up. And you just might get the divine answer.

Secret Ingredient: **God knows every language and created every word. The words of your mouth are only as effective as the meditation of your heart.**

❋ JULY 29 ❋

Don't get burned.

I grew up with this pervasive attitude when it came to sun tanning: *You're black enough already, what do you need to tan for?*

Then the "Black Is Beautiful" philosophy changed the paradigm, and all of a sudden it was a big deal to come back to college after spring break with a tan. After a trip to Panama, where I hung out on an island beach that was said to be near the equator, I went back to school jet black and thought I was all that! Even black people could get blacker. Stokely Carmichael would be proud.

I was so dumb. I knew that we melanin-rich people have built-in sun protection that soaks up UV light and scatters the photon radiation, keeping it from penetrating more deeply. But what I didn't know is that even deep-brown pigment provides only as much protection as a sunscreen with an SPF of 4 or 6. That's far below the SPF of 15 that dermatologists recommend as protection against skin damage. In addition, we *can* and do burn (ouch! I've been there) when we are overexposed and underprotected. And the long-term effects of baking in the sun can damage our skin in ways we may think are the result of something else—like aging.

We're not *totally* immune to skin cancer either. Black is beautiful in a wide range of shades. The more fair-skinned we are, the greater our chances of contracting it. And brown-skinned folks can get it too; typically, on the bottoms of our feet and on the palms of our hands, places where we are less melanin-endowed.

Let me tell you, I was a person who *worked* on my tan every chance I got. But ever since I noticed a big brown splotch on my cheek, I've become a recovering sun-aholic. I'm slathering on the lotion, collecting straw hats, and discovering the joys of sitting under a big, shady umbrella.

Secret Ingredient: **Just because you've got African sun in your blood doesn't mean you don't have to wear sunscreen. An SPF of 6 to 8 is adequate for everyday use. If you're going to be vacationing in the sun or engaging in outdoor sports or other summer activities, use a waterproof sunscreen with an SPF of at least 15.**

❋ JULY 30 ❋

Make a positive impression.

My cousin Melanie Smith records a "food for thought" message at the end of her telephone answering machine greeting. One day when I called, I was told to "remember that you have only one chance to make a first impression. Make it a good one." I liked that, and have tried to act on it.

Two occasions of meeting people I admired have illustrated the impact of first impressions for me. Both happened to be academicians. I was pretty nervous to meet the illustrious, muckety-muck of a prestigious university, who shall remain nameless. In Europe for an arts conference one winter, my girlfriend and I had brought only our fur coats, not knowing that the weather would be mild. We felt self-conscious about our mistake and couldn't wait to go shopping. But first, we saw an opportunity to meet The Man, and we gathered the nerve to walk up to him and extend our hands. He pointed to our coats and said, "There must not be any more animals left in the jungle!" He had made fun of us before we could even be introduced. We were so disappointed!

On another occasion, I had the pleasure of meeting Dr. Johnetta B. Cole, who was then president of Spelman College. She was visiting Susan Taylor in the *Essence* offices when Susan invited the staff in to meet her. "I'm so proud to meet you . . ." I began. She interrupted my fumbling with a warm handshake: "And I am proud of *you!*" I thought, *How gracious of her to say she was proud of someone she didn't even know anything about.* Recently, I had the pleasure of telling her how much her gesture had meant to me, and that I try to replicate it with young people I meet.

I don't always succeed. Sometimes, I, too, talk before I think. But Cousin Melanie (whose bubbly personality probably always makes a positive first impression) has definitely got the right idea.

Secret Ingredient: **If you or someone else makes a bad first impression, help them out, the way Dr. Cole helped me. Remember the Golden Rule: Do unto others as you would have them do unto you.**

❋ JULY 31 ❋

Breathe deeply.

We all take breathing for granted, don't we? It usually seems to come so naturally.

But when it becomes belabored because of asthma or emphysema or maybe just because we've been crying, it becomes the most important thing in the world.

Give the breath of life some appreciation today. Stop now and take a deep breath. Feel the air fill up your lungs. Exhale slowly, experiencing its movement down to your abdomen. Repeat two more times. Give thanks for the unencumbered, unaided exchange of oxygen and carbon dioxide.

Then breathe easy.

Secret Ingredient: **If you want a long life of deep breathing, avoid any and all contact with tobacco. Stay away from people who smoke and the areas in which they smoke. Do not allow smoking in your home, your car, your work area, or anywhere near you. Teach your children these guidelines early. Start them early loving the air they breathe.**

❋ MIND

❋ AUGUST 1 ❋

Boost your confidence.

Everyone loses self-confidence at some time or another. When the boss says something disparaging about your work. When you realize you were wrong and have to admit it. Or maybe your love life is giving signals that you need to "get a life."

Yet you don't have time to sit around and stew about it. Duty still calls. When you're feeling down but have to be up, how do you do it? Here are some sisterly suggestions:

❖ **Hold your head up.** It's a thin line between eating humble pie and wanting to throw the pie in someone's face! Let your demeanor show the strong stuff you're made of. Author and editor Rosemary L. Bray wrote an essay about the women of her childhood who had "a real sense of themselves: who . . . shared, among other things, a wonderful sense of fun, yet they were neither frivolous nor self-absorbed." Their demeanor said: "I laugh and I joke, but I don't play."

- ❖ **Act the part.** Literally *act* like you've got it all together (they don't call it a balancing act for nothing). Play the role of self-confidence as if you were competing for an Academy Award. Look people in the eye. Speak with self-assurance. Project an air of conviction but not arrogance.
- ❖ **Keep calm.** Contrary to how we may feel, blowing off steam doesn't make us look confident—it often makes us look foolish. Calm down and listen to the criticism or advice from others. How can you learn if you're doing all the talking? It will help boost your confidence to find out ways not to repeat a mistake.
- ❖ **Imagine a positive outcome.** Think about how you want to resolve the conflict. Do your research, then strategize a winning plan. It will help you feel more in control.
- ❖ **Wear your "confidence clothes."** Put on that killer suit that always makes you feel on top. Lively up yourself with makeup. Paint your nails, do your hair. *Feeling* confident goes a long way toward *being* confident.

Secret Ingredient: Smile. As Maya Angelou would say, you're still a child of God.

 BODY

❋ AUGUST 2 ❋

Build on the soul food pyramid.

You've heard of the food pyramid, right? That's the plan the federal government unveiled in 1992 to define a balanced diet. Well, in 1996, three registered dietitians in Orlando, Florida, developed the soul food pyramid. The founding partners of Hebni Nutrition Consultants, Roniece Weaver, Fabiola D. Gaines, and Ellareetha Carson, felt that the USDA pyramid was a good guideline, but that there was a need to acknowledge the traditional soul food diet of African Americans.

Envision the shape of a pyramid, with these food groups from the base up:

Eat Liberally: Breads, Cereal, Rice, and Pasta Group (6–11 servings daily): Brown bread, biscuits, rice, grits, macaroni, noodles, non-sugar-coated flake cereal, oatmeal or Cream of Wheat, crackers, bagels

Eat Generously: Vegetables Group (3–5 servings daily): Collard, okra, snap beans, pole beans, turnips, kale, mustard greens, green cabbage, potatoes, sweet potatoes, squash, corn, carrots, onions; low-sodium vegetable juice

Eat Generously: Fruit Group (2–4 servings daily): Apple, banana, peach, mango, orange, pear, grapefruit, cantaloupe, grapes, strawberries or blackberries, 100 percent fruit juice (not fruit punch or presweetened drink), canned fruit packed in light syrup, natural fruit juice

Eat Moderately: Meats, Poultry, Fish, Dry Beans, Eggs, and Nut Group (2–3 servings daily): Poultry, lean beef, fish, lean pork, eggs, lean lamb, lean ground meats, cooked dried peas or beans, peanut butter, nuts

Eat Moderately: Milk, Cheese, and Yogurt Group (2–3 servings daily): One percent or skim milk, buttermilk, or lactose-free milk, ice cream, ice milk, or low-fat frozen yogurt, natural cheese (cheddar, provolone, mozzarella), cottage cheese, low-fat yogurt

Eat Sparingly: Snacks and Sweets Group: Snack foods such as chips, cheese puffs, corn chips, and pork skins should be eaten only occasionally because they are high in sugar, fat, and salt. These foods do not have enough nutrients to fit in any of the basic food groups. Go easy on rich desserts, candies, soft drinks, and alcoholic beverages.

Eat Sparingly: Fats, Oils: The small tip of the pyramid shows high-fat meats, snacks, vegetable fats and oils, salt, and sweets. Foods such as chitterlings, sausage, bacon, pork neckbones, fat back, hog jowls, and pigs' feet are traditionally used in the African American diet as meats. Due to the high fat content, these foods belong to the Fats, Oil, Sweets Group and should be used sparingly. Foods in this group provide calories that are low in nutrients.

Secret Ingredient: **Watch what you eat! Get into the habit of reading the labels of the foods you buy. Canned food contains a surprisingly high amount of sugar and salt.**

❋ AUGUST 3 ❋

Jump for joy!

You got the promotion you'd been working toward. Or you married and started the family you'd planned. Or maybe your joy comes in the absence of any problems—for the time being. However it may manifest itself, happiness needs to be acknowledged and accepted.

Too often we wallow in our problems so long that when something wonderful happens, we can't accept it or don't believe we deserve it or we suppress it so someone else won't be jealous. But jumping for joy is empowering to the spirit. Here are ways to bask in the moment:

❖ **Make a joyful noise.** Let out a staccato "Yes!" Let others know when things are going well, in a comparable manner to the "Oh, no!" you moan when things fall apart. I'll never forget the TV news clips of Myrlie Evers-Williams shouting for joy when the assassin of her first husband, civil rights leader Medgar Evers, was finally brought to justice after thirty years. It marked a moment of triumph for us all. Some things just shouldn't be taken quietly.

❖ **Make a joyful gesture.** Whom does it hurt when football players make a touchdown, then do a dance in the end zone? Acknowledging your breakthrough relieves the pressure. Uninhibited joy about your own win doesn't mean that you want anyone else to lose. Don't be arrogant, but don't let others kill your spirit either.

❖ **Make a joyful showing.** Got another big, bad bill paid off? Post your zero-balance statement on your bulletin board. Surrounding yourself with your success reminds you that "you can do it!"

❖ **Make a joyful sharing.** Did others help you reach your success? Was it teamwork all the way? Share your good news with those who wish you well. Thank the people on whose shoulders you stand.

❖ **Make a joyful prayer.** Don't forget to give God the glory.

Secret Ingredient: If it seems that you sing the blues more often than you jump for joy, consider keeping a Joy Journal. Document all the things that give you joy. Then, when you feel down, take out the journal, give it a read, and give it a chance to turn your mood around.

✸ AUGUST 4 ✸

Perfect being imperfect.

Many of us think of ourselves as perfectionists—and that's okay if your definition means that you're a striver toward the highest degree of excellence. But if in your heart you know what you're really doing is trying to be flawless, to never be wrong, to never make or admit mistakes, it's time to be real.

"My parents were perfectly imperfect, but they were the perfect parents for me," says actress Sheryl Lee Ralph. That's a high compliment. As others will tell you, some of your charming imperfections are exactly what make you perfect.

In trying to be perfect parents, we run the risk of making our children resentful that we show no vulnerability, no forgiveness. Plus, doing everything by the book can stress you out. If you're a new parent, and the book says "let the baby cry" but your instincts say "pick her up and cuddle her," then which one is the perfect solution? Which one will make you a more caring parent? Then again, there are times your instincts will tell you that letting the baby cry is okay. Those are the times in which you are guided not by some perceived rules of perfection, but by your feelings.

Then there's perfection at work. Say you're an artist and you've done rendering after rendering but don't make deadlines. Or you take up other people's time making sure things are your way.

I remember that when I graduated from college, my boyfriend, in his effort to impress my parents, went to get his car washed before picking them up from the hotel to transport them to my commencement. What he *thought* he was doing was making sure his car (and, by association, he) was perfect. What he accomplished was nothing, because going to the car wash meant running late to pick them up, and that was one time my family definitely wanted to be *early.* They didn't care about how his car looked—they wanted to see how *I* looked getting that diploma. After waiting for him and becoming anxious, they took a taxi. So, my poor boyfriend's attempt at perfection was a total bomb. Being on time, and using his charm, would have been the better move.

Secret Ingredient: **Follow your instincts to put priorities over perfectionism. As the old folks used to say, "You got to know when to leave 'well enough' alone."**

✹ AUGUST 5 ✹

Treat your feet.

There are few things more un-cute than a pair of crusty feet in a pair of chic sandals. There are women who think getting a professional pedicure is a self-indulgent waste of time and money. There are those who couldn't live without the luxury. And somewhere in between are the rest of us. But all of us, at some time or another in the summer, could use these treats to banish funky feet:

Do the prep. Remove any nail polish. With a toenail clipper, cut your nails straight across, squaring off the sides rather than rounding them, to avoid ingrown toenails. Then gently shape them with a nail file.

Smooth. Use a pumice stone to smooth the bottoms of your feet, the calluses, the heels, your toes.

Soothe. Soak both feet in a mini bubble bath. Or, for the ultimate moisturizing experience, submerge them instead in a half gallon of warm milk. Allow ten minutes, then rinse.

Massage. Rub on your favorite body or foot cream.

Push 'em back, push 'em back . . . Using an orange stick, push the cuticles. Then top off all your toes with a wet nailbrush. I put on brightly colored foam toe separators for the next step.

Polish. Here's the nail polish routine: Base coat. Wait one minute. Two coats nail polish. Wait three minutes. Top coat. While it dries, sit back, relax, and admire your fancy footwork.

Secret Ingredient: **An all-time favorite ashy-feet fighter: good old petroleum jelly. Apply liberally before going to bed and cover feet with cotton socks. There will be a noticeable difference in the morning!**

❋ AUGUST 6 ❋

Expect the best.

Because the quote is one of my favorites and is fresh in my mind, I hadn't expected to look through so many back issues of *Essence* to find it. But finally, after searching my home archives, I dusted off the February 1991 love story of Randall and Hazel Robinson. The interviewer, *Washington Post* columnist Donna Britt, had asked Hazel if her life with the founder of TransAfrica, whom she describes as "the perfect husband," ever seemed too good to be true. Looking surprised at the notion, Hazel answers, "I don't think anything could happen to me that would be too good to be true. I was raised to expect the best in life."

That was so affirming for me! I had been raised the same way by supportive parents, a loving extended family, and encouraging teachers. All topped off by messages received in church in songs such as the one that goes: "It is no secret what God can do/What he's done for others, he'll do for you." I had seen wonderful things happen to other people, and I never doubted that wonderful things would happen to me too. And they have and still do.

The Sudanese model Alek Wek expresses a similar belief. When asked in *Oneworld* magazine if she was suspicious when model bookers, agents, and photographers suddenly declared her the "hot new thing," she responded, "I'm never suspicious of life."

On *60 Minutes,* journalist Mike Wallace talked with singer Tina Turner as they walked around her magnificent pool that overlooks a dramatic scenic view. "Do you think you deserve all this?" Wallace asked.

With a teasing laugh and a toss of her head, Tina jumped into her Hummer and answered, "I deserve more!"

Secret Ingredient: **Expect that life has wonderful things in store for you. It's not arrogant or conceited to have this mind-set. It's called faith.**

❉ AUGUST 7 ❉

Garden your way to good health.

My mother enjoys what she calls "working in the yard." When we were children, my sister and I thought Mom spent so much time there that we dubbed her "Flower-tendin' Flora." Of course, we were being brats who were making fun of the time and effort our mother put into creating the lovely garden that surrounded our happy home, but now we know that Mom's the one who had the last laugh. That's because of the health and fitness benefits of gardening:

- ❖ **It's good exercise.** Mowing the lawn can be a serious aerobic workout.
- ❖ **It builds muscle tone** doing all that squatting and lifting.
- ❖ **It gives you good stretches** when you're reaching for this tool, pulling up that weed.
- ❖ **Has a calming effect** that can reduce stress and help lower blood pressure.
- ❖ **It can give you a sense of pride** in the achievement of a creating something beautiful. Community gardens have brought neighbors together for a common cause that cuts across income, gender, and race.
- ❖ **Gardening boosts mental and spiritual health** in the admiration of God's growing things.

Secret Ingredient: Whether you're an avid gardener or have a literal "brown thumb" like me, you can reap the joys of cultivating the beautiful plants of nature. Have at least one plant in your apartment, house, or office. If you're a novice, ask your nursery salesperson for a low-maintenance plant. Is there a community garden you can help out with? Whether in your own yard or around the 'hood, you can help make your neighborhood a lovely place.

❈ AUGUST 8 ❈

Hit the numbers.

Knowing the target numbers for healthy blood pressure, cholesterol, and body mass is a first step in working toward your fitness goals. Here are some important numbers for you to try to hit.

BLOOD PRESSURE

What it is: When the pressure of the blood pumped from the heart through the arteries is elevated, making the heart work harder, it's called high blood pressure. When the heart doesn't have to work very hard, it's low to normal.

How it's determined: By two numbers, the *systolic,* the pressure exerted when the heart beats, over the *diastolic,* when the heart is at rest between beats. *Normal:* 135/85 or lower; *Borderline:* 135/85 to 140/90; *High:* 140/90 or above.

The number that's a winner: 120/80

CHOLESTEROL

What it is: Elevated blood cholesterol produces plaque-filled fatty deposits in the arteries, impeding blood flow.

How it's determined: Cholesterol travels through the body by *lipoproteins.* There are two types of lipoproteins: *high-density lipoproteins* (HDLs, the good cholesterol) and *low-density lipoproteins* (LDLs, the bad cholesterol). The total of both are measured, along with the ratio between the total and HDL.

The number to hit: Less than 200 total cholesterol. A healthy ratio is below 4.

BODY MASS INDEX (BMI)

What it is: A measure of fitness that determines weight in relation to height.

How it's determined: Divide your weight in pounds by the square of your height in inches and multiply that number by 705. For example, at 5 feet 5 and 115 pounds, I calculate my BMI like this: 65 times 65 equals 4,225; divide 115 by the 4,225; then multiply that 0.0272189 by 705 to equal 19.18.

The number that's the winner: Below 27 (women with 19 or less have the lowest death rates).

Secret Ingredient: **Your doctor should conduct the first two tests and advise you on all three if you need to improve.**

❋ AUGUST 9 ❋

Give somebody a soul hug.

Sammy Davis, Jr., gave one to President Richard Nixon on national TV and stunned the country. When the Queen of England toured the United States, she got one from a woman she visited in a housing project, who was just following the "protocol" she was accustomed to in the 'hood. And it's reported that the chief executive of the largest black business in the nation greets people with a big, warm *hug*.

As Alice Walker writes in her book *The Same River Twice* observing the difference between her book and the movie version of *The Color Purple*, "A hug in our culture has always seemed more soulful than a kiss."

The soul kiss gets all the buzz, the air kiss is the New York fashion-crowd custom, but the soul hug is the worldwide people connector. A kiss is intimate, romantic, sexual. A hug is personal, sociable, literally embracing. It's a signal of acceptance, of affection, or warmth. It's down home.

TLC Beatrice International Holdings, Inc., is number one on the *Black Enterprise* list of one hundred largest black-owned businesses. Loida N. Lewis, the petite CEO of TLC (The Lewis Company), is known for the big hugs she dispenses. *Working Woman* magazine reported that "a hug from Lewis has become a key corporate incentive, and she hands out copies of *The Little Book of Hugs,* a baby-blue compendium of the theory and practice of embracing." The secret to her success, perhaps? Lewis speaks five languages, but her hugs speak a universal language. Maybe TLC (The Lewis Company) could also stand for tender loving care?

Men are starting to hug each other more. It's becoming common to see brothers extend a hand to another for a handshake that pulls them into a bear hug. A beautiful sight in our hard, tough world.

And despite the hard-core music our children are exposed to, it seems that they are embracing each other more than ever. "Have you noticed how much Anique and her friends hug each other?" my husband asked me while we were observing our daughter with a group of friends. "They hug way more than we did." And that's a good sign for the future.

Secret Ingredient: "Border babies" need hugs. Senior citizens need hugs. Volunteer to administer "hug therapy" to people in need. Your reward? Giving a hug means you also get one in return.

❈ AUGUST 10 ❈

Cruise away the blues.

I love to cruise. Somehow, getting on a boat makes me feel that I've left my worries behind at the pier. Looking at the world from the vantage point of the sea can give you a new perspective. The soothing rocking of the boat has lulled many an insomniac into sleeping like a baby.

I've experienced three types of boat trips that I've found soothing and have given me peace of mind:

❖ **Day cruises.** Recently, as a result of whining about not having had a date in too long, my husband took me on a "blues cruise." We didn't even know the female vocalist or anyone else on the boat, but we had a good time with each other, hugged up watching the sights and the folks. In New York City, New Orleans, and other coastal areas, there are also "jazz cruises." I've been on a Gil Scott-Heron jam, and just missed one starring Angela Bofill. Check the entertainment sections of local newspapers and listen out for radio promotions.

❖ **Weekend cruises.** This is a good way to wet your feet and see if you even like spending the night at sea before you go on a full-fledged cruise. Reg and I once went on a "cruise to nowhere," just out to sea on Friday and returning on Sunday. Other trips go to ports nearby, say, a round trip from Seattle to Victoria, Canada. I find the cost of these trips to be pretty reasonable. In port cities, check the travel sections of the newspaper, or your travel agent, for more information.

❖ **The black boat and other floating hotels.** Just like resorts, there are cruise ships for every whim. The current hot thing is the "black cruise." Patricia Yarbrough, president of Blue World Travel in San Francisco and organizer of the popular cruise events called Festival at Sea, says her full-ship charters are "designed to reflect the African American community." Besides the celebrity entertainment, bid whist tournaments, and community service events, there are health and fitness activities such as volleyball, funky aerobics, water aerobics, step classes, and a spa and gym on board.

Secret Ingredient: **Not to worry, if you can't afford to go away. Consult your local phone book and head toward the closest park with a body of water. If you live in the desert, find a quiet place and** listen to an environmental tape of a waterfall or ocean. The tapes are available at most libraries or can be purchased at most record stores or bookstores.

☀ AUGUST 11 ☀

Wear shades.

If you like sporting a hat with a brim and sunglasses, you aren't just being cool, you're being smart. New studies show that exposure to ultraviolet B (UV-B) can lead to cataracts, a condition that forms a clouding of the eye's lens and impairs vision.

One study, from the Wilmer Eye Institute at Johns Hopkins University in Baltimore, studied more than twenty-five hundred people, including twenty-six percent who were African Americans. The research showed that the higher their lifetime exposure to UV-B radiation, the stronger their chances of developing cataracts after age sixty-five. Sunlight includes radiation, which includes invisible ultraviolet light that's absorbed in large doses by the eye's lens and cornea. Aging is another cause of cataracts, but unlike aging, UV-B exposure can be prevented.

How? Three easy ways:

* **By wearing plastic glasses.** The most popular type of eyeglasses today, plastic lenses absorb ninety-eight percent of the light.
* **By wearing plastic sunglasses.** The best kinds have stickers or hang tags that inform you of their degree of UV-B protection. Wraparound glasses prevent rays from "sneaking" in the sides.
* **By sporting a hat.** The wider the brim, the better the protection from the sun. Even if you don't get sunburned when you're outdoors, the sun could be damaging your eyes. Cataracts tend to develop slowly and painlessly.

There are other eye conditions you can get from overexposure to sun and sand. I remember a Bahamian tourist board executive telling me he was about to have eye surgery for sand buildup in his eyes over the years. More frequent use of sunglasses would have helped. He got the message, so can you.

Secret Ingredient: Don't keep just babies in cute sun hats, but kids of all ages. Develop the habit in children early of wearing sunglasses and hats.

✳ AUGUST 12 ✳

Become your own victory.

Several years ago I had the pleasure of attending a Spelman College commencement. The graduating class that year was the largest in the school's history to date. The soulfulness of African American womanhood permeated the program, with the school's first "sister-president," Dr. Johnetta B. Cole at the helm. Renowned poet and activist Sonia Sanchez composed and read "A Love Song for Spelman." And the senior class president, Kyra Stinson, gave a farewell address that sounded like the beginning of an adult life of leadership.

So it was appropriate that the commencement speaker be someone who cared about African American women too. Indeed, this one did to the degree of providing a $20 million gift to the school, sixty percent of which would be used for an impressive academic center that today is clearly visible from the front gates of the school. The commencement speaker was—you guessed it—Camille Olivia Hanks Cosby. "Victory" was her spirited theme.

"Despite all the adversity we have known in this country, we have had our victories," she told the overflow crowd, and I reported it in *Essence.* "Given the odds, we weren't supposed to stop being slaves. Given the opposition, we weren't supposed to have an education. Given the history, we weren't supposed to have families. Given the blues, we weren't supposed to have spirit. Given the power of the enemy, we weren't supposed to fight back. Not only have we achieved victories, we have—despite the powers against us—become our own victories."

Cosby's own life has shown that she's a strong woman, "self-defining," as she would say. Every young sister there was a victory—for themselves, for their families, for our community, and our country. Every sister who is entering Spelman, or any other school, from prekindergarten to grad school, this month is a victory for a people for whom it was once illegal—for centuries!—to learn to read and write.

One of Sonia Sanchez's poems sums it up: We a baddDDD people!

Secret Ingredient: **As Dr. Cornel West, professor of Afro-American studies at Harvard University, says, "Don't look for heroes. Be the hero you're looking for."**

✹ AUGUST 13 ✹

Give a lefty a hand.

Today is International Lefthanders' Day. I'm going to celebrate because I'm left-handed—along with Natalie Cole, Whoopi Goldberg, Oprah Winfrey, and some people you may know and love.

Being left-handed is like being in a tribe with its own rites of passage—such as learning how to write pushing the pen and then smearing the ink when your hand goes over it, instead of pulling the pen and being able to see what you're doing! There are all kinds of other inconveniences of living in a right-handed world, such as:

❖ Using a computer mouse made for right-handers, like I'm doing right now! I always have to move the mouse and the pad to the left side of the computer after others have used it.

❖ Trying to ladle punch at a party when the lip is on the outside

❖ Using mechanical can openers with the crank on the right

❖ Trying to read a measuring cup through the food you're pouring in it

❖ Reading the measurements on a ruler from left to right, when your propensity is to go from right to left (I got a left-handed ruler that says "Lefties Rule the World!")

❖ Rarely finding a student desk with the writing surface attached on the left

❖ Using scissors (fortunately, I've noticed, the design is increasingly more ambidextrous)

Now, you know me—Patsy Positive. I just had to find some *good* things about being left-handed, including the fact that at least left-handed people are in their right minds! Language skills can be located on the right side or both sides of the brains of lefties, which means a better recovery rate for left-handers from stroke and other head or brain injuries. We're also more likely to be able to use our right hand more dexterously than right-handers can use their left hand. And while dining, after using a knife to cut food, we don't have to change our forks back to the right hand. Left on, my sister!

Secret Ingredient: **For more information about left-handedness, browse the Web. Some good sites include: www.io.com/~cortese/ left/southpaw.html and www.indiana.edu/~primate/left.html. For left-handed products and gifts, visit www.thelefthand.com or www.wh4.com/lefty.**

✺ AUGUST 14 ✺

Make your own natural toothpaste.

When I was a child, I often saw my father brush his teeth in the way he had as a child: by pouring baking soda into the palm of his hand, then dipping his wet toothbrush bristles into the powder and brushing his teeth with it. I would tease him about having been raised in the "golden olden days" as I squeezed my toothpaste from the tube. Then I'd run off to watch *The Jetsons.*

But facing some periodontal problems myself about twenty years later, I was advised by my periodontist to use the following recipe for combatting plaque:

1 teaspoon hydrogen peroxide
1 teaspoon baking soda
1 cup water

Pour the peroxide into a bathroom cup. Dip your toothbrush in the peroxide to completely wet it. Dip the brush in the baking soda. Brush your teeth and massage your gums with this concoction. Use the water to rinse out thoroughly. Avoid swallowing the peroxide.

The dentist's recipe for homemade plaque-fighting toothpowder was almost the same as my father's "old-timey" way of doing it. I made sure I brushed after eating humble pie!

Try it out sometime. I recently saw a similar recipe in the Heloise column of the newspaper that suggested adding a choice of flavoring to the baking soda, either a few drops of peppermint flavoring, vanilla extract, or several dashes of powdered cinnamon. Brushing your teeth will become an adventure.

Secret Ingredient: **Think of it as a "face mask" for your teeth. On days when you're giving yourself a special pampering or beauty treatments, do something special for your teeth too. (And don't forget to floss afterward.)**

✸ AUGUST 15 ✸

Use the language of affirmation.

It was a happy day. I was feeling good and thinking, *I am content. I have everything I want or need. The only problem I have is . . .* Whoa! My inner voice behind the thinking voice jumped up in my face: *Don't even go there! It's not a* problem—*it's just a little challenge.* And instantly I felt better about not having as much cash flow since I became a full-time writer as I used to when I was working overtime in a corporation.

It's a spiritual exercise to change your language from put-downs to affirmations. That's because it takes *believing* to make the difference. You can say positive, empowering things, but then you have to make yourself believe that what you are saying is true. I realized it had worked for me lately when I stopped thinking of the boyfriend of someone close to me as a horrible person. He had never done anything to deserve that image, but I thought he was "beneath" her. Eventually, I came to think that if I loved her, and she cared for him, he must not be all bad. After all, he was some mama's child.

Then there is the friend of mine who "hates" a certain well-known celebrity. "How can you hate her if you've never even met her?" I keep asking. My husband Reggie's litmus test is: Have they ever done anything to *you?* If they're not bothering *you,* why bother to hate *them?* It's just wasted energy.

So, try making an effort to change the language, and thus the feeling behind the words. Instead of:

I can't do that, make it: That would be a new experience for me.

I'm unlovable, make it: My prince is still looking for me.

My body is too fat, make it: My body is a divine creation.

I'll never reach my goal, make it: I'll reach it in God's time.

Secret Ingredient: **Whatever the tape is that's playing in your mind, change it to a positive spiritual tape. Just as you can change the channel from a station that's airing a depressing show to one that makes you laugh, you can change the channel of your thoughts.**

❋ AUGUST 16 ❋

Be a surrogate mother.

I'm a stepmom, and proud of it. I call Amena, Aleeyah, and Ahmondyllah my three precious "wedding presents." They gave me some good lessons in Mothering 101 before I birthed my only. I share a special bond with my girls. And I know the feelings are mutual, primarily because of what they call me—their "other mother."

Stepmothers are just one of the many kinds of "other mothers" our African American family structure has blessed us with. These women nurture, give advice, teach, listen, and are just plain *there* for us. I'm talking about every one of our kind of "surrogate" mother:

* Grandmothers, who love us always, and raise us sometimes when our own mothers cannot
* Foster mothers, who take in children and rear them as their own
* Adoptive mothers, who give the love and care of any "real" mother
* Mothers-in-law, whom we love for birthing the loves of our lives
* Our mothers' and fathers' sisters, who are our real aunts . . .
* . . . and our mothers' friends whom we call "aunt" but who are not related at all.

Generations of black churchgoers have witnessed a tradition of blessing newborns in dedication ceremonies and christenings. In recognition of the African proverb It takes a village to raise a child, new parents ask a man and woman to serve as godparents. The Reverend Samuel B. McKinney tells me that the tradition of godparenting is more ceremonial than legally binding, but that the godparents should assume the attitude that "if something should happen to the parents, the child should want for nothing."

Dorothy, a family friend, says she doesn't like the term *godmother* because, "there's only one God." Instead, she prefers to call the other mothers in her three daughters' lives their guardmothers. These women, she says, "are available to guard and protect your child and pledge that support to you."

Secret Ingredient: **Whether you call it mothering or mentoring, giving time to our children enriches the lives of our youth—and our own lives as well.**

❋ AUGUST 17 ❋

Control your sugar jones.

Registered dietitian and nutrition consultant Grace Wilson-Woods of Sun Lakes, Arizona, is an expert in the eating habits of black folks. I saw her in action when we shared a panel discussion at the Today's Black Woman Expo in Chicago a couple of years ago. She asked the audience, "How many of you put one teaspoonful of sugar in your coffee?" A few hands went up. "How many put two?" More hands shot up. "Three?" Even more women raised their hands. "How many of you use *more* than three teaspoons of sugar in your coffee?" As many as or more than those who had already raised their hands admitted that they use a *lot* of sugar.

That habit may make the coffee taste sweeter, but it can mask a bitter truth: excessive sugar consumption is detrimental to your health. That's because it can cause tooth decay, it can aggravate diabetes, and it can contribute to obesity. Although health experts recommend getting ten percent or less of our calories from sugar, on average, studies show that Americans are getting twenty percent.

Here's how Wilson-Woods advised the sisters in Chicago to curb their sweet teeth and help their health.

- ❖ **Use one less teaspoon of sugar in your coffee** or other beverage.
- ❖ **Reduce intake of all sugars,** brown or white, honey, syrups, etc.
- ❖ **Buy canned fruit packed in its own juice** rather than in heavy syrup.
- ❖ **Use fresh fruit** as dessert more often, instead of pies, cakes, and cobblers.
- ❖ **Adjust recipes** by reducing the sugar by one fourth and then try reducing it by one half.
- ❖ **Sweeten waffles or pancakes with fresh fruit** instead of syrup.
- ❖ **Use vanilla, cinnamon, or other spices** in recipes to heighten the sweetness.
- ❖ **Select sugar-free versions of your favorite foods.**
- ❖ **Drink fewer sodas.** Replace one soda with one eight-ounce glass of water each day.
- ❖ **Don't use sweet foods as a reward.**

Secret Ingredient: Nature provides the secret ingredient. The natural taste of fruit—an apple, an orange, a juice—is the best sweetener.

❋ AUGUST 18 ❋

Use the healing force of affirmation.

I've got to admit it: I used to think that affirmations, chanting, all that New Age stuff, was a bunch of hocus-pocus. But the constant search for self-improvement and enlightenment kept taking me back past the path of affirmation. Finally, I came to realize that I affirm myself everyday in my own way. You don't have to follow any guru's formula to do what is in your mind and heart. You don't even have to follow what I'm going to tell you next! But if you're interested in exploring using affirmations, feel free to see if any of the suggestions below fit your personality and lifestyle.

Ten Everyday Ways to Affirm Yourself

1. When you get dressed in the morning and give yourself that last look in the mirror, say aloud, "Looking good!" Give yourself a thumbs-up.
2. The next time you figure out a problem, acknowledge your worth with a big "Yes, I can do this!"
3. Buy yourself flowers.
4. For one whole day, concentrate on your beauty, not your perceived imperfections.
5. Deliver a pep talk to yourself in a tape recorder and listen to it whenever you need it, or pop it in the tape deck of your car and play it each morning on the way to work.
6. Keep an affirmation journal. Write down your favorite words of inspiration and encouragement, and refer to them when you need a boost.
7. Post words of motivation on a bulletin board at home.
8. Recall encouraging words of others.
9. Keep a "kudos" folder. When someone sends you a thank-you note, or a compliment in a letter or e-mail, retain it for future reference.
10. Go easy on yourself.

Secret Ingredient: **Each time you think something positive about yourself, each time you acknowledge your worth or help someone else, you are a living affirmation. Be yourself.**

❋ AUGUST 19 ❋

Affirm someone else.

Now that you've got it going on in the self-affirmation department, don't keep it to yourself! Let someone else know they are worthy, capable, smart, important.

When I left *Essence,* I expressed to editor in chief Susan Taylor that I felt confident that I could do the job as editor in chief of *Heart & Soul,* but I had misgivings about producing good covers for the magazine because I didn't have much experience in it. She responded, "Oh, you'll be able to do it." Very simply. She may not even remember that she said that, but I do because I recall an immediate feeling of confidence come over me. And sure enough, the covers of the magazine became one of the facets of my work of which I was most proud.

Are there people in your life you can affirm today? Let them know you think they are VIPs. Try these ways:

1. Find something to compliment about everyone you encounter today.
2. Send a "thinking of you" card to someone with whom you've been out of touch.
3. Catch your children doing something right. Make as big a deal of it as you do when you catch them "being bad."
4. Listen without interruption. See if you can have a conversation in which the other person feels your full attention. Interject only affirming words.
5. Express your pride in others. According to Dr. Joyce Brothers, "The best thing to say in a relationship is 'I'm proud of you.' The worst thing to say is 'I told you so.' "
6. Let someone know you appreciate him or her. So often, people close to us feel taken for granted.
7. Tell someone when you'll be praying for them.
8. Let those in your life know when you think they are right.
9. Be in someone's corner.
10. Watch their back.

Secret Ingredient: **Never underestimate the power of encouragement.**

❋ AUGUST 20 ❋

Don't be "old school" about food.

African Americans are at the cutting edge of popular culture. We invent new language that permeates the mainstream. We wear our clothes in innovative ways that cross over. Our music sets the beat all over the world. Yet when it comes to our eating habits, too many of us are die-hard "old school." Some of the same people who would make fun of someone for doing last year's dance step are still following the eating habits of their grandmama's grandmama.

As nutrition consultant Grace Wilson-Woods says, "We cling to the old habits that encourage us to eat more than we need of fat, salt, and sugar. Yes, it is true that 'Aunt Sue and Grandmother Jones lived to be ninety and they ate our traditional foods.' But they also worked harder and longer than most people do today. Just as we shorten our working hours and add modern conveniences to our lives, we must make a change for a healthier lifestyle."

Old habits are comfortable and hard to break, but it can be done. Wilson-Woods suggests that one way to do it is to make small changes in the foods we eat, not eliminate them. Here's how to go from old school to new jack.

Old School: Pile your plate with as much food as it can hold.
New Jack: Don't fill it up, or else change your plate to a smaller size. Keep food off the outside rim.

Old School: Eating high-fat foods all the time, and high-fiber foods rarely.
New Jack: Some foods need to be eaten *less* often (like high-fat meats), and some foods need to be consumed *more* often (like high-fiber grains). This will automatically reduce the fat intake and increase total fiber consumption.

Old School: Salting food before tasting it.
New Jack: Not adding salt at all, or at least tasting the food to see how the cook intended it to be flavored.

SOME EASY CHANGES

Old School	New Jack	Even Better
French fries	Baked potato	
Fried chicken	Baked chicken	Baked chicken
Pie	Low-fat pudding	without skin
Bacon and eggs	Whole grain cereal	Fresh fruit

Secret Ingredient: **You don't have to stop eating the foods you love, just think of them as soul food with a new attitude.**

 SPIRIT

 AUGUST 21

Help somebody.

I still have Earth, Wind & Fire's first album, which featured the song "Help Somebody." Then there's the spiritual "If I Can Help Somebody." So it must be "in the blood," as Sade would say, to help others.

Did you know, though, that being of service to others can help *you?* It can give you a sense of well-being to be able to "give back." Helping others can boost your self-esteem because you know you are making a difference in someone's life. It can reduce stress by providing a calming sense of satisfaction. Being charitable gives you a feeling of taking control and countering society's ills.

In fact, volunteerism has been shown to be beneficial for health. One study revealed that people who "get involved" stay in better health than those who don't, and they live longer. The mental and physical rewards of "doing good" are great. And the ways in which you can help somebody are countless, but allow me to try to count a few ways anyway:

Be a community activist. Get involved in good causes in your neighborhood.

Help out at a senior citizens' home.

Tutor a child at a school or after-school program.

Be a mentor, Big Sister, or scout leader.

Volunteer at a homeless shelter.

Help out at a food kitchen.

Donate old clothes to drug rehab houses and other charities.

Give to a scholarship fund.

Secret Ingredient: **Commit to doing something you enjoy on a regular basis, and make it a family affair. Children can learn early that helping others is rewarding—and the right thing to do.**

 MIND

☀ AUGUST 22 ☀

Be a warrior, not a worrier.

Everybody worries over something sometime. But it's the folks who worry over everything all the time that I worry about.

Like stress, there is good worry and bad worry. It's good to be concerned about, say, safety. If a loved one is making a cross-country airplane trip, and you express the hope that they "have a safe trip," that's normal. But if you fret about whether the plane is a wide-body or a prop, you call the airline to check the plane's progress every hour, and you can't think about anything else during the entire time the plane is in the air—that's not normal.

And that makes two kinds of people:

Worriers are people whose obsessive anxiety holds them back and makes them risk averse. Their brooding can result in stomach knots, chest pain, headache, and a racing heart. They epitomize the phrase "worried to death."

Warriors are people who successful fight worry with healthy concern. They tend to "go with the flow" and "let go and let God."

So how do you go from worrier to warrior? First, *acknowledge the difference* and examine your feelings when you are in a worrying situation. Try to *anticipate events* that may cause worry and attempt to plan safeguards. *Head off worrisome tasks,* such as performance on tests, public speaking, first day of a new job jitters by being prepared. *Take positive action* rather than sitting around stewing. *Share your concerns* with relatives or friends; or if it continues to be a problem that hinders you, discuss it with a therapist. *Take a hike:* getting away from the source of your worry to exercise can give you a different perspective on the matter—and a healthier heart rate.

Secret Ingredient: **Why worry? For more worry-busting advice read *Worry: Controlling It and Using It Wisely* by Edward M. Hallowell, M.D., and *Meditations for People Who (May) Worry Too Much,* by Anne Wilson Schaef (Editor), Cheryl Woodruff (Editor).**

❋ AUGUST 23 ❋

Live to be 100.

I've read all the Delany Sisters' books. Don't you just love them? Although "baby sister" Bessie passed away at 105, her spirit lives on in the books she wrote with her sister, Sadie (who recently passed away at the age of 109): *Having Our Say* and *The Delany Sisters' Book of Everyday Wisdom.* From their books, the Broadway play, and the articles I've read about them, I've collected some of their secrets of living to old age that can be put to use at any age.

❖ Get up with the sun.
❖ Exercise every morning.
❖ Make breakfast the biggest meal of the day.
❖ Drink a full glass of water, followed by a teaspoon of cod liver oil and a whole clove of garlic.
❖ Take vitamin supplements (their daily intake: vitamin A, B complex, C, D, E, zinc, and tyrosine).
❖ Take more vitamin C if you get "a tickle in your throat."
❖ Drink lots of purified water.
❖ Wash your hands often.
❖ Don't smoke.
❖ Don't drink.
❖ Watch what you eat.
❖ Always clean your plate.
❖ Stay pure of heart.

Secret Ingredient: "God gave you one body, so you better be nice to it."

❋ AUGUST 24 ❋

Visit the Motherland.

Journeying to the land of your ancestors can be a spiritual experience. It gives you a connection with the past, a sense of pride, and a cultural education.

I remember the first time I went to Africa, I was blessed to go as an editor at *Essence* to produce a lifestyle story on the Ivory Coast. Before the journey, I had been busy with all the details the preparations, leaving no time to "trip" about the trip's significance. Of course, it was planned with more excitement than my usual business travel, but I didn't give it much deeper thought.

Once we were on the airplane, as guests of Air Afrique, I noticed that our team had the unexpected privilege of riding in first class. Comfortably seated, looking at all the beautiful black flight attendants, I felt a sudden *knowing*—and I lost it. I was flying first class over the Middle Passage that my ancestors had journeyed by sea in the most horrific of circumstances. They had arrived in America as slaves, yet my "return" to Africa was a trip that could have been described as "royal treatment." I felt an incredible sense of joy and gratitude. I recently read that *Roots* author Alex Haley's brother George W. Haley was overwhelmed by a similar humbling feeling when he became the United States ambassador to The Gambia—the country of origin of his ancestor Kunte Kinte.

Secret Ingredient: **If you've ever dreamed of going to the Motherland, devise a plan and start saving today! Senegal is only six hours from the United States East Coast—about the same as making a domestic cross-country flight. Think of your pilgrimage as an investment of a lifetime.**

❋ AUGUST 25 ❋

Face your fears—then do it anyway!

Of course you want that big promotion. Who wouldn't want to move up, not to mention make more money? But behind your joy at the opportunity, there may be fear: *How can I manage the same people with whom I used to work on an equal level? What if my team doesn't perform as well or better than the previous boss did? How will my family take my longer working hours?*

Or maybe you're starting a business. Although it's always been your dream to be your own boss, to be an entrepreneur, now that the time seems right, it still feels scary not to have a regular paycheck, to possibly use your 401K savings, or to have others looking to you for *their* paycheck.

Whether you're in a life-changing situation such as childbirth, or facing an everyday fear such as a root canal, the process of feeling the anxiety, stepping out of your comfort zone, and going with the flow remains the same. Here's a strategy for getting to the desired result—courage and bravery!

❖ **First name the fear.** What is it about what you are facing that is making you upset?

❖ **Then face the fear.** Is it something you really can't avoid? Is it something that will, if you succeed, bring you great joy? Would you feel better if you could only do it?

❖ **Draw up a plan of attack.** Write down ways to approach the situation step by step. If the task seems too difficult, draw on the strength of "making a way where there's no way."

❖ **Enlist your army.** Make note of who can help you along the way. To whom can you delegate tasks? Who can advise you? Whom can you talk to if you need emotional support?

❖ **Be prepared.** It may seem obvious, but whether you're in school or not, it's important to study before the test. Do your homework. Research the company, your opposition, or what a root canal entails. Many unnecessary fears are born of ignorance. When we don't know what to expect, our anxiety can get out of hand. Let knowledge put you in control.

❖ **Learn from your setbacks.** Few people succeed without making mistakes. You'll get over it.

Secret Ingredient: Take a moment to get quiet. Make a promise to do just one thing today that you are afraid to do. After you've completed your task you'll feel a wonderful sense of accomplishment and relief. Remember the adage, "A journey of a thousand miles starts with a single step." For steps to confidence and action, read *Feel the Fear and Do It Anyway,* by Susan Jeffers, Ph.D., and the companion guidebook, *Feel the Fear . . . And Beyond.*

 BODY

☀ AUGUST 26 ☀

Have a hot and healthy sex life.

I'm not going to begin to tell you how to heat up your sex life. You've probably already got your technique grooving for you. And if you don't, you can pick up any women's magazine any month of the year and find tips on that. Such information is a staple of what drives magazine sales. But while attempting to titillate you, very few articles do you the favor of sharing the secrets of healthy, wholesome sexuality—the kind that brings a mutual sharing of loving respect and consideration as well as habits that can keep you alive and well to experience a lifetime of luscious lovemaking.

So let your sister-friend here pull your coat—before the next time you take it all off.

Carefully choose your sexual partners. That may seem a given, but so many women feel intimidated about asking for the respect they deserve in bed. Your partner should be someone with whom you feel comfortable talking about sexual habits and preferences *before* you ever have intercourse. Aim not only to please, but to be pleased.

Be conscientious about condoms. To avoid the risk of STDs such as HIV, herpes, syphilis, and chlamydia, as well as unintended pregnancy, condoms should be used every time you make love. And that includes oral sex. Contrary to popular opinion, STDs *can* be contracted through preejaculate.

Have forethought before foreplay. Take control of your own sexual health rather than rely on your partner. If he doesn't have a condom, that's no excuse for you not having one. I suggest the Reality female condom; it's made just for your protection.

Make two dates: to get tested. One Rx for healthy sexuality is monogamy. If that is what the two of you are committed to, get an HIV test, continue to use condoms for the next six months, then get tested again. Only after the second test with negative results should you relax your condom use. It may seem a hassle, but believe me, your health—and your life—are worth it.

Secret Ingredient: Sexual education is the key to sexual health. For free pamphlets or a consultation, call your local Planned Parenthood or 1-800-230-PLAN; Web site: www.plannedparenthood.org.

✳ SPIRIT

✳ AUGUST 27 ✳

Be attached to spiritual, not material, matters.

We were in a jungle—and it was beautiful beyond words. I felt I had caught the Tarzan movies in *another* lie about Africa—they never conveyed the peacefulness and grandeur of the jungle.

NO CELL PHONES BEYOND THIS POINT read the sign on the expansive deck of the sister-owned Lily's Lodge, where my friend Gail and I sat on the edge of a jungle overlooking the ocean in Eastern Cape, South Africa. It's so important to see the world, we agreed, awestruck. Of course, it is quite expensive to see the world too. To travel from the United States to Lily's Lodge in South Africa would cost a few thousand dollars. But we were pleased to see so many African Americans on the South African Airways flight we took to get there making that investment. I would bet that many of those people felt like Gail, whose philosophy is "I don't spend money on material things. I use my money for experiences."

Gail is a senior vice president at a public relations firm in New York City, and can afford pricey material things, but the experiences she prefers are those that are priceless. Family time spent with her husband and two children are on the top of her list: cheering her son on at his ice hockey games, taking golf lessons with her daughter, and planning family vacations together at Hilton Head.

Recently, rushing out of my driveway, late as usual for an event with my daughter, I forgot that I had left my tote bag on the back bumper of the car! While we were gone, a kindly neighbor rang the bell and handed my husband a tattered bagful of my belongings he had picked up from the busy street in front of our house: a smashed cell phone, cracked credit cards, lipstick (that Reg mistook for blood) smeared everywhere. Not having heard from us yet (I was incommunicado without my cell phone),

Reg was afraid something even worse than my stupidity had happened to us. But once I realized what I had done, I couldn't even panic. *Those are just material things,* I thought. *At least we are safe.* And Anique and I returned home to a loving reunion.

Secret Ingredient: Remember: Material things come and go. The pleasurable memories of delightful, enlightening experiences last a lifetime.

 MIND

☀ AUGUST 28 ☀

Think young.

The older we get, the more we slow down. One way to keep moving and maintain vitality is to think young. Here are sixteen tips from my sixteen-year-old daughter of young things not-so-young folks can do:

1. Do something spontaneous, such as going roller skating ("They play old-school music at the rinks," Anique says, "so even if you don't skate, you can dance!").
2. Go to an ice cream parlor and have a (low-fat) cone.
3. Go to an amusement park—if you're no longer a thrill-seeker, just the walking will do you good.
4. Visit your local zoo. Another opportunity to get exercise walking—while observing the ways of animals, reptiles, and amphibians.
5. Go for a joy ride.
6. Wear sneakers.
7. Run.
8. Jump double Dutch.
9. Drink your juice.
10. Don't drink.
11. Don't smoke.
12. Buy yourself a toy. (She suggested this while looking at my own new toy, a leopard Beanie Baby.)
13. Throw a house party in your basement. Change the lightbulbs to blue.
14. Support your former sport. Bill Cosby, a student track star, still goes to the Penn Relays, the annual track competition.

15. Remembering how it was before you had a driver's license? Ride your bike to the store.
16. Take a hip-hop dance class (Anique's specialty).

Secret Ingredient: **Before you go to sleep tonight, commit to doing four of Anique's tips in the next week. Schedule four more for the week after, and so on, until you've done everything!**

✳ AUGUST 29 ✳

Warm up to your workout.

There are three common mistakes that people make when working out. And there's the clue—they work out but they don't take time to warm up, cool down, and stretch.

Why warm up? Gradually beginning to use the muscles that will be in action during your workout helps acclimate your body to the increased heart rate and prevents injury. If jogging is your workout, try walking briskly as your warm up. If power walking is your exercise, start out with a stroll.

Skipping your warm-up may seem like a good idea for saving time, but don't do it. Getting committed to your warm-up will give you more energy for the workout, and your body won't get jolted. The more out of shape you are, the longer you need to warm up, so allow between five and fifteen minutes, depending on your own condition. Once you get in the habit, you'll feel something's amiss if you skip it.

Why cool down? Just like you need to ease into your exercise, it's best to ease on out. Think of it as a reverse warm-up. A cooldown allows your body temperature to decrease before you jump into a hot or cold shower. Take a few minutes to lower your heart rate and to stretch.

Aren't you supposed to stretch first? I know, I know, that's what your high school gym teacher said, but many experts now agree that it's best to stretch when the muscles are already flexible. This will prevent strained or pulled muscles. Stretching after you've warmed up and also after your cooldown can give you maximum benefit.

Stretching is good for your posture, for flexibility, for injury prevention. Hold the stretch for several seconds (the more you work out, the longer you should be able to hold it), and try to build up to a minute. Don't bounce, just ease into the stretch. And don't forget to breathe.

Secret Ingredient: You can take stretching classes at your local gym or dance theater. Also, just about any workout video will feature warm-ups, cooldowns, and stretches. Yoga videos are also great for stretching techniques.

 SPIRIT

✸ AUGUST 30 ✸

Wait on God.

Think about it: so many of the ills of the world are a result of the desire for instant gratification. People steal because they want it *now,* not "someday" when they can afford it. Folks lie on their résumés because they want that top job *now,* not when they've earned it. Credit card debt is out of control because people want those material things *this minute,* not after they've saved for them.

Many of us miss making our health and fitness goals because of instant gratification. The chocolate cake was just sitting around—it had to be eaten right away or it would go bad! Eat now, worry about exercising later.

We may not lose the weight when we want to, but perseverance is the way. You may reach a plateau and have trouble breaking through, but determination combined with patience is a sure bet. You might not want to wear that cumbersome, inelegant brace for as long as the doctor said, but it will help in your full recovery. Sex is hot when spontaneous, but safer—even life-saving—when you take an instant to put on the condom. It may be painful to mourn the loss of a loved one, but going through all the stages of grief will aid your healing.

Whether it's a matter of a simple thing, like waiting until you've warmed up to jump on the treadmill, or a big thing, such as following doctor's orders after surgery, waiting can be a test of self-control, of commitment, of your maturity, patience, and even of your spirituality.

To make the wait more do-able, concentrate on the reasons for waiting. Know why and how having patience will benefit you. *Believe* that doing the right thing can make the difference.

As your mother always said, good things come to those who wait. As the gospel song says, wait on the Lord. Either way, you can't go wrong.

Secret Ingredient: Think of times in your life when instant gratification has tempted you. List five instances you gave in to it with negative results, and five times you successfully managed temptation. Decide how, in the future, you can make sure each situation falls in the category of success. Then say a prayer asking for the wisdom and patience of delayed gratification.

AUGUST 31

Don't trip on yourself.

"You can't lift yourself up by putting other people down," said Patti La-Belle in her memoir *Don't Block the Blessings.* "And you will never impress everyone by stepping on anyone. In fact, there is really no need to impress people at all. Those who really care about you don't have to be impressed. Those who don't care never can be."

Words of wisdom from a great lady of song who knows of what she speaks; the entertainment business is full of people with big egos. But as in any industry or community, there are also people with big hearts—like Patti—whose sincerity will get them where they want to go and keep them there longer.

It's so easy to fall into the schoolgirl trap of petty jealousy and rivalry. It's a no-brainer to "talk about people." It uses energy that could be geared to something positive. And most important, it gives you good karma. You know the saying, what goes around . . .

A friend of mine shared this story in which she learned a lesson: In church one Sunday, someone sang a solo all off key. After the service my friend asked a choir member, "Who in the world was that singing that awful solo? I didn't have my glasses, so I couldn't see who it was. I should have gone to choir rehearsal, I would have sung it better than that!"

The choir member just looked at her and said, "You're right, girl. I was off key today."

The embarrassment and humiliation my friend felt was her own self-inflicted punishment. And the fact that she rarely spoke ill of anyone only compounded her regret. So whether you're in the habit of putting others down or you find yourself slipping every once in a while, keep trying to stay out of the dirt and refrain from spreading it. It's so easy to pass along destructive gossip, to agree when someone is dogging someone else, to chime in like the amen chorus. But it's more honorable, more intelligent, just plain smarter, to catch yourself.

Secret Ingredient: For more of Patti LaBelle's pearls of wisdom, read *Don't Block the Blessing: Revelations of a Lifetime.* If you find yourself in a sticky situation, try to identify a good quality in the other person, turn the conversation around—or don't say anything at all.

✿ BODY

🍁 SEPTEMBER 1 🍁

Make small changes for big results.

"Food is not the enemy," says Grace Wilson-Woods, M.H.S., R.D., L.D. "As a registered dietitian, I am often asked, 'How can I eat healthier without sacrificing the taste?' or 'How can I eat healthier and still celebrate family traditions?' One way is to make small changes in the foods we eat, not eliminate them."

How do we do that? Just follow what Wilson-Woods describes as "ten small things we can do to make big changes."

1. Don't skip meals, just reduce the portion sizes.
2. Count servings, not calories.
3. Don't snack at night.
4. Increase your fiber intake to decrease the risk of heart disease and cancer.
5. Drink plenty of water (eight glasses a day).
6. Use salt in moderation. Ask yourself, *do I salt food before tasting it?*
7. Use sugar in moderation. Ask yourself, *do I add extra sugar to everything?*
8. Eat five fruits and vegetables a day.
9. Read and compare food labels. They can help you control serving sizes, fat, saturated fat, sodium, fiber, sugar, and calories.
10. While you decrease the amount of fat in your food, increase physical activity to reach and maintain a reasonable body weight. Get moving.

Secret Ingredient: For more tips on nutrition, contact the American Dietetic Association's consumer nutrition hotline at 1-800-366-1655, where you can listen to recorded nutrition messages or receive referrals to registered dietitians in your area.

🍁 SEPTEMBER 2 🍁

Bend, but don't break.

Terrible things happen to good people. There are so many circumstances beyond our control. We may not be able to prevent them from occurring, but how we react to them determines what we're made of. How we deal with disaster either makes us or breaks us.

I've heard several people with diverse points of view comment on coping with adversity. Their remarks may give you strength:

> "Only the slave can liberate himself. When someone is on your back, you may get bent over, but the only way to get him off is to stand straight up!"
>
> —Historian John Henrik Clarke

> "Without a test, you won't have a testimony."
>
> —Author Iyanla Vanzant

> "If you think the game is worth it, you play the hand you're dealt."
>
> —Actor Christopher Reeve

> "Just because what you want to do is hard—that's no reason to quit!"
>
> —Comedian Richard Pryor

> "If you want to follow the rainbow, you have to put up with some rain."
>
> —Numerologist Cheryl Lee Terry

> "Knowledge is the thing that makes you smile in the face of disaster."
>
> —Actor Avery Brooks

> "Revenge puts you even with your enemy. Forgiveness puts you above her."
>
> —Seen on church marquee in Seattle

> "You may not be responsible for getting knocked down, but you are responsible for getting back up."
>
> —Activist Jesse Jackson

> "You can survive the worst—and there's whole lot more to do."
>
> —Anti-crime advocate John P. Walsh

> "God sees. He knows. He cares."
>
> —Singer Cece Winans

Secret Ingredient: How do you deal with adversity? If any of the quotes above strike a chord with you, write them down or memorize them and use them as armor in bad times.

 MIND

 SEPTEMBER 3

Start anew.

Labor Day marks the end of summer vacation and the beginning of the school year. Much like January 1, it's time to make a fresh start. As the temperature drops, and the leaves fall, think of ways to break out of any unhealthful habits. Make plans to start a year of learning, of educating yourself, of preparing for new opportunities. School yourself on beneficial habits of health and fitness.

Go back to school. Dance classes, yoga courses, cooking school, meditation instruction—just about anything you're interested in is open for registration in September. Don't enroll just your children in meaningful activities; further your own education as well. As an adult, over the years I've started fall classes in modern dance, tennis, and calligraphy, in addition to career courses.

Rededicate yourself to your goals. Whether it's weight loss, weight gain, or overall toning that you are pursuing, it's time to sign up for the gym, dust off your dumbbells, and take the clothes off your treadmill.

Start a fitness journal. Note the days you workout. Keep track of how often you succeed at working your plan. You may be surprised to see that you exercise more often than you thought you did.

Inaugurate a new diet. After a season of light summer salads, it's a good time to make "cooking light" a part of your eating lifestyle. Avoid falling back into the winter, heavy-food habit by extending your hot weather meals into the fall.

Secret Ingredient: Every day is an opportunity to leave the past behind and start anew. What can you choose to do anew today?

✤ SEPTEMBER 4 ✤

Give sports support to a girl.

The Women's Sports Foundation is passionate about the benefits of sports in the lives of girls and young women. As a former trustee now on their advisory board, I've had the opportunity to see this advocacy group in action. Their excitement is infectious!

Another passion of mine is teen pregnancy prevention. So it was with great interest that I read the foundation's report on the benefits of sports in preventing premature pregnancy. After-school sports help to lower girls' risk of pregnancy by keeping them busy and chaperoned. Coaches tell stories about the boost in self-esteem girls acquire that helps them to ward off peer pressure to have sex. Pregnancy jeopardizes athletic performance and participation. Sports foster discipline and a positive appreciation of a girl's developing body. Here are some additional benefits of a sports program:

1. **Female athletes are less likely to get pregnant.** In the nationwide survey, it was shown that female athletes are less than half as likely to get pregnant as female nonathletes.
2. **Female athletes are more likely to be virgins.** Female athletes are significantly more likely than female nonathletes to report that they had never had sexual intercourse.
3. **Female athletes had their first intercourse later in adolescence.** Female nonathletes are twice as likely as female athletes to experience their first intercourse between the ages of ten to thirteen.
4. **Female athletes have sex less often.** Less than a third of athletes acknowledged having sexual intercourse four or more times during the past year; almost half of nonathletes did so.
5. **Female athletes have fewer sex partners.** Thirty-seven percent of nonathletes said they had two or more partners during their lifetime; twenty-nine percent of athletes said the same.
6. **Athletes are more likely to use contraceptives.** Female athletes are significantly more likely to report condom use than female nonathletes.

Of course, sports are no quick fix for teen pregnancy prevention, but they can be part of the solution.

Secret Ingredient: **Are there girls or other women athletes in your life that you can encourage and support? Seek them out; send a card, or an e-mail, or simply call someone up.**

 SEPTEMBER 5

Be alone—with your own funny bone.

When we were growing up, my brother and I shared an indoor deck that was intended as a homework room or study, but "playroom" was more like it. It was accessible by a door from my bedroom on one end, and another door into André's room on the other end. If he was lounging on the floor, watching television, I could push back the curtain over the glass window of my door and spy on him. Quite often André would be in there watching cartoons or something else humorous on television, and he would laugh unabashedly or say something aloud. Then I would swing open the door and yell, "Ah-ha! I caught ya talking to yourself!"

Accustomed to the frequent nuisances of his little sister, he would reply, "Well, why not? I'm the most intelligent person to talk to in here!" Or else he would say, "I'm not by myself. I'm here with three people: me, myself, and I." Although I would never admit to being "ranked on," as we used to say when someone won a "snap," or "the dozens," I now realize that this was his way of saying that he was totally comfortable being by himself. No wonder I could never think of a good comeback.

A few years later André went off to college three thousand miles away, then, four years later I left home for a school that was also on the other side of the country. At Howard, when people would ask where I was from and I would reply "Seattle," the second thing (after "I didn't know there were any black folks in Seattle!") they would say was "Gee, you're a long way from home." This sorry look would cross their face. But it was hard to explain that I rarely felt forlorn. As long as I could find a Baptist church, I felt at home. There is something about the universal church invitation: "If you're looking for a 'church home,' we invite you to look no further." As long as I can "get the Spirit," I am never lonesome.

When you feel alone, get in touch with your funny bone. Seek the intelligent company of "me, myself, and I," and know that Spirit is closer than your breath.

Secret Ingredient: **If you've been feeling lonely, check in with yourself and reconnect with the Spirit. Go to church, pray or meditate, and take care of "me, myself, and I."**

❧ SEPTEMBER 6 ❧

Decide on your "life's work."

One day recently, it hit me: I don't have a job!

For twenty-five years I had gone to work in an office building in midtown Manhattan—on swanky Madison Avenue, on Broadway in Times Square, on Third Avenue near the United Nations. I was part of the New York state of mind. I had the New York walk down pat. The New York talk and *all that.*

And now, by my own choice, I was living my dream as a SOHO writer. Not SOHO as in South of Houston in New York City, but as in Small Office/Home Office—the new lingo, perfect for my new life! But the reality of not having a traditional job for the first time in my adulthood hit me, and I saw that I could have gone on with it and just freaked on out (No weekly paycheck! No paid vacation! No benes or bonuses!). But a tandem thought rose up and overpowered the panic-attack-in-the-making: *I may not have a job, but I still have a job to do.*

I still had a message: our health is our wealth. And I still had opportunities to spread it. I had started a media consulting business I was calling SSO Communications, Inc. I had my book deal. The Boston Coalition of 100 Black Women had invited me to speak at their Between Sisters conference, and I already had my plane ticket and was preparing my remarks. I felt a sense of mission, and deep down I knew that *it's the mission, not the management that gives our lives meaning.* Suddenly, my thinking changed, and with it, my attitude. I realized I had discovered my "life's work."

You can look at a piece of art and think, *That's a nice painting.* Then someone will come up to you and say, "That's a Romare Bearden painting," and all of a sudden it's not just a nice painting to you anymore— it's a masterpiece. Stephen R. Covey, author of *The Seven Habits of Highly Effective People,* calls this a "paradigm shift." "Our perceptions come out of our experiences," he says.

We can create positive paradigms to change our "slave mentality" to a "life's work" attitude.

Secret Ingredient: **Read all about Covey's philosophy of success in his bestselling book.**

 BODY

Learn more about sickle cell disease.

One person can make a difference. Tionne Watkins sings alto as T-Boz of the hip-hop female group TLC, and she also raises her voice for sickle cell disease awareness. As the first celebrity spokesperson for the Sickle Cell Disease Association of America (SCDAA) who has the disease herself, Watkins wants to inspire people of childbearing age to get a test for the sickle cell trait, and to get counseling if the test is positive. September is National Sickle Cell Month, so take this opportunity to familiarize yourself with sickle cell disease, a health problem that affects more than sixty thousand Americans, mostly African Americans. Here are some answers from the SCDAA to commonly asked questions about sickle cell disease.

What is sickle cell disease? Sickle cell disease is a disease of the red blood cells. People with sickle cell disease have red blood cells that become hard and pointed instead of being soft and round. Sickle cells cause anemia, pain, and many other problems.

Why is it called sickle cell? Many red blood cells in people with sickle cell disease look like a sickle, a tool used by farmers. So a red blood cell that looks like a sickle is called sickle cell.

What is the sickle cell trait? If you have the sickle cell trait, you have the gene for sickle cell disease. You do not have a disease, and there are no health problems associated with the trait. Over 2.5 million Americans, mostly African Americans, have the sickle cell trait, and if both parents have it, they can have children with sickle cell disease.

How will I know if I have sickle cell trait? A simple, painless blood test will detect the sickle cell trait. In most states, newborn screening programs have enabled physicians to detect the trait or disease in infants and to recommend that other family members be tested for the sickling gene.

Is there a cure? About a dozen patients in the United States have been cured with bone marrow transplantation. Gene therapy, which would be less risky, and one medication, hydroxyurea, are being tested.

Secret Ingredient: **Your physician can give you a sickle cell detection test. If you test positive, contact your local Sickle Cell Disease Association of America (SCDAA) for counseling.**

SEPTEMBER 8

Respect the sacred moments of others.

We were touring Robben Island, the place where Nelson Mandela spent most of his twenty-seven years in incarceration. Somber and solemn, our group of Africans and African Americans peered into his former jail cell. This felt like sacred ground.

But someone on her cell phone kept disturbing our moment! One of our guides had invited a colleague, a South African yuppie who had been there several times before, so she was mainly killing time on her lunch hour accompanying her friend and us—and yapping on her phone. At that moment our visit just didn't mean the same thing to her as it did to us. Fine. But why ruin it for us?

We each need to find our sacred moments, our spiritual communion, our time of reflection. Maybe it's your twenty minutes of meditation twice a day. You do everything you can to keep others away. You turn off the phone, the TV, the radio, you lock up the kids. But do you afford others the same respect?

Theoretically, of course you do. But realistically, it's hard to not let someone know when there's a delivery at the front door for them—even if they are in meditation. Or someone is saying grace at the table but you don't stop taking the food out of the oven—it might burn!

It's courtesy, it's karma, it's the right thing to do to give deference to the spiritual. Don't expect and demand it only when it's you in the spiritual zone. Make sure you extend to others the privilege of a total spiritual experience as well.

Secret Ingredient: **Be a gracious guest when invited to a house of worship other than your own by making sure you understand the protocols and rituals of the religion. In the book *Basic Black: Home**

Training for Modern Times authors Karen Grigsby Bates and Karen Elyse Hudson, along with other wonderful advice, give guidelines for proper etiquette when attending religious services decidedly different from your own.

 MIND

 SEPTEMBER 9

Practice counter-procrastination.

I call it counter-procrastination because I think it needs a name of its own. It's not enough to think we can just *stop* procrastinating. Sometimes it takes an *effort* to do the things we have to do, to do the things we need to do, to do what is expected, and even what we *want* to accomplish. So I think that procrastination takes a counter effort, an opposite force, a concerted action of its own.

When it comes to our well-being, we procrastinate about starting a fitness plan, beginning to eat right, in making that doctor's appointment, or getting a mammogram. Maybe some of my counter-procrastination strategies can help:

Psych yourself up. Be your own motivational speaker. I often tell myself what my father used to say to me: "Come on, Steph. You've got it to do, so just do it." Convince yourself that not only can you do it, you're the best person to do it, and you'll feel better when you're finished.

Tell your business. If you put the word out about tasks you have to complete, next thing you know people will ask at every turn, "Have you done it yet?" or say, "How's it going?" You don't want to look bad when they ask, so prevent embarrassment by getting to it.

Make appointments. Mark on your calendar the day the next fitness session starts at the gym. Enter a note in your electronic organizer if you want to start eating right the Monday after Thanksgiving. Computers, telephone answering machines, and other kinds of technology can provide task reminders nowadays.

Plan a meaningful reward. Have a victory dinner. Buy yourself a gift that will constantly remind you of your perseverance. Make your reward reinforce your goal, and think of it whenever you're tempted to say "later for it!"

Secret Ingredient: For more help, read *Stop Procrastinating: Understand Why You Procrastinate—and Kick the Habit Forever!,* by Frank Joe Bruno.

❧ SEPTEMBER 10 ❧

Decode the food label.

Of course you know how to *read* a food label. But if you're not *familiar* with the lingo, the federally regulated labels can make you feel as though you're trying to decipher hieroglyphics. It was pretty confusing to me, too, until I learned the secret code. I'm only too happy to crack it for you:

❖ **% Daily Value:** The important element on the label is this thing, "% Daily Value." The numbers that read down the column under it are the total percentages of each of the nutrients listed.

❖ **Four Low:** Of those nutrients, the first four under "Calories" are the ones that are detrimental to your health. So you want these percentages (and probably, the calories) to be as low as possible. Just remember "four low" as if you were bidding in a card game. Based on the fact that the average woman eats about 1,800 calories a day (men eat 2,000 or more), the following four nutrients for the whole day should be *lower* than:

NUTRIENT	TOTALS	% DAILY VALUE
Fat	50 g	75
Saturated fat	14 g	70
Cholesterol	300 mg	100
Sodium	2,400 mg	100

In general, a nice, low percentage would be five or less.

❖ **Head high:** For the next good-for-you nutrients listed on a food label, such as total carbohydrate, dietary fiber, and protein, you'll want the numbers to be *high* (with the exception of sugar, if listed). Look for percentages of twenty or more, and make the foods you select for the entire day add up to at least one hundred percent of the % Daily Value.

Secret Ingredient: Remember that the % Daily Value on labels are guidelines for the whole day, not just one meal, so if you eat three meals a day, divide those g's and mg's by three. Still confused? Go to the source; the Food and Drug Administration's Web site, www.fda.gov (click on Food Label) has a Nutrition Facts image that you can click on any part of the label for more information.

 SPIRIT

 SEPTEMBER 11 🍁

Boost your team spirit.

When I attended Howard University, every school basketball or football game started with the black national anthem, "Lift Ev'ry Voice and Sing." And if you didn't want to look like a fool, you had to know the words to the song! But more important, there was something about singing that anthem along with the "Star-Spangled Banner" that gave us all immense pride in our country, in our race, in our school, and in ourselves.

Then came the entertainment of baddest cheerleaders with the fiercest moves of any team on the planet! And the brothers on the team (and in the stands) were too fine! By the time you finished with all that excitement, it almost seemed incidental who won the game.

Whether you're in school or rooting for Michael Jordan, Lisa Leslie, Sammy Sosa, or Venus Williams, team spirit helps us to:
- ❖ Leave our daily travails behind and immerse ourselves in the game
- ❖ Release tension by shouting, yelling, clapping, and cheering
- ❖ Feel a sense of camaraderie by being part of the "fans in the stands"
- ❖ Have a common goal with others in the crowd, including strangers
- ❖ Express aggression in an acceptable manner (like by booing the ref)
- ❖ Feel triumphant; when "we" win our spirits soar.

Secret Ingredient: You can find game schedules for many of your favorite teams on the Internet. For example, to get information about the National Football League, visit www.nfl.com. You'll find news, statistics, inside scoop on players and teams, and special areas for kids. It's a great way to get team spirit!

❦ SEPTEMBER 12 ❦

Adopt a wealth mentality.

The U.S. Census Bureau reported recently that the rate of poverty for African Americans had declined in the last three years to 26.5 percent, the lowest since the government began reporting in 1959. That is good news for so many reasons, among which is the fact that higher income means better health care.

The higher the income, the more likely a family is to have health insurance, to pursue preventive care, to eat better, and to have the means to take better care of themselves in general. When we are able to pursue good health, we are more likely to get prenatal care, which can help us avoid low-birth-weight babies and infant mortality. We are more likely to get regular dental checkups, instead of waiting for a toothache. The eye doctor gets paid a visit and "gets paid" whether we have health insurance coverage for it or not. We're more likely to use contraception. With a little money, we can afford to take vitamins.

As poverty falls and incomes rise, we can experience less stress and focus on our quality of life rather than on plain survival. To have a strong community, we need every person to be in robust health.

None of us may be making as much money as we would like to, but if you are blessed with gainful employment and relative comfort, you owe it to yourself and the community to use your resources to keep yourself in top shape and to help someone who may be struggling financially. The Black Panther Party was known for many things in the sixties, but the one thing I recall most vividly was their effort to carry out a free breakfast program among low-income children. Today we can make sure our schools have breakfast programs, or that our churches help feed the hungry. Many community-based organizations sponsor health fairs with mobile vans for free blood pressure checks and mammograms. It's in the best interest of the 'hood when we do what we should: share the wealth and spread the health.

Secret Ingredient: **If your church or community organization would like to sponsor a health fair, ask doctors, dentists, and optometrists in your area to participate, and call your local hospital's public affairs department for information on providing free services.**

❦ SEPTEMBER 13 ❦

Strike a pose; do yoga.

Have you ever tried yoga? I have. It's fun, and makes you feel very New Age and hip. Yet it's been around for thousands of years. If you'd like to change the pace from the bounce, the beat, and manic moves of aerobics, stretch your body and quiet your mind with yoga.

What it is: Yoga is a series of poses designed to affect body, mind, and spirit. Classes can be taken at health clubs and fitness gyms, and can include stretching, strengthening, and postures. Varying widely, some yoga classes may feature aerobic moves, while others have a spiritual component to them, complete with incense and silence.

What it does: Improves your posture, alignment, and flexibility. Teaches you breathing techniques. Stretches all muscles, warding off injury when you participate in other fitness activities or sports.

Benefits: It's a stressbuster. It can lower blood pressure. Yoga has also been found to decrease heart rate, which can prevent heart disease. It can serve as your overall workout, or you can use it to compliment your regular aerobic exercise. Just think of it as a component of crosstraining.

The celebrity endorsements: Madonna told *Vanity Fair* magazine she does yoga every day, that it's the only workout she needs. **Kareem Abdul-Jabbar,** who has been practicing yoga since 1978, said in *Heart & Soul* that "it filled a void in my training, and my flexibility. The fact that I didn't have any injuries while in the NBA is one of the biggest things in its favor. . . . It really connected me to my whole body." **Ali McGraw** liked it so much that she made a yoga video for an intermediate- to advanced-level workout. Check it out: Ali McGraw's *Yoga Mind and Body* with Erich Schiffman.

Secret Ingredient: **Ready to get started? Begin your yoga journey by taking a beginner course at a health club, gym, or yoga center. Or try it out in the privacy of your own home by getting a video. For beginners, try *Easy Yoga for Busy People,* by Bobbe Norrise, a book that features black participants.**

❧ SEPTEMBER 14 ❧

Seek spirituality in sexuality.

If I see another hoochie mama on a music video representing the sexuality of black women, I am going to scream—and it won't be in orgasm. I'm tired of sex jokes and gratuitous titillation in media too. Not that I have anything against sex. *Au contraire.* Because I have a daughter, and therefore feel the responsibility of helping to shape her attitudes and values, I am all the more adamant about extolling the virtues of sexuality. Wouldn't the highest level of sexuality be somewhere near spirituality?

I started pondering this one day, when I heard Alice Walker, who was on a morning television program talking about her book *By the Light of My Father's Smile,* say, "Sexuality is a door to spirituality." *Yes,* I thought. That sounds beautiful. And that's what sexuality should be—beautiful. What can make this most primal and universal of acts a heavenly experience?

When it is between loving adults. Lovemaking is *superb* between people mature enough to be consistently responsible for its consequences. If you're old enough to have a patient-doctor relationship with a gynecologist, to earn the money it takes for contraception and safe sex, and to take care of a baby if you should get pregnant—you're most likely an adult.

When it is not only sensual, but consensual. No matter how old you are, sex is nothing close to spiritual if you don't want it. Having someone ask you if you would consent to making love can be one of the most sensual moments of a sexual experience.

When you are both free to love each other. When neither person is emotionally attached to a third person, when he's not "somebody else's guy," when you aren't a mistress. Single, sassy, taboo sex may get all the hype—and may be exciting—but the highest *spiritual* ground is married (to each other) sex.

When the love is "divine." If you feel that God is doing the matchmaking, then the lovemaking is the highest form of intimacy and truly a sacred gift.

Secret Ingredient: **Think about your own "spiritual sex principles." Before you have sex again, have an honest conversation with your mate and share your highest ideals of lovemaking.**

❧ SEPTEMBER 15 ❧

Have a hobby.

The word *hobby* sounds so old-school, doesn't it. Well, actually, it is a time-tested way of pursuing an interest that provides a feeling of relaxation. If you have a hobby that you share with an elder, such as needlepoint, crocheting, or knitting, you can have the added benefit of time spent with that beloved person. And sharing the fruits of your pursuit with your loved ones can be a way of developing family heirlooms. Maybe you are one of those lucky folks who has a quilt made by your great-grandmother, and you took up quiltmaking yourself. I remember that my grandmother enjoyed making fudge that I enjoyed devouring! And her sister, Aunt Bootsie, made lovely crocheted novelties.

Today our hobbies can run from the traditional to the high-tech. Surfing the Internet can be a relaxing pastime. And in doing so, you can find people online who share your interests. Actor Billy Dee Williams paints as a hobby. He has exhibited his work in galleries across the country, and when Avon introduced his Undeniable fragrance line several years ago, they made scarves using one of his designs (I have one!).

Pursuing a hobby can relieve the stress of an intense profession. It can be a creative outlet for someone who feels she has little opportunity for creativity at work. Plus, it can help you make some money on the side. I know a little about that. When I was in my twenties I took up calligraphy, and before I knew it, I was moonlighting, making stationery, wedding invitations, place cards, signs, and certificates. Once, after placing my calligraphy business card in a photocopy shop, a soap opera star called to hire me to write a letter to her fans that they would think was handwritten by her! For eighteen months or so, I put all the money I made aside, and by the time my daughter was born I had enough to hire an interior designer to decorate her nursery. So having a hobby can be lucrative.

Stamp collecting, a cappella singing, gardening, reading, refinishing furniture, playing cards, are just a few of the fun and relaxing ways to ease your mind. Pursue your passion, and it just could change your life.

Secret Ingredient: **If you don't have a hobby, develop one, or if you do have a hobby but have neglected it of late, take a few minutes today and pick up where you left off!**

❧ SEPTEMBER 16 ❧

Exercise with your pet.

Of course you already know that you can get a pretty healthy workout by walking your dog. But just in case that gets tired, here are some other ways to use Shaka Zulu for a workout partner:

Take your dog for a jog. When walking the dog, you're constantly stopping to let her relieve herself, sniff this, look at that. But if you go for a run, the dog will be following your lead rather than you just tagging along while it stretches its legs. Plus, the workout will be good for both of you.

Play Frisbee. Dogs love to run, jump, and catch. And you can get a good workout as well.

Play catch. Go out to a big field or park and throw his favorite ball. If he can tear up your house chasing a ball inside, he can really have fun in a wide open space.

Play dodge dog. Chase the dog. Let the dog chase you. Get your kids in the act. Now that fall is approaching, it's a great time to play in the autumn leaves.

Secret Ingredient: What if you don't have a dog? To tell the truth, I don't have one myself! So here's what to do: Take yourself for a jog. Play frisbee with a friend. Get a softball game going with folks from work or people in your neighborhood. Dodge raindrops. What's important is that you exercise.

❧ SEPTEMBER 17 ❧

Explore Islam.

You don't have to be interested in converting to another religion to learn something about your own spirituality. I'm always amazed at how much Muslims acknowledge Christianity, yet Christians know so little about Islam. It seems that people are afraid that learning about other religions means they are not being true to their own faith. When actually, studying the faith of others can strengthen your own.

I'm a Baptist, but I married a Muslim. Mutual respect and acceptance of our differing religions is a cornerstone in our relationship. I enjoy listening to my husband's stories of his journey to make hajj in Mecca, Saudi Arabia, back in 1970. And my understanding of the religion has given me a better appreciation for the concept of faith in general, and the greatness of God, specifically.

If you would like to broaden your knowledge of Islam, I suggest the following:

Go online. Start with the Islamic Information & News Network's Web site, muslims.org. With links such as "Misconceptions about Islam," testimonies from recent converts, facts about Islam, Q&A pages, prayers, and an "Islam Internet Guide," the site is user friendly and very comprehensive. "Islam sometimes seems strange to non-Muslims because it is a religion that impacts every part of life, from eating and sleeping to working and playing. It is not only a personal religion, but also a social one," the home page explains. "Muslims believe that God is One, indivisible, and they believe in all the prophets of the Christians and Jews, including Adam, Noah, Abraham, Ishmael, Isaac, Jacob, Joseph, Job, Moses, Aaron, David, Solomon, Elias, Jonah, John the Baptist, and Jesus (peace be upon them)."

Get a book. If you haven't read *The Autobiography of Malcolm X,* start there. Then read Steven Barboza's *American Jihad: Islam After Malcolm X,* and *Islam in the African-American Experience,* by Richard Brent Turner.

Go to a mosque. On Fridays, congregational prayers are held in mosques around the world. Cover your head, and join in prayer.

Secret Ingredient: **Read the Quran (also spelled Koran) for the ultimate understanding of the faith. In addition to bookstores, the Quran can be found in libraries. Check it out.**

❋ SEPTEMBER 18 ❋

Pull the trigger on emotional eating.

What are the emotional triggers that cause women to overeat? Health experts site:

- ❖ Depression
- ❖ Anger
- ❖ Anxiousness
- ❖ Stress
- ❖ Boredom

If any of those feelings give you the impulse to get busy in the kitchen or stop by the fast-food place when you know you're not hungry (or, worse, when you just ate), try some of these techniques to trigger a change—and stop the ensuing guilt:

Go to the phone, not the fridge. Share your feelings of *depression* with someone you trust who may be helpful in aiding your behavioral change. Seek a buddy in reinforcing positive thoughts.

Confront your anger. Take time to calm down, then nip frustrating situations in the bud by expressing your concerns or disappointment with the source of your *anger.*

Meditate, not medicate. When *anxiety* causes you to feel worry and the desire to overdose on food, just relax. It may sound easier said than done, but meditation, relaxation, and a good night's sleep can calm your nerves far better than packing on the calories.

Stress exercise. Experts say again and again that a good workout can help you work out the *stress* in your life. Not only are you not concentrating on your problems when you are exercising, you are doing your body good.

Get busy. If you're too busy to eat, you are more likely to wait until you're really hungry. Keep yourself occupied with activities that are engrossing—and far from the fridge. Outdoor pursuits, community service, and learning a new task can banish *boredom.*

Secret Ingredient: **If overeating is a problem for you, check the local library or the Internet for more information and consult your doctor.**

❧ SEPTEMBER 19 ❧

Save your sight.

Dr. John P. Mitchell is committed to taking care of the eyesight of people of African descent. He's assistant professor of clinical ophthalmology at Columbia University College of Physicians and Surgeons in New York City, as well as director of ophthalmology at North General Hospital. In addition, every year he travels to Haiti, volunteering his services performing eye surgery and dispensing medication and eyeglasses in a remote countryside town, where his group of medical activists, Friends of the Children of Lascasobas, Haiti, Inc., have just built a hospital after many years of struggle. Here he shares his top tips for all of us:

"My first tip would be to have an eye examination by an ophthalmologist at least every two years, to check for glaucoma or to see if you need glasses. If you have sickle cell disease or diabetes, the checkup should be annual and include dilation.

"Second, to strengthen and protect eyes from the oxidative process, take antioxidants.

❖ Vitamin C: 1000 mg
❖ Vitamin E: 400 units
❖ Beta-carotene: 1 tablet a day
❖ Ginkgo Biloba: 1 to 2 tablets a day

"Lastly, if you wear contact lenses, know the rule of 'RSVP' to help you remember when to remove them and seek help from an eye specialist:

Redness: If redness should persist over two or three hours.

Secretions: If secretions persist throughout the day, and your eye is stuck together in the morning. This could be a sign of conjunctivitis.

Vision: If your vision is blurred and not cleared with rewetting drops.

Pain: Any persistent pain should signal a problem."

Secret Ingredient: **If you haven't had an eye exam in at least two years, make an appointment today. For more information, visit the American Academy of Ophthalmology's Web site at www.aao.org.**

❧ SEPTEMBER 20 ❧

Believe in your heart that dreams come true.

"I didn't think that for a girl from the ghetto, dreams come true. But if you believe, it can happen," said singer Mary J. Blige on BET a couple of years ago. "Out of my mouth I would say, 'Naw, it won't happen,' but in my heart I prayed that it would." And as we know, it—success in the music business—happened big for Mary J. Blige.

The song sung most ardently during the civil rights movement, an anthem that spread to liberation movements around the world, told us to believe deep in our hearts that we shall overcome someday. The jury may still be out on whether we *have* overcome yet, but at least it is a better day.

"Believe in yourself. Ooooooouuuuuu . . ." Lena Horne sang with conviction in *The Wiz*. And according to her, there were times when she had to believe deeply in herself while pursuing her acting and singing career through segregation, racism, and the personal tragedies of her life. It must have worked, because look at her now! Glorious and resplendent.

Whether you are in your twenties like Mary J. Blige, or your eighties like Lena Horne, there is reason and testimony for believing in your dreams. Keep having faith in things unseen, in personal goals, and in public aspirations for our children and their children. And be sure you believe with all your heart.

Secret Ingredient: **Take time out today to dream. It's never to late to start something new. Believe in yourself. As the saying goes, "Whatever you dream, you can achieve."**

❧ SEPTEMBER 21 ❧

Step together as a family.

Whitney Houston is one. So is B. Smith. And I am too. We're stepmothers.

I love being a stepmom. I tell people that when I got married, my husband gave me three precious wedding presents. My stepdaughters, Amena, Aleeyah, and Ahmondyllah, are very much a part of my life. Having met them when they were adorable little girls, having shared in their parenting, and now seeing them as productive, independent adults is so gratifying. And the sisterhood they share with their baby sister, the one I gave birth to, is strong and enduring.

Over the years I've come up with my own little guidelines for nurturing the relationship. For any of you who are dating or marrying a brother with children, here's my five-step strategy to good steppin':

1. **Never say anything negative about their mother** in their presence. On the other hand, if anything positive or complimentary comes to mind, don't hesitate to say that. (But don't be patronizing; kids are smart enough to detect it right away.)

2. **Don't try to be their mother.** Respect the fact that they already have one. If she is deceased or otherwise absent, respect her memory by not trying to replace her. The aim is to carve your own *unique* place in your stepchildren's hearts.

3. **Establish how they would like you to refer to them.** They may resent you calling them your "sons" when they have parents who can rightfully make that exclusive claim. I'm trying to change the negative connotation of the prefix *step*. Too bad the English language isn't more like the French. In French, the prefix translates to "beautiful"—*belle-fille, belle-mère,* literally means "beautiful daughter" and "beautiful mother." I think that gives a more positive spin on the relationship than the "wicked stepmother" model. I remember after Reg and I married, I asked Reg's six-year-old daughter if she knew how I was related to her now. "My godmother?" she pondered, I loved that answer. I still pray she sees in me a mother figure who tries to exhibit godliness.

4. **Show affection as well as discipline.** It's easy to fall into the trap of thinking you exhibit authority by laying on the discipline, but a loving parent also shows gentleness, caring, and pride.

5. **Establish your own relationship** with the children apart from that of your spouse. That was my hardest lesson. At first I kept feeling so left out of the loving relationship my husband had with his kids, but one day it occurred to me that I could have my own special bond with them. Doing things together—just us girls, when Dad was working—made all the difference.

Secret Ingredient: **The Stepfamily Association of America is dedicated to educating and supporting stepfamilies, and creating a positive image of the "blended" family. Visit their Web site, www.stepfam.org, or call 1-800-735-0329 for materials, facts, book suggestions, and membership.**

✹ SEPTEMBER 22 ✹

Energize to the max.

How come some sisters always seem to have so much energy and pep? You know the kind, the ones you *never* hear say "I'm sick and tired of being sick and tired"—because they're never sick, and they're never tired. Like the Energizer bunny, they just keep going, and going, and going.

But this isn't a battery commercial, so what's the secret? Healthy habits.

Exercising "religiously": My friend Kathryn, for example, runs her own consulting business that takes her all over the world, and she solo-parents a teenage daughter. At the end of a telephone conversation with her the other day, she said, "Well, I gotta go—have to do my powerwalk before it gets dark." Having known her to take regular dance classes at Alvin Ailey as well, I asked her how she did it all. "I do it *religiously,*" she replied, "because I'm sitting on so many eighteen-hour flights to Japan and to South Africa. I just have to move!" Even if you can't find time to work out like Kathryn, being *active* helps.

Eating nutritiously: Energetic women don't skip meals, yet they don't overeat either. They snack for energy and strength, rather than recreation.

Managing time wisely: Energetic women manage their time. It does not manage them. To avoid getting bogged down and overwhelmed, they make lists, schedule priorities, delegate, and stay focused.

Self-indulging regularly: Energetic women know how to make beauty regimens feel like rejuvenation. Hair appointments at the salon with the best scalp massage, as well as the latest styles, can make you feel ready for anything.

Sleeping soundly: *More* magazine reported that studies conducted at Henry Ford Hospital's Sleep Disorders and Research Center, in Detroit, found that some people who increased their nightly sleep by an hour or two were more alert, more productive, less accident-prone, and less irritable and edgy. Go to bed an hour earlier tonight, and see what a difference it makes tomorrow.

Secret Ingredient: The best source of natural food energy are carbohydrates. So when you are looking for a pick-me-up, choose fruits, vegetables, and whole grains.

🍁 SEPTEMBER 23 🍁

Worship with Supreme Love.

Music can touch our spiritual core. That's why some of it is called sacred music, gospel, or praise songs.

Saxophonist John Coltrane's music was generally called jazz. But seven years after experiencing what he called a "spiritual awakening," Coltrane released an album entitled *A Love Supreme* in 1964 that entered that spiritual realm. The liner notes to this album are almost as well known to jazz buffs as the music. In a letter to "Dear Listener," Coltrane shared how he had asked God "to be given the means and privilege to make others happy through music." He explained that the music was presented in four parts, the last entitled "Psalm." And that *A Love Supreme* was a humble offering, an attempt to say, "THANK YOU GOD" (capitalization his) through his music.

A year after *A Love Supreme* was released, a brother named Franzo Wayne King heard John Coltrane play in concert. The music so moved him that he says he felt a "call to God." A few years later he had converted a room of his apartment into a chapel. On Coltrane's birthday, September 23, 1972, Saint John Coltrane African Orthodox Church was established on Divisadero Street in San Francisco, and remains there today. "We are grateful to lift up the Name of Jesus Christ through John's music," says King, who was made a bishop by the African Orthodox Church in 1982. The multiracial congregation that reaches out to those in need by providing food, shelter, counseling, and education, believes that Coltrane deserves sainthood because of the spiritual path he found in his last decade. Like many people, Coltrane, who suffered drinking and drug problems, gained sustenance through his faith in God's supreme love. Then—like no one else—he turned his unique musical gift into a homage to that love.

Just think of how high a calling we would all feel if we made our work, our gifts, our talents an offering, a thank-you to the Creator. May we all find a way to give gratitude for the most supreme of all love.

Secret Ingredient: If you are in the San Francisco area and would like to worship to the sounds of John Coltrane's spiritual music, contact the Saint John Coltrane African Orthodox Church on Divisadero Street. Or visit the Web site: saintjohncoltrane.org. If you have never heard Coltrane's music, start by checking out *A Love Supreme* or *My Favorite Things* at the local library or record store.

❧ SEPTEMBER 24 ❧

Start a "sister circle."

When I had the pleasure of meeting Julia Boyd, bestselling author of *Girlfriend to Girlfriend: Everyday Wisdom and Affirmations from the Sister Circle* at the Between Sisters conference in Boston, I invited her to share some words with you in this book. Including her contribution here has made me feel like I have a special person in my *Daily Cornbread* guest room. Here's the wonderful advice she shared exclusively with me about how to start a support group—which she so fondly calls a "sister circle:"

"Sis, pass me the macaroni and cheese."

"Zoey, did you make this cornbread all by yourself, or did you have a little help from Mr. Jiffy?"

"Ella, honey, you need to quit. You know me better than that. I don't do nothin' quick, and that includes makin' cornbread. Now, pass me the hot sauce for my chicken."

"Yeah, girl, a little hot sauce can really spice up your life."

"Speakin' of spice, girl, did you check out Danny Glover in *Beloved*. Honey! Honey! Honey! My man was too hot."

Pull up a chair and pass your plate, you've just joined my sister circle. Girlfriend, all I can say is be ready, 'cause with this group of *sistahs*, anything and everything goes. The food is delightful, the company is cozy, and the atmosphere—while laid back in style—is fully charged by stimulating conversation, easy laughter, and the warmth of sisterhood at its best.

I grew up in a family of five sisters and three brothers, so there was never a shortage of playmates. We've always been close and remain so to this day. In 1978 when I moved from San Jose, California to Seattle, Washington, I missed my family, and looking for the kind of comfort I received from them, I decided to create what I call my family of choice— my sister circle. Now, while my sister circle will never replace my family, it does allow me the freedom to explore all the different aspects of my life, from physical to spiritual. My sister circle serves as my main support system. We try to get together at least once every couple of months, sometimes more frequently to give each other comfort, support, and most of all a shared sense of unconditional love as individuals.

Sisters always ask me how do you get a sister circle going? Well, I'd love to share my recipe:

- Gather a generous heap of friends, choose those you know and a few you'd like to know better.
- Pick one date/time; we like weekends best.
- Choose a cozy meeting place, we generally take turns meeting at each other's homes.
- Plan for plenty of good food, everybody bringing a dish prepared from the heart.
- Stir it all together and let the fun begin.
- Keep the atmosphere casual and open so that conversation can be an easy flow.
- Set the food out buffet style; that way folks can help themselves, and there's no need for formal hosting.
- Set the date/time for the next gathering before everybody leaves; that way it's on the books ahead of time.

A good sister circle is a treasure. It can consist of two sisters or thirty. The important thing is coming together in the company of your sisters.

Secret Ingredient: **Do something positive for yourself and your female friends and relatives. Start a sister circle today.**

 BODY

SEPTEMBER 25

Fit in the five facets of fitness.

Women often ask me, "What exercise do *you* do?" Since I'm the big blabbermouth about working out, surely, I must have the workout routine of all time. *Wrong.* I'm just trying to make it, like everyone else. Always too busy to exercise. Forever procrastinating about taking my powerwalk. Rarely out there three times a week, as I profess. If I weren't a longtime vegetarian, I'd probably be overweight.

Sometimes, just the plethora of exercise choices are enough to make you wanna holler and call it an excuse for not doing anything! But on the contrary, I was inspired (for one whole week) on a trip to the Rancho La Puerta spa resort in Tecate, Mexico, to see what it would be like if I were to work out every day. As a guideline, guests are given a fitness schedule that features the Five Facets of Fitness. The aim is for you to balance your fitness program with at least one activity from each category a day. At home, I knew I would be accomplishing something if I did one activity from *one* category a day. What about you?

1. **Cardiovascular workouts (aerobic)**
   Aerobic activities to strengthen the heart and respiratory muscles and increase metabolism
   Choices: Hiking, walking, aerobics, aerobic circuit training, running/jogging, biking, lap swimming, step aerobics, StairMaster, treadmill, water walking
2. **Strengthening (anaerobic)**
   Activities that firm and strengthen muscles
   Choices: Dynabands, abdominal workout, dumbbells, yoga, Pilates, back exercises, hiking, resistance weight training
3. **Stretching and flexibility**
   Activities that stretch and lengthen the muscles and make them more flexible while minimizing soreness
   Choices: Morning stretch, yoga, back exercises, Pilates
4. **Coordination and balance**
   Stop/start activities, sports, dance. Proficiency in thee activities requires full application of first three facets, plus coordination.
   Choices: Yoga, hiking, self-defense, aerobics, tennis, volleyball, dance, basketball
5. **Relaxation**
   A time to recharge and revitalize while you relax deeply.
   Choices: T'ai chi, meditation, massage, herbal wrap, manicure, pedicure, pool lounging, sauna, Jacuzzi

Secret Ingredient: **Create your own spa retreat without leaving home. Incorporate the "five facets of fitness" into your life.**

❋ SPIRIT

🍁 SEPTEMBER 26 🍁

Have gratitude for sister love.

Besides the relationship between black men and their mothers, is there any bond closer than between black women who are sisters? Ask Sister Sledge about it. Ask the Delany Sisters, or Debbie Allen and Phylicia

Rashad. Ask Tamara and Tia Mowry—even the name of their television show is a testimony to the bond, *Sister, Sister.* African American women love their sisters so much that anyone else they feel even half that much affection toward gets the moniker "Sister." It's an honorific title, comparable to Reverend, Mrs., Doctor, or Attorney.

My mother always said she would do anything for her older sister because Aunt Katie helped pay for her college education—at the same time Aunt Katie was struggling to pay her own tuition. My aunt took such good care of my mother because, she always said, "That's my mama's baby!"

Because today is the birthday of my own sister, Vicki, my mentor and confidante, I am inspired to contemplate the unique bond of sisters that we and other sisters blessed to have sisters enjoy:

- ❖ **The bond of shared history.** The story of your lives is written on the same pages. Family events, joys, and sorrows are experienced and remembered together for a lifetime. Historically for black women in particular, after being separated from our sisters in slavery, we feel blessed to have each other now. I'm convinced the bond involves "race memory" that can't be taken for granted.
- ❖ **The security of trust.** Secrets are shared and kept, knowing that blood ties protect them from violation.
- ❖ **The absence of envy.** Women who are sisters are more likely to be not only genuinely happy for, but *proud of,* each other's successes and triumphs.
- ❖ **Unconditional love.** When Daddy's passed and Mama's gone, sometimes the most enduring love left is that of our first friend.

Secret Ingredient: **Enrich your day by calling your sister(s) or sister-friends and saying "thank you" and "I love you."**

 MIND

 SEPTEMBER 27

Speak in the affirmative.

Here's a riddle for you: *What is the most famous affirmation of all time?*

Hint: In the Muhammad Ali biography *King of the World,* author David Remnick quotes boxer Floyd Patterson as saying, "I always knew that all of Clay's bragging was a way to convince himself that he could do what he said he'd do. I never liked all his bragging. It took me a long time to understand who Clay was talking to. Clay was talking to Clay."

Affirmations are just a positive way of talking to yourself. Pumping yourself up. On *Entertainment Tonight* recently, I saw an interview with actor Will Smith in which he was asked if he gave himself a pep talk before doing a challenging scene in a movie. Smith said yes, that he looks in the mirror and exclaims, "You're the man! You're the man! You can do this!"

There are some things that Will Smith's affirmations have in common with the one in the riddle:

* ❖ **It is said in the present tense.** Notice he didn't say, "You will be the man," but *you are now!* It makes the outcome happening now, and that makes it more powerful than *whenever.*
* ❖ **Don't worry about whether you believe the affirmation** or not, at first. After you say it long enough, you will.
* ❖ **Make the affirmation have power.** Don't pussyfoot around. Men are better at this bravado than women, so take a lesson from the brothers and give it assertiveness and punch.
* ❖ **Say it over and over.** Write it down.

In the 1960s, Muhammad Ali had the nerve to not only utter affirmations such as "Float like a butterfly, sting like a bee," he also shared them with the world. He wrote poetry. And he's still being quoted today. When former professional wrestler Jesse Ventura won the election for governor of Minnesota in 1998, he quoted Ali by saying, "We shocked the world!"

Secret Ingredient: Answer to the riddle: Muhammad Ali's famous affirmation, "I am the greatest!" Develop your own personal mantra/affirmation. Let it bring out the you that you want to be.

❀ BODY

 SEPTEMBER 28

Defeat the agony of "de feet."

Did you know that your feet are each composed of a network of twenty-six bones, twenty-nine joints, and many muscles? Taking an average of several thousand steps a day, the feet are capable of bearing great loads over many miles. When functioning properly, your feet can handle all the demands you place on them, but when your feet get to aching, watch out! What you need is the right treatment for rapid results, complete healing, and full function. Knowledge of some of the most common foot problems, and the remedies suggested by the American College of Foot and Ankle Surgeons, is a first step:

Corns and calluses, frequently caused by ill-fitting or poor quality shoes, or various foot deformities.

What to do: Purchase well-constructed shoes that fit properly, allowing ample space between the toe and the end of the shoe to prevent irritation.

Bunion, an enlargement of the bone on the inside of the foot at the big toe.

What to do: Obtain shoes of greater length and width to provide space for the bunion. Avoid pointy-toed shoes. Wear shoes of softer material to decrease irritation. If pain persists, a podiatric surgeon may prescribe orthoses (special shoe inserts) or recommend treatment alternatives, including surgical correction.

Hammertoe, an abnormal contraction of one or more toes that often causes them to run on the top of the shoe.

What to do: Buy shoes of larger size with roomier toe boxes to decrease pressure on the toes. Consult a podiatric surgeon for possible surgical straightening of one or more hammertoes if careful shoe selection doesn't relieve the discomfort.

Ankle sprain, a condition that results from an inherently unstable ankle, trauma, or as a result of an athletic injury.

What to do: Rest, ice, compression, and elevation (RICE). See a podiatric surgeon immediately to rule out a fracture or ligament tear.

Secret Ingredient: **If pain, discomfort, or fatigue of the feet persists, consult a podiatrist. For your choice of thirteen free brochures on foot and ankle health, contact the American College of Foot and Ankle Surgeons at 1-888-THE-FEET.**

❧ SEPTEMBER 29 ❧

Reclaim the drum.

One of the most powerful experiences I ever had was attending the funeral of author and activist James Baldwin. In New York's Cathedral of St. John the Divine in 1987, I sat transfixed by the moving eulogies of Baldwin's renowned contemporaries, which included Toni Morrison, Maya Angelou, and Amiri Baraka. What I wasn't prepared for, however, was the awesome processional and recessional that featured the African drumming of the great percussionist Babatunde Olatunji and his ensemble. The powerful drumbeats that accompanied the casket down the cathedral aisle made me feel in my *soul* that the ancestors were indeed coming to take Baldwin home that day. I had never heard anything in my life even close to those deep and mournful rhythms that reverberated with the dignity and honor fit for a king. James Baldwin deserved no less.

Prohibited during slavery in America, communication with African skin drums was largely lost for centuries. But Nigerian-born New York–based Olatunji says he "reclaimed the drum" in 1959 with his first album, *Drums of Passion,* and more recently he was nominated for a Grammy for his 1997 CD *Love Drum Talk.* When my family and I went to see Olatunji perform in Harlem recently at the Schomburg Center for Research in Black Culture, he told the audience that he had just performed in Ghana for the fortieth anniversary of that country's independence. At the Schomburg he was accompanied by his ensemble, Drums of Passion, which included seven other drummers and five dancers. The music was upbeat and joyous, and had the audience clapping and joining in. "The rhythm," Olatunji said, "is a powerful form of communication, of healing, of thanksgiving." At the end of the concert, young and old danced on the stage and in the aisles. Then Olatunji and his drummers came into the crowd and led us all out to the vestibule in a recession that this time was a celebration of life.

Secret Ingredient: If you would like to "reclaim the drum," get an African drum to play at home. In most major cities across the country, you can find African drum and dance classes, at local gyms, dance studios or recreation centers. Or pick up Olatunji's Grammy-nominated CD, *Love Drum Talk* and listen to the music of our ancestors.

❧ SEPTEMBER 30 ❧

Plan some fall foliage fun.

In the newspapers around this time of year, there are tons of ads for fall foliage tours and bed-and-breakfast inns in scenic settings where you can observe the turning of the leaves. If you've never done this before, make it a point to get away one weekend and try it. Need more coaxing? Some of the reasons it's well worth the journey, include:

❖ **You can recharge.** Being in the midst of nature's beauty just can't be beat. Be sure to drive to your destination to get the full view of the changing of the leaves. If you live in a warm climate and need to fly there, rent a car from the airport. Going by train is scenic too.

❖ **Take the kids.** Of course, it will be hard to "do nothing" if you take young children, but no matter what age they are, being out in the open air and new environment will do them, as well as you, a world of good. It's educational to boot.

❖ **Don't take the kids.** Hey, whichever option suits you! If you need a break after breaking in the back-to-school routine, it's a good time to fly the coop. I'm always up for a couples weekend. Tell your baby-sitting angel that you'll bring back plenty of brochures for them to make their own reservations soon.

❖ **Take all the books and magazines you've got piled up.** I read once in the *New York Times* travel section about a couple who take an annual long weekend just for reading. They save their best books for their much-anticipated trip, making sure the inn has an active fireplace and a rocking chair.

❖ **Be enriched.** When I was a college student, I once spent a fall weekend visiting Harpers Ferry in West Virginia, the site of the John Brown insurrection. Years later, Reg and I went to an inn in New England that, we discovered upon our arrival, had been a rest stop on the Underground Railroad. If you think you might get cabin fever just reading and relaxing, plan your weekend near history.

Secret Ingredient: **Check out** *Hippocrene Guide to the Underground Railroad,* **by Charles L. Blockson, for locations along the mid-Atlantic states and Canada. Contact the Department of Parks and Services in Washington, D.C., and inquire about other Underground Railroad sites.**

🍁 OCTOBER 1 🍁

Do your best to save your breasts.

"I was in bed watching TV when a commercial came on about breast cancer and it said you should check your breasts every month," my cousin Deborah Chisholm told me. "I had never done this before, because no one in my family that I knew of ever had breast cancer. So I was just kidding around, checking my breast, when I noticed one of them had a very small, hard lump that felt like a rock."

Deborah, forty-one, called her doctor, who scheduled a mammogram, which "came back okay, so I didn't give it another thought," she said. "Well, six months later I had bought a house and the lady who lived there before me had left a card in the shower showing a woman checking her breasts for cancer on one side and, on the other side, a man checking himself. One night while I was sleeping I dreamt that there was a large lump in my breast and that I was lying down on the bed with my hand over it. When I woke up, I was lying with my hand directly on the lump—and it had grown three times larger than when I felt it before."

Now, five years later, because of Deborah's early detection, a biopsy, lumpectomy, radiation, and chemotherapy, she says there are "no signs of cancer. My cancer blood count is extremely low," she told me in an e-mail message. "My oncologist said I am doing extra well. **God is good all the time,**" she typed in boldface.

Deborah is grateful that examining her own breasts saved her life. It can work for you too. For instructions on how to do it, see October 2. Don't be afraid; take control of your health.

Secret Ingredient: Deborah finds helpful the Web site AOL Keyword: Breast Cancer, which has information on awareness, self-examination, facts, books, organizations, support groups, and experts to answer your questions. For woman-to-woman information on getting to know your breasts, the female doctor who performs my mammograms recommends *Dr. Susan Love's Breast Book,* by Susan M. Love, M.D., with Karen Lindsey.

❧ OCTOBER 2 ❧

Take your self-exam once a month.

You may have taken the PSAT, the SAT, maybe even the GRE, but are you in the habit of taking the BSE (breast self-examination)? Women aged twenty or older should perform a BSE every month. By doing it regularly, you can get to know how your breasts normally feel and therefore be more aware of any changes. The best time for BSE is about a week after your period ends, when your breasts are no longer tender or swollen. If you're postmenopausal, pick a particular day each month (i.e., the first, or payday). Here are BSE instructions from the American Cancer Society:

How to Do the Breast Self-Examination

1. Lie down with a pillow under your right shoulder and place your right arm behind your head.
2. Use the finger pads of the three inner fingers of your left hand to feel for lumps in the right breast.
3. Press firmly enough to know how your breast feels. A firm ridge in the lower curve of each breast is normal. If you're not sure how hard to press, talk with your doctor or nurse.
4. Move around the breast in a circular up-and-down line or wedge pattern. Be sure to do it the same way every time, check the entire breast area, and remember how your breast feels from month to month.
5. Repeat the exam on your left breast, using the finger pads of the right hand. (Move the pillow to under your left shoulder.)
6. Repeat the examination of both breasts while standing, with one arm behind your head. The upright position makes it easier to check the upper and outer part of the breasts (toward your armpit). This is where about half of breast cancers are found. You may want to do the standing part of the BSE while you are in the shower. Some breast changes can be felt more easily when your skin is wet and soapy.

Secret Ingredient: If change occurs, such as development of a lump or swelling, skin irritation, dimpling, nipple pain or retraction (turning inward), redness or scaliness of the nipple or breast skin, or a discharge other than breast milk, you should see your doctor as soon as possible. Remember that most of the time, these breast changes are not cancer. For a free self-exam instruction card illustrated for black women, call the Celebrating Life Foundation at 1-800-207-0992. Visit their Web site at www.celebratinglife.org.

❊ NATIONAL BREAST CANCER AWARENESS MONTH

🍁 OCTOBER 3 🍁

Dispel the myths; get the facts.

Like my cousin Deborah (see October 1), many women feel that they may not need to be concerned about breast cancer prevention because they are unaware of any family history of it. That is a common myth that results in only fifty-eight percent of African American women forty and older ever having had a mammogram, and many more who don't get them often enough. While black women are less likely than white women to develop breast cancer, our mortality rate is five percent higher, in part because black women do not seek treatment until the cancer is more advanced. In order to be effective, mammograms must be obtained regularly. Here are three common myths and the facts.

Myth 1: There's no history of breast cancer in my family, so I don't need to worry about it.

Fact: While a family history of the disease is one risk factor according to the National Cancer Institute, eighty percent of women who develop breast cancer have no history of the disease in their families. All women are at risk for developing breast cancer. Breast cancer is the most common form of cancer in American women, striking one in nine. Just being a woman and getting older puts you at risk for breast cancer.

Myth 2: My doctor didn't recommend a mammogram, so I don't need one.

Fact: African American women are more likely to develop breast cancer under age forty, and your doctor may or may not be aware of that ethnic-specific fact. Don't wait for your doctor; follow this guideline from Brenda Blane, eastern regional director of the National Black Leadership Initiative on Cancer: Get your baseline (a first X ray for future comparison) mammogram at age thirty-five. The American Cancer Society suggests that women forty and older should have a mammogram every year.

Myth 3: I don't have any symptoms, so I don't need a mammogram.

Fact: Mammography can detect breast cancers when they are extremely small, up to two years before they can be felt by a woman or her doctor. When detected and treated early, breast cancer need not be life-threatening. The exam is easy to arrange. Your doctor can set it up for you. Or you can get a mammogram at a local hospital, health clinic, or mobile van.

Secret Ingredient: If you have a history of breast cancer in your family, or are thirty-five or over, you should have a mammogram once a year. Insurance coverage is becoming more widespread. If cost is a concern, various health agencies, organizations, and women's support groups provide referrals to low-cost or free mammography services. For more information, call the National Cancer Institute's Cancer Information Service at 1-800-4-CANCER.

❦ OCTOBER 4 ❦

Bless yourself. Bless your pet.

My daughter and her friend Aftynn were having a conversation about the new leopard collar someone would be wearing to church the next day. It took me a moment to realize that the "person" was actually Aftynn's dog, Spice Girl. Why would a schnauzer be getting all gussied up and going to *church?* Turns out, it was for a blessing of animals held at Aftynn's family's Episcopalian church as well as at other churches—particularly Catholic—throughout the world. The ceremony coincides with the Feast of St. Francis of Assisi, which is celebrated every October 4. Known for his kindness to pets, St. Francis, who lived in Italy in the eleventh century, is considered the patron saint of animals.

When I asked Aftynn's mom, Brenda, my good friend, why the family decided to take their doggie to church, she immediately detected the whimsy in my question and responded, "I felt if there was any chance Spice Girl could be saved, I'd have to take her. I used to see pets going into the Catholic church, and I'd holler [with laughter], but when our interim pastor said we were going to do this too, I said okay."

Brenda told me that the pets sat right in the pews. "One started howling!" When it came time for the blessing of the pets, the owners took them up to the altar. "They sat down nicely, and the canon blessed them with prayer and by sprinkling holy water on them," Brenda reported. "The sermon was on the value of having pets." Quite apropos.

If you don't attend a church that has this tradition, you can visit a Catholic church in your area. Brenda tells me that all are welcome, whether you belong to the church or not. It's a community service. Or, you can have your own little ceremony at home. Ask God's blessing that your pet might have strong health and safety. Thank God for the joy and companionship the pet brings. And don't forget to let the pet know how special he is by making sure he wears his Sunday best.

Secret Ingredient: If you're just crazy about your little poochie or parakeet, you're likely to enjoy *Chicken Soup for the Pet Lover's Soul,* by Jack Canfield et al. The book features short stories about the love and lessons that pets offer.

 MIND

❧ OCTOBER 5 ❧

Know this: we can win!

With the disproportionate number of black men in prison; the higher propensity of African Americans to contract HIV-AIDS, diabetes, heart disease, and hypertension; the pervasive veil of racism; and just the general sense of "the struggle," it's a miracle that African Americans don't have a collective sense of feeling like "losers."

But if you know your history, you know that we "keep hope alive" not just because Jesse Jackson tells us to do so, but because our ancestors did. And if they could prevail under worse conditions, who are we to give up?

Every individual achievement is a step toward our collective winning victory. When heavyweight champion Muhammad Ali, who was so vilified by the American majority in the 1960s, becomes a beloved international icon in the 1990s, it's a sign that we can win.

When the presidential appointment for "America's family doctor," the United States surgeon general, happens to be an African American twice in a row, the phrase "there's a doctor *in the house*" has new meaning.

When Magic Johnson can announce that he is HIV-positive, yet ten years later still be robust and making a difference as a business owner in black communities, we all feel a little better.

And when *Fortune* magazine calls Oprah Winfrey one of the most powerful women in American business, the cotton field seems farther and farther away.

A couple of years ago, my husband, Reggie, found himself at a party with attorney Johnnie Cochran, and after introducing himself he said, "After the victory you had in the O.J. trial, it makes me think that maybe we *can* win in court." To that, Cochran replied, "Oh, yes, we can win. We can *win!*"

Secret Ingredient: **If this book had a sound track, I'd play *We're a Winner* by the Impressions featuring Curtis Mayfield right about now! If you've been feeling low lately, jot down your own list of victories in your life, in the lives of others around you, in our history, and in our present that prove that "we're movin' on up."**

 BODY

 ## OCTOBER 6

Kick a cold.

Does it seem like everyone around you is sneezing, coughing, and blowing their noses? If you're afraid that you or your children will be next, there are four effective ways to reduce your odds of catching a cold:

1. **Wash up.** Scientists and doctors say that washing your hands often is the most important thing you can do to prevent catching a cold. Contrary to popular belief, antibacterial soaps are no more effective than other types of cleansers, plus it's the rinsing of the germs with water that gets rid of the germs. With young children, however, the lathering with soap may make them rinse off longer.
2. **Use lots of paper cups, plates, and bowls.** Colds can be contagious as soon as forty-eight hours before the onset of symptoms and as long as five days or more after the signs of a cold appear. So sharing of drinks from the same cup, or snacks from the same bowl, should be avoided.
3. **Keep your distance.** On buses, subways, trains, and planes, it's hard to avoid proximity to a sneezer or cougher, but try to stay at least

three feet away. If that's not possible, turn your back to the cold culprit.

4. **Stop rubbing your eyes and nose.** I always thought it was odd that my husband and daughter had a similar habit of rubbing their eyes with the heels of their hands, but experts say this is actually less hazardous to your health than using a fingertip, which is more likely to be loaded with germs. It's best to stop rubbing at all, but if you can't, use your knuckle, the heel of your hand—or better yet, a clean tissue.

Secret Ingredient: **Even the most fastidious among us are likely to catch a cold sometime, so in case you do, drink lots of fluids (such as water, herbal tea, or chicken gumbo), and try echinacea (an herb that is believed to help your resistance to colds) at the first sign of your cold and continue throughout the duration. If symptoms persist, pick cold medicines that offer relief specifically for your symptoms of running nose, dry or mucous cough, or stuffy nose. And do like your mama told you: Cover your mouth when you cough and keep your germs to yourself.**

❋ SPIRIT

🍁 OCTOBER 7 🍁

Go gospel surfing.

My cousin Deborah, who shared her breast cancer story, and I have laid eyes on each other only once in our entire lives—and that was almost thirty years ago. She grew up in the South, I was raised in the Pacific Northwest; she now lives in the Midwest, and I'm on the East Coast. Yet, after years of letters, photos, messages relayed between now-deceased relatives, and long-distance phone calls, Deborah and I keep in touch easily through the technology of e-mail. We may be miles apart, but our spirits are as close as our ages (we're only months apart).

One day she sent me by e-mail some inspirational passages for the week that were posted on the NetNoir Web site. That started something new for me; I had done a lot of surfing the Net, but never any gospel surfing! Here's what I found:

❖ **A praise party:** If you log on to www.netnoir.com or AOL Keyword:NetNoir, in the area called black gospel chapel you can find Weekly Inspirations, Words of Wisdom, Prayer Hour and

Praise Party, Sermons, and info on gospel jazz and gospel rap among other things. It's very comprehensive. You could be in there for hours getting your spiritual groove on!

❖ **Prayer for the week:** Motivational teacher and author Iyanla Vanzant has a Web site that features a weekly prayer. Visit her on www.innervisionsworldwide.com.

❖ **Thought for the day:** *Essence* magazine editor in chief Susan Taylor posts a thought of the day on www.essence.com.

❖ **Inspiration for any time:** Tying in to the spiritual on her television show, Oprah Winfrey has a Remembering Your Spirit area on www.oprah.com and on AOL Keyword: Oprah. Under the heading Spiritualife, you can contemplate your Gratitude and find a Thought for the Day.

Secret Ingredient: For additional online inspiration, go to Net-Noir's Related Web Sites in the black gospel chapel area. You'll find a motherlode of Afrocentric links.

❀ MIND

 OCTOBER 8 ❧

Lose the blues.

When I was on the road constantly, promoting *Heart & Soul* and talking with women about their health concerns, one of the recurring requests sisters approached me with across the country was to address depression and mental illness in the magazine. "It's something no one wants to talk about, but it's a big problem," I heard again and again.

In an effort to bring attention and treat this overwhelming illness, the American Psychiatric Association has initiated National Depression Screening Day (NDSD). Held around this time each year, NDSD was created to call attention to the illness of depression, to educate the public about its symptoms and effective treatments, to offer the opportunity to be screened for depression, and to connect those in need of treatment to a mental health care professional. On NSDS, some three thousand sites at hospitals, clinics, primary care doctors' offices, college clinics, and other health organizations nationwide offer free, confidential screenings for depression. At the sites you can learn more about depression, take a ten-question screening test, meet with a mental health professional, and get a referral for further evaluation if necessary.

Depression will strike one in five women and one in ten men over the course of their lifetimes. Sufferers feel hopeless, sad, anxious, and that they no longer enjoy their usual activities. Physical symptoms such as headaches, stomach problems, difficulty sleeping or sleeping too much occur. Changes in weight and appetite can also be signs of depression. Unfortunately, nearly half of people with depression do not seek treatment, although treatment is readily available and extremely effective.

African American women are among those numbers. Our perception of what it means to be a "strong black woman" often prohibits our reaching out for help. But you don't have to suffer to be strong. In fact, you don't have to suffer at all. With treatment, you can lose the blues.

Secret Ingredient: **For more information about depression/ anxiety screening sites near you, call the National Mental Illness Screening Project at 1-800-573-4433, or visit the Web site www.nmisp.org. Two books for African American women may also be helpful. Read** *Can I Get a Witness?: For Sisters, When the Blues Is More Than a Song,* **by Julia A. Boyd, and** *What the Blues Is All About,* **by Angela Mitchell with Kennise Herring, Ph.D.**

 MIND

❧ OCTOBER 9 ❧

Hold a fire drill.

The dreaded fire drill. From the classroom to the boardroom, the fire drill is regarded as an inconvenient nuisance that makes preschoolers shiver outside without their coats in wintertime, and has corporate execs sucking their teeth when important meetings get interrupted. But no one mandates a fire drill at home, and that may be where we need it most. According to the National Fire Protection Association (NFPA), eight in ten fire deaths in the United States take place in the home.

When my daughter was in grade school, one of her homework assignments was to draw a map of the escape route from her bedroom out of the house in case of fire. Anique took this assignment very seriously, and voiced her complaint that she couldn't get her father and me to conduct a home fire drill. Taking our daughter's lead, our family became more prepared. As the Bible says, ". . . and a little child shall lead them."

According to a National Fire Protection Association (NFPA) survey, we were typical—only sixteen percent of respondents had planned and practiced how they'd escape if they had a fire in their home. That means that nearly eight-five percent of the population would be ill prepared if fire should strike. Since 1925, National Fire Prevention Week has been observed during around October 9, the anniversary of the great Chicago fire of 1871. This is a time to:

- ❖ Hold a home fire drill. Review escape tips such as getting out the house quickly and carefully and calling the fire department from a neighbor's phone, a portable phone, or call box.
- ❖ Clean the lint out of your clothes-dryer screens and vent hoses. Clothes dryers start more residential fires than any other appliance.
- ❖ Remember that most fatal home fires happen at night, when people are asleep. The top five causes of home fires that kill are: 1) smoking, 2) arson, 3) heating equipment, 4) children playing with fire, 5) electrical systems.

Secret Ingredient: **Make sure every member of your household knows what to do in the event of a fire. Get out your calendar and schedule a fire drill every three months in the upcoming year. For more information about Fire Prevention Week, or a kit to plan a campaign in your community, call 1-800-344-3555, or visit www.nfpa.org.**

❋ SPIRIT

OCTOBER 10 ❧

Journey toward ultimate inner peace.

My friend Michael Coakley was formerly a resident manager at a chic golf and tennis club in the Bahamas. Most folks would think that was a successful enough job, full of glamour, beach parties, and pretty women from around the world. But following his truer path to self-fulfillment, he got an MBA and began to work in hospital administration in Fort Lauderdale. "People may not think so, but both of the jobs I've had are similar," he says. "They both deal with people. On my first job I en-countered people when they were vibrant and healthy, and now on this one I'm working with people when they are sick and dying. Yet, what is the same is that I observe human nature."

On his hospital job he feels the reward of helping people in need, of service to humanity. But mainly, Mike says, he is learning so much about life. "One day I walked into a hospital room when a hospice volunteer was asking a patient, 'Are you afraid?' And the woman replied, 'Yes, I'm afraid, because I never took control of my spiritual life, of my core beliefs, of who I wanted to be religiously.' " This woman, he says, was over ninety years old. "Yet, it doesn't matter how old they are, very few are ready, no one wants to go." Some people in the hospital who are terminal even scream out in fear.

On the other hand, he says, there are some young people he sees who have inner peace! "I saw a girl one evening who had the most peaceful, beautiful expression on her face, like a glow," he tells me. "And the next day, when I came to work, they said she had passed."

What makes the difference? Faith. Pure and simple. No one wants to think about dying, much less prepare for it, which takes not only thinking about it but contemplating and planning and taking charge. But that was the regret of the first woman—that she hadn't taken control of her spirituality. When we think about the concept of taking control, it is rarely in connection with our spiritual life. More often we follow like sheep.

It often takes courage; it takes stepping out of your comfort zone to find your real essence. When we travel down the freeway, where are we all going? Although the traffic may be heavy, we all have our individual exits, our own destinations, our own final stops. The journey to inner peace may seem to be a daunting one. But when you're ready to go, God will take you there.

Secret Ingredient: **Take control of your spiritual life by studying first what's in your heart and then what's in holy books, churches, mosques, and temples. Search your soul, and there you'll find peace.**

 MIND

☙ OCTOBER 11 ☙

Come out, come out, wherever you are!

In September 1998, speaking at a dinner of the Human Rights Campaign (HRC) at which Vice President Al Gore also spoke, Maya Angelou made a powerful analogy that people who are gay and in the closet are like caged birds. In her remarks printed in the *HRC Quarterly* she said, ". . . all of us are caged birds. . . . Caged by somebody else's ignorance. Caged because of someone's else's smallmindedness. Caged because of someone else's fear, hate, and, sometimes, caged by our own lack of courage. When we have enough courage to come out—I don't mean just out of a closet, I mean out of your spirit—when you have enough courage to stand and say, 'I came here to stay,' it's amazing."

Held every October 11, HRC's National Coming-Out Day commemorates the 1987 March on Washington for Lesbian and Gay Rights, and promotes honesty and openness about being lesbian, gay, or bisexual, at home, in the workplace, or on campus. As part of HRC's public education program to help turn ignorance into acceptance, the organization publishes a resource guide that includes these five facts:

1. Homosexuality is not a choice; it chooses you.
2. Being gay or lesbian is not a "lifestyle," it's a life.
3. Gay people are mentally healthy.
4. Gay men and lesbians constitute families.
5. Some of the most talented people are gay or lesbian.

No one knows how many people are gay, lesbian, or bisexual. According to the HRC, the current estimates are around three to six percent of the population. However, because of discrimination, many people are afraid or unwilling to be identified as gay or lesbian, even in an anonymous survey. Chances are someone you know, someone in your family—maybe even you—are homosexual. Coming out, being yourself, can be psychologically healthy, but it is a major life decision. The HRC advises that as with reaching any personal milestone, a person might seek professional help through the process.

Secret Ingredient: **To receive free copies of the Human Rights Campaign's *Resource Guide to Coming Out*, call 1-800-866-NCOD or e-mail ncop@hrc.org. Stay up-to-date on current issues by visiting www.hrc.org.**

 SPIRIT

 OCTOBER 12

Establish a "day of caring."

When you work under deadlines and pressure, you always feel stressed out and as if you're trying to play catch-up. That was the general feeling in the office on the day that our company, Rodale Press, mandated that all employees would be expected to participate in a corporate initiative called A Day of Caring.

Well, you should have seen all the eyes rolling and the hands on the hips. No, better that you didn't. "It's a nice gesture," someone said to me, "I just don't like being forced to do it. If I want to give back to the community, I will on my own."

Long story short, just about every single person who participated in some way by choosing to hold a "border baby," or volunteer at a teen pregnancy center, or perform some other community service was rewarded with that feeling of making a difference that experts call the "helper's high."

I can testify to that. I signed up for the team that was going to a senior citizen residence. When the office e-mail announced that the center would need someone to play the piano for the weekly sing-along, I volunteered. As we ate a sandwich lunch with the residents, a handsome gentleman introduced himself to me as the cousin of a long-gone jazz great. I in turn immediately developed a crush on him, and we sang duets from the hymnal long after the official sing-along time was over. I had noticed that the cardigan sweater he was wearing was a bit tattered, so I sent him a new one for a Christmas gift. Yet, the gift of caring he gave *me* was the more valuable present.

If you feel you just don't have the time to do the community service you would like to, know that you are normal, and don't feel guilty. But do try to take at least *one* day a year to help those in need. Or advocate that your company start a program. There are many organizations that need assistance and helping them may fit into your lifestyle, like contributing clothes to women making the transition from welfare to work, or donating children's books to underprivileged children. Help others— and help yourself.

Secret Ingredient: **Start a Columbus Day alternative. The United Way Corporate Volunteer Program helps coordinate companies with charitable organizations. Call your local United Way for the office nearest you.**

❧ OCTOBER 13 ❧

Take it from Donna.

If you are a fitness buff, you probably know Donna Richardson. A *Heart & Soul* cover model twice, an often-quoted expert in the magazine, and an editorial adviser, Donna has proven her commitment to getting women fit. And the sisters love her! Once, when the magazine had special events at gyms in four cities, everywhere I went sisters wanted to know, "Where's Donna?"

Recently, I caught up with her on the heels of promoting her recently published book *Let's Get Real! Exercise Your Right to a Healthy Body* and between radio appearances on *The Tom Joyner Morning Show.* I asked her for her secrets—and she gave them to me! So, here are Donna Richardson's seven top fitness tips, exclusively for the readers of *Daily Cornbread*—you!

1. **Consult with your doctor** before starting any fitness program.
2. **Set realistic goals.** Set short-term and long-term goals. Decide what you wish to accomplish and develop an action plan to achieve it.
3. **Choose activities that will help you meet your goals.** Realize, though, that you will like doing some of them, and some you won't. Do it because it's good for you!
4. **Combine healthy eating with daily physical activity.** Drink plenty of water.
5. **Get in stride by walking.** My favorite aerobic activity, walking, is low impact, burns lots of calories, strengthens your heart and lungs, and you can do it anytime and anywhere.
6. **Consider weight training.** It strengthens and tones your muscles, and if you're trying to lose weight, the more muscle you have, the more calories you burn.
7. **Make a commitment and be consistent.** Dedication on a daily basis becomes a lifestyle, so work it out!"

Secret Ingredient: You can "work it out" with Donna Richardson on her videos *30 Days to Thinner Thighs* and *30 Days to Firmer Abs and Arms.* Or call 1-800-745-1145 to order, or to receive a free catalogue that includes Donna's videos.

🍁 OCTOBER 14 🍁

Let your spirit lead your body.

One evening when I was busy writing, the phone rang, I answered it, and the caller was David Harris, my husband's charming, handsome young protégé.

"Hey, Steph, what's up?" he asked.

"Just writing my book, David."

"Yeah? Put me in it!"

"Do you have a mind/body/spirit lesson to share? You got something to say?" I started, egging him on. "You can't just be *in* it, you gotta drop some knowledge."

He didn't skip a beat. "Say this: Let your body be led by your spirit; don't let your body lead your spirit."

"What do you mean by that, Dave?" For some reason, my mind went straight to Sunday sermons on temptations of the flesh.

"I mean, like what happened to me today. I really didn't want to go jogging, but my spirit knew it was the right thing to do, so I followed the spirit—not the body. That's what we've got to do, follow the spirit, because the body is not always willing."

Jogging, he was talking about (do you hear the little slaps I'm giving my wrists?). *Motivation* to get up and do it when you don't feel like it. Working out when you don't want to. Doing it anyway. Pushing yourself. Letting the spirit move you toward your goal.

Okay, okay, Dave. I'm feeling it. That can work. I hear ya. Thanks.

Secret Ingredient: **The secret to staying motivated is to do an exercise you enjoy. For example, if your routine is jogging or walking, but you really enjoy dancing, on your under-inspired days, just put on some music and see what happens. You just might find your spirit *moving.***

❧ OCTOBER 15 ❧

Take inventory of your "woman things."

My friend Teresa sent me an e-mail that had a list, What Every Woman Should Have. It was a fun message that included such gems as: One old boyfriend you can imagine going back to and one who reminds you of how far you've come. And, One friend who always makes you laugh, and one who lets you cry."

Using that format, I thought I'd come up with my own list of "woman thangs" for mind, body, and spirit.

Ten Things Every Woman Should Have for Health and Well-Being

1. **A spiritual core** that sustains you
2. **Family members** who care about you
3. **A love relationship** that affirms you
4. **Someone to talk to** when you're blue
5. **An exercise** that you take pleasure in doing regularly
6. **Several delicious low-fat meals** that you enjoy preparing
7. **A doctor** whom you trust
8. **A job** that fulfills you
9. **A cause** you're passionate about
10. **A purpose**

Secret Ingredient: Go down the list and contemplate each point. Keep in mind that few women have all these things at one time, and that not having any particular one is no reflection on your self-worth. For example, if you are not currently in a love relationship, that is better than being in one that doesn't affirm you.

❦ OCTOBER 16 ❦

Be a natural beauty.

Bobbi Brown, the founder of Bobbi Brown Cosmetics, happens to live in my town. One day, when my friend Erlene and I went to pick up my daughter from her Saturday job at a local toy store, Anique informed us that Brown was making an appearance in the bookstore next door to her store to promote *Bobbi Brown Beauty: The Ultimate Beauty Resource.* Having positive vibes about Brown and her products, I said, "Hey, let's go in!"

Brown was at the tail end of her talk before her book signing, but I heard her say as we were walking in that the most important beauty tools were brushes. "I suggest two cosmetic brushes," she said. "One big blush brush—not the kind that comes in the case; they streak your face—and one eyeliner brush." Being addicted to my eye pencils, I paid attention when she explained that liner applied with a wet brush was less oily than using a pencil. *That makes sense,* I thought. *So that's why my contact lenses are always so filmy!* Duh.

After the talk, Brown took questions. My hand shot up. "Tyra Banks says her makeup routine includes four coats of mascara," I began, quoting advice from Tyra's cover story for *Heart & Soul* that I had used myself on special occasions. "What's your top beauty tip?" I asked.

"Really?" she asked thoughtfully about Tyra. Then she said something that surprised me: "My top tip is to get on the treadmill!" With other people waiting to ask questions and get books signed, there was not enough time for her to elaborate, but once I went home and started reading her book I came across the beauty philosophy that fostered that answer: "Exercise will get rid of the puffiness in your face and open up your pores. It will help energize you for the day and will always make you feel better."

Secret Ingredient: **Take Bobbi's advice: Exercise for a healthy glow, and be a natural beauty! Check out Brown's book, which includes a chapter on African American beauty.**

🍁 OCTOBER 17 🍁

Let your flower blossom.

Bessie Love has the perfect name. She loved herself enough to get out of an abusive relationship. Now she has devoted her life's work to helping other women do the same. Here's her story:

"My abusive husband told me, 'You have no purpose in life. You are merely taking up space and breathing air that someone else would be breathing.' But God had a plan for me, and today I know what my purpose in life is. The last eight years have been spent advocating for women who cannot or will not speak for themselves. I speak about survival, not the terrible crime, because I have chosen to turn my nightmare into something positive. I strongly believe it does not matter what has happened to you—it is what you *do* about it that matters. When I decided to end fourteen years of marital abuse, here's what I did:

- ❖ I stopped denying (by minimizing, intellectualizing, rationalizing, and justifying) what was happening to me
- ❖ I detached emotionally (by severing the love issues that once kept me connected)
- ❖ I started rebuilding my self-esteem and validating myself
- ❖ I took control of my fears by not allowing them to control me (I realized he did not have an all-seeing eye, as he had told me)
- ❖ I realized that I needed to seek help. I couldn't do this by myself, so I established a strong support system of family, friends, and a domestic-violence agency that understood my issues
- ❖ And finally, I decided it would serve no purpose to be resentful, angry, or to retaliate. Women ask me what I did for revenge. I view that as a waste of time and energy that would not be productive to my healing process. When you retaliate, you shift the focus from being positive, and you're allowing him to pull your strings

"In the prison camp of my own home, I was a rosebud. Fortunately, on March 18, 1990, a beautiful ray of light touched my bloom. Today I am continuously learning and exploring what happened to me. This crime happened for fourteen years, and my healing process will be ongoing for the rest of my life. But I am one of the lucky women, a survivor, an advocate, a dreamer, a beautiful blossoming rose."

Secret Ingredient: I met Bessie Love in May 1997, when she was the inspirational keynote speaker at the White House for the unveiling of the National Domestic Violence Hotline number on the cover of two United States Postal Service stamp books. If you purchase a book of either the Statue of Liberty or the American flag stamps, you will find the number: 1-800-799-SAFE. Help is only a phone call away.

OCTOBER 18 🍁

Know the warning signs.

Many health experts now agree that domestic violence prevention is a public health issue. When choosing a mate, or analyzing his behavior, you are taking into consideration your own health, safety, and well-being. And maybe also that of your children or other loved ones.

Even if you are not in an abusive situation yourself, it helps to know the following warning signs of potentially violent behavior in order to educate our daughters or help a friend.

- ❖ He's overprotective or extremely jealous.
- ❖ He gets angry easily.
- ❖ He puts you down.
- ❖ He threatens to hurt you, your family, or friends.
- ❖ He has ever hit, punched, slapped, kicked, or shoved you.
- ❖ He fights with you in front of your friends or family.
- ❖ He tries to keep you from seeing friends or family.
- ❖ He uses intimidation or manipulation to control you or your children.
- ❖ He tries to control your finances.
- ❖ He has ever forced you to have sex.
- ❖ He harasses you at work.

Secret Ingredient: Be realistic; Know that it is not likely that you can change his behavior, or that he will change it on his own, unless he wants to enough to seek treatment. For more information, read *Chain Chain Change: For Black Women in Abusive Relationships,* by Evelyn C. White.

❦ OCTOBER 19 ❦

Plan a safe escape.

People who have never experienced domestic violence seem to see it simplistically, asking, "Why doesn't she just leave?" As Bessie Love says, "Women in abusive situations don't want the relationship to end—they want the violence to stop. Women are not helpless victims who are unable or unwilling to help themselves or leave their abusers; rather, they are courageous survivors who work hard to preserve their families. However, many have demonstrated that they can and do leave abusive relationships when they deem leaving to be the best alternative and when they are given the help and support they need."

Like having a fire-escape plan, it doesn't hurt for women still living with their abuser to develop a safe-escape plan, like this one:

* **Develop a support network:** Get in touch with folks at the local domestic violence coalition or shelter; talk to someone you trust.
* **Memorize important phone numbers:** These include your local precinct, battered women's shelter, hospital, and domestic violence hotline.
* **Pick a code word** to alert a friend or neighbor that you're in danger.
* **Pack a survival kit** and keep it in a safe place such as with a neighbor. Pack a change of clothing; some money, including coins for phone calls; extra house and car keys; medications; glasses; pictures and other items of sentimental value; and so on.
* **Collect important items** and keep them safe. You may want to give a friend or family member copies of certain documents. Your list might include your ATM card and credit cards, checkbook, passport, driver's license and registration, social security card, birth certificate, medical ID card and records, lease, address book, legal documents, and police records.
* **Know your escape routes:** If you live in an apartment building, be aware of all fire escapes and stairwells. Know which doors in your house have locks.
* **Decide when to leave:** Think about leaving when he's asleep—or passed out. Also think of reasons to leave the house at night.
* **Decide where to go** once you're out of the house and how to get there: Pick a public place open 24-7 that also offers help—

such as a police station or hospital—a hotel, or somewhere else *where he can't find you.*

Secret Ingredient: Where to turn for help depends on the urgency of your situation. Local sources can be found either in the front section of the White Pages or in the Yellow Pages. In an emergency, dial 911.

 SPIRIT

🍁 OCTOBER 20 🍁

Follow the rule that's worth more than gold.

On *The Tonight Show* recently, I saw Jay Leno ask people on the street, "What is the Golden Rule?" Everyone fumbled. No one got it right.

I always ask my daughter these "man on the street" questions, just in case someone should approach her to air her answer on national TV (Hey, you never know!). "Anique," I asked, "what is the Golden Rule?"

"The one with the gold rules!" she responded in typical teenage, hip-hop fashion, and then she cracked up, amused at her own self.

"Wrong!" I said.

She stopped laughing and thought for a minute—much longer than they give you on TV, I noted—before she said carefully, "Do to others as you would have them do to you." I was satisfied.

Her initial answer, I'm afraid, may say more about the prevailing mind-set. The way we treat people with money differs from how we treat people without money. And people with money often act as though they are immune to rules of common courtesy and fairness. So, I've come up with "the rules" about everyday situations that can test our spirituality.

Greet people with the courtesy you expect from others.

Order people around only if you like to be spoken to in that way (which I doubt).

Love as you would like to be loved.

Don't treat others generously and expect anything in return.

Envy not, and be not envied.

Never hesitate to treat someone *better* than you think anyone will ever treat you.

Secret Ingredient: Compassion is the key. Develop your humility as well, and the Golden Rule will come naturally, and the good works in your life will reflect it. Read Matthew 7:12 in the Bible.

OCTOBER 21

Try this tension tamer.

When teenagers are distressed with their parents, what do they threaten to do? Run away.

When someone in the movies is upset and fretful, what do they do? Pace the floor.

And what do these two scenarios have in common? They both point to the fact that under stress, people get to *moving.*

It happened to me today. I had a phone fight with a health care administrator who *really* pissed me off. As soon as I hung up, I threw on my sneakers and hit the park. *Better to hit the park than to punch her out!* I said to myself (although that was just wolfin' because I am nonviolent). But it just goes to show that exercise is a perfect antidote to violent behavior, right? It's better to take out your frustrations in, say, an aerobic-boxing class, hitting a punching bag, than hitting a real person!

Exercise may not solve your problems, but it can help balance out a bad day. When things seem to be going downhill, try jogging uphill. Working out works because when you are upset, you feel wound up and uptight, and moving your body makes you loosen up and feel calmer. You think more levelheadedly and you're more energized to take on your challenges. Your body seems to say, *Bring it on! I can deal with this!* If you take a dance class or lift weights, your mind will be too preoccupied with the steps or the reps to dwell on anything disturbing. Plus, you'll be having too much fun.

Although I ran out to a park that my family has frequented for years, as I power-walked around the perimeter, I discovered for the first time a tree with branches low enough for even me to climb. So I did. I sat up in that tree and felt as young and carefree as the little boy being pushed in his stroller who looked up, spotted me, and waved with a serious, knowing look. When I returned home, there was a message on the answering machine: a resolution to my problem and an apology from the administrator.

Secret Ingredient: Always have your "secrete weapon" ready. Know what kind of exercise calms your tension. A hot bath may work for a generally busy and overwhelming day, but when you need a quick tension-tamer at work, take a walk instead of a coffee break. When you're in the middle of a pickle, get with the exercise that moves your mind and puts problems behind.

❋ BODY

❧ OCTOBER 22 ❧

Beat back pain.

You know how it goes: you make the wrong move, and your back is out of whack. The ache in the lower part of your back near the sacroiliac can last for hours, days, and maybe even put you out of commission, unable to move without pain for weeks. There may not be a "quick fix" method of treatment, but before you resort to taking it lying down, try these natural methods of relieving the pain—or preventing it.

Strike a pose. Stretch and strengthen your back muscles, and keep your spine loose and limber with this exercise: Lie on the floor. Bring one knee to the chest, then bring up the other. Hold for a few moments, feeling the stretch in your back, up and down your spine. Repeat ten times.

Keep moving. Stay as active as you can. Walking, swimming, and cycling also relieve the pain by increasing blood flow to the back muscles and promoting healing. Continuing to stay physically fit is a key to prevention.

Check out your chair. If you have a job that requires hours of sitting, your desk chair may be the culprit. Most office catalogues contain ergonomic choices with lumbar supports. Automotive supply companies offer special inserts for your car seats too. Also, consider a better bed.

Relax. Studies have shown that back pain can be related to stress. Try relaxation techniques, meditation, yoga, or your own brand of shaking stress.

Evaluate your diet. Nutrition plays a large part in how we feel. Allergies, for example, can produce inflammation that can cause backache. A healthful diet and certain supplements can help. Ask your doctor or consult with a nutritionist.

Massage the ache. My favorite remedy (for almost anything). Massage therapy with a trained professional can help if you make sure you discuss your pain with the masseuse in advance.

Secret Ingredient: **For more on these natural remedies and also alternative treatments such as chiropractic, osteopathy, Chinese and Ayurvedic medicines, herbal remedies, and homeopathy, read** *Natural Medicine for Back Pain,* **by Glenn S. Rothfeld, M.D., and Suzanne LeVert.**

 SPIRIT

 OCTOBER 23

Get your prayers answered.

"Prayer is one of the most powerful forces available to us," writes Reverend Herbert Daughtry in his booklet *Effectual Prayer, Volume One: A Simple Guide to Getting Your Prayers Answered.* "God wants us to pray and He has promised to answer." Reverend Daughtry has developed a six-point approach to prayer:

1. **See it clearly.**
   Be as definitive as you can. One good practice is to write your request on two or more pieces of paper. Keep one in your prayer box (a special place where you keep all your prayer requests and prayer answers). Keep one out in the open, and carry one with you. The point is to fix it clearly in your mind.
2. **Believe it has happened or is happening.**
   Believe that what you have prayed for is happening even while you are praying. You don't have to try to figure out how it will be answered. If you are to be involved in the answer, you will be shown what to do.
3. **Feel it.**
   Feel as if you have the concrete answer to your prayer. That is no small challenge; most of the time we feel the opposite of what we are praying for. In fact, in some instances that is why we are praying. But we can still try.
4. **Act it.**
   Act as if your prayer is already answered. If you are praying for wealth, money to meet obligations, or just praying to prosper, act as

if you have it already. Don't think, talk, or act impoverished; act prosperous.

5. **Be grateful.**
   Thanksgiving should accompany every prayer. Thank and praise God for answering your prayer.

6. **Share it.**
   One of the reasons God does good things for us is so we might share with others. In so doing, we increase our blessing. We become part of God's recycling plan. Try giving what you are praying for.

Secret Ingredient: **Put Reverend Daughtry's six-point approach to prayer to work today.**

 MIND

❧ OCTOBER 24 ❧

Test your workstyle.

Quick—what's your work style? Hardworking or hardly working? Based on twenty-five years of observing employee work habits, here's a totally unscientific quiz I thought up to help you understand where you (or those people you work with) stand. Be honest, now!

1. When you have a project to do that you don't enjoy, do you:
   A. Do a half-assed job
   B. Do it with a vengeance
   C. Do just enough to get over
   D. Give it my best

2. In meeting do you:
   A. Try to liven it up by doing all the talking
   B. Say nothing and think your own, more exciting thoughts
   C. Always volunteer to take minutes
   D. Take your own notes; every meeting has its merits

3. During the workday, do you:
   A. Visit with other employees at work whenever you feel like it—I get *all* the gossip
   B. Have the slogan: I mind my own business and leave other folks' alone

C. Chitchat only with the boss. Why bother with anyone else?

D. Socialize with others at lunchtime or after work.

4. When a project has a deadline, I
    A. Know I can always ask for an extension
    B. Tackle it right away to get it over with
    C. Cram at some point before it's due; I've got all this other work!
    D. Evaluate how long it will take, and schedule the time

5. At quitting time
    A. I'm outta here
    B. I'm known as the last one to go home
    C. I go home when the boss does
    D. I start to wind down

Answers: If you answered mainly A's with #2 a B, **you are hardly working.** You should pay the company for keeping you.

If your answers were primarily B's with #2 a C, **you're a workaholic.** Take a sabbatical ASAP.

If you answered all C's with #2 an A, **you're a kiss-up queen.** *Pulease,* girl!

If you answered all D's, you're doing all the right things. Congratulate yourself.

Secret Ingredient: **Sit in solitude today and think about how you can improve your workstyle. On an index card, write down the five essential points of your revised workstyle. Keep the card in your wallet or desk drawer for easy reference and inspiration. Read** *Success Strategies for African-Americans: A Guide to Creating Personal and Professional Achievement,* **by Beatryce Nivens—but not at work.**

 BODY

 OCTOBER 25

Make a change to lose weight.

"Many of us have depended on food to soothe and heal ourselves," says author Julie Waltz Kembel, who herself was fifty pounds overweight. "But if we use food as the only means of playing and indulging ourselves, we create a cycle that is almost impossible to break. If we need to eat to have fun, reduce stress, nurture ourselves, or otherwise make our lives temporarily better, why would we want to stop eating excessively?"

In her book *Winning the Weight and Wellness Game*, Kembel answers her own question. "We have a logical answer: lower weight, better health, improved self-esteem, acceptance by others. But the resolve to eat differently doesn't always hold firm when emotional need is strong, or when something we enjoy eating is within reach."

Kembel, whom I met at Canyon Ranch in Tucson, is such a lean lady, you wouldn't think she was ever overweight. But from experience in losing weight and keeping it off, she offers these guidelines for change:

- ❖ **Set specific study time aside each week for reading, planning, and practicing.**
- ❖ **Share your learning and progress with someone who will give you reinforcement and support.**
- ❖ **Focus on the process rather than on the result.** If you change your eating behavior, the result you want will occur. Look daily at what you are doing, and if your eating behavior is not changing in the way you want it to, do something different.
- ❖ **Recognize the ways you sabotage your own progress and take action to avoid doing so.**
- ❖ **Talk about your success, not your failures.** This task is not easy, since most of us have been trained to notice our errors and failings, and are equally quick to minimize our successes. Share your newest strategy for controlling evening snacks. Other people will enjoy what you have to say, and you will have positive feelings about what you are doing.

Secret Ingredient: **If you've been struggling to lose weight, take some tips from Julie Kempel and make a change for the better.**

 SPIRIT

 OCTOBER 26 🍁

Commune with God.

When you pray, do you ever wander off into meditation or daydream? And when you meditate, do you ever find yourself in prayer? If so, it may be because prayer and meditation have something in common: communion with God.

"Prayer is talking to God. Meditation is listening to God," says Reverend Herbert Daughtry, national presiding minister of the House of the Lord Churches, headquartered in Brooklyn, New York. "Pray and/or meditate as often as you can. Keep your mind on God and the things of God."

Here are some reflections from Rev. Daughtry on the distinctions between prayer and meditation.

Prayer is . . .
the soul's sincere desire, uttered or unexpressed.
the primordial cry for communion with the Creator.
the search for oneness with the ultimate Source of our being.

Meditation is . . .
the act of the soul in receiving, through listening and reflecting.
how the soul is refilled: by allowing God to rejuvenate, replenish, and restore.

Use both prayer and meditation each day, and you'll have the blessing of double the ways of communing with God.

Secret Ingredient: Says Reverend Daughtry, "In Psalm 19:14, the psalmist sets forth a request that embodies both prayer and meditation, and which we would do well to actualize: *Let the words of my mouth* [prayer], *and the meditation of my heart* [meditation], *be acceptable in thy sight, O Lord, my strength, and my redeemer."* If you live in or plan to visit Brooklyn, New York, Reverend Daughtry invites you to join his Sunday worship service at the House of the Lord Church, 415 Atlantic Avenue, Brooklyn, NY.

 MIND

❦ OCTOBER 27 ❦

Remember that every ending ain't over.

Every Good-bye Ain't Gone is the name of a family memoir written by journalist Itabari Njeri. I thought of that title today when I read my horoscope, which said: What you think is the end really isn't. I was just finishing a project that I wanted to be finished with pretty badly, so I was disappointed. But when I talked with my friend Marlene, she interpreted it another way and turned it into a positive message.

"Just think of all the endings people experience that give them sadness," she said. "If they could just remember that when one thing ends, another door opens, it would help them cope with it better." We talked more and agreed that there are several types of situations in which an ending doesn't have to mean The End.

- **The end of a job** can be a new beginning for the career you've always wanted. How many times have we heard people say they started a successful business after they were laid off? Or they were offered a better position in another department when the one they were in was reorganized? It happens.

- **The end of a relationship** may make you unhappy but turn out for the best. As one person leaves your life, the door swings open for someone sweeter to step in.

- **The end of a stage of your life** can signal new freedom. After someone I know had a hysterectomy, she said, "The worst thing that ever happened to me was one of the best things." The end of having a menstrual cycle—although abrupt and unplanned—relieved her of the worry about an unplanned pregnancy.

- **The end of childrearing** may be just the start of a wonderful new relationship with your child (or if you're the child, an adult closeness with your parent). And eventually, the "empty nest" may be replaced by the joys of grandparenting.

> You know what they say, when one door closes, another one opens, so the end ain't always over. It's just a stop on the continuum of life.

Secret Ingredient: **Look back on your life and think of things you experienced with a feeling of gloom and doom. Then analyze the lesson learned and what turned your lessons into "happy endings."**

✺ BODY

OCTOBER 28 🍁

Put baby "back to sleep."

"Back to sleep" is the catch phrase for the campaign held this month to persuade parents, day-care providers, baby-sitters, grandparents—anyone who might have a sleeping infant in their care—to place the baby on his or her back at night and naptime to reduce the risk of sudden infant death syndrome.

Sudden infant death syndrome (SIDS) is a medical disorder that claims the lives of thousands of young children primarily between the ages of one week to one year. Once known as crib death, these infant deaths can affect families of all races and income levels. It usually occurs during sleep, and strikes without warning. Its victims appear to be healthy.

Although it is not known how or why SIDS happens, researchers have offered risk factors. Babies who sleep on their stomachs have an increased risk of SIDS. More babies die of SIDS whose mothers smoked during and after pregnancy. Boys are at slightly higher risk than girls. And SIDS occurs most often in infants under six months of age.

I remember that my infant had colic her first four months, and I desperately wanted to place her in *any* position just to get her to stop all that crying! But I was more afraid of SIDS than of her noise or my fatigue. I still have vivid memories of witnessing from my bedroom window as a teenager the horrible, overwhelming, sudden grief of a neighbor who had so recently welcomed a new baby home. I recall the ambulance, and the other neighbors standing helplessly outside the house. Although this baby was white, black babies are 2.4 times more likely than white babies to die of SIDS. But it's a scene—and a deep, painful grief—no one should ever have to experience.

You might find that the baby goes to sleep faster on the stomach. But that's no reason you can't turn the child over once he or she falls asleep. A few minutes of vigilance is worth a lifetime of joy.

Secret Ingredient: **Other SIDS-busters include providing a smoke-free environment for your baby, using a firm, flat mattress without a pillow, comforter, or other soft item under the baby or covering the child's head or face, and avoiding overheating baby with too much clothing, bedding, or too warm a room. SIDS counselors and additional information are available by calling 1-800-221-SIDS.**

 SPIRIT

 OCTOBER 29

Find happiness on your spiritual path.

Harriette Cole, former fashion editor of *Essence,* is the author of *How to Be: Contemporary Etiquette for African Americans.* Outward success came smoothly for my friend Harriette, but inner happiness took some soul-searching. Her story may help you find your path.

Like many others, I spent quite a few years searching for a way to be happy. During lonely moments of need I used to ask myself, Why can't I find happiness through what I do or who I'm with? That sentiment was quickly followed by a barrage of finger-pointing: If only he would be different, I would be happy. If only my employer gave me better opportunities, I would be just fine, thank you.

It took the breakup of a marriage and wandering into too many dark corners before I realized my way wasn't working. That's when I accepted what my mother and my younger sister had been whispering into my ear for so long, "Just pray, Harriette. If you ask God to help you, He will." My prayer started rather desperately: "Please God, help me to be happy. Help me to live, really live." To my surprise, my world immediately brightened. Opportunities began to appear that made me feel good about myself. So, with a little more prayer, a little more goodness crept in to replace the gloom.

Within a few months I met a wonderful man. Together we discovered a spiritual path that supported the philosophy lying dormant within me—that inside of me was a reflection of God, and that all I must do is nurture that presence in order to have peace and happiness in my life. I found Siddha Yoga at Thanksgiving of 1990, and from that day to this, my life has changed both dramatically and subtly. Although at first the ritual of his path seemed far distant from my original Christian roots, the basic spiritual practices promised to support me in my daily life, and I could still maintain my Christian faith.

Daily (well, *almost* every day), I follow a number of spiritual practices:

❖ When I get up in the morning, I thank God for giving me a beautiful day to experience.

❖ Then I chant or sing a holy mantra. The practice of singing God's name settles me down and helps me to get centered as I start my day.

❖ Next, I meditate; a time when I sit quietly, intent upon stilling my mind so that I can hear the message that God has for me in that day.

❖ Throughout the day I carry with me the promise that I will celebrate the greatness in everyone—starting with myself. In this way, no matter what happens, I am able to be grounded, as well as clear, strong, and loving.

❖ At the close of each day I offer a prayer of gratitude for all of the great lessons—both uplifting and tough—that have come my way. I also contemplate how I can improve tomorrow. When I close my eyes at night, I can sleep peacefully, knowing that I have done all in my power to shore up my own Spiritual Self.

Secret Ingredient: **For information about "In Search of the Self," a home study course in the Siddha Yoga meditation teachings, call 1-914-434-2000, ext. 1900.**

 BODY

🍁 OCTOBER 30 🍁

Toy with soy.

Tofu—yum! yum! yum! Tofu has a bad rap as the "rabbit" food of vegetarians, but I love it. Found in tofu is soy protein, which has all kinds of benefits:

* ❖ Soy lowers blood cholesterol, which may reduce the chances of developing heart disease.
* ❖ It may prevent hormone-related cancers of the breast, ovaries, and prostate.
* ❖ It may reduce menopausal hot flashes.

I eat tofu in several different ways. My favorite and easiest way is in Chinese food. I order the hot spiced bean curd dish (although I prefer it prepared mildly spiced) or have it in my vegetable fried rice. At Japanese restaurants, order the miso soup. Often, they have a sautéed tofu dish as well. The other night I ordered a dish that could be described as sautéed tofu cubes in a soy sauce (that tasted like barbecue sauce) served with spinach. Tasted like soul food.

At home on occasion, I've made quick-and-easy tofuburgers: buy tofu cakes from the grocery store, slice them in half lengthwise, and sauté them on both sides until cooked through. Serve the "patties" on burger buns with your favorite fixings.

You can also use tofu as an ingredient in your favorite dishes: in chili, in lasagna, in scrambled eggs, in tuna salad, in potato salad.

On the recommendation of Dr. Andrea D. Sullivan, author of *A Path to Healing: A Guide to Wellness for Body, Mind, and Soul,* I'm trying to acquire a taste for soy milk instead of cow's milk. Dr. Sullivan says it's a great alternative for folks who are lactose intolerant, and will make you feel better even if you're not. Soy milk comes in delicious flavors like vanilla and chocolate. You can get it at grocery stores as well as health food stores.

For years I also used soybean margarine. Tastewise, you can hardly tell the difference between it and "regular" margarine. Toy around with soy. It's a versatile, fun food. Check it out.

Secret Ingredient: Recent reports state that women who consume a healthy amount of soy products have a lower risk of developing breast cancer.

 MIND

 OCTOBER 31

Keep kids safe on Halloween.

Witches, goblins, ghosts, and thieves
They'll all be at your door
On this Hallows Eve!

Today is Halloween, and here are some tips for you and yours:

- ❖ Take children trick-or-treating early in the evening, between six and eight P.M., so they won't be out too late in the dark.
- ❖ Make sure costumes are light in color or have reflective material so your child can be seen at night.
- ❖ Baggy may be the "in" style, but don't let costumes fall so loose or long that they cause tripping. Also, make sure shoes are the child's own, not your high heels or other ill-fitting footwear.
- ❖ Check to see that costumes are flame retardant.
- ❖ Because masks can obstruct a child's vision, they are best worn at parties. Use face makeup for trick-or-treating.
- ❖ An adult or responsible teenager should accompany children. If you send them with a teenager, make sure you know and approve the route they'll be taking. They should stay in the most familiar parts of the neighborhood. Tell them to approach only those homes that are well lit (and not to go to homes where there's no front porch light on), and to be back home by a certain time. For maximum protection, have the teenager carry a cell phone or a pager, with plenty change to be able to call home. Give them a flashlight too, then scoot the little spooks out the door.

Secret Ingredient: Sugarless gum—that's the number one choice of dentists for Halloween treat giving, followed by mini granola bars, and other less sticky treats. Help the children weed out the stale, unwrapped, and suspicious candies, then allow them one to three treats a day (tightly wrapped nonchocolate candy stored in a cool place can be kept for several months). And after every binge, make sure they brush their teeth.

 BODY

NOVEMBER 1

Be a pumpkin eater.

Gerald W. Deas, M.D., really cares about the health of the community. A full-time physician, he makes time to write a weekly column called "House Calls" for *The New York Amsterdam News*. Here's a day-after-Halloween piece he shared with his readers that he's given me permission to share with you. Now, you be sure to pass it on to the fellas in your life—and bake a pumpkin pie together tonight!

If the pumpkin was human, I bet he or she would be indignant, realizing that he or she was only being used for Halloween night as a decoration and then carelessly thrown away. I am sure the pumpkin would say: "There's more to me than a smiling face." And that would be right. Inside this beautiful round orange vegetable is a seed that contains unsaturated fat and zinc that is capable of keeping the prostate gland healthy.

The prostate gland enlarges because of testosterone, a male hormone. Often, as the prostate enlarges, the male may experience obstruction of the urinary outflow, causing frequency in urination, burning, and a slow stream. The enlargement of the prostate gland may be due to just an overgrowth of tissue or a tumor within the gland. To determine the difference, a simple blood test known as a prostatic specific antigen (PSA) can be done. Usually, if the value of the PSA is below four, the enlargement of the gland is referred to as benign prostatic hypertrophy. If the value is above four, a biopsy of the gland is necessary to rule out a prostatic tumor.

Pumpkin seeds contain a wealth of nutrients, such as zinc and unsaturated fats, that can maintain the prostate gland in a healthy condition. The wonderful flesh of the pumpkin also contains carotenoids like beta-carotene, lutein, and zeaxanthin, which are free-radical absorbers. These are capable of preventing cancer of the stomach, esophagus, lungs, and colon.

The pumpkin isn't just a scary, toothless smile on a cold Halloween night. It is a wonderful vegetable that should be used for more than decoration. There are many nutritious dishes that can be prepared from the meat of the pumpkin. So enjoy this beautiful gift from God and keep your body healthy.

Secret Ingredient: Dr. Deas tells me that roasted pumpkin seeds make a cheap treat. "Just suck the seeds, crack them open, and spit out the shells," he says. "It's like a bag of chips!"

 MIND

NOVEMBER 2

Complain with compassion.

What's your way of voicing complaint or criticism? I had never given this a thought until I heard an expert on a talk radio show say that people need to "complain with compassion." He explained that doing so would not only get better results, but that it would be more healthy for our well-being.

From my own observation, I would say that we complain in three general ways:

With hostility: Meaning that when things don't go our way, we respond with animosity and antagonism, often beyond the scope of the problem, but just because we are annoyed that we *have* the complaint. The act of having to "go there" gets on our last nerve. We can just feel our blood pressure rising. Our stress level goes sky high. And somebody's going to get it!

By whining: At work one day during the course of discussing staffers, my boss and I identified several people that could be described as "whiners and complainers." These are people who "tell" on other people but never think to come up with a solution to the problem in a constructive way. The opposite of hostile complainers, they'd rather whine than take control.

With compassion: When we voice our dislikes in this middle-ground way, we give the benefit of the doubt as our first resort. We assume good intentions. Maybe your toddler really wanted to learn about how the toy worked, not drive you nuts with anxiety looking for him. Perhaps the maître d' seated you near the kitchen so that you wouldn't have to wait for a table, not because you're black. Just maybe, it was fate that the flight was canceled so you could get on a safer one, even though it made you late for the wedding. What would be accomplished by yelling at the airline employee at the gate?

Aggressively voicing our displeasure may get the results we desire, but doing so *assertively* is usually more productive. Complaining with compassion may mean that you not only get resolution, but that you, in turn, get treated with compassion. And isn't that the best outcome for your health?

Secret Ingredient: Practice compassion by recognizing the little things that set you off. When they occur, think of how to handle them with patience and without anger. Practice with the little stuff and then move on to bigger things.

🍁 NOVEMBER 3 🍁

Reclaim our soul.

Once upon a time in America, people used to talk about having "soul" with pride. What is soul? As the saying went: If you have to ask, you don't have it (or more Ebonically, you ain't got it).

It's that undefinable feeling, that inner quality of negritude, of unique Afrocentricity. It was found in African American music, in our walk, in our talk. James Brown had it. He was the godfather of it. Aretha Franklin had it. She was the queen. Ellington was the Duke. Basie was the Count. So we even had Soul Royalty. The Brits had nothing on us!

Soul brothers slapped five on the street whenever they would meet and greet. Soul sisters wore Afros with pride. "Soul Man" was in the lyrics Sam & Dave sang live.

If this sounds like a poem, it's because that was the rhythm of the time. Sonia, Haki, Nikki—keeping it real in rhyme.

We've got to reclaim our soul, my sisters and brothers. It's deep. It's spiritual. It's us.

Secret Ingredient: Keep oldies alive—I tell you no jive. Play the songs, read the poetry, get the books, study our history, be black and proud!

❋ NOVEMBER 4 ❋

Eat less fat.

No one wants to *be* fat. But did you know there are reasons not to *eat* fat?

- ❖ Eating less fat can assist in weight loss or weight maintenance because you'll be eating fewer calories.
- ❖ It can help reduce your risk of heart disease by reducing saturated fat, which will help lower blood cholesterol levels.
- ❖ It may help reduce your risk of cancer.
- ❖ Eating fewer high-fat foods means more room for fruits, vegetables, grains, and beans.

Here are a whole bunch of ways the National Cancer Institute suggests you cut back on the fat.

Eat fewer of these foods: fatty meats, nuts, peanut butter, mayonnaise, sauces, butter or margarine, ice cream, potato chips, doughnuts, and cakes

Try not to fry foods.

Save French fries and other fried foods for special occasions: have small servings; share with a friend.

Ditto high-fat desserts (ice cream, pastries)

Use less fat meat. When fat cooks out of meat, pour the fat off and throw it away (don't recycle in a can, y'all).

Eat bread with little butter or margarine.

Use reduced-fat or nonfat salad dressings.

Use nonfat or lower-fat spreads such as jelly or jam, fruit spread, apple butter, nonfat or reduced-calorie mayonnaise, nonfat margarine, or mustard.

To top baked potatoes, use nonfat or reduced-fat sour cream, plain nonfat or low-fat yogurt, nonfat or low-fat cottage cheese, nonfat margarine, nonfat hard cheese, salsa, or vinegar.

Switch to one percent or skim milk and other nonfat or lower-fat dairy products.

Secret Ingredient: Treats you *can* eat: ginger snaps, fig bars, vanilla wafers, raisins, angel food cake, hard candy, low-fat puddings, nonfat frozen yogurt, ice milk, sherbet, fruit Popsicles, pretzels, or popcorn without butter or oil. Fruits and vegetables *anytime.*

❧ NOVEMBER 5 ❧

Exercise your right to vote.

The first time I learned about "voter apathy," I was personally affected by it. I ran for cheerleader in eleventh grade. I really, really wanted to be a Franklin High School cheerleader too. Sixteen girls made the finals, but only eight would be elected. But because too many of the black students (my primary constituency in a school that was one third black, one third Asian, and one third white) chose hanging out in the gorgeous spring weather over voting during lunchtime, the lack of a "black voting block," left me number nine.

I soon turned eighteen and was informed by my parents that I definitely would be registering to vote, because just one vote could be the difference in whether my father, an elected judge, would have a job or not. Then, over the years, I learned about the people who marched, protested, caught hell, and some who even died, for the right of African Americans to vote. So voting is serious stuff for me. I am passionate about it—and I get a "voter's high" every time I push down those little levers.

What does voting have to do with health and fitness? Well, since the president, for example, appoints the person who heads the Health and Human Services department of the government, it has a lot to do with forming our federal government's health policies. The president also appoints the United States surgeon general, who as I write this is an African American, David Satcher, and also makes appointments to the President's Council on Physical Fitness and Sports. Similar appointed positions are made on the state and local levels too. So if you vote someone into office, you are more likely to agree with the decisions and regulations made about your health. And often the referendums on the ballots themselves have to do with health or the environment, giving you a chance to directly approve or disapprove of things that will affect you.

So exercising your right to vote is a good move. Make the ancestors, who were disenfranchised, proud.

Secret Ingredient: **If you are not registered to vote, call your local NAACP, Urban League, or League of Women Voters for information on how to do it.**

❧ NOVEMBER 6 ❧

Practice an ancient custom.

In many parts of Africa, if you walk up to someone and ask an impersonal question, for example, "Which way is the market?" the person you asked just may turn and walk away. You're likely to think that he was being rude. The African will have thought the same of you, which is why he walked off.

That's a scenario from a magazine I read when boning up on the Ivory Coast before I led a team from *Essence* there several years ago. In explaining African customs to travelers, the article pointed out the difference between the Western mode of thinking, called "low context," where people have minimal interaction, and the African way, called "high context," of acknowledging one's humanity before asking a favor. I have observed in the many years since my trip that here in the United States, people of African descent are more likely to be high context than the American norm. I call that race memory. Here's what I mean:

Low context: When people are outside, they are primarily in cars, or walking looking straight ahead. When another person passes by them, there is no acknowledgment of that person even if the stranger does not seem threatening. They walk as if they are the only one on the street.

High context: People "sit a spell" on front porches or stand on street corners, talking, joking, and telling tales. When walking, passing strangers are met with a pleasant glance, a nod, maybe even a "hello."

Low context: Before you can take off your coat, your colleague walks up to your cubicle and demands, "Hey, Tiffany, you got that report you're supposed to turn in this morning?"

High context: In an office setting, you prefer that a colleague say, "Good morning, how're you doing?" Or that the person inquire about your weekend or the child who was home sick the day before. Then, after this preliminary sharing, however brief, the tasks at hand get discussed.

In Africa, the person who wanted directions would have been more warmly received if she had said, "Hello, my name is Nia, and I am from America. This is my family. What is your name? How are you? How is your family?" before asking directions. Acknowledging another's humanity is essential in any context.

Secret Ingredient: **Think about whether you have a high or low context spirit. Practice being high context and see if you don't get wondrous results. Ancient custom can't be all wrong.**

❧ NOVEMBER 7 ❧

Eat more fiber.

Now that you're eating *less fat*—good for you!—let's move on to eating *more fiber*. Finally, there is something we can eat *more* of. A high-fiber diet protects against cancer of the colon.

A survey conducted by *Heart & Soul* magazine and the Food Marketing Institute in 1996 found that only four percent of African American respondents chose fiber as one of the top three nutrients they look for on a food label. And only five percent buy foods specifically for the fiber content. Since a healthy diet should include at *least* twenty to thirty grams of fiber daily, we've got to change those stats! Let's get to eating some good ol' fiber, family!

According to the Fox Chase Cancer Center in Philadelphia, good sources of fiber are:

❖ **Whole grain cereals.** Those with "bran" in the name usually have the most fiber. Some good choices: All-Bran with extra fiber, Fiber One, 100% Bran, All-Bran, Bran Buds, Corn Bran, Shredded Wheat, oatmeal, Wheaties

❖ **Beans, peas, and lentils.** Eat high-fiber soups such as bean, lentil, corn chowder, cabbage, and vegetable with beans. Add beans to salads. Use kidney beans, green beans, and chick peas. Black-eyed peas top the list in dietary fiber, with 12.4 grams in one-half cup cooked.

❖ **Fruits and vegetables.** Choose fruits and vegetables with edible skins and seeds. Eat fresh fruit instead of drinking fruit juices whenever possible. Pears, apples, bananas, peaches, and oranges top the high-fiber fruit list. Peas, corn, potatoes, zucchini, and collard greens are great vegetable choices.

❖ **Whole grain breads, brown rice, and whole grain flours.** Use whole grain breads such as pumpernickel, whole wheat, and rye. Use brown rice instead of white. When cooking or baking, substitute whole wheat flour for white, since whole wheat has almost three times the fiber.

Secret Ingredient: **For free material about nutrition and cancer, call the Cancer Information Service at 1-800-4-CANCER.**

❧ NOVEMBER 8 ❧

Seek therapy.

Let's face it. We just can't handle everything on our own. Sometimes the problems we face seem overwhelming and insurmountable. That's when we need professional help.

Don't let the folklore of the Strong Black Women keep you suffering in silence. Forget the common taboo of black women not seeking treatment. The effects of our socioeconomic status mean we probably need it more than anyone. Here are some other myths to step over, with the real-deal answers from my psychotherapist friend, Marlene F. Watson:

I need therapy only if I'm going absolutely crazy. "Actually all of us could use it," Marlene says. "That's because therapy is an investment in yourself. It's time that you devote exclusively to *you*. And you have someone who is there to listen closely to you, and who is able to hear and pick up on things that you don't. Therapy is for anyone who would like to spend time learning more about themselves, and dealing with any issues from grief to loss to job stress. Or to the more severe conditions, such as depression or schizophrenia."

It's too expensive. "Therapy can be expensive, but it doesn't have to be. Prices range, and you may have insurance that may pay all or some of it. The more important question is, what price do you put on a higher quality of life, rather than staying stuck with old behaviors that can cost you love, commitment, jobs?"

I can just talk with my mama or my girlfriends. "The difference between therapy and doing that is that people close to you are likely to be 'inside the same frame' as you and when that happens they can't see the picture clearly. They may also have a vested interest in you taking their advice, or become annoyed when you don't. And they don't have the training to see the things that therapists do."

I'll get dependent on it. "Any good therapist isn't looking to have you stay. It's a temporary arrangement; you're there to learn how to deal with your own life, and the therapist is there to give you the tools. Like parents, therapists want to see the client go on and be in charge of her life. When looking for the right one for you, interview the therapist, and ask about the end at the beginning."

Secret Ingredient: For help in finding an African American therapist, contact the Association of Black Psychologists, P.O. Box 55999, Washington, D.C. 20040-5999; 1-202-722-0808.

🍁 NOVEMBER 9 🍁

Make your appointment for a checkup.

The year is winding to an end. Have you had your annual medical examinations yet? Here are some general guidelines for women that will help you know what to expect.

Test: GENERAL PHYSICAL EXAM, including blood pressure check, eye exam, and lifestyle counseling
Who should have it; how often: Ages eighteen to thirty-nine, every three years; ages forty and over, once a year
Why: To find anything that seems abnormal. A good time to discuss with your doctor any minor or recurring ailments

Test: BLOOD CHOLESTEROL
Who: Everyone; every five years if first test result is normal, as recommended by doctor if level is elevated
Why: Checks the level of fats in your blood

Test: PELVIC EXAM WITH PAP SMEAR
Who: Sexually active women or by the age of eighteen, whichever comes first; once a year if test result is normal; as recommended by doctor if abnormalities are found
Why: Looking for abnormalities of the uterus, ovaries, and lower pelvic area, as well as cancer of the cervix, and sexually transmitted diseases

Test: CLINICAL BREAST EXAM
Who: Everyone; once a year
Why: Can detect cancer or precancerous condition in the breast

Test: MAMMOGRAM
Who: Black women ages thirty-five to forty-nine, every one to two years. Ages fifty and over, once a year
Why: Early detection of cancer or precancerous breast conditions

Test: RECTAL EXAM
Who: Everyone over age forty, once a year
Why: Checks for colon or rectal cancer

Test: FECAL OCCULT BLOOD TEST
Who: Everyone over age forty, once a year

Why: Detects blood in the stool, which can indicate minor problems such as hemorrhoids, or more serious conditions such as colon or rectal cancer

---

Test: DENTAL EXAM
Who: Everyone, every six months
Why: Looking for signs of tooth decay, gum disease, or other dental problems

---

Test: EYE EXAM
Who: Everyone, every two years
Why: Checks for sight problems, glaucoma in people over forty

Secret Ingredient: **Take a copy of this page with you to the doctor, dentist, and optometrist to be sure to get a thorough checkup. Keep notes for comparison each year.**

SPIRIT

❧ NOVEMBER 10 ❧

Focus on spirituality.

Do you think about getting rich? Nothing wrong with that, but try this: focus on what you could do *spiritually* if you had wealth. Maybe you could help others in need, maybe you could contribute to your church's building fund, perhaps you could afford to go to Mecca for pilgrimage, or to walk where Jesus walked in Jerusalem.

Tuning our sights not on the material, but on the spiritual, is always the way to express desire with purpose and mission. It pleases God for your wishes to be not only for you, but for the greater good. It shows an intention to spread the blessing, literally share the wealth.

Think of other things you may desire, such as having time to exercise. What could be a spiritual purpose in that? Well, some women have found it. For example, fitness expert Victoria Johnson tells me that she has decided to turn her workout sessions into praise-songs. Her goal to get more black women healthy through exercise has grown into a series of Gospel Urban Praise classes at which women use movement to give God the glory!

Kids need clothes? Buying new ones could allow the outgrown

clothes to be given to charity and help another child dress warm. Want a new car? Consider the spiritual "why?"

What does your heart desire today? Write it here:

_____

_____

_____

Now focus on the spiritual aspect of your desire. Jot it down here:

_____

_____

_____

Giving our wants and needs spiritual power takes them from *selfish* to *serving.*

Secret Ingredient: **Get in a habit of focusing** *all* **your desires through the prism of spirituality. As the Bible says, to whom much is given, much is expected.**

 MIND

 NOVEMBER 11

Break free of slave mentality.

It's so close to the millennium that it can seem depressing to think of slavery, but as the saying goes, "You don't know where you're going until you know where you've been." There are still ramifications of the effects of our ancestors' oppression under the American institution of slavery on us today. Here are some ways to escape them:

Change your name: If you feel there's a moniker more powerful than your "slave name," change it. If Queen Latifah (Dana Owens), Aminata Moseka (Abbey Lincoln), and Whoopi Goldberg (Caryn Johnson) can do it, so can you. When I was fifteen, I changed the spelling of my first name to Stephani. I kept it like that for ten years, and my high school and college diplomas are proof. However, the twenty-five-year-old me again preferred the spelling my parents gave me, so I changed it back. You'll need to notify Social Security, the IRS, and other institutions that keep public records.

Take calculated risks. The most slaves could hope for was a plantation on which they would be treated civilly, and not be sold away. We don't have to settle for ill treatment, underpayment, or stagnation on the job. We are now free to pursue meaningful, pleasant work with a purpose. Education and calculation is key to stepping outside our comfort zone.

Strengthen relationships. Families were separated. Mothers from children. Fathers from families. What held us together was our African tradition of extended family, and it continues to sustain us today and will in the future. Work to keep family ties close.

Eat nutritiously. Many of the unhealthy foods we eat are the leftovers from an era of deprivation. Necessity made our foremothers doctor up the parts of the pig no one else would eat. Too much sugar sweetened the taste of foods with little nutritional value. Yet, the traditions of eating fresh vegetables have been slipping away. Know what's healthy and what's not, and eat to live in the millennium.

Secret Ingredient: Take time today to think about how this legacy affects your life today. Knowing the ramifications is the first step in healing.

✺ BODY

❧ NOVEMBER 12 ❧

Curb your sweet tooth.

For years, about once a month, I have had a craving for one Hershey bar without almonds. I have absolutely no shame in admitting that I always cave in to it. That's because I am proud to have pulled back from supplementing that candy bar with brownies, chocolate chip cookies, yellow cake with chocolate icing, and a bowlful of Hershey's Kisses to pop like pills each day until the next month.

You guessed it. It's my menstrual cycle that brings on the chocolate cravings. Why does it do that to me and millions of other women on the planet? According to a study conducted at MIT, during the three days prior to their periods, when women were able to eat anything they wanted, they devoured an average of five hundred calories a day more than normal, with almost all of them coming from sweet and starchy carbohydrates. The reason? Around the time of our periods, women need more of the brain chemical serotonin, which controls our moods. The sweets set off a series of biochemical events that help the brain make more serotonin.

In addition to having cravings during our periods, we can get them when we're happy or sad. Either emotion can make you want to bring on the hot fudge sundae! Believe me, I mention that indulgence, in particular, from personal experience! Sweets are comfort foods. That's okay as long as we don't overindulge. *That* can cause weight gain and tooth decay, among other problems.

So how do you kick your craving to the curb?

- ❖ Know your body and what triggers your cravings. Then, when you get a "jones" for sweets, instead of trying to submerge your craving only to eventually wolf down more than you need, you'll be prepared.
- ❖ Stash pre-bagged portions of healthy "sweets" such as dried apricots, prunes, or raisins, and eat all you want.
- ❖ Substitute a high-fat craving for a low-fat version.

Secret Ingredient: **The strategy that works best for me is to give in to a reasonable amount (my one candy bar a month isn't bad, is it?) of the craving. It takes only a little to raise your serotonin level. The goal is quantity-control, not total denial of your sweet tooth.**

❋ SPIRIT

❧ NOVEMBER 13 ❧

Vanquish your vanity.

Platform shoes were in vogue then in a big way. And of course I was wearing them just like everyone else. On one particular Saturday, I had on a sharp pair of beige, butter-suede mules that were about six inches off the ground at the heel. Returning from a shopping spree, I was walking from the bus stop, cutting across campus to my dorm, when I noticed coming toward me a pretty woman with long, flowing hair walking arm-in-arm with a fine brother. At second glance I recognized the sister to be someone with whom I had a friendly rivalry in some of my classes. As far as I could tell, there were only the three of us on the expansive grounds.

Lifting my head up high and throwing my "soulful strut" into motion, I was almost about to pass the couple, when, all of a sudden, my shoe got caught on an uneven slab of cement in the walkway. In a split second I was down on the ground in front of these beautiful people with a busted lip!

Fortunately for me, the couple treated me with compassion, getting me to the college infirmary. The person I had perceived as a rival never made fun of me or laughed in my face; she only expressed concern and caring. I was humbled.

Sitting up in my dorm room with an ice pack on my swollen lip but with nothing hurt more than my ego, all I could think of was the Bible passage: Pride cometh before the fall. I had been full of pride about my silly platform shoes, and what had happened? My butt fell right at the feet of one of the *last* people in the world in front of whom I would have wanted that to have happened!

Let my lesson be one for you. Don't let vanity or pride get to your head. (It might bust your lip!)

Secret Ingredient: **My husband, Reggie, is a handsome man, yet people remark that he never seems affected by it or to even acknowledge it. Recently, I learned his secret. In sharing a passage from the *hadith*, the Muslim prayer book, he admitted that for the last thirty years whenever he looked in the mirror and felt that he was looking particularly good, he would silently say this prayer: O Allah! As Thou hast made me well in appearance, so do Thou make me good in morals.**

 MIND

 NOVEMBER 14

Decide to make stronger decisions.

Sometimes the decisions are easy and routine, like what to have for dinner. Occasionally, however, we all have to make decisions that can have a major impact on our lives. Is it time to end that marriage? Should you look for another job or keep the one you've got? What is the best way to love a troubled child?

Our decisions reveal our beliefs. They also show our character. Inherent in most major decision-making is a test of our intuition, our insight, and our integrity. To make informed choices, consider these points:

- **The reality of the situation.** What is the "real deal"? Examine the facts, the actuality of what you are considering, not what you *wish* they were.
- **The truth of the matter.** Accept and agree with the reality and you'll come across the truth. Avoid distorting or misrepresenting the reality or you'll obscure the facts.
- **Consider your intuition.** What do you sense about arriving at the decision? Does it feel right to *you?* Don't put more weight into others' opinions on the situation than you do your own.
- **Figure out if the choice is complex or complicated.** If it's complex, it has many parts to it. If the decision is complicated, it means you can't distinguish one part from another, and this may involve a component of fear. Bring all the parts together for analysis, and you'll be better prepared to formulate an answer.
- **Proceed with integrity and honesty.** Tell yourself the truth and keep telling the truth to others. When you hold your integrity close and speak honestly, you know you have truth on your side.
- **Make your decision based on that truth.** If you're deciding whether you should marry someone, for example, and you know in your heart the relationship is not good for you, then that truth should be the basis of your decision. If the truth is that the love is enduring and joyous, then go for it.

Secret Ingredient: The Bible says: Let your "yes" be "yes" and your "no" be "no." All else is of the devil. Read *"Yes" or "No": The Guide to Better Decisions,* by Spencer Johnson, for more advice on making decisions that show character and leadership.

 BODY

NOVEMBER 15

Be drug-free and healthy.

A health news bulletin I read recently reported that a new study described in the *Journal of the American Medical Association* found that blockages in the arteries can be significantly reduced without the use of drugs if patients with heart disease follow what was called an "austere lifestyle regimen." That meant:
- a very low-fat vegetarian diet
- exercising "religiously"

- ❖ practicing stress reduction daily
- ❖ meditation
- ❖ avoiding smoking

After going down the list that defined this "austere" lifestyle, I thought, *Hey, that's pretty close to my lifestyle!* (With the exception of "religious" exercise, I do admit.) But never have I ever considered it austere, or characterized by any strict discipline or restraint. For me and my family it's just a healthy way of life. And I'm sure that it is for millions of other people who are vegetarians, who exercise, make a conscious effort to minimize stress, and don't smoke. It's not deprivation to enjoy a full life without the sicknesses that can require drugs, and maybe even, in the case of heart disease, balloon angioplasty and bypass surgery.

Putting your life on this healthful track can be the abundance in itself. Becoming a vegetarian shouldn't mean eliminating meat as much as trying out new foods and recipes. Exercising can be the start of learning new skills and making new friends. Reducing stress can led to pleasurable activities with your family or your girlfriends. Meditation leads to quality time with yourself. Abstaining from smoking can give you peace of mind knowing that you are not only not harming your health, but that the secondhand smoke is not endangering the health of your loved ones. And the longer you adhere to this "austere" lifestyle, the longer life you'll have to live.

Secret Ingredient: **Try just one of these lifestyle changes today. Haven't exercised in a while? Do something to move your body before the day is through. Then work on the others day by day.**

 ❀ SPIRIT

 ❧ NOVEMBER 16 ❧

Share Victoria's secrets.

Victoria Johnson is a fitness expert, health activist, and star and producer of *Victoria's Body Shoppe,* a TV show on the nationwide Prime Sports Network. To see her so fit and trim now, you'd never know that she was once overweight and out of shape. Committed to helping other women reach their fitness goals, Victoria shares her secrets for getting and staying wholly fit, inside and out.

I love to work out. It is one of the purest forms of discipline. It is a true test about obedience and consistency. To me it's not enough being physically fit and spiritually unhealthy. We are the most blessed creatures on earth. We have the ability to think, reason, act, react, and make our own choices.

There was a time when I would eat whatever I wanted because I worked out a couple of hours per day. I was doing the activity, talking a good talk, but behind closed doors I was bingeing and purging. I was on a destructive cycle headed for disaster. I went to my doctor because I was experiencing blackouts, severe depression, and poor circulation. I was not physically fit nor was I spiritually fit. I thought that since I was going to church every Sunday and saying my prayers, I was covered.

Through kicking my negative behavior patterns and truly understanding the Lord's words, I was released from the disease of diabetes. I now know that I am supposed to be healthy physically, emotionally, and spiritually. I realized that my purpose was much bigger than eating, sleeping, and going to work.

The number-one killer of women today is heart disease. A lifestyle disease, it is preventable and controllable. I know we can beat this man-made problem. We have all the tools we need right now. We just have to take action, the right kind of action. Here are some positive suggestions to get you started on the road to creating a healthy and fit body:

❖ **You must engage in *positive prayer* to experience *spiritual fitness.***

❖ **You must engage in *positive thinking* to become *emotionally fit.***

❖ **You must engage in *positive physical activity* to become *physically fit.***

Secret Ingredient: **For more of "Victoria's secrets," check out her Web site at www.victoriajohnson.com.**

🍁 NOVEMBER 17 🍁

Work your ideal weight.

As we get more and more bombarded by advertisements for year-end sales, you may find yourself deciding whether to go out and buy a lot of pricey exercise equipment. Well, according to fitness expert Victoria Johnson, you can put your money in the bank and sleep easy. Instead of breaking the piggy bank, she suggests a simple pair of five-pound dumb-bells, available for about $15 at most local variety stores or fitness shops.

"The most accurate test of what brand to buy is how comfortable the weight feels in your hand," Victoria says, "However, I recommend buying metal ones, which last longer than plastic or sand-filled ones."

Now, after you've picked up your pair of weights, try these two ex-ercises from Victoria Johnson to help you weight-lift in effective, smart, noninjuring ways:

Lunges: Standing sideways to a chair, place your left hand on the back of it for balance. Place your left leg out in front of your right leg. Keeping your ear, shoulder, hip, and right knee vertically aligned, clutch the dumbbell gently and lower yourself toward the floor so that the right knee almost hits the floor. Technique is everything! Make sure the left knee is directly over the ankle and the toes of your left foot are lifted. Do two or three sets (ten to fifteen lunges on each side) every day to increase your lower body strength.

Wall sits: Stand with your back flat against a wall. Feet should be shoulder-width apart and ten to twelve inches in front of you. With arms at your sides, holding five-pound dumbbells, slowly lower yourself to-ward the floor until your knees are at a ninety-degree angle. Keep your quadriceps parallel to the floor for ten to thirty seconds. Return to start-ing position. Repeat five to ten times. Do five to ten repetitions every other day.

Secret Ingredient: Would you like to work out with Victoria Johnson? If you're waving your five-pound weight in the affirmative, then order her *Power Shaping II* video, which uses light hand-weights and takes you through a forty-five-minute workout. Call 1-800-635-3893.

❧ NOVEMBER 18 ❧

Change the tape.

Reading Malcolm X's autobiography when he was in prison, Nathan McCall says he began to "understand the devastating effects of self-hatred" that often lead to the anger and violence that he and other African Americans have experienced. And, he says on a TLC program called *The Human Experience,* he learned a universal principle: If you change your self-perception, you can change your behavior.

How to change our self-perception and collective sense of low self-esteem is a complex issue. For McCall, it meant applying to college and eventually becoming a reporter at *The Washington Post.* But subtle steps of enlightenment come before big ones like that. It's almost impossible to become self-empowered without changing "the tape" in your head—that constantly running voice with the negative messages—and replacing it with a positive one.

Respect yourself. It's an affirmation. The Staple Singers made a song about it. Radio talk show host Bob Law greets callers with "Respect yourself" and they in turn respond, "And I respect you, brother!" Unchanged for years, Law's positive message is repeated over and over—like an affirmation.

Reverend Jesse Jackson is the crown prince of collective affirmation. Long before all the current New Age thought swept in with the accompanying chants, meditations, and repetitions, Jackson was leading crowds in call-and-response:

> *I am somebody!*
> *I am beautiful!*
> *I am to be protected!*
> *I am to be respected!*
> *I may be poor,*
> *But I am somebody!*
> *Keep hope alive!*

Secret Ingredient: **Think of your own collective affirmation and put it to use.**

❦ NOVEMBER 19 ❦

Embrace the circle of unity.

Growing up in Seattle, a city named after a great Native American tribal chief, I was surrounded and influenced by Native American culture. One of my best childhood friends was a black Indian. We didn't know it then though; Juanita was considered a "Negro" like the rest of us, but now, as I recall her mother was Native American and her father was African American, I realize she was definitely biracial.

Historically, Africans and Indians have lived side by side so harmoniously that many African Americans claim to be "part Indian," and, in fact, so many blacks *are* that it is estimated that up to one third could claim reservation rights. But the most important fact is that there has been a spiritual bond between the two peoples since the first days Africans arrived in this country.

Author and historian William Loren Katz has done extensive research on the relationship between the two peoples, most notably for his book *Black Indians: A Hidden Heritage.* I asked him to point out some common bonds as we approach Thanksgiving—the one day of the year in which the United States acknowledges any contribution of Native Americans:

- ❖ The cultures of both groups stem from tribal societies and village life.
- ❖ Religious practices are a matter of daily reflection, not just relegated to Sundays.
- ❖ Africans and Indians believe nature is to be protected. Mountains and hills represent spirits and divinities. Their economies avoid harm to the environment.
- ❖ Both cultures reject the pursuit of worldly treasures and ownership.
- ❖ Both venerate kinship, old people, and young children.
- ❖ The circle is a symbol of unity for both peoples. They sit in circles during rituals and ceremonies.
- ❖ Unlike Western society, which exalts the individual (and still does), both Native American and African American cultures have an ancient creed of owing the community.

Secret Ingredient: **Embrace these principles and renew the bonds. Read William Loren Katz's informative *Black Indians*. Or visit his Web site at www.thefuturesite.com/wlkatz. For a whole community of Black Indians (articles, links, commentary), visit www.thefuture-site.com/nzingha.**

❦ NOVEMBER 20 ❦

Kick some butt . . .

. . . If you smoke, that is.

Shelia Baynes of Berkeley Heights, New Jersey, did it. Judy Dothard Simmons of Anniston, Alabama, did it. Beverly Logan-Morrison, M.D., of St. Louis, Missouri, did it too. So did Karen Johnson of New York City. Lucille Anderson of San Francisco won the fight. And Nikki Giovanni of Christiansburg, Virginia, kicked some serious butt.

Around this time each year, the American Cancer Society encourages all smokers to abstain from cigarettes for twenty-four hours. The Great American Smokeout, as it's called, is an opportunity for folks who smoke to prove to themselves that they can quit for life—and for a healthier life. Almost twenty-five years since the campaign started, just about everyone understands the health hazard of cigarette smoking: it causes cancer and aggravates many other diseases to start sooner—and sometimes kill quicker. Each year, forty-five thousand African Americans die from a smoking-related disease that could have been prevented. All of us can observe the Smokeout in one or more of the following ways:

- ❖ Decide to stop smoking if it's your habit now, like the sisters mentioned above.
- ❖ Help a friend to quit; my sister, Vicki, credits her friend Emily with making an enormous difference in Vicki's determination to quit (see January 4).
- ❖ Remind your organizations and churches to support the Smokeout.
- ❖ Spread your own "don't you even start" messages to our youth.

I once asked former United States surgeon general M. Joycelyn Elders, M.D., who writes a column for *Heart & Soul*, what her advice would be about smoking. Here's what she said: "Just because smoking cigarettes is legal doesn't mean it isn't deadly. A cigarette is a bomb with a long fuse. You can either make the tobacco companies wealthy or you can stay healthy. Don't smoke."

Secret Ingredient: To find out how to observe the Great American Smokeout in your area, call your local American Cancer Society.

❧ NOVEMBER 21 ❧

Work smarter, not harder.

Are you a workaholic? See how many of the following scenarios get your adrenaline flowing:

❖ Do you get a rush when you turn on your computer and see you have three hundred e-mails—since yesterday?

❖ Does checking your voice mail excite you?

❖ Do you love your job more than just about any other pursuit— or person—you can think of?

❖ Do you feel guilty when you're not working—like at bedtime?

❖ Do friends and relatives tell you often that they miss seeing you?

❖ At parties, do you make sure people know what you do for a living?

❖ Do you skip most party invitations because you're "busy"?

❖ Is your workplace where you feel most at home?

You get the picture. Well, for those of us brought up with the philosophy that we're the "last hired and the first fired," we have to be workaholics to keep up, right? Not really. Productiveness is always better than perfectionism. Working smart is the objective. Workaholism is an addiction that we mistake for success. The rush of adrenaline gets mistaken for excitement and enthusiasm of the job. The desire for a promotion is normal; wanting it at the cost of a normal life isn't. Plus, the stress that comes with being a workaholic can mean burnout, absenteeism, chronic headaches, high blood pressure, depression, ulcers, or a heart attack.

To find the balance, first acknowledge that you need to. Take the clues of family and friends. Check out your home life (are you on the computer late at night, when your mate is asleep?). How are your eating and sleeping habits? Make time for exercise and de-stressing. Take a time management course. Delegate. Love your job, but love yourself more.

Secret Ingredient: **If you feel you need help getting your work life back in balance, contact the American Self-Help Clearinghouse in Denville, New Jersey.**

❦ NOVEMBER 22 ❦

Be thankful.

Bea Gaddy of Baltimore is one of my heroes. In 1981 she had five children and was on welfare, with fifty cents to her name, but that didn't stop her from inviting her whole neighborhood for Thanksgiving dinner. She played the lottery with the coins and won $290—enough to feed the thirty-nine people. Today she has an organization, the Bea Gaddy Family Centers, that serves thousands of Thanksgiving dinners to needy families each year, and has branched out to provide mortgage payment and cancer support.

We may not all be Queen Beas, but we can remember that Thanksgiving is not about overeating or pigging out. It's about godliness, gratefulness, and helping others who don't have the abundance that we do. Here are twelve ways to give thanks this Thanksgiving.

1. **Say grace.** Giving thanks for the food which you are about to receive is the most common way to express gratitude during the gathering of family and friends. (And bless the hands that prepared it.)
2. **Count your blessings.** You know the procedure: name them one by one.
3. **Tell loved ones why they are precious to you.**
4. **Write down the reasons you have to be grateful.**
5. **Attend a Thanksgiving religious service.**
6. **Share your meal** with someone in need.
7. **Forego the overeating** and help out in a soup kitchen.
8. **Donate a turkey** to a charity that dispenses them to families who can't afford to buy them.
9. **Duplicate your shopping cart** and give the groceries to a food pantry.
10. **Donate gently used coats** to a homeless shelter.
11. **Organize a Thanksgiving church supper** for the community.
12. **Give thanks every day.**

Secret Ingredient: If you would like to form a community service organization, be sure to first volunteer at other centers to learn the proper methods of record keeping, obtaining resources, and working with the public. To help or donate to Bea Gaddy's organization, call 1-410-563-2749.

🍁 NOVEMBER 23 🍁

Eat, drink, and be healthy.

And they're off! The official eating season has begun! From now until New Year's, we'll all be afraid of adding on extra pounds caused by the delicious tastes, flavors, fats, and desserts of Thanksgiving, Christmas parties, Christmas dinner, the Kwanzaa *karamu,* the New Year's Day good-luck feast, the leftovers of all those meals, and others in between. Yum, yum, yum!

If you've been trying hard to develop good eating habits this year, though, don't stop now! Here are some ways to eat using your head instead of adding to your hips.

- ❖ **Prepare your soul food favorites in a different way.** Use low-fat cheese and skim milk in the macaroni, cook the greens with herbs or turkey, use brown rice instead of white rice.
- ❖ **Season foods with herbs and spices** instead of salt.
- ❖ **Don't forget the cornbread**—dressing, that is. Prepare the dressing in a separate dish rather than stuffing it inside the turkey to avoid the fat drippings during cooking, and the bacteria hazard of leaving it in the cavities when storing. Use broth instead of butter to flavor it. Not stuffing the bird can reduce cooking time by up to an hour.
- ❖ **Eat a healthy breakfast** before you start cooking so your tasting doesn't turn into eating.
- ❖ **Opt for white turkey meat over dark meat; it has half the fat.**
- ❖ **Avoid eating the turkey skin.**
- ❖ **Make sure your plate has more vegetables and fruits than meat.**
- ❖ **Don't drown the food in gravy.** The added calories can defeat your whole game plan.
- ❖ **Serve hot spiced cider** instead of egg nog (which is seriously high in calories). Cider's fat-free.
- ❖ **Avoid the driving hazard and the calories of wine** by serving nonalcoholic sparkling cider.

Secret Ingredient: Plan a "turkey trot" after dinner for the whole family. Get everyone outside to "walk off" their calories—it's something the whole family, from the babies to the grandparents, can enjoy. My former colleague, Claire McIntosh, says her family started taking a walk "for dessert" as a new annual tradition. Your family can do it too.

🍁 NOVEMBER 24 🍁

Share your abundance.

It was the first time we had worshipped in this church, a Unitarian Universalist congregation in our town. We went there to hear our friend Rosemary Bray give the sermon. But we had no idea that our visit would bring us not only a memorable sermon on caring about the homeless, but an unimaginable Thanksgiving that carried out that theme just ten days later.

During a time of sharing in the service, two women stood up—one white, one black. Jane,* the petite, older white woman, introduced her guest, a tall, stocky woman wearing impeccable cornrows, and an exile from the civil war that was being fought in Sierra Leone. She explained that she was hosting the other woman, Antoinette,* who was seeking political asylum here in the United States. For the Thanksgiving holiday, Jane planned to be away. Was there anyone with whom Antoinette could stay while she was gone? Seeing Antoinette's eyes tear up, my daughter whispered to her father that we should volunteer. After the service, the three of us approached the two women and offered our guest room to the African sister. "Jane asked why I chose you," Antoinette told me later, saying that five families had extended invitations. "I said I didn't really know, but it just seemed to me that your family would be fun." I was honored and surprised that in her intensely distressed state of uncertainty about her future she had used the word "fun." And I think both Jane and I had expected her to say that it was because we were one of the few black families in attendance that Sunday. But instead, Antoinette took the higher ground of family fun.

During our visit together, we did have fun when my childhood friend, Olivia, who now lives in France, came for a one-night stay that had been planned long before. We extended our fax, phone, and Internet service (where we found news of Special Envoy to Africa Reverend Jesse Jackson's peace mission to Sierra Leone) to Antoinette, and Reggie took her to an African restaurant in Harlem. Antoinette shared with us stories of the beauty of her country, and the heartbreak of the war. She told us about her arrest in Sierra Leone for activism, of coming to the States for an international women's conference on peace and freedom, and of being told by her own five children that it would not be safe for her to return home—many of her neighbors had been arrested and killed, and she had

---

* *A pseudonym.*

been targeted also. Providing her with a few winter clothes ("It is too cold here for me"), a Baptist church experience ("I want to go there; Baptists are full of life!"), and after the holiday returning her to Jane's house, I kept being visited by the spirit of the blacks and whites who had provided safe haven along the journey of the Underground Railroad. We vowed to celebrate peace and freedom together in Sierra Leone someday. And as we said grace before Antoinette's first Thanksgiving Day feast, we gave thanks for our new friendship.

Secret Ingredient: Invite someone who would otherwise be alone or who cannot afford a feast to your table this holiday. Or look in the newspapers for solicitations for volunteers to prepare food, give groceries, deliver dinners, and otherwise spread our country's abundance. You'll find that opening your heart and/or home will not just help someone else, but will enrich your own life.

 MIND

❦ NOVEMBER 25 ❦

Find common ground.

During the five days around Thanksgiving that our guest from Sierra Leone visited with our family, the more we talked about our lives, the more we realized that people are the same everywhere. Antoinette* would lament that while she has been in America in exile, back in Africa her sixteen-year-old son has been running up her phone bill without a thought as to who would pay it. And I would say, "My sixteen-year-old child does the same thing!"

"The challenge," she said, "is to keep the school grades up and the phone bills down." And after we agreed on that, the conversation turned to how both our teenagers, in different parts of the world, were totally obsessed with getting their driver's licenses.

In her moments of despair over her uncertain situation, Antoinette would pull herself out by uttering, "God is good *all the time.*" I had thought that was an American expression.

The common ground Antoinette found wasn't just with us black folks either. She told me that she sympathized with Jane,* the white

* *A pseudonym.*

woman who had been helping her obtain asylum, because Jane's best friend was terminally ill with lung cancer. Antoinette had also lost friends who smoked to lung cancer in her homeland. In addition, Antoinette had been caring for a senile grandmother, running a business, and raising her children as a single mom. Like so many women of every color in this country, she felt the stress of the "sandwich generation."

When strangers look at one another, we assume that things like skin color, country of origin, hair texture, income, and language make us different. These presumptions, and often stereotypes, keep us skeptical and at arm's length from one another. We assume differences before similarities.

Develop a habit of finding common ground with others and you'll broaden your self-esteem, be less afraid to approach people who could be of genuine assistance, and expand your mind. You'll be more adventurous because you know you'll be able to make friends out of strangers anywhere you go. Realizing that all of us on this planet are more alike than different could even change the world.

Secret Ingredient: Share a meal with someone "different." It's an ancient custom (consider Thanksgiving's origin). Political strategist James Carville had the right idea when he exclaimed on *The Today Show* a few years ago: "A lot of differences can be settled over a pot of gumbo!"

 BODY

❧ NOVEMBER 26 ❧

Fight those fibroids.

Why fifty percent of black women get fibroids, no one knows. But the fact remains that we develop these tumors at a rate of more than twice that of white women. Because they are so common, there are some basic facts every sister should know:

What are fibroids? Fibroids are noncancerous tumors found in the muscles of the uterus. As their size can vary, they are often compared to fruits, with sizes described as ranging from apple seeds to grapefruits.

What causes them? Although fibroids are common, very little is known of their cause. Many physicians do agree that excessive weight causes fibroids to grow, and that heredity plays a part.

What are the symptoms? You can have fibroids without any symptoms (like the little one I have that was found in a test for something else), but the most common complaints that may indicate the need for treatment include heavy menstrual bleeding, anemia or fainting as a result of the blood loss, abdominal swelling, pain or pressure in the pelvic area, painful intercourse, and frequent urination.

What can I do about them? Treatments range from simply monitoring the tumors if they remain small and pain-free, to nonsurgical embolization, to the controversial last-resort major surgery of hysterectomy.

Any way to prevent them? Because so little is known of the cause, little is known of the prevention. However, as weight seems to be a factor, eating healthful foods and exercising to keep your body at a normal weight may discourage the estrogen production that causes fibroids to grow.

Secret Ingredient: A popular resource is the book *Uterine Fibroids: What Every Woman Needs to Know,* by Nelson H. Stringer, M.D. Web sites www.thriveonline.com, www.BeWell.com, and www.fibroids.org also have information on fibroids.

 SPIRIT

🍁 NOVEMBER 27 🍁

Turn to The Word.

Do you have a favorite passage of the Bible, Quran, or other spiritual or religious book that you turn to for strength? I've taken note of some of the sacred passages that people in media and folks I know cite:

Quran (2:286). My husband, Reggie, suggests this prayer for those who feel heavy burdens. It asks for mercy, protection, and strength to bear.

Bible, Psalm 130. According to the A&E *Biography* show, "Cinque," this song of ascents, was read by a young girl who was formerly a prisoner on the *Amistad* ship, in a farewell event in New York before return to Sierra Leone in 1842.

The Book of Job. My present-day Sierra Leonean friend in exile took refuge in this book of the Bible about a man who was very rich, and lost everything—but through it all he kept his trust in God.

The Book of Nehemiah. *Jesus CEO* author Laurie Beth Jones says she gets inspiration from this book, the story of a man who provided spiritual leadership for his people.

Jeremiah 8:22. Reverend Meriann Taylor of Balm in Gilead, a resource center in New York City that helps establish AIDS ministries in black churches, says the organization took its name from this passage.

Psalm 27. During four years of a federal investigation that ended in acquittal, Mike Espy, the former Secretary of Agriculture, took solace in this passage. "Each and every day I read the twenty-seventh psalm," *The New York Times* reported him as saying. "And it basically says that the Lord is my light and my salvation. Whom shall I fear? Certainly not Donald Smaltz." Smaltz was the special prosecutor who brought the charges against him. Oprah Winfrey, who also was acquitted of charges against her, filed by Texas cattle ranchers, says this is her favorite psalm as well.

Secret Ingredient: Reverend Wyatt T. Walker, in *The Story of Gospel Music,* a documentary, sums it up simply by citing Psalm 150: Praise the Lord.

❈ MIND

NOVEMBER 28 ❈

Lady, sing the blues.

Believe it or not, singing the blues or playing a blues CD just may help prevent getting them.

Trumpeter Wynton Marsalis explained how this works on a televised "White House Millennium" jazz program. "There's a difference between having and listening to the blues," he said after having played "St. Louis Blues" by W. C. Handy. "Listening to the blues keeps you from getting the blues. It's like getting an innoculation for smallpox. A little shot of it keeps you from getting it."

We already know that music can make you feel better. And soul music is medicine for the mind. The blues, being an original African American music form, is one that we can relate to, that comes from the black experience. Although the blues is internationally popular now, we need to hold on to it, keep a claim on it as our own, and remember its original purpose—preventive medicine.

Some of my favorite blues songs are those by Billie Holiday and B. B. King. I also have a personal infinity for the late Muddy Waters, because on my twenty-first birthday I went to see this legend perform, and when he found out that I had the blues (because I'd been stood up on my special day!), he made several gracious efforts to make the performance memorable for me. Got my blues cured, sure 'nuff.

Blues is not only a music form, however. It's also a type of poetry. In college I had a class on African American poetry that included the blues. What I learned is that the blues stanza is pretty standard: two lines that repeat themselves (the second line may embellish the first), and a third rhyming line. Like this:

> *The blues ain't nothing but a song.*
> *The blues, it ain't nothing but a soulful song.*
> *It's so easy that anyone can sing along.*

I just made that up. If I can sing and write some blues, I know you can. Try it out!

Secret Ingredient: **Keep the blues alive! Blues tunes are some of the easiest to sing along to. Buy the CDs, attend concerts of the blues singers who perform in your area. Visit the House of Blues in Chicago, immerse yourself in blues culture in New Orleans, take a blues cruise in New York. Feel better.**

❁ BODY

🍁 NOVEMBER 29 🍁

Exercise without really trying.

Pick out a few of these things you can start doing *today* to get in a habit of being active and moving that body:

- ❖ Take the stairs *everywhere.*
- ❖ Do some jumping jacks, like you did in high school.
- ❖ Park walking distance from the mall entrance (except when it's dark).
- ❖ Find out if the mall has "morning fitness walks" before stores open.
- ❖ Walk your dog.
- ❖ Walk to the grocery store, like you did when you were a kid.
- ❖ Rake your leaves.
- ❖ Take your children to an amusement park and don't sit down unless they do.
- ❖ Vacuum your whole house or apartment.

* Shovel snow.
* Wash your car yourself.
* Exercise while you watch television. Try leg lifts and sit-ups.
* Walk while you talk. Move around the house while you're on the telephone.
* Whenever you sit on the floor, try getting down and standing up without using any hands.
* Get one of those exercise strollers to commit yourself to pushing baby all over the park—often.
* Use your baby to "lift weight." Lie on your back and lift baby toward the ceiling.
* Take a walking vacation.
* Party!
* Have mad (safe) sex!

Secret Ingredient: **Today incorporate at least five of these activities into your schedule.**

NOVEMBER 30 🍁

Eat better without really trying.

Pick out a few of these things you can start doing *today* to get in a habit of cutting out extra calories and shaping up by eating right:

* Eat slowly and in small amounts.
* Fight hunger pangs by eating a green salad or drinking a clear soup or tomato juice before a meal.
* Stick to lean meats like chicken, veal, and turkey as much as possible.
* Pick "swimming fish" like tuna, cod, and flounder. Shellfish like shrimp are richer in cholesterol.
* Broil or roast. If you have to fry, use a nonstick pan or spray coating.
* Sauté with chicken broth, soy sauce, or wine.
* Cook Chinese, Indian, and Turkish for low-calorie, low-fat cooking methods. Use recipes with a high proportion of vegetables.
* Steam vegetables to preserve the flavor and nutritional value.
* Squeeze a lemon on top of veggies for added flavor.

- ❖ Flavor vegetable dishes with herbs instead of butter.
- ❖ Eat a plain boiled or baked potato (only seventy-two calories) to satisfy that craving for "starchy" food.
- ❖ Eat cheeses for protein. The ones lower in fat content are Swiss, mozzarella, ricotta, and cottage.
- ❖ Drink skimmed or one percent milk.
- ❖ If you crave sweets, use dietetic syrups, sodas, jams, and jellies. Read the labels to be certain that they're low in calories.
- ❖ Drink more water than anything else.

Secret Ingredient: **If you are trying to lose weight, look for a pocket calorie-counter at your bookstore. It can help you track what foods and dishes are loaded with calories and which ones contain only a few.**

✸ BODY

✸ DECEMBER 1 ✸

Protect yourself against HIV-AIDS.

Gary C. Dennis, M.D., is the president of the National Medical Association (NMA), the organization of African American physicians that is over one hundred years old. In a conversation with me about the NMA's focus during his year as president, Dr. Dennis cited black men's health, diabetes education, and HIV-AIDS prevention. On this, World AIDS Day, and with African Americans contracting fifty-seven percent of this country's new HIV cases, it's an appropriate time to heed Dr. Dennis's advice to African American women about preventing HIV-AIDS exposure. His words were down to earth and direct, spoken like a true brother-doctor.

"A woman needs to know the man she's dating before she has sex with him," he says simply. "If you don't know the background, you shouldn't have sex. Women should ask these questions before beginning any sexual relationship," Dr. Dennis advises:

"Have you been incarcerated?" "If so, he may have been exposed to AIDS and not been tested," says Dr. Dennis.

"Have you ever had a bisexual experience?" "There are men who have been incarcerated—including many educated black men—who are bisexual. You need to make sure you know all you can."

"Will you be tested with me?" "Some men won't be tested, or have an irresponsible attitude about AIDS."

In addition, Dr. Dennis had some advice for the sisters: "If you're single or married, and think you could have been exposed to AIDS, *get tested if you want to have a baby.*" We discussed the fact that some women may not be trying to get pregnant, yet they do not insist on condom use to prevent HIV-AIDS or contraceptives to prevent pregnancy. "That's a passive-aggressive pregnancy," says Dr. Dennis. "You know you will get pregnant even though it wasn't 'intended.' That is irresponsible. If your baby is HIV-positive, the infant will be sick and hard to care for. If you know before you become pregnant that you're HIV-positive, you can take medication that dramatically reduces the chances of having a baby born HIV-positive."

The most important thing Dr. Dennis wants us to remember is that "if you feel you may have been exposed to AIDS, you should be tested. Don't wait until you have a sick baby to find out your HIV status. An educated woman should *know,* instead of getting pregnant and finding out when the baby's born."

Secret Ingredient: **The Centers for Disease Control and Prevention (CDC) has a National HIV/AIDS hotline; call 1-800-342-AIDS.**

 MIND

❄ DECEMBER 2 ❄

Make your list, and check it a bunch of times.

Stores are already luring you with holiday sales. The radio may be playing the first Christmas songs of the season. And if you're like me, you're bugging out!

So much to do—and so little time or money to do it with. When your life turns into shopping, cooking, entertaining, office partying, decorating, caroling, giving, and playing Santa Claus, it can also turn into that "good stress" we talked about before. And that can result in bad habits such as overeating, smoking, drinking . . . well, you get the picture.

We can change the picture to a tranquil scene. Get a jump on keeping it all under control with a simple tool: a blank book. Buy a special little notebook, small enough to carry in your handbag, that you will want to keep for years to come. I use my electronic notebook, but I have a Christmas-red bound notebook that a friend gave me that would have been perfect (if I had thought of it before using it to record business expenses!). Use your notebook to keep yourself organized and sane. Jot down inside:

- ❖ Your holiday gift list
- ❖ Your holiday gift budget and expenditures
- ❖ Things to do, errands to run
- ❖ Recipes for nonalcoholic egg nog and other drinks to serve guests that are driving
- ❖ Kwanzaa activities in the community, ways to celebrate at home
- ❖ New Year's Eve plans
- ❖ Special thoughts of the holiday season

If you do this every year, you can compare your notes, feelings, and gift giving and receiving. If you decide to hold on to the books as keepsakes, you might also paste inside gift tags from presents you receive, snippets of ribbon, samples of holiday stamps, return-address labels, and a photo or two. As years go by, and loved ones move, grow up, or pass away, your little red book will be as precious as a family album.

Secret Ingredient: **Look for blank books at bookstores, stationery stores, or art supply houses.**

❄ DECEMBER 3 ❄

Find God in yourself.

The Broadway play *For Colored Girls who have Considered Suicide/When the Rainbow is Enuf* was a landmark work of the 1970s. Playwright Ntozake Shange struck a chord in portraying the lives and challenges of everyday, strong black women.

My favorite lines of the Obie Award–winning play, often described as a choreopoem, are:

i found god in myself
& i loved her/i loved her fiercely

It was a profound thought. Onstage, it was like the punch line, the "ah-ha!" to the whole show. Although it seems a given now, it was ahead of its time then, because it just wasn't common to acknowledge God *within* us. God was always "up there" or "in heaven." Who were we to think God could be inside *us?* And then, to call God *her*—well, that was really revolutionary, and to some, downright blasphemous.

Oz Scott, the television and film director, was the director of *For Colored Girls.* Talking with him recently, I asked if he remembered how avant garde that particular line of the play was, and if there had been any reaction to it. He said that indeed, a brother well known in drama circles came backstage after seeing a performance and said in all sincerity, "The show was good—but everyone knows God is a man!"

God is Spirit. And Holy Spirit dwells within each of us, male or female, and that manifestation is whatever we are, and whatever we feel it to be, because what we feel is what is real. When I pray, I acknowledge both genders by saying, "Father Heaven, Mother Earth," in the Native American way.

Some folks think God is black. Or God is white. I like the title of James McBride's book *The Color of Water*—that's the color James's Jewish mother told him God is. On my bulletin board is a clipping of the comic strip "Family Circus" by Bill Keane in which the little girl asks her mother, "Is God white, black, brown, yellow or red?" The mother answers, "Yes."

Secret Ingredient: **Do as Ntozake instructs the actresses in the script: Repeat softly to yourself, "i found god in myself & i loved her" until it becomes "a song of joy."**

 B O D Y

❄ DECEMBER 4 ❄

Live each day to the fullest.

My mother, Josephine Stokes, whose birthday is today, has more energy than I will ever have in my lifetime. In 1999 she's planning to celebrate her seventy-fifth birthday with a big bash of a party, which, she says, must include dancing! No sitting around for this still-size-eight little lady! Here she shares more of her secrets of an energetic, healthy life.

❖ **Keep singing and dancing.** "Even back when people said those were stereotypes, I didn't care, because I enjoyed them. When I was in college, I was voted 'best dancer,' and now I like line dancing (because it doesn't require a partner). I sing in all the choirs of my church."

- ❖ **Don't smoke or drink.** "I never smoked because I liked dancing and singing, and thought the smoking would affect my breathing. And I just never did like drinking."
- ❖ **Watch how you eat.** "I eat breakfast (because it breaks the fast), a hot lunch, and a balanced dinner. I cut down on sugar, salt, and white flour, and eat more raw fruits and vegetables. I use one percent milk to cut cholesterol."
- ❖ **Look good, and you'll feel good.** "I believe in getting my hair done, and in regular manicures and pedicures." Mom, who was once photographed in *Ebony* for bringing the Fashion Fair to town, still shops and dresses with a vengeance—"I love it!" she says.
- ❖ **Take care of yourself.** "No one can take better take of you than you." (She always says that.) "That means taking responsibility for birth control and STD prevention, not relying on anyone else to do it."
- ❖ **Get an annual checkup.** "Early in the New Year, I get a complete physical, my eyes checked, and a mammogram. After all those tests, it makes me feel better to know I'm healthy."
- ❖ **Stay active.** "I've been president of everything: the church choir, my circle, the preschool board." Still running for office, she's currently president of the North Pacific Baptist Women's convention.
- ❖ **Stay positive.** "My [late] husband used to call me Pollyanna because I always looked for the good in a situation. You live longer if you're positive."

Secret Ingredient: **Mom's most frequent advice to me is "Live each day to the fullest. No matter how old or young you are, you never know if this day will be your last, so enjoy every moment."**

❀ MIND

❄ DECEMBER 5 ❄

Hold family-wellness meetings.

When I was a child, our family "held court" at the kitchen table. If one of us kids was accused of a "misdemeanor," my father would have us present our case, and then the jury (the other two kids) would be asked to decide guilt or innocence, and if guilty, the punishment. I guess my father was practicing on us—he actually did become a judge. And we kids got a big kick out of being the "jury of our peers."

A similar method of family decision-making has continued in the next generation. At my house we have family meetings every Wednesday at eight P.M. I find them to be a good way to air issues that one might hold in, waiting for the right time to say something—and that time never comes. It keeps people from holding grudges, and lets you air them when you're not upset. Like meetings at work, you can plan an agenda and discuss things calmly when all parties are listening, not when someone is doing their homework, cooking dinner, or watching the Bulls game.

You don't even have to live with the person to have issues you might want to share on a regular basis. Have your powwow with a roommate, boyfriend, or elder parent. Do it by phone or online.

Some things we discuss include making up a schedule for sharing the cooking and kitchen-cleaning duties, our daughter's school progress, upcoming events, the bills, preparations for guests, family values. Health and wellness discussions could also include:

- ❖ Reminders about doctors' appointments
- ❖ Airing any disagreements or hurt feelings
- ❖ Counseling someone's problems
- ❖ Letting others know if they did something that was appreciated. Always end on a positive.

Secret Ingredient: Give children equal time. We allow our daughters to say anything that's bothering them—even if it's about us—as long as it's said respectfully. Even children have stresses and need to be heard. And believe me, if you provide the forum in a "zone" in which they feel safe and free to speak up, they'll tell you what's on their mind.

 SPIRIT

❄ DECEMBER 6 ❄

Smile.

It won't cost you nothing! And it'll make you and those around you feel so good.

It may seem silly, but smiling is very powerful gift from God. When babies are born, the first act of intelligence parents look for is in the smile. When a loved one is terminal and no longer speaking, those gathered around look only for that final sign of reassurance, a smile. It's universal, it doesn't require language lessons. Flashing a smile is global communication.

Recently, my husband Reg and I went to the Blue Note jazz club in Manhattan to see Roberta Flack perform. As anyone who's ever been there may know, like most clubs, the place is crowded with folks who may not know each other sitting at the same table. We were seated at the end of a table for six, the other four people were young Japanese tourists. Immediately, I could tell that the woman I sat down next to did not speak English, but she smiled and nodded, and I smiled and nodded, and instantly we were communicating. After the fabulous show, Reg and I got up to leave, and again my tablemate and I smiled and nodded—this time we smiled more broadly and nodded more vigorously, pointing up to the stage. And we both knew that that meant we agreed that we sure had enjoyed the show.

I'll bet you think you smile all the time. But make a conscious effort today and see how mentally gratifying—and fun—it turns out. Try these "smile therapies."

- ❖ When someone gives you "road rage," smile at them when they pass instead of giving them the finger. Watch them drive off totally baffled!
- ❖ Smile at people who pass you on the street. (I don't mean flirt, just acknowledge their existence and keep on walking.)
- ❖ Think of smiles that warm our hearts. I give Nelson Mandela the prize for "best smile" (His whole handsome face lights up!). Remember that a gap-toothed smile is a sign of African beauty. The toothless smile of any baby is good luck. And the smile of anyone you love is priceless.

Secret Ingredient: Smile, Smile, Smile! is a book of thirty-one poems by Gurumayi Chidvilasananda that encourages you to "smile at your destiny." To order the book or tape, call 1-888-422-3334.

 BODY

 **DECEMBER 7**

Put it on—or take it off.

When I was editing *Heart & Soul,* the magazine often published articles on how to lose weight, because women would see those stories and think *That's what I need to do,* and then they'd buy the magazine. We always sold more copies of the magazine when we carried stories on weight loss. And with almost fifty percent of African American women overweight, there was a need for information on how to take off the pounds.

But for every dozen or so overweight sisters, there are those who want to *gain* weight. And they let us know! So we gave information on that too, and published some stories of women who wanted to get that "sister body."

The ironic thing is that women who want to lose weight and those who want to gain pounds have a lot in common. Both need more physical exercise to tone their bodies. Both can benefit from eating five or six mini-meals a day instead of three big ones. If you're trying to gain, it makes adding on those high-calorie foods less of a struggle, and if you're trying to lose, you can curb hunger pains by eating less but spreading it out. And both women need highly nutritious foods. What each eats is often just a variation on the same theme: both should eat many of the same kinds of foods, often the same size portions, but prepared differently. If you're tying to gain, add sauces and plenty of high-calorie extras. If you're trying to lose, cut them to the barest minimum. Here are some guidelines I kept from *Glamour* magazine, when I worked there years ago, that can work for you today:

TO PUT WEIGHT ON:

Fried chicken (3 oz.) = 201 calories

Beef pot pie (4^{1}/$_{2}$" dia.) = 560 calories

Creamed corn (^{1}/$_{2}$ c.) = 102 calories

French fries (20 pcs.) = 233 calories

Apple pie (1 slice) = 360 calories

TO TAKE WEIGHT OFF:

Broiled chicken (3 oz.) = 115 calories

Lean roast beef (3 oz.) = 182 calories

Unbuttered green beans (^{1}/$_{2}$ c.) = 22 calories

Baked potato, dash Worcestershire sauce = 104 calories

Apple (1 med.) = 80 calories

Secret Ingredient: Whether you're trying to gain or lose weight, a pocket calendar with calorie counter can help you keep tabs on everything you eat each day.

❄ DECEMBER 8 ❄

Relax.

Sharon Morgan and Barbara Mitchell of New Jersey are two women who know from experience the stress involved in juggling busy careers and families. As an antidote, they decided to take weekend retreats to relax and refresh themselves. Now they sponsor Creative Escapes, stress-management and spa retreats, which for more than six years has helped hundreds of women take time out for themselves. Barbara and Sharon share their top relaxation techniques:

Start each day celebrating yourself. Your thoughts set the tone for the day. Make positive thoughts about yourself part of your morning routine. Better known as self-affirmations, positive thoughts should always pat you on the back and build confidence. Use thoughts such as "I'm a good person and deserve to be happy," or "I am calm, relaxed, and confident," or "I can handle all my challenges today." These reduce feelings of being overwhelmed and underappreciated. Post your positive thoughts where they can be seen first thing in the morning.

Take deep breaths. Slow, rhythmic, deep inhalation and exhalation soothes the nerves, quiets the rapid heartbeat, brings life-giving oxygen to the cells, and aids in the removal of toxins from the body. The next time you're feeling tense or nervous, try this breathing exercise: Inhale to the count of four; hold the breath to the count of four; exhale to the count of four; mentally say the word "relax" to the count of four. Repeat until you begin to feel calm.

Practice relaxation throughout the day. The quickest way to relax tight muscles is by progressively contracting and relaxing large muscle groups in the area of tension. Soothe frayed nerves by slowing the breath and focusing your awareness inward while saying, "I am calm and relaxed." Break the tedium of the workday by mentally finding your place of beautiful memories or by gazing out a window and savoring the wonders of nature. These exercises take only moments and help to center you and balance your day.

Secret Ingredient: Take ten minutes today to practice Barbara & Sharon's exercises. Afterward notice how much better you feel. For relaxation techniques on an audiotape produced by Barbara and Sharon called *The Gentle Art of Relaxing with Creative Escapes,* check out the web site: www.creativeescapes.com.

❄ DECEMBER 9 ❄

Get a daily dose of a Good Book.

When it comes time to make New Year's resolutions, there's one I vow to do every year: read the entire Bible in a year. I haven't finished it yet, but every year I try again. When I finish the Bible, the next year I'm going to start in on the Quran, then on to other books of the world's religions. I want to read all of God's best sellers!

If it's your goal to read the Bible in a year, it may be helpful to do a little legwork now so that when the New Year starts, you'll be ready to read.

- ❖ Look to see if your Bible contains a listing of passages to read over the course of the year. (I recently discovered that my grandfather's Bible, almost sixty years old, had a reading plan in the back.)
- ❖ Read *Our Daily Bread* pamphlets, starting in January, which in the past few years has published a schedule of "The Bible in One Year" on each day's page.
- ❖ Ask your pastor to print the weekly reading assignments in the church bulletin. Some churches sponsor annual Bible-reading programs with acknowledgment during a year-end service of those who successfully complete the program.
- ❖ You can buy a Bible edited for this purpose. I picked up *The One-Year Bible* (Tyndale) that features the entire New American Standard Bible arranged in 365 daily readings. Do look through these types of texts to familiarize yourself with the format first, however. I didn't realize until too late that the book mixed Old Testament with New Testament readings every day, when I preferred a chronological read. But if you can keep up with two stories and a psalm-a-day too, this one's for you.

Secret Ingredient: If you've got a good memory, and even better discipline, here's the rule of thumb: To read through the entire Bible in one year, read three chapters each day, Monday through Saturday, and read five chapters each Sunday. To take your time over two years, read two chapters each day. If you're a Christian, you may prefer to start with the New Testament, then go back to the Old Testament. Even if you've already read the Bible, it never hurts to reread the Greatest Story Ever Told.

❋ DECEMBER 10 ❋

Have a bright, not white, Christmas.

I think we smile more often this month. We're smiling at children who are on their best Santa-won't-come-if-you're-bad behavior, we're grinning at cute salesclerks in the men's department, and flirting at holiday parties. So the teeth have got to be as white as snow, right?

Not necessarily. Dentists say that most folks are too obsessed with the fact that teeth should be white, and that's almost impossible to obtain. Instead, think natural, clean, and bright.

Now, stains can occur that can make your teeth darker than you want them to be, or than they need to appear. For example, your teeth can get discolored from:

❖ coffee

❖ tea

❖ cranberry or grape juice

❖ certain medications

Foods that have the opposite, cleansing effect are those primarily with roughage, such as:

❖ apples

❖ carrots

❖ cauliflower

❖ broccoli

❖ celery (also makes a great body-double for a chew stick)

All these foods are perfect for a holiday crudité tray.

So don't rush out and buy some expensive bleaching kit you saw on a late-night infomercial. First try these simple, tasty, natural cleansers.

Secret Ingredient: **Toss out your hard-bristled toothbrush. It doesn't make your teeth any whiter to scrub them as if you were using a scouring pad. In fact, that can be damaging. A soft toothbrush used with an easy stroke is less abrasive for your teeth and gums and is best for getting teeth gently clean.**

❋ DECEMBER 11 ❋

Take care of the elders—and yourself.

African American extended family bonds keep us close to our elders. And at that point when they need us, we want to be able to give back to them. "Grandmama took care of me," we say, "so now it's time to take care of her." But often when that time comes, we feel overwhelmed and unsuited for the constant care that an illness or total dependence can bring. And being in what is called the "sandwich generation," taking care of young children as well as our elders, puts us under enormous strain. If that's your situation, take this quick quiz adapted from the Housecall Medical Resources "Home Health Care Needs Checklist" to determine if you could use help with the care of your loved one. Answer yes or no:

1. She lives alone.
2. Her physical condition does not permit her to care for herself and do the things she used to.
3. No other family members are able to care for her needs.
4. Her doctor has prescribed a special diet.
5. She has difficulty selecting and preparing her own meals.
6. She doesn't understand her disease and how to control it.
7. She has more than one medical problem.
8. She takes many prescription medicines.
9. Her doctor has prescribed some new medicines she's never taken before.
10. She had an operation during a recent hospital stay.
11. She has an unhealed wound and needs assistance with dressing changes.
12. Physical limitations make it difficult for her to use the bathroom at home.
13. She has trouble bathing herself.
14. She has to learn to use a wheelchair, walker, or other assistance device to manage at home.
15. She is homebound, making it difficult to do errands, etc.

If you can answer yes to any of these questions, consider discussing the need for assistance at home with your family and your loved one's doctor.

Secret Ingredient: You can get a wealth of information about community programs, financial services, housing, and health issues from the Web site www.housecall.com. Or call Housecall Medical Resources at 1-800-342-9809.

❅ DECEMBER 12 ❅

Get in touch.

When we haven't talked with a dear friend in a long time, we often get that feeling that we'd like to "get in touch." *I need to get in touch with my long-lost girlfriend,* we might think.

Not connecting with someone as often as we would like makes us feel "out of touch." *I don't know what's going on with her; I feel so out of touch.*

We crave that contact, that emotional state of being in close association. When we do get in touch, we feel better, satisfied, fulfilled, maybe relieved.

That's also how we feel when we get in touch with our spirit. It's usually the last connection we make. We're more often dealing with our physical lives. Looking in mirrors every day, we see our bodies. We get up each day making a determination of whether we feel well or sick. We make evaluations throughout the day as to whether we're tired or energized. We're constantly in touch with the body.

And also with the mind. Quick, right now, are you happy or sad? Feeling blue or breezy? In love or out of it? You probably know because you're in touch with your emotional self.

But the spirit—now, that's another matter. Many of us haven't been in touch in a *long* time. Some of us won't even go there. Getting close to our spirit, our inner light, our center is just too scary for some folks. But let me tell you—the mind and the body can't do it all alone. We all need the balance, the centering, that finding our spirit brings. It may mean resting the mind and body in meditation. It may mean taking a yoga class or going to midweek prayer session. Reading a spiritual book does it for many people. Listening to gospel music. Feeling your heartbeat. Concentrating on your breathing. They're all pursuits of the spirit. Ain't nothing spooky about it.

Secret Ingredient: At the end of a busy day—which is just about every day for most of us—it's essential to exercise your unique way of getting in touch with your spirit. No one else can really tell you how to do it or what to do. It's something you have to go deep within yourself to find. And when you do, you'll discover it with joy.

 MIND

❄ DECEMBER 13 ❄

Downsize your holiday stress.

Over the years, companies have downsized. They've cut back on expenditures, pared down operations, and laid off employees. Corporate Christmas parties aren't as lavish as they used to be, holiday bonuses are less generous—if given at all.

Many of us have been affected by those corporate cuts, yet it hasn't occurred to us to downsize our holiday lifestyles. Some of us aren't sure just how to cut back on Christmas gift expenditures, pare down decorating and partying, or lay off people from our Christmas card list. Although many of us complain about the commercialism of Christmas, we still fall into the trick bag: the average amount spent per family on Christmas is around $1,300. And when we get those bills in January and can't pay them, we experience our own personal "post-traumatic stress" or "sticker shock." If you don't want that to happen to you, but you still want to enjoy the holiday season, here are some suggestions for downsizing:

❖ Buy only one box of holiday cards, and send them only to people with whom you've been out of touch, owe a response from an earlier kindness, or to elderly relatives. Give personal, verbal greetings to friends you will see socially over the holidays, and call (locally) or e-mail (anyone out of town) everyone else.

❖ Save on expensive tree ornaments by using colorful costume jewelry and trinkets you have around the house. When I couldn't find my whole box of decorations, I draped the tree with gold ribbon, lights, and Afrocentric jewelry—and everyone thought it was deliberate and creative.

❖ Have a "children only" Christmas gifting. One year when money was tight for me and my siblings, we all agreed not to exchange gifts among ourselves but to spend only on the children. You'd be amazed at how much less stress buying just two or three fewer gifts can be.

❖ Instead of buying this year's holiday CD's for your house party, turn on your favorite radio station, which is bound to be playing *all* the latest jams—for free.

Secret Ingredient: **For one hundred tips on how to "reduce the stress and recapture the joy of the holidays," read *Simplify Your Christmas*, by Elaine St. James.**

✴ BODY

❄ DECEMBER 14 ❄

Give gifts of health.

Another way to simplify your gift giving and your expense is by having a theme. Of course, I would recommend that theme be gifts of health and fitness. In an *Essence* interview with Bill Cosby about Christmas traditions, he told me that people often try to impress him with expensive gifts, but inexpensive presents, such as the tennis sweat bands his daughter once gave him, mean the most. The Women's Sports Foundation suggests these gifts, like the kind Cos favors:

Arm or ankle weights	Leotard
Athletic gloves	Pedometer for walking or biking
Athletic shoes	Sports bag
Bike/skating helmet	Sports bra
Books on women in sports	Sports lesson or fitness class
Boxing gloves	Sports watch
Exercise mat	Sports water bottle
Exercise video	Subscription to women's sports
Free-weight set	or health magazine
Gift certificate for a massage	Swim goggles
Golf balls	Tennis racket
Inline skating accessory	Tickets to a sports event
pack	Warm-up suit
Jump rope	Weight-training belt

Secret Ingredient: **For $20, you can give an athletic girl some encouragement and a youth athletic membership in the Women's**

Sports Foundation. She'll get a membership pin, T-shirt, and a quarterly newsletter, *Sports Talk,* which features female athletic role models. Call 1-800-227-3988.

❄ DECEMBER 15 ❄

Thank your guardian angels.

Have you said "thank you" to your guardian angels lately? Well, if you're not in a habit of talking with them, or even ever thinking about them, you're not the only one.

Plus, if you're black, you may not have embraced them because art and media almost exclusively represent angels as white-faced, pink-cheeked, blue-eyed cherubs. Oprah Winfrey once said on her show that she had never seen angels depicted as black. On a later show she made a point of announcing that people had sent her so many angels—figurines, dolls, ornaments, etc.—that they could have filled a room or two, and that she was going to donate them to a museum for display. So maybe there are a good number of us who believe in black angels after all.

Like God, though, angels come in every color, I think. There are two types of angels: angels on high, and angels on earth. Whether we are black, white, red, yellow, or brown, we need to acknowledge that either kind provides divine protection and may come to us in a race different from our own. I found this out when my father was being visited in his home by a hospice nurse. My mother told me that one day the nurse approached his bedroom and stood in the doorway to greet him before she entered. My father, who was never known to be a teller of tall tales and who was sharp of mind to the very end, asked her, "Do you see those angels?" She replied, "Do *you* see angels?" "Yes," he told her, "they're on both sides of you." I believe that angels *were* with that woman, and that she was one on earth herself. Although she was white and my father black, she had administered care and kindness to him. Our American society is accustomed to the nurturing of whites by blacks, but this woman had transcended the baggage of race to be an angel who aided my mother and helped my father find comfort in his last days. Hospice volunteers are earth angels.

Who have been the angels in your life? More important, make an effort to *be* an angel to someone else. If you do, you just may get touched by an angel yourself.

Secret Ingredient: For inspiration, watch Della Reese on the *Touched by an Angel* TV show or Denzel Washington (who makes a fine angel) in the film *The Preacher's Wife.* A beautiful book for children is *Brown Angels: An Album of Pictures and Verse,* by Walter Dean Myers.

❋ BODY

❄ DECEMBER 16 ❄

Curb your cholesterol.

We've talked a lot in this book about cholesterol, so you know it's something you want to keep low. And you know that the problem with high cholesterol is that it can lead to another high—blood pressure—as well as heart disease and stroke.

Hit the number
- ❖ The goal is keep your cholesterol rate at a level of 200 milligrams or below.
- ❖ If it's 200 to 239, the level is on the border, heading in the wrong direction.
- ❖ If it's 240 and above, it's *in* the wrong direction—it's high, and needs to get under control.

How to hit it
- ❖ The American Heart Association suggests a diet dominated by fruits, vegetables, cereals, and grains. Lean cuts of meat with the fat trimmed away can be a small part.
- ❖ Keep away from saturated fats found in meats and shortening. They kick off the production of cholesterol in the liver. Use oils in moderation; lay off the lard completely, and substitute with olive oil, which is considered by many health experts to be salutary.
- ❖ Cut down on fried foods; that's one area in which you'll feel the difference quickly.
- ❖ Eat lots of fish and poultry. Instead of frying, prepare them by baking, broiling, roasting, or grilling.
- ❖ Read food labels to avoid (or at least limit) ingredients with high cholesterol such as butter, beef fat, coconut oil, egg, hydrogenated or hardened oil, lard, palm oil, and whole milk.

- Remember that some foods that you eat on the run customarily don't have labels, such as doughnuts, and may be made with lard or shortening. Bagels are a better choice.
- From the dairy counter, choose: skim, low-fat (one or two percent), or nonfat milk; soft tub margarine or soybean margarine, nonfat yogurt; ice milk, sorbet, low-fat ice cream, or nonfat frozen yogurt.

Secret Ingredient: **Lowering cholesterol can taste good and be easier than you think! For more tips, contact the National Heart, Lung, and Blood Information Center in Bethesda, Maryland, e-mail: nhlbiic@dgsys.com.**

 MIND

❄ DECEMBER 17 ❄

Be creative!

One good thing about the holiday season is that it gives us a chance to use our creativity. Christmas trees need to be decorated, how the lights will be displayed has to be decided, the way gifts will be wrapped can be your choice.

Every bit of effort you put into these projects shows how much you care—as well as how talented you are. Share the gifts of your creativity by doing any of the following projects that give you joy and self-expression:

- Personalize holiday cards. My friend Brenda sent store-bought Christmas cards that had a photo pocket on the cover, in which we received a much-appreciated picture of her two daughters. Iqua, another friend, had a photo of her family that had been taken for a newspaper story made into a holiday card. She had it printed with envelopes at the local business center.
- Bake cookies and cakes. If you're known for being allergic to the kitchen, your friends will be delightfully surprised to get homemade cookies or a low-fat pound cake. My favorites: Choc-Oat-Chip cookies (for recipe, see inside top of Quaker Old-Fashioned Oatmeal).
- Have your children and their friends make up a Kwanzaa play. You be the director.
- Pull out old photos of Christmases past, and substitute them for

the family photos you usually have on display. Or make a collage out of them in the shape of a tree or wreath.

❖ Create your own gifts of "assembly required." My daughter, Anique, bought soaps, candles, lotions, and other pampering products and assembled them into cosmetic bags as gifts for her sisters. For me, she bought a picture frame of faux leopard (my passion), and inserted a favorite photo of the two of us. Inexpensive gifts such as these are priceless.

Secret Ingredient: **Think of special talents you have and tap into them. But if you aren't "feeling it," don't do it, because loved ones will be able to tell that your heart isn't in it. Delegate, pay someone else, or think of something else to give instead. Always be a cheerful giver—whether you created the gift yourself or not.**

 BODY

❄ DECEMBER 18 ❄

Help yourself to health information.

The doctor has just told you that you've been diagnosed with a condition. Maybe it's fibroids, lupus, sarcoidosis, cancer—or maybe it's happy news, like you're pregnant. You'll be more prepared to deal with whatever it is and take control of your health if you know how to gather information that will help you better understand it. As the former health research chief at Rodale Press, Carol Lindner instituted the research procedures for all the health and fitness information published during the launch of *Heart & Soul.* Here's her advice on how to conduct your own research:

❖ **Partner with your health-care professional.** Many providers gather valuable information with their patients in mind and often know how just what resources are available.

❖ **Check with your local hospital.** Many hospitals have developed community outreach programs focusing on health and wellness, and may be an untapped source for you. Some of the more innovative ones have created health libraries and learning centers—one-stop medical malls staffed by nurse educators—where you can get helpful information and referrals to hundreds of traditional and natural treatments for just about any health problem.

❖ **Stroll through your favorite bookstore.** Books are a wonderful source of inspiration and information, but use good judgment and find books that are accurate, up-to-date, and written by a leading medical authority specializing in your particular health problem.

❖ **Surf the Internet.** If you don't have a computer, check with your local library. Most libraries have computers, and librarians can be extremely helpful in directing you on how to do your search. As with books, be careful. You'll want to find sites that are reliable, trustworthy, and up-to-date.

❖ **Join a self-help group.** Becoming a member of a support group will offer you a wonderful opportunity to meet others who share your concerns, and who may be able to provide real-life counsel. To locate a group in your area, contact the American Self-Help Clearinghouse at 1-973-625-3037.

Secret Ingredient: **Contact key organizations. The National Health Information Center at 1-800-336-4797 can refer you to organizations and government offices best able to answer your questions. For alternative and natural therapy treatments, call the National Center of Complementary and Alternative Medicine at 1-888-644-6226 to tap into their seven-million-record database. Referrals to Overeaters Anonymous groups in your area, may be obtained by calling the America Self-Help Clearinghouse in Denville, New Jersey.**

❋ SPIRIT

❄ DECEMBER 19 ❄

Experience "everyday spirituality."

During the month of December, it's easy to satisfy the soul's desire for the sacred. Christmas concerts, religious services, home decorations—even department store window displays—remind us of the holy-day season. But how can we make each day of the year a holy day? How can going to work, cleaning the house, and working out be considered spiritual?

Actually, with a little effort, we can experience "everyday spirituality." Here are some ways I've discovered.

Get up and get blessed. I don't know about you, but going from sleeping to standing is one of the hardest things I do each day. But I have a special way to make it easier: I just think, *Get up, girl, and get today's blessing!*

Be one with the sun. When was the last time you watched a sunrise or a sunset? Getting up early in Seattle to catch a plane one morning, I caught a sunrise so magnificent, so majestic, that all I could do was pray.

Find the good and praise it. That's what *Roots* author Alex Haley used to say. Catch your kids doing something *right* today—and let them know it as readily as if it had been wrong.

Clean the house. Your mother always told you that cleanliness was next to godliness.

Work out your worries. Get regular exercise. Thirty minutes of aerobic activity at least three times a week can help cut your stress level in half. Feel your heart beat with the pulse of life.

Laugh it up. In her book *Embraced by the Light,* Betty J. Eadie says that one thing she remembers of her near death experience is that God has a sense of humor. Tap into yours. Pick up a humorous book, such as anything by Bertice Berry, Kim Coles, or Whoopi Goldberg. Get a Chris Rock or Eddie Murphy video. Let your children amuse you—now, there's a free ride for the spirit.

Secret Ingredient: **Go to bed. The bed is where we are born, and the cradle of renewal. Escape the daily chaos; read an inspirational book each night (like this one!). Then drift off into the spirit world.**

 BODY

❄ DECEMBER 20 ❄

Dance to your heart's content.

Dancing is good for the heart. Beyond great exercise, it gives us cultural expression, a creative outlet, and makes the spirit soar.

Katherine Dunham is a living dance legend. Dunham's life work as a dancer, choreographer, anthropologist, and founder of the Dunham Dance Company that performed around the world, has secured her place in history as a pioneer in the world of dance. When I spoke with her recently, she was eighty-eight and still overseeing dance workshops at the Katherine Dunham Centers in East St. Louis. I asked her to share with you her philosophy on the joy of dance.

. . .

"Many people don't know their spirit or ever feel great joy. Some people think of dance only as an exercise. But dance lets you feel and express emotion. Rhythm and form can give you self-expression. You can discover your spirit through dance and recognize it as beautiful and wonderful.

"The first thing we notice as babies is our bodies. Yet, I was in high school before I knew I could experience the spirit of movement in dance. I was taking dance class in school, and at some point when I got beyond the muscles hurting, I found this bright spirit.

"My professors said that dance isn't separated from the other parts of life. So I looked beyond the social traits into how other cultures experience dance. This led me to travel as an anthropologist to Haiti, Martinique, and other places. I realized I couldn't just *do* their dance. I had to experience their cultures, so my dance would be *truth*.

"When you see someone on a stage, you can tell if they're having feelings when they dance. If you're dancing at a carnival, you're extremely joyous. It's a continuous joy for me to see people dancing."

Secret Ingredient: Katherine Dunham theory classes are offered as summer seminars at the Dunham Centers in East St. Louis. Dunham theory is also offered at the Alvin Ailey American Dance Theater in New York City. To find classes in your area, inquire about Dunham theory at local dance studios that offer modern dance courses. To educate a young reader about this great dancer's life, look in the library for the book *Katherine Dunham: A Biography,* by Ruth Beckford.

 MIND

❄ DECEMBER 21 ❄

Be real.

Most of us understand the concept of having a "love that's real." We can recognize when a brother isn't being real with us. When we want to know the true story, or the honest facts, we ask for the "real deal."

But the question is: Are we being real with ourselves? Do we live each moment striving toward our purpose? When at a crossroads, do we take the advice of others to placate them, or do we do the things we know are best for us?

If you would like your life to reflect the real you, take these steps:

Accept yourself. Accept that you are unique and have your own special talents and gifts to share with the world that no one else has. How can anyone tell you how to use what is special within you? Ask for advice but make your own decisions based on your very valid intuition.

Know your strengths and your flaws. No, you don't have more flaws than strengths. And sometimes your flaws can also be your strengths. At *Glamour* magazine, I had a boss once who could talk your ear off. She was known at work as "the talker," but because she could drive a point home, she was also a great salesperson. When she was out selling our retail promotions, her charm, wit, and easy conversations made the sale every time. She made her flaw work in her favor, and it became a strength.

Forgive yourself. We can't be perfect no matter how hard we try. So accept your mistakes, apologize to anyone you may have hurt, learn the lesson, and humbly move forward.

Love your body. Not tall enough? Not slim enough? Unfortunately, too many of us are still wishing we had lighter skin or darker skin, straighter hair or longer hair. When we focus too much attention on changing superfluous things that are not in harmony with our nature, it never turns out better anyway. If you are as chocolate as an African queen, do you really think you'll look better as a bottle blonde? And how many blondes dye their hair black? Society's beauty standards are false and unequal. Natural beauty is what is real. Love your natural-born self.

Secret Ingredient: Work on seeing yourself exactly as God intended. Tell yourself through repeated affirmations that you are a divine creation. You may not feel perfect, but God is.

❋ SPIRIT

❄ DECEMBER 22 ❄

Feed an animal, heal the soul.

My friend Dr. Gerald W. Deas is a physician in Queens, New York. He cares not only about the lives of human beings, but of all living creatures. He has a message for you on how caring for animals can be good for what ails you too:

"God must have loved animals to have had His son born among them. The manger was surrounded by animals.

"Inner-city stray animals and birds experience hazardous conditions during the winter months while they try to survive. Often there is little water for them to drink. Warm shelter is scarce, and there is little food to be gotten from the barren trees and secured garbage cans. During the winter, birds and animals die by the thousands. This is usually not the scene found on the joyous Christmas cards showing happy animals and birds playing in the snow.

"We must make a commitment to not only our unfortunate brothers and sisters, but also to the little creatures who cannot beg for food or shelter. In front of my house, which is in the inner city, I have a large fir tree under which I spread corn and seeds for the survival of our flying creatures. When I go out to feed them, you can hear them singing with great vitality and vigor. As I go under the tree to spread the manna, the birds become very silent, as if they are praying and thanking God. As soon as I leave, they begin to swoop down and enjoy the magic harvest spread before them.

"It has been proven that elderly people who care for a pet in their home live longer than those persons without a pet. Often, when I visit a seniors' home and see them rocking in a chair with a pet on their lap, I know that they are extending their lives many years. This form of therapy is greater than any medicine I could prescribe to my patients.

"During this season of celebration of life, I would suggest that you save your scraps of food and place them outside in a convenient area for the stray animals. Also, buy a few pounds of birdseed and spread it outside your window or on your fire escape. For these acts of love and compassion for Mother Earth's creatures, I guarantee that as you sleep in your house, you won't hear even the stirring of a mouse!"

Secret Ingredient: Dr. Deas says he was inspired by a book called *Reverence for Life,* by Dr. Albert Schweitzer, that espouses Schweitzer's philosophy that every creature on the planet should enjoy their existence, and that they have a right to survive.

✳ DECEMBER 23 ✳

Turn your vice into something nice.

Okay, I've got a confession to make. I am an ice cream addict.

There, I've said it! If anyone knows the number to Ice Cream-aholics Anonymous, let me know.

If I were to lie on a psychiatrist's couch and uncover the roots of this, I would say: It all started when I was finishing school in Washington, D.C., and some fine brothers were raving about this new kind of ice cream we could find in Georgetown at a health food store. We all took off to check it out and found flavors such as honey vanilla, carob, and rum raisin. Yum, yum, yum! And that started my love affair with a certain brand of ice cream (and with one of the brothers, but that didn't last half as long!).

But I know that too much of anything is not a good thing, so I've tried to not OD on this potentially high-calorie, high-cholesterol indulgence. So, I don't eat whole *pints* at a time, like some folks I know. But I do admit that I use a couple of scoops to make milk shakes several times a week. Many people have asked me how I could possibly do that and not get fat. *Here's the secret: I've given my addiction a makeover.* First, the shakes hardly compare with the size of an extra-large fast-food shake; I make it in a small mug. Second, I add nutritious ingredients. My secret recipe follows:

Steph's Hearty Health Shake

2 scoops ice cream
1 tablespoon wheat germ
1 tablespoon brewer's yeast
2 tablespoons chocolate or vanilla malted milk
one percent milk to cover

Stir it up (or make it in a blender and turn it on), and enjoy!

Secret Ingredient: **For lower cholesterol, use nonfat frozen yogurt instead of ice cream and try soy milk instead of cow's milk. I make it this way too sometimes, and it's still yummy!**

Think of your own vice and how you can make it nice. For example, if you drink wine, try the new nonalcoholic brands. It's hard to give up *everything*, but if your "addiction" is not dangerous to your health (like smoking, drinking excessive amounts of alcohol, or drugs) moderation is a good first step.

❄ DECEMBER 24 ❄

Give the best gift.

The song may say it's the season to be jolly, but for many people it's the season to be depressed. My girlfriend Marlene Watson, a psychotherapist in private practice in Philadelphia, says that many clients she sees at this time of year have the holiday blues.

"Why?" I ask.

"Because they focus on what they don't have," she says, "on losses, on bad childhoods, on not having someone special for the holidays, or on being in relationships not worth having."

Those feelings seem to be quite common. According to a *Dateline NBC/Prevention* magazine holiday stress survey, sixty-four percent of respondents reported feeling nervous or stressed during the holidays. In addition, people sometimes experience family conflicts, loneliness, substance abuse, or excessive eating.

"What to do?" I ask Marlene.

"I advise people to give of themselves in the spirit of Christmas," Marlene answered. "Give time at a homeless shelter. Adopt a child for the holidays. Spend time with the children in your family. God gave His son on this day, so we should give of ourselves. Christmas is a day in which we all need to be in the present."

When she said that, it reminded me of a poem I heard nutritionist Grace Wilson-Woods recite:

Yesterday is history.
Tomorrow is a mystery.
Today is God's gift,
That's why it's called the present.

—Unknown

Secret Ingredient: Focus on what you do have and give the gift of yourself. At this time of year, newspapers often list agencies that would like help in assisting children with special holiday requests. Check your local paper as well as your nearest Urban League, NAACP, and your church for families who would appreciate your "playing Santa Claus" to some little ones in need.

❋ DECEMBER 25 ❋

It's Christmas—enjoy!

I saw a Christmas package that had these words stacked on the wrapping: EN

JOY

As in the French phrase "en vogue" that we know best as the name of a singing group, the "en" simply translates to "in" in English. So I thought it was apropos to be "en joy," or in the state of joy at this wonderful time of year.

I rarely get into the Christmas spirit until Christmas Eve. All the deadlines, shopping, decorating, and travel home to Seattle from New York just point to my being "en stress." But come the actual holidays, I'm transformed by the joy of it all. Here are some of the joyous reasons for the season:

- ❖ Glad Tidings: **The birth of Christ**
- ❖ O Christmas Tree: **The whole neighborhood is lit up.**
- ❖ O Come, All Ye Faithful: **Family togetherness**
- ❖ Hark! the Herald Angels Sing: **Christmas concerts and caroling**
- ❖ Go Tell It on the Mountain: **Catching up on gossip with family and friends**
- ❖ Silent Night: **It must be snowing.**
- ❖ God Rest Ye Merry Gentlemen: **Try copping a nap with your honey**
- ❖ Joy to the World: **Just think—people are celebrating just like you are all over the planet.**
- ❖ African Noel: **By the way, Kwanzaa starts tomorrow.**

Merry Christmas to all!
And to all: You're outta sight!

Secret Ingredient: Pray and be thankful for another Christmas Day. Count your blessings and encourage the people you see today to do the same.

❋ DECEMBER 26 ❋

Celebrate Kwanzaa.

Kwanzaa is an African American holiday that was first celebrated in December 1966 by Maulana Karenga and members of the black nationalist organization called Us. Celebrated each year from December 26 through January 1, Kwanzaa is a cultural observance that in no way conflicts with or serves as an alternative to Christmas. You can have your Christmas and your Kwanzaa too!

According to Karenga's book, *Kwanzaa: A Celebration of Family, Community and Culture,* the holiday is based on the seven-day, first-fruits-of-the-harvest celebrations of ancient Southern Africa, particularly Zululand. It is a time to *gather the family and the community* to renew and reinforce the bonds between them. Kwanzaa observances should *express special reverence for the Creator* and be a time of thanksgiving. It should *commemorate the past great legacies* as well as the "Holocaust of Enslavement." During Kwanzaa, we are encouraged to *focus on and practice our highest ethical values*—"values of the good life, truth, justice, sisterhood, brotherhood, and respect for . . . elders and for nature." And lastly, Kwanzaa is a time to *celebrate the good*—of life, family, community, friendship, the elders, the young, our history, our struggle for justice and liberation, and of humanity.

My husband and I have observed Kwanzaa for years. We started out by giving his three daughters Kwanzaa gifts *(zawadi)* of books. As the years went by, we attended community Kwanzaa events such as the one given by the Museum of Natural History in New York City, and we had fun at intimate parties, such as one we attended at a friend's home in Seattle in 1984. By 1998 our teenage daughter was an old hand at assembling a Kwanzaa table with a *kinara* (candleholder), *mishumaa saba* (the seven candles), *mkeka* (straw mat), *kikombe cha umoja* (the unity cup), *Nguzo Saba* poster (of the Seven Principles), and other things we added to make it our own style, such as Kente cloth, children's books about Kwanzaa, African art, and a poinsettia. We had a *karamu* (feast) and invited our friends to meet my mother, who was visiting. There are so precious few times of the year that the whole family can share together. Kwanzaa is definitely one of them.

Secret Ingredient: For the "official handbook" of the holiday, pick up a copy of Karenga's book. Also, ask for the Kwanzaa stamp, designed by Synthia St. James, at your local post office.

❋ DECEMBER 27 ❋

Live the Seven Principles.

Kwanzaa's *Nguzo Saba* are the seven principles that define the core values and consciousness of the cultural celebration. Each day, "illuminate" the principle of that day, founder Maulana Karenga suggests, by lighting a Kwanzaa candle and saying a few words about what the theme of the day means.

The *Nguzo Saba* are, in Swahili (and English):

December 26: *Umoja* **(Unity)** To strive for and maintain unity in the family, community, nation, and race.

December 27: *Kujichagulia* **(Self-Determination)** To define ourselves, name ourselves, create for ourselves, and speak for ourselves.

December 28: *Ujima* **(Collective Work and Responsibility)** To build and maintain our community together and make our brothers' and sisters' problems our problems and to solve them together.

December 29: *Ujamaa* **(Cooperative Economics)** To build and maintain our own stores, shops, and other businesses, and to profit from them together.

December 30: *Nia* **(Purpose)** To make our collective vocation the building and developing of our community in order to restore our people to their traditional greatness.

December 31: *Kuumba* **(Creativity)** To do always as much as we can, in the way we can, in order to leave our community more beautiful and beneficial than we inherited it.

January 1: *Imani* **(Faith)** To believe with all our hearts in our people, our parents, our teachers, our leaders, and the righteousness and victory of our struggle.

Secret Ingredient: Kwanzaa kits that include a *kinara* and candles can be found in Afrocentric stores. Or make your own.

✳ DECEMBER 28 ✳

Celebrate with the community.

In general, there are three ways to celebrate Kwanzaa:

* ❖ At a community event
* ❖ At a gathering in someone's home
* ❖ At your own home with your family

On this and the following two pages, I'll discuss suggestions for how these activities may be carried out, but the most important thing to remember is that any celebration that comes with good intentions from the heart is *the* perfect way to do it. There's no Kwanzaa police to get you if you do it wrong, and there is no wrong to do. Remember: African Americans are the jazz people—we improvise, create on the spot, do it all with good humor and joy, and it all turns out all right! So, any way you celebrate Kwanzaa is the right way.

Here are some suggestions for a community celebration:

* ❖ Ask a storyteller to present an African fable. The Jack & Jill of America chapter to which I belong does this every year. Salik Cuevas, a Yoruba storyteller, had young ones and parents alike enthralled with his story of an African child. He brought African clothing for the youngest children, and had them acting out all the parts.
* ❖ Invite respected elders in your community, and pour a libation to them and the ancestors.
* ❖ Take African friends with you. Last year we invited our friend from Sierra Leone to go with us, and in so doing, we introduced her to this uniquely African American celebration and she gave us a link with the Motherland.
* ❖ Consider a *umoja* night, in which community leaders are invited to plan and discuss local, national, and political issues. Light the candles for community unity.

Secret Ingredient: Ask a cultural institution to sponsor a community event if you don't already have a local celebration in your area. Museums, libraries, and social organizations make perfect backers and can provide a venue and publicity.

✳ DECEMBER 29 ✳

Establish a family tradition.

Kwanzaa offers a unique opportunity to establish your very own annual family traditions. Each year, you can observe the week-long holiday in ways that are most reflective of your own family style of tradition, culture, and ritual.

If your family is formal and ritualistic, you will probably want to light the candles each night and have discussions about the meaning of that day's theme. You might also want to make sure you have all the elements on your table, including the *mazoa,* symbols of the crops of the harvest, and the *muhindi,* the corn that symbolizes your children and the future they embody. To really follow the celebration to the letter, be sure to read up on the Swahili words and greet others by saying *"Habari gani?"* (literally, "What news?" Or colloquially, "What's up?"). The answer is the principle of the day. For example, if someone greeted you, *"Habari gani?"* on the second day of Kwanzaa, you would answer, *"Kujichagulia!"*

If you have a casual, more informal family (like mine), you may do one or two of the many things that make Kwanzaa special. We traditionally set up a Kwanzaa display, usually on our dining table, but this year because we had friends over and needed the table for the food, we draped Kente over a card table and set it up near the entry of the house (One friend said it looked like an altar!). I also like to give the children a *zawadi* because I learned that Kwanzaa gifts should not cost more than $10, so that was a special challenge to find a bargain! I usually buy books—my favorite things! If you have small children, you'll find a great selection of Kwanzaa books. Our favorite is *Seven Candles for Kwanzaa,* by Andrea Davis Pinkney. I do admit to a bias toward it, though, because the illustrator, Brian Pinkney, used our daughter, Anique, as the model for the girl character illustrated in the book. So you can imagine that we think it's pretty special.

Secret Ingredient: **Instruct your kids not to light Kwanzaa candles unless you are in the room. Also, don't leave the house with candles lit. If the candles burn down to the bottom, the *kinara,* which is usually made of wood, can burn and become a fire hazard. Believe me, I know about this from firsthand experience!**

❋ DECEMBER 30 ❋

Throw a karamu.

Everyone likes a good feast! New Year's Eve is traditionally the night for the *karamu*, with mainly adults in attendance, but according to founder Maulana Karenga's Kwanzaa book, if you change the date or include the children, that's okay too!

Being the reluctant cook that I am, one thing I like about the spirit of the Kwanzaa feast is that it is communal, so everyone is expected to bring a dish. Collective cooperation is the order of the day! Of course, I would strongly advise you to prepare dishes that are healthful, low calorie, and low on the fat, sugar, and salt. What better time than Kwanzaa to show the ones we love how much we love them and that we want them to live a long, healthy life than by serving them the most health-conscious foods we can think of? At our house, the *karamu* is always vegetarian— just as we eat year-round. If you are not a vegetarian, perhaps this could be the one meal you serve each year that is. Who knows, it could start something good!

Other ways to make the *karamu* special include:

❖ Decorations in the Kwanzaa colors of black, red, and green
❖ African music or drumming
❖ African dancing
❖ Libations poured in memory of the ancestors
❖ Candle-lighting ceremony
❖ And, of course, nonalcoholic beverages

Secret Ingredient: **End your *karamu* with a *harambee* chant. *Harambee* means "let's all pull together." This call to unity and collective work and struggle begins by raising the right arm with an open hand, then pulling down and closing the hand into a fist. *Harambee!***

❋ DECEMBER 31 ❋

Make merry tonight, meditate tomorrow.

As I mentioned, although Kwanzaa is not a religious holiday, it does have a spiritual aspect to it. It would be hard to be a successful African American observance without some acknowledgment of the Creator. It wouldn't honor the ancestors without giving thanks for their lives. Kwanzaa would be an empty celebration without "the Spirit."

In reading *Kwanzaa,* I discovered a particular aspect of this culture fest that I hadn't known about: The day of meditation. In my years at *Essence,* I had been the unofficial "keeper of the Kwanzaa culture," always making sure we did articles on Kwanzaa, and when I was at *Heart & Soul* I even appeared on the weekend *Today* show talking about Kwanzaa. So I thought I knew just about everything when it came to Kwanzaa. After more than twenty years, I was pleased to learn that January 1, the last day of Kwanzaa, had been designated as a time for self-reflection, contemplation, and meditation.

Founder Maulana Karenga suggests that we focus on three questions:

1. Who am I?
2. Am I really who I say I am?
3. Am I all I ought to be?

I for one like to party every New Year's Eve like it's 1999! I have a group of friends who gather together every New Year's as though we belonged to some secret New Year's club or something. This year, though, things changed. After we boogied to The Artist's song for the millennium, our hosts, Benilde Little and her husband, Cliff Virgin, turned off the music and asked everyone to share a meaningful passage. Some were poignant, some humorous, some even erotic! But one that touched us most was shared by Terry Lee, who recited what his mother told him before she died when he was quite young:

> *The gift God gives us is Life.*
> *What we do with it,*
> *is our gift to God.*

Secret Ingredient: Have a healthy, soulful, Happy New Year!

Afterword

By David Satcher, M.D., Ph.D.
Assistant Secretary for Health and United States Surgeon General

Now that you've gone through one year of commitment to healthy habits for a strong mind, body, and spirit, plan ahead for the future through the year 2010 and beyond with this inspiration from the Surgeon General of the United States, David Satcher.

Every ten years, Federal health agencies work with various public and private sector organizations to establish a set of national health goals for the next decade. This effort is known as the Healthy People Initiative. As Surgeon General of the United States, I have been attending meetings around the country to solicit comments on the goals that will guide the nation's health improvement agenda for the first decade for the new century—Healthy People 2010.

The U.S. Department of Health and Human Services has coordinated the Healthy People Initiative for three decades. This effort might seem abstract unless you realize how far we have come in this decade alone—how many less adults smoke and suffered related diseases, how many more babies were born healthy, how many women have survived breast cancer because they have a mammogram sooner than they might have. Maybe you too have been helped by advances in medicine and personal health.

Because improving health for a nation really means improving the health of a whole lot of individuals, I want each American to ask yourself what you would like your own health to be in ten years, to be your own personal goals. Then go about improving your exercise or diet or whatever other changes you can make that will help you achieve your personal health goals.

Let me share with you my priorities for Surgeon General, because in them are some lifelong lessons for healthy living. **First, I want to make sure that every child has an opportunity for a healthy start in life.** When I raise that topic, I am referring to babies being born to parents ready to be parents and being born into nurturing environments. It means ensuring healthy pregnancies by making sure mothers have access to quality prenatal care. It means addressing teen pregnancy so that babies are born to parents who are ready to be parents. It means a safe and nurturing environment for babies.

Second, we must promote healthy lifestyles. That applies at any stage in life. It refers to good nutrition, physical activity, responsible sexual behavior, and the avoidance of toxins. A healthy lifestyle means taking care of yourself so that you develop a regimen of good habits, while eliminating bad ones. I often like to point out that it is just as easy to develop healthy habits as it is to develop harmful ones.

For example, I am hooked on jogging. I like to jog every day, but if not, at least several times a week. When I am unable to fit jogging into my schedule, I am not a pleasant person to be around. That's what I mean. You can get attached to good behaviors, like physical activity, as easily as you can to bad ones.

We're not talking about running marathons or becoming an all-star athlete. But by engaging in simple, consistent physical activities like walking, gardening, swimming, and cycling, we can improve the nation's physical health significantly.

Nutrition is the same. By getting into the habit of eating at least five servings of fruit and vegetables each day, you can much more readily turn away those foods that are not healthy. The American diet is too loaded with fats and sugar, and too lacking in fruit, vegetables, and grains.

The next priority deals with mental health. No priority yet has generated as much interest and enthusiasm as this one. We must develop a mental health system that is caring and supportive. We must remove the blame and stigmatization that surrounds mental health in this nation. Mental health problems often relate to other serious health problems, including substance abuse and violence.

We live in a high pressure, fast-paced, frenzied, chaotic world. Not only should you pay attention to your physical health, you must be mindful of your psychological and emotional health. Just as things go wrong with the heart, lung, kidneys, and liver, things also go wrong with the mind—and you must be aware of that. Too many of our communities are environments of hopelessness. What we are trying to do is to remove the stigmas and shame that often surround mental health. These stigmas often prevent those who need help most from seeking it.

Fourth, we must strengthen support for an effective community health system. You can provide a great deal of help in this area. We envision a health system that is based on health promotion, disease prevention, early detection, and universal access to care. We must rethink our health system so that we focus more of our efforts on prevention, so that we'll have to devote less time to care. Currently, we spend $1 trillion each year on health care, and yet only 1 percent of that amount is spent on population-based prevention.

The fifth priority is this: We must view health from a global perspective. We cannot afford to view our health as if diseases stopped at borders. It now takes an individual a mere twenty-four to thirty-six hours to travel around the globe, increasing significantly the threat of outbreaks of disease. Beyond that, tobacco and violence are increasingly becoming larger health concerns. In the twenty-first century, our efforts will be focused on maintaining a system of global health surveillance, particularly with regard to:

1. coordinating the national response to emerging infectious disease
2. leading the national response to health consequences of bioterrorism, and
3. promoting the safety and availability of the nations; food and blood supply.

An overriding factor of each of these objectives is the goal of eliminating racial disparities in health. Back in February of 1998, the President unveiled his Initiative on Race and Health. In it, he announced a goal of *eliminating* racial disparities in health by 2010, coinciding with the Healthy People 2010 Initiative. This means that we have proposed one target for all population groups. For all the medical breakthroughs we have seen in the past century, we still see significant disparities in the medical conditions of racial groups in this country.

As I mentioned, too many of our communities are environments of hopelessness. When I left home for college, my parents did not have a lot to offer me in the way of material things, but what they did offer me amounted to much, much more. In my hands was placed not wealth, not clothing, not even a solid plan for success, instead, what they gave me was hope.

I started out in medicine, wishing to do biomedical research. So I completed the M.D. and Ph.D. in cytogenics. I wound up doing research in sickle cell and starting a sickle center.

It was hope that led me to want to teach community health, but I wound up chairing the Department of Family Medicine at Drew and Community and Family Medicine at Morehouse. It was hope that prodded me to want to become involved in medical administration, but I wound up as president of one of the greatest medical schools in the country, Meharry Medical College. It was hope that inspired me to want to understand and improve the health of the poor; and I wound up leading the world's premier prevention agency at the Centers for Disease Control.

And it was hope that brought me this far today. And now, **I challenge you to hold on to your hope, and to inspire hope in others.** In the immortal words of Langston Hughes, "Hold fast to dreams." Be part of your own future—take good care of yourself. You hold in your hands each day the future of the health of this nation.

Secret Ingredient: Dr. Satcher adds, "I invite you to contribute to the health objectives of the nation. Accessible to those of you who get on the Internet is our interactive Healthy People 2010 Web site: www.health.gov/healthypeople. If you don't use the Internet, then I invite you to order our plan in book form. To order *Healthy People 2010 Objectives: Draft for Public Comments,* call (800) 367-4725."

Notes and Credits

The author gratefully acknowledges these publishers and individuals for permission to reprint the following material:

Portions of this work were originally written by the author, Stephanie Stokes Oliver, and appeared in *Heart & Soul* Magazine as "Word From the Editor." Reprinted with permission of the publisher, Clarence Brown.

Portions of this work were originally published in *Essence* Magazine in various articles written by the author, Stephanie Stokes Oliver. Reprinted with permission of the editor-in-chief, Susan L. Taylor.

January 12: "Nikki-Rosa" by Nikki Giovanni. *The Selected Poems of Nikki Giovanni* (Morrow, 1996); page 42. Reprinted with permission of the author, Nikki Giovanni.

February 20, 21: Excerpts from "An Agenda for Empowerment," a speech delivered by Marian Wright Edelman at the Congressional Black Caucus Awards dinner, September 26, 1987, and published in *Essence* Magazine, May 1988, are reprinted with the permission of Marian Wright Edelman and *Essence* Magazine.

April 12: "Low-Sodium Creole Oven-Fried Chicken" recipe from *The Dooky Chase Cookbook* by Leah Chase. Reprinted with permission of the author, Leah Chase.

April 22: Two lines from "And Still I Rise" by Maya Angelou. Copyright © 1978 by Maya Angelou. Reprinted by permission of Random House, Inc.

May 16: Statistics quoted from the *Christian Science Monitor* article, "A Frontier of Medical Research: Prayer," reprinted with permission of United Media.

May 18: "Joke of the Weak" was originally published in the *Seattle Post-Intelligencer.* Reprinted with permission of the editor and publisher, J. D. Alexander.

May 21: The "Least Stressful Jobs" List: From *The Wall Street Journal Almanac '98* by Editors of *The Wall Street Journal.* Copyright © 1997 by Dow Jones Co. Inc. Reprinted by permission of Ballantine Books, a division of Random House, Inc.

May 23: Information from *Exercise and Your Heart* was reproduced with permission of the American Heart Association. *Exercise and Your Heart,* © 1993, American Heart Association.

July 15: Excerpt from *Role Play: Personalities in Action* (LifeChange Partners) by Julie Waltz Kembel. Copyright © 1996 by Julie Waltz Kembel. Reprinted with permission of Julie Waltz Kembel.

October 25: Excerpt from *Winning the Weight and Wellness Game* (Northwest Learning Associates) by Julie Waltz Kembel. Copyright © 1993, 1994 by Julie Waltz Kembel. Reprinted with permission of Julie Waltz Kembel.

November 16: "Victoria's Secrets" reprinted from the Web site of Victoria Johnson International with permission of Victoria Johnson.

Afterword by David Satcher, Assistant Secretary for Health and U.S. Surgeon General, compiled and edited from "Holding Fast to Hope for Education and Health" commencement address for the University of Texas at El Paso, delivered December 19, 1998; "Building the Next Generation of Healthy People" address delivered at the National Healthy People Consortium Meeting and Public Hearing, Washington, D.C., November 12, 1998; "Healthy People Initiative" press release, November 13, 1998. Printed with permission of David Satcher.

Expert advice, individual contributions, and quotes in the public domain are not listed here, however, the author would like to thank all the people that have been quoted or cited in this book for their wisdom and insight. If there were any errors, it was purely unintentional.

The information in *Daily Cornbread* is meant to increase knowledge of health and fitness for the purpose of disease prevention and self-improvement. For best results, also seek the advice of a physician and other health-care professionals.

Resources

BOOKS MENTIONED OR THAT I'VE FOUND HELPFUL TO GOOD HEALTH

American Jihad: Islam After Malcolm X by Steven Barboza (Doubleday)

Autobiography of Malcolm X by Malcolm X with Alex Haley (Ballantine)

The Basic Money Management Workbook by Glinda F. Bridgforth (Bridgforth, 1992)

The Best Kind of Loving: A Black Woman's Guide to Finding Intimacy by Dr. Gwendolyn Goldsby Grant (HarperCollins)

Black Indians: A Hidden Heritage by William Loren Katz (Aladdin, 1993)

The Black Man's Guide to Good Health by James W. Reed, M.D., Neil Shulman, M.D., and Charlene Shucker (Perigee Books, 1994)

The Black Woman's Guide to Financial Independence by Cheryl D. Broussard (Viking Penguin)

Bobbi Brown Beauty (HarperPerennial, 1997)

Brothers on the Mend: Understanding and Healing Anger for African-American Men and Women by Ernest H. Johnson (Pocket Books, 1998)

Brown Angels: An Album in Pictures and Verse by Walter Dean Myers (HarperCollins Children's, 1996)

B. Smith's Entertaining and Cooking for Friends by Barbara Smith (Artisan, 1995)

Can I Get a Witness?: For Sisters, When the Blues Is More Than a Song by Julia A. Boyd (Dutton, 1998)

Chain Chain Change: For Black Women in Abusive Relationships by Evelyn C. White (Seal Press, 1995)

Chicken Soup for the Pet Lover's Soul by Jack Canfield, Mark Victor Hansen, Marty Becker, Carol Kline (Health Communications)

Coming from the Light: Spiritual Accounts of Life Before Life by Sarah Hinze (Pocket Books, 1997)

The Domestic Violence Sourcebook: Everything You Need to Know by Dawn Bradley Berry (Lowell House, 1998)

Dr. Susan Love's Breast Book by Susan M. Love, M.D., with Karen Lindsey (Addison Wesley Longman, 1995)

Easy Yoga for Busy People by Bobbe Norrise (Total Health Institute, [510] 530-8220; also available at Marcus Books in Oakand). Has accompanying audiotape.

Even the Stars Get Lonesome by Maya Angelou (Random House, 1997)

Fitness for Dummies by Suzanne Schlosberg and Liz Neporent (IDG Books Worldwide, 1996) *for colored girls who have considered suicide/when the rainbow is enuf* by Ntozake Shange (Collier Books, Macmillan Publishing, 1989)

Go, Girl! The Black Woman's Book of Travel and Adventure edited by Elaine Lee (The Eighth Mountain Press, 1997)

Good Health for African Americans by Barbara M. Dixon, L.P.N., R.D. (Crown)

Hippocrene Guide to the Underground Railroad by Charles Blockson (Hippocrene Books)

In the Company of My Sisters: Black Women and Self-Esteem by Julia A. Boyd (Dutton)

In the Meantime by Iyanla Vanzant (Simon & Schuster)

Introduction to Yoga (Yoga Zone, [888] 264-YOGA)

Islam in the African-American Experience by Richard Brent Turner (Indiana University Press, 1997)

Jesus CEO: Using Ancient Wisdom for Visionary Leadership by Laurie Beth Jones (Hyperion, 1995)

Just Between Girlfriends: African-American Women Celebrate Friendship by Chrisena Coleman (Simon & Schuster)

Katherine Dunham: A Biography by Ruth Beckford (Marcel Dekker, 1979)

Kwanzaa: A Celebration of Family, Community, and Culture by Maulana Karenga (University of Sankore Press, 1998 [Commonwealth Edition])

Love Lessons: A Guide to Transforming Relationships by Brenda K. Wade (Amistad)

Love Poems by Nikki Giovanni (William Morrow)

Makes Me Wanna Holler by Nathan McCall (Vintage Books, 1995)

The New Soy Cookbook: Delicious Ideas for Soybeans, Soy Milk, Tofu, Tempeh, Miso, and Soy Sauce by Lorna J. Sass (Chronicle Books, 1998)

One Day My Soul Just Opened Up: 40 Days & 40 Nights Toward Spiritual Strength & Personal Growth by Iyanla Vanzant (Fireside/Simon & Schuster)

A Path to Healing: A Guide to Wellness for Body, Mind, and Soul by Dr. Andrea D. Sullivan (Doubleday, 1998)

ROLE Play by Julie Kembel (Northwest Learning Associates. [520] 881-0877)

Sacred Pampering Principles: An African-American Woman's Guide to Self-Care and Inner Renewal by Debrena Jackson Gandy (William Morrow, 1998)

The Spirited Walker by Carolyn Scott Kortge (HarperSanFrancisco/HarperCollins, 1998)

The Spiritual Life of Children by Robert Coles (Houghton Mifflin, 1991)

Success Strategies for African-Americans: A Guide to Creating Personal and Professional Achievement by Beatryce Nivens (Plume, 1998)

A Testament of Hope: The Essential Writiings and Speeches of Martin Luther King, Jr. Edited by James M. Washington (HarperCollins)

This Far by Faith: How to Put God First in Everyday Living by Linnie Frank and Andria Hall (Doubleday, 1998)

Transform Your Life by Reverend Dr. Barbara King (Perigee)

Tyra's Beauty Inside & Out by Tyra Banks (HarperPerennial)

The Value in the Valley: A Woman's Guide Through Life's Dilemmas by Iyanla Vanzant (Simon & Schuster, 1995)

What the Blues Is All About by Angela Mitchell with Kennise Herring, Ph.D. (Perigee Books, 1998)

Winning the Weight and Wellness Game by Julie Waltz Kembel (Northwest Learning Associates, [520] 881-0877; 1994)

"Yes" or "No:" The Guide to Better Decisions by Spencer Johnson (Harper Business, 1993)

EXPERT SOURCES

Glinda Bridgforth
Financial adviser
Oakland, CA
(888) 430-1820
www.electra.com (AOL Keyword:
   Electra)
www.bridgforthfmg.com

Cheryl D. Broussard
Financial adviser
Palo Alto, CA
(415) 688-1188

Rev. Herbert Daughtry
The House of the Lord Church
415 Atlantic Avenue
Brooklyn, NY 11217
(718) 596-1991

Julie Waltz Kembel
Northwest Learning Associates
3061 North Willow Creek Drive
Tucson, AR 85712
(520) 881-0877

Ann J. Lemon
Vice President, Investments
Paine Webber
1251 Avenue of the Americas
New York, NY 10020-0363
(800) 458-1764, ext. 8557
in New York City, (212) 626-8557

Barbara Mitchell
Sharon Morgan
Creative Escapes
P.O. Box 1257
Piscataway, NJ 08855-1257
(973) 761-4573 or phone or
   fax (732) 463-3794
Web site: www.creativeescapes.com

Jewel Diamond Taylor
The Enlightened Circle
4195 Chino Hills Pkwy., #180
Chino Hills, CA 91709
(213) 964-1736
e-mail: JEWELDIAM@aol.com or
   Gem@aol.com
To hear Jewel's positive thought for the
   day, call (323) 964-4070

Dr. Ivan Van Sertima
347 Felton Avenue
Highland Park, NJ 08094

Iyanla Vanzant
Inner Visions Worldwide Network
P.O. Box 3231
Silver Spring, MD 20910
E-mail: innervisions@innervisions
   worldwide.com
http://Innervisionsworldwide.com

Marlene F. Watson, Ph.D.
Couple and Family Therapist
(in private practice)
(215) 762-6781

Grace Wilson-Woods
Nutrition Consultant
10233 East Stoney Vista Drive
Sun Lakes, AZ 85248
(602) 895-8818

Zarif
Zarif Fitness Center
3310 West Manchester Blvd.
Inglewood, CA
(310) 671-7676

HOT LINES

California Smoker's Helpline
(800) 7-NO-BUTTS

Dial-a-Hearing-Test
(800) 222-EARS

Lupus and Rare Disorders
(800) 999-6673

National AIDS Hotline
(800) 342-AIDS

National Cancer Institute
Cancer Information Service
(800) 4-CANCER

National Resource Center on
   Domestic Violence
(800) 537-2238

Sickle Cell Disease
(800) 421-8453

The Blues Line (Depression)
(800) 826-3632

The National Domestic Violence
   Hotline
(800) 799-SAFE (7233)
or TTY: (800) 787-3224

ORGANIZATIONS

American Cancer Society
National Headquarters
1599 Clifton Road N.E.
Atlanta, GA 30329-4251
(800) ACS-2345
(404) 320-3333

American Heart Association
7272 Greenville Avenue
Dallas, TX 75231
(800) AHA USA1

American Lung Association
1740 Broadway
New York, NY 10019-4374
(800) LUNG-USA
(212) 889-3370

American Medical Association
535 North Dearborn Street
Chicago, IL 60610
(312) 464-5000
www.ama-assn.org

American Menopause Foundation
Madison Square Station
P.O. Box 2013
New York, NY 10010

American Psychiatric Association
1400 K Street N.W.
Washington, DC 20005
(202) 682-6220

Arthur Ashe Institute for Urban
   Health, Inc.
State University of New York at
   Brooklyn College
Room 2118, Boylan Hall
2900 Bedford Avenue
Brooklyn, NY 11210
(877) 270-4258
(718) 951-5000

Association of Black Psychologists
P.O. Box 55999
Washington, DC 20040-5999
(202) 722-0808

Balm in Gilead
New York, NY
(212) 730-7381

Bea Gaddy Family Centers, Inc.
140 North Collington Avenue
P.O. Box 38501
Baltimore, MD 21231
(410) 563-2749
*Call to help: donations also welcome and
needed*

California State African American
   Tobacco Education Network
1721 Second Street, Suite 102
Sacramento, CA 95814
(916) 556-3359

Consumer Credit Counseling Service
(888) 462-2227
www.credit.org

Consumer Information Center
Pueblo, CO 81009
(888) 8-PUEBLO
www.pueblo.gsa.gov

Debt Counselors of America
(800) 680-3328
www.dca.org

Health Watch Information &
   Promotion Service
3020 Glenwood Road
Brooklyn, NY 11210
(718) 434-5411
E-mail: healthwatc@aol.com [note:
   correct spelling; no final h]
www.health-watch.org

International Society on Hypertension
   in Blacks
Atlanta, GA
(404) 875-6263

Lupus Foundation of America
1300 Piccard Drive, Suite 200
Rockville, MD 20850-4303
(800) 558-0121
(301) 670-9292

Martin Luther King Center for
  Nonviolent Social Change
449 Auburn Avenue N.E.
Atlanta, GA
(404) 526-8900
www.thekingcenter.com

National Association of Personal
  Financial Advisors
(888) 333-6659

National Black Nurses Association
1511 K Street N.W.
Suite 415
Washington, D.C. 20001
(202) 393-6870

National Black Women's Health
  Project
1211 Connecticut Avenue N.W.,
  Suite 310
Washington, D.C. 20036
(202) 835-0117
E-mail: NBWHPDC@aol.com
National Center of Complementary
  and Alternative Medicine
(888) 644-6226

National Coalition Against Domestic
  Violence
P.O. Box 18749
Denver, CO 80218-0749
(303) 839-1852
www.ncadv.org

National Coming Out Project
919 Eighteenth Street N.W. #800
Washington, DC 20006
(800) 866-NCOD
(202) 628-4160
ncop@hrc.org
www.hrc.org

National Dental Association
5506 Connecticut Avenue N.W.
Suite 24-25
Washington, DC 20015
(202) 244-7555

National Health Information Center
(800) 336-4797

National Heart, Lung, and Blood
  Information Center
P.O. Box 30105
Bethesda, MD 20824-0105
(301) 251-1222
(301) 251-1223 (fax)
nhlbiic@dgsys.com (e-mail)
Information on cholesterol education

National Kidney Foundation
(800) 622-9010

National Medical Association
1012 Tenth Street N.W.
Washington, DC 20001
(202) 347-1895

National Mental Health Association
1021 Prince Street
Alexandria, VA 22314-2971
(800) 959-6642
(703) 684-7722

National Minority AIDS Council
1931 Thirteenth Street N.W.
Washington, DC 20009
(202) 483-6622
www.nmac.org

National Men's Health Foundation
14 East Minor Street
Emmaus, PA 18098
(610) 967-8620
www.menshealth.com

Planned Parenthood Federation of
  America
810 Seventh Avenue
New York, NY 10019
(212) 261-4628

Sickle Cell Disease Association
200 Corporate Pointe, Suite 495
Culver City, CA 90230-7633
(800) 421-8453
(310) 216-6363

Siddha Yoga Meditation
371 Brickman Road, P.O. Box 600
South Fallsburg, NY 12779-0600
(914) 434-2000

SIDS Alliance
1314 Bedford Avenue, Suite 210
Baltimore, MD 21208
(800) 221-SIDS
(410) 653-8226

Sisters Together: Move More, Eat
  Better
1637 Tremont Street
Boston, MA 02120
(617) 432-2048

Sudden Infant Death Syndrome
  Alliance
1314 Bedford Avenue, Suite 210
Baltimore, MD 21208
(800) 221-SIDS
(410) 653-8709 Fax
sidshq@charm.net
www.sidsalliance.org

The Centers for Disease Control and
  Prevention
1600 Clifton Road MS D-25
Atlanta, GA 30333
(800) 311-3435
Prerecorded messages: (404) 332-4555

The Stepfamily Association of America
(800) 735-0329
www.stepfam.org

The Susan G. Komen Breast Cancer
  Foundation
5005 LBJ Freeway, Suite 370
Dallas, TX 75244
(800) IM-AWARE

Transcendental Meditation ® Program
(888) LEARN TM
www.tm.org

United Way of America
701 N. Fairfax Street
Alexandria, VA 22314-2045
(703) 836-7100
www.unitedway.org

Women's Sports Foundation
Eisenhower Park
East Meadow, NY 11554
(800) 227-3988
(516) 542-4700
e-mail: wosport@aol.com

WEB SITES

Alternative Health News Online
www.altmedicine.com

American Academy of Ophthalmology
www.aao.org

American College of Obstetricians and
  Gynecologists
www.acog.org

American Heart Association
www.americanheart.org

Better Health
www.betterhealth.com
AOL Keyword: Better Health

Julia A. Boyd
www.jetcity.com/-gumbomed/
  JuliaBoyd.html

Feminist Majority Foundation's
  Domestic Violence Information
  Center
www.feminist.org/other/dv/
  dvhome.html

Institute on Domestic Violence in the
  African American Community
www.dvinstitute.org

William Loren Katz
www.thefuturesite.com/wlkatz

National Depression Screening Day
www.nmisp.org

National Men's Health Foundation
www.menshealth.com

Nzingha
www.thefuturesite.com/nzingha.

The Stepfamily Association of America
www.stepfam.org

Jewel Diamond Taylor
www.jeweldiamondtaylor.com

Transcendental Meditation ® Program
www.tm.org

United Way of America
www.unitedway.org

Victim Assistance Online
www.vaonline.org

Victoria Johnson International
www.victoriajohnson.com

Yahoo!
www.yahoo.com